An Introduction to

NINETEENTH-CENTURY EUROPEAN HISTORY
1815–1914

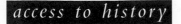
access to history

An Introduction to

NINETEENTH-CENTURY EUROPEAN HISTORY 1815–1914

Alan Farmer

HODDER
EDUCATION
AN HACHETTE UK COMPANY

ACKNOWLEDGEMENTS

The front cover shows Proclamation of Kaiser Wilhelm, 1871, by Anton Alexander von Werner, reproduced courtesy of Schloss Friedrichsruhe, Germany/Bridgeman Art Library.

The publishers would like to thank the following individuals, institutions and companies for permission to reproduce copyright illustrations in this book:

© Bettmann/Corbis, page 251; © Christel Gerstenberg/Corbis, page 154; David King, page 258; Edward Arnold, page 18; Hulton Deutsch Collection, page 26; Hulton Getty, page 176; Illustrated London News Picture Library, page 16; Illustrated London News Picture Library/Peter Newarks Military Pictures, page 22; Index Firenze, page 123; Mary Evans Picture Library, pages 12, 31 bottom, 34 top, 34 bottom, 35 top, 35 middle, 35 bottom, 202; Museo Centrale Del Risorgimento, page 129 bottom; Photo RMN-Daniel Arnaudet, page 219; Photo RMN-Hervé Lewandowski, page 31 top; Punch, pages 110, 139 top, 139 middle, 139 bottom, 188, 201, 222, 233, 234, 275; Rex Features, pages 116, 129 top; © Scheufler Collection/Corbis, page 245; Proclamation of Kaiser Wilhelm, 1871, by Anton Alexander von Werner, Schloss Friedrichsruhe, Germany/Bridgeman Art Library, page 169.

Every effort has been made to trace and acknowledge ownership of copyright. The publishers will be glad to make suitable arrangements with any copyright holders whom it has not been possible to contact.

Orders: please contact Bookpoint Ltd, 130 Milton Park, Abingdon, Oxon OX14 4SB. Telephone: (44) 01235 827720, Fax: (44) 01235 400454. Lines are open from 9.00 – 5.00, Monday to Saturday, with a 24 hour message answering service. You can also order through our website www.hoddereducation.co.uk

British Library Cataloguing in Publication Data

A catalogue record for this title is available from The British Library

ISBN - 13: 978 0 340 78113 5

First published 2001

Impression number   15

Year   2016

Copyright © 2001 Alan Farmer

Typeset by Hardlines Ltd, Charlbury, Oxford

Printed in Great Britain for Hodder Education, an Hachette UK company, Carmelite House, 50 Victoria Embankment, London EC4Y 0DZ by the CPI Group (UK) Ltd, Croydon, CR0 4YY

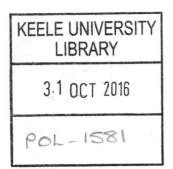

CONTENTS

List of Figures	*vii*
List of Profiles	*viii*
List of Tables	*viii*
Series Editor's Preface	*1*
Chapter 1 Europe 1815–48: The Domestic Scene	**5**
1 Europe: general trends 1815–48	5
2 Nationalism, liberalism and radicalism	9
3 France: 1815–48	11
4 The Habsburg Monarchy	20
5 Russia	25
Working on Europe 1815–48: The Domestic Scene	30
Further Reading	32
Chapter 2 Europe 1815–48: The International Scene	**33**
1 The great powers in 1815	34
2 Peacemaking at the Congress of Vienna	36
3 The Vienna Settlement	38
4 The 'Concert of Europe' 1815–23	41
5 The impact of Canning 1823–7	48
6 The Eastern Question: 1823–33	50
7 The revolutions of 1830–1	53
8 Near Eastern crises 1831–41	56
9 The Concert and diplomatic alignments 1830–48	58
Working on Europe 1815–48: The International Scene	59
Further Reading	61
Chapter 3 The 1848 Revolutions	**62**
1 Economic and social problems	63
2 Political problems	65
3 The 1848 revolution in France	68
4 The revolutions in the Habsburg Empire	73
5 Revolution in Germany: 1848–9	81
6 The revolutions in Italy	88
7 Conclusion	90
Working on The 1848 Revolutions	91
Further Reading	93
Chapter 4 The Impact of the Crimean War	**94**
1 The causes of the Crimean War	94
2 The war: 1854–6	102
3 The effects of the Crimean War on international relations	107
Working on The Impact of the Crimean War	109
Further Reading	111
Chapter 5 Italian Unification	**112**
1 Italy in 1815	112
2 The growth of opposition: 1815–48	113
3 The revolutions of 1848–9	118

4 Piedmont and Cavour 1848–60   121
5 Garibaldi and 'the Thousand'   128
6 Italy 1861–70   132
Working on Italian Unification   136
Further Reading   140

Chapter 6   The Unification of Germany: 1815–71   **141**
1 Germany in 1815   141
2 The *Vormärz*: 1815–48   144
3 Germany's economic development pre-1850   148
4 The 1848–9 revolutions   149
5 Developments in Prussia 1849–62   150
6 Prussia 1862–6   153
7 The Seven Weeks War and the North German Confederation   160
8 The Franco-Prussian War   164
Working on The Unification of Germany: 1815–71   170
Further Reading   173

Chapter 7   Bismarck's Germany: 1871–90   **174**
1 The German Empire   174
2 Bismarck's domestic policy   180
3 Bismarck's foreign policy   188
4 Bismarck's fall   197
Working on Bismarck's Germany: 1871–90   199
Further Reading   201

Chapter 8   Russia, Austria and France c.1850–80   **202**
1 Russia: Alexander II   202
2 Austria 1848–80   211
3 France 1848–80   218
Working on Russia, Austria and France c.1850–80   232
Further Reading   235

Chapter 9   Germany, France and Russia 1880–1914   **236**
1 General European trends 1880–1914   236
2 Wilhelmine Germany   242
3 France: the Third Republic   249
4 Tsarist Russia   254
Working on Germany, France and Russia 1880–1914   263
Further Reading   264

Chapter 10 The Origins of the First World War   **265**
1 Colonial rivalry   266
2 European relations 1890–1907   272
3 Increasing tension: 1908–1913   277
4 The July Crisis   281
5 Which country was most to blame for the war?   284
6 What were the main causes of the war?   287
Working on The Origins of the First World War   291
Further Reading   293

Glossary   *294*

Index   *295*

List of figures

Chapter 1

Figure 1	Europe in 1815	6
Figure 2	Portrait of Louis XVIII	12
Figure 3	Portrait of Louis-Philippe	16
Figure 4	Caricature of Louis-Philippe by Honoré Daumier	18
Figure 5	Map showing the Austrian Empire	20
Figure 6	Portrait of Alexander I	26

Chapter 2

Figure 1	Europe's great powers in 1815	34–5
Figure 2	Central Europe in 1815	39
Figure 3	The Ottoman Empire	50

Chapter 3

Figure 1	The Habsburg Empire	73
Figure 2	Revolutions in Italy	89
Figure 3a	Long-term problems	91
Figure 3b	The situation in 1845–8	92

Chapter 4

Figure 1	Map of the Near East	102

Chapter 5

Figure 1	Italian revolutions 1820–1 and 1831	115
Figure 2	Mazzini	116
Figure 3	The Unification of Italy 1859–70	127
Figure 4	Garibaldi in 1849	129

Chapter 6

Figure 1	Germany and the Austrian Empire 1815	143
Figure 2	Germany and Austria-Hungary in 1867	162
Figure 3	Map of the Franco-Prussian War	167
Figure 4	William I proclaimed Emperor of Germany, 1871	169

Chapter 7

Figure 1	Map of the German Empire 1871	174
Figure 2	How was Germany ruled?	175
Figure 3	Bismarck in 1877	176
Figure 4	*Punch* cartoon 1873	188
Figure 5	The Balkans 1878	192

Chapter 8

Figure 1	Alexander II (1855–81) – The 'Tsar Liberator'?	202
Figure 2	The impact of emancipation of the serfs in Russia	205
Figure 3	Russian industrial progress	208
Figure 4	The Dual Monarchy	215

| *Figure 5* | Constitutional organisation of Austria-Hungary | 216 |
| *Figure 6* | *Punch* cartoon | 222 |

Chapter 9
Figure 1	Rate of economic growth 1880–1900	243
Figure 2	Kaiser William II	245
Figure 3	General Georges Boulanger	251
Figure 4	The Russian Empire in 1905	254
Figure 5	Photograph of Nicholas and Alexandra	258

Chapter 10
Figure 1	Africa in 1914	269
Figure 2	China and the Far East	271
Figure 3	*Punch* cartoon 1905	275
Figure 4	The Balkans in 1912 and 1913	279
Figure 5	The Schlieffen Plan	283

List of Profiles

Klemens Metternich	22
Count Camillo di Cavour	123
Giuseppe Garibaldi	129
Otto von Bismarck	154
Louis Napoleon	219

List of Tables

Chapter 6
| *Tables 1 & 2* | Statistical comparisons: France, Germany and Austria-Hungary | 156 |

Chapter 7
| *Table 1* | German production: 1870–90 | 179 |
| *Table 2* | Germany's political parties | 181 |

Chapter 9
Table 1	Population table	236
Table 2	Share of world industrial production	237
Table 3	*Reichstag* election results	244
Table 4	Diagram showing major nationalities in Russia	255
Tables 5a)–f)	Diagrams showing Russia's economic performance	262

Chapter 10
| *Table 1* | The strengths of the powers in 1900 | 265 |

PREFACE

Access to History Context

Structure

In some ways *Access to History Context* volumes are similar to most text-books. They are divided into chapters, each of which is focused on a specific topic. In turn, chapters are divided into sections which have self-explanatory headings. As is the case with most textbooks, *Context* authors have organised the chapters in a logical sequence so that, if you start at the beginning of the book and work your way through to the end, everything will make sense. However, because many readers 'dip' into textbooks rather than reading them from beginning to end, care has been taken to make sure that whichever chapter you start with you should not find yourself feeling lost.

Special features in the main text

Points to consider – at the start of each chapter this shaded box provides you with vital information about how the chapter is organised and how the various issues covered relate to each other.

Issues boxes are a standard feature of each chapter and, like points to consider boxes, are designed to help you extract the maximum benefit from the work you do. They appear in the margin immediately following most numbered section headings. The question(s) contained in each issues box will tell you which historical issue(s) the section is primarily going to cover. If the section you intend to start with has no issues box, turn back page by page until you find one. This will contain the questions the author is considering from that point onwards, including the section you are about to read.

Boxed sections appear in both the margin and the main column of text. In each of the boxes you will find a self-explanatory heading which will make it clear what the contents of the box are about. Very often, the contents of boxes are explanations of words or phrases, or descriptions of events or situations. When you are reading a chapter for the first time you might make a conscious decision to pay little attention to boxed entries so that you can concentrate your attention on the author's main message.

Q-boxes appear in the margin and contain one or more questions about the item they appear alongside. These questions are intended to stimulate you to think about some aspect of the material the box is linked to. The most useful answers to these questions will often emerge during discussions with other students.

Activities boxes – as a general rule, the contents of activities boxes are more complex than the questions in Q-boxes, and often require you to undertake a significant amount of work, either on your own or with others. One reason for completing the task(s) is to consolidate what you have already learnt or to extend the range or depth of your understanding.

Profiles – most of these are about named individuals who are central to an understanding of the topic under consideration: some are about events of particular importance. Each profile contains a similar range of material. The two aspects you are likely to find most useful are:

▼ the dated timeline down the side of the page; and
▼ the source extracts, which provide you with ideas on what made the subject of the Profile especially notable or highly controversial.

Profiles also provide useful points of focus during the revision process.

End-of-chapter sections

The final pages of each chapter contain different sections. It is always worthwhile looking at the **Summary chart** or **Summary diagram** first. As their names suggest, these are designed to provide you with a brief and carefully structured overview of the topic covered by the chapter. The important thing for you to do is to check that you understand the way it is structured and how the topics covered interrelate with one another.

The **Working on...** section should be studied in detail once you have finished your first reading of the main text of the chapter. Assuming that you read the Points to Consider section when you began work on the chapter, and that you followed any advice given in it when you read the chapter for the first time, the Working on... section is designed to suggest what form any further work you do on the chapter should take.

The **Answering extended writing and essay questions on...** sections, taken as a whole throughout the book, form a coherent body of guidance on how to tackle these types of examination questions successfully.

The same is true of the **Answering source-based questions on...** sections which have been carefully planned bearing in mind the ways you need to build on the skills you have already developed in this area. You may find these sections particularly helpful during the time you are preparing for an exam.

The last part of each chapter contains a **Further Reading** section. These are of vital importance to you in chapters covering topics you are expected to know about in some detail. To do well in any History course it is essential to read more than one book. However, it is possible to find individual books which can act as your guide and companion throughout your studies, and this is one of them. One of the major ways in which it fulfils this function is by providing you with detailed guidance on the way you can make the most effective use of your limited time in reading more widely.

This book is an integral part of the Access to History series. One of its functions is to act as a link between the various topic books in the series on the period it covers, by drawing explicit attention in the Further Reading sections to where, within the series, other material exists which can be used to broaden and deepen your knowledge and understanding. Attention is also drawn to the non-Access to History publications which you are likely to find most useful. By using material which has been written based on the same aims and objectives, you are likely to find yourself consistently building up the key skills and abilities needed for success on your course.

Revision

Context books have been planned to be directly helpful to you during the revision period. One of the first things many students do when starting to revise a topic for an examination is to make a list of the 'facts' they need to know about. A safer way of doing this (because it covers the possibility that you missed something important when you originally worked on the topic) is to compile your lists from a book you can rely on. Context volumes aim to be reliable in this sense. If you work through the chapter which covers the topic you are about to revise and list the events contained in marginal 'events lists' and in boxed lists of events, you can be confident that you have identified every fact of real significance that you need to know about on the topic. However, you also need to make a list of the historical issues you might be asked to write about. You can do this most conveniently by working through the relevant chapter and noting down the contents of the 'Issues boxes'.

For almost everybody, important parts of the revision process are the planning of answers to all the main types of structured and essay questions, and the answering of typical questions (both those requiring extended writing and those based on source material) under exam conditions. The best way to make full use of what this book has to offer in these respects is to work through the two relevant sets of End-of-chapter sections (Answering extended writing and essay questions on… and Answering source-based questions on…) in a methodical manner.

Keith Randell

EUROPE 1815–48: THE DOMESTIC SCENE

POINTS TO CONSIDER

In 1815 most of Europe was again ruled by absolute monarchs who had survived the French Revolutionary and Napoleonic Wars. Committed to preserving the *status quo*, the monarchs faced challenges as a result of accelerating economic and social change and the spread of new ideas, especially nationalism and liberalism. What were the general problems facing most European governments in the years 1815–48? How did these problems affect continental Europe's three main powers – France, Austria and Russia?

1   Europe: general trends 1815–48

a) The impact of the French Revolution and the Napoleonic Wars

ISSUE:
What were the main political, economic and social features of Europe 1815–48?

The French Revolution and the Napoleonic Wars had a profound impact on most of Europe. In 1789 the French had risen in revolt against an absolute monarchy and set up a government based on the notion that power should ultimately lie with the people. The revolution eliminated the old privileged groups in France. By 1793 King Louis XVI had been guillotined and revolutionary France was at war with most of Europe. French military success ensured that revolutionary ideas spread. Whether Napoleon Bonaparte, who took over control of France in 1799 and proclaimed himself emperor in 1804, was a supporter or an opponent of the revolution is debatable. His conquests, however, certainly changed the map of Europe. By 1811 most of Europe was under his control. Old rulers were swept away as he reorganised Europe in a way that he hoped would benefit his own – and French – interests. Across Europe traditional values and ways of life also came under attack as French soldiers and officials introduced new practices. Some of the changes were seen by some, if not most, people as improvements.

▼ Serfdom was abolished.
▼ Religious toleration was introduced.
▼ Careers were now open to talent.
▼ New improved legal systems were introduced.

However, those areas occupied by French armies were subjected to conscription and heavy taxation. Whatever the French proclaimed about liberation, it seemed that one form of tyranny had simply been replaced by another. In economically backward areas of Europe, like Spain, Naples and Russia, loyalty to God and the old order remained strong.

Figure 1 Europe in 1815

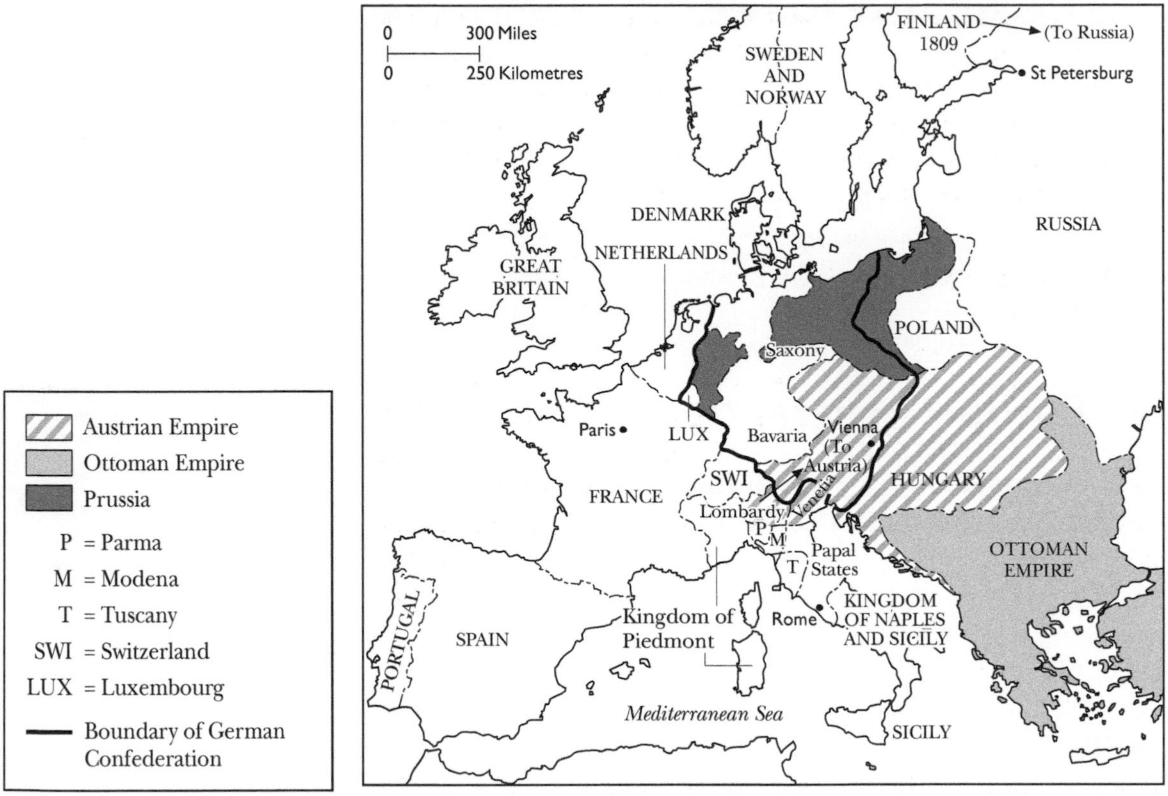

The memory of the revolutionary-Napoleonic experience had a massive impact in shaping the political ideas of Europe after 1815. The revolution proved that the established order could be overthrown: it thus provided a precedent for future generations who were opposed to the *status quo*. The belief that only representative government is legitimate and that sovereignty – ultimate power – lies with the people was another major revolutionary legacy. For conservatives the revolution was a warning and a threat. Fears of revolution often determined the decisions of rulers and their advisers post-1815.

b) The political situation

By 1815 Napoleonic France and the ideas associated with the French Revolution seemed to have been defeated. Across Europe the traditional ruling classes were back in control. The Vienna peace settlement (see chapter 2) was more than just a set of territorial arrangements: it was also a general political settlement that aimed to restore the old order – monarchy, the power of the church, and aristocratic influence. There was almost universal acceptance of hereditary monarchy as the normal constitutional form. However, the actual powers of Europe's monarchs varied widely. At one extreme, British kings had limited powers. Parliament effectively ruled. At the other extreme, Russian tsars had absolute power.

c) The economic situation

i) Rising population

Europe's population grew from 187 million in 1800 to 266 million in 1850. The increase was unevenly spread. The population of Russia and Prussia rose by 75 per cent. The French population, by contrast, only grew by 30 per cent. The rate of increase was generally higher in the countryside than in the towns. However, many capital cities and industrial towns, attracting people from the countryside, more than doubled in size. People generally had more children and lived longer. However, limited medical progress, poor sanitation and outbreaks of smallpox, typhoid and cholera still inflicted heavy losses of life and there was an appallingly high infant mortality rate.

ii) Agriculture

Most Europeans still lived, worked and died in the countryside. The introduction of new crops, fertilisers, machinery, and improved breeding of animals began to have an impact on farming in some regions. Agricultural colleges, societies and journals encouraged new development. The general picture is one of rising output which helped sustain, and helps explain, Europe's population growth. However, across much of Europe there were few major changes. While some large landowners were able to take advantage of new techniques, peasants lacked the means to do so. Bad harvests remained a serious threat.

iii) Transport and communications

There were considerable, if patchy, improvements.

▼ The development of canal and river traffic enabled goods to be moved more easily.

▼ Extensive road building programmes were begun in France, Austria and Prussia.

▼ The main transport development came in the 1830s with the construction of railways.

iv) Industrial development

In the first half of the 19th century fewer than 10 per cent of Europeans were directly involved in some form of industrial enterprise and no more than a quarter of these worked in factories. Pockets of industrial development were the exception in what remained an essentially rural landscape. While the impact of new, invariably British, inventions led to a gradual acceleration of industrial growth, this should not be exaggerated. Massive industrial development did not occur until after 1850.

d) The social situation

i) The aristocracy and gentry

The aristocracy's wealth and power came from the ownership of huge landed estates. This class dominated positions in the government, church and army virtually everywhere in Europe.

ii) The middle classes (or bourgeoisie)

Industrialisation led to an increase in the political and economic power of the middle class. This class was divided into an infinite number of groups with different interests and degrees of prosperity.

iii) The peasantry

The vast majority of Europeans were peasants. However, there were many different types of peasants. In eastern Europe many peasants were serfs who had to pay a variety of feudal dues, including working on nobles' land several days a week. In western Europe most peasants were small landowners. Some prospered. In general, however, the growth of population led to rural poverty and migration to the cities. Peasant unrest, arising from wretched conditions, was normal across much of southern and eastern Europe.

iv) The urban working class (or proletariat)

There were at least three 'working classes'.

▼ *The factory proletariat* was small in number. In France in 1848, only a quarter of manufacturing workers were employed in factories and mines.

▼ *Craftsmen, handweavers and artisans* were far more common. Most industrial workers worked in small workshops of less than five people.

The new factories and mechanisation threatened the livelihoods of craftsmen.

▼ The 'lumpen' proletariat, the unskilled and often unemployed, was growing, swollen by an exodus from the countryside.

2 Nationalism, liberalism and radicalism

a) Nationalism

In 1815 the political organisation of most of Europe was not based on nationality. Italy, for example, was divided into eight states while the German Confederation comprised 39 states. Dynastic empires were once again triumphant. Nevertheless, the French Revolutionary and Napoleonic Wars had stimulated the development of nationalism. In France a new emphasis on national unity was evident during the Revolution. This was intensified by the experience of war which instilled a sense of national pride and mission. After 1815 Napoleon claimed that he wished to free Germans and Italians from foreign oppression, creating a single national body for both peoples in the process. This was a Napoleonic afterthought. Apart from redrawing Europe's frontiers, he had done little while in power to deliberately encourage nationalism. Even so, French victories may have stirred national feeling elsewhere in Europe. On the positive side, they displayed the power which a united nation could possess. On the negative side, resentment of French conquest provoked a hostile reaction and led to some degree of unity among various national groups. Historian M. S. Anderson has claimed that the growth of nationalism was the 'most important political fact of the nineteenth century'. Few would disagree with him. However, national movements were not particularly strong or successful in the early 19th century. Moreover, they varied considerably from place to place and from time to time.

For much of the 19th century nationalism's strongest appeal was in countries divided by foreign occupation (like Italy) or artificial political barriers (like Germany). The desire to make the political boundaries of states coincide with the boundaries of a nation, coupled with demands for political autonomy or independence, placed nationalism firmly on the side of those opposed to the *status quo*. It threatened to undermine multinational empires like the Austrian Empire. However, the strength of nationalism in 1815 should not be exaggerated. In Italy and Germany nationalism was essentially limited to the liberal middle class and to students. In Poland and Hungary nationalist feeling was limited to the landowning classes. Across Europe the mass of peasants had little interest in nationalism in 1815 or for many decades thereafter.

ISSUE:
How much of a challenge did liberal/nationalist movements pose to the existing regimes pre-1848?

NATIONALISM
Nationalism arises from the belief that a group of people have something in common which binds them together in a national community, making them different from other communities. Nationalists stressed all or some of the following national elements:

a common language;
a common religion;
a shared history;
ties of blood and community arising from long settlement in a particular area.

Nationalists believed that national groups should come together to form nation states – the ideal and only legitimate form of political organisation.

LIBERALISM AND NATIONALISM

While many liberals were nationalists not all nationalists were liberals. Some nationalists were conservatives; others held republican views. Nevertheless after 1815 in many parts of Europe, but especially Italy and Germany, liberal and nationalist aspirations – particularly the idea that sovereignty should rest with the people – were so closely linked that it was impossible to distinguish between them.

REVOLUTIONARY OUTBREAKS

▼ In 1820–1 revolutions occurred in Spain, Portugal, Sicily, Naples and Piedmont. They were caused by general discontent with despotic and incompetent governments and with the restoration of clerical and aristocratic privileges. The revolts either began with an army mutiny or took the form of a military coup. Discontented officers found natural allies among the urban middle class and some of the lesser nobility. The revolutionaries' main demand was for a constitution. All the revolutions were ultimately defeated.

b) Liberalism

Most liberals were middle class. Most wanted:

▼ A guarantee of individual liberties and rights – freedom of speech, press and worship and the right to form political associations and to a fair trial – for all citizens.

▼ A constitution which would limit the powers of absolute monarchs and establish some form of parliamentary government. Liberals supported various 'model' constitutions but, fearing the uneducated masses, they were generally opposed to full democracy. They favoured limiting the vote to a small section of the wealthy upper middle class. The demand for effective parliamentary government was strongest in western Europe. Britain provided an important stimulus to this feeling. British power and wealth seemed to many observers to be the result of the excellence of Britain's parliamentary system. However, liberals also drew support from ideas released by the American and French Revolutions.

c) Radicals, republicans and revolutionaries

Various radical – usually republican – groups existed. Most insisted that any representative assembly should be elected by universal male franchise. Some radicals, particularly in France, wanted social reform and a redistribution of wealth. Socialist theories, however, did not begin to develop until the 1830s and did not have much consistency – or influence – until the second half of the 19th century. Some extremists believed that violent revolution was the only way to achieve their aims.

d) Secret societies

To escape arrest, opponents of existing regimes usually had to operate in secret. Secret societies, with radical and/or liberal aims, spread rapidly during the first two decades after 1815, especially in Italy. The Carbonari, the strongest society, probably had between 300,000–600,000 members in 1820. Poorly organised and lacking unity, the societies were never a serious threat to the established regimes. However, the spectre of revolutionary societies, organised on a European and not merely a national scale, haunted the thoughts of conservatives.

e) The power of the press

Rising educational standards and improved printing technology meant it was possible to disseminate information and ideas on a hitherto unheard-of scale. (In 1810 the best rate of hand press printing was 200 copies an hour: by 1847 steam-powered presses could print 16,000 copies an hour.) The power of the press explains why conservative rulers were determined to control it by repression and censorship.

3 France: 1815–48

a) Introduction

After 1815 France was the most politically unstable of all the major European powers. The main reason for this was the legacy of the Revolution – a complex affair that went through many different stages. Initially in 1789–90 a parliamentary system of sorts was set up which aimed at the destruction of all forms of privilege. The Revolution, however, quickly became more extreme. In 1793 the Bourbon King Louis XV1 was guillotined. Later Napoleon Bonaparte took over as Emperor. In 1815 France was politically divided:

▼ *Republicans*: Small in number, they were committed to the democratic and social ideals of the early Revolution.
▼ *Monarchists*: Many Frenchmen were prepared to accept a constitutional monarch who would maintain traditional values.
▼ *Bonapartists*: There was still sympathy for Napoleon's cause and the hope that he or some member of his family might return to rule.

The legacy of Revolution: the losers

▼ The aristocracy had lost its traditional privileges. The émigrés who had fled abroad had also lost their lands.
▼ The Catholic Church had been deprived of its privileges and its huge landholdings.

The legacy of Revolution: the winners

▼ The peasants were freed from irksome feudal dues. Many had also acquired former church or émigré land.
▼ The bourgeoisie benefited from the fact that appointments to government posts were now on the basis of merit rather than of birth.

(Continued)

▼ In 1830 a revolution in France led to the overthrow of the Bourbons. Revolution proved contagious. Within weeks there were revolts in Belgium, Switzerland, Poland, Germany and Italy. The Belgian revolt was successful but the rest failed.

THE IMPORTANCE OF RELIGION

There was something of a religious revival after 1815 and keen – often bitter – religious debate. In France there were clashes between Catholics and non-Catholics; in Germany between Catholics and Protestants; in Poland between the Catholic masses and the Orthodox rulers; and in the Balkans between Christians and Muslims. Liberals generally opposed the influence of the (perceived reactionary) Catholic Church.

ISSUE:
Why was France politically unstable between 1815 and 1848?

Figure 2 Portrait of Louis XVIII

THE CONSTITUTIONAL CHARTER OF 1814

On the civil rights front:

▼ Freedom of conscience, a free press and legal rights were guaranteed.

▼ All Frenchmen were equally eligible for civil and military appointments.

On the political front:

▼ A Chamber of Deputies of substantial property holders (scarcely 10,000 qualified as candidates) was to be elected (every five years) by voters restricted by age (over 30) and property qualifications. Less than one in a hundred French males could vote.

▼ In addition there was an hereditary Chamber of Peers.

▼ The king had the right to initiate and to veto legislation, to issue emergency laws, to dissolve the Chamber of Deputies, to nominate members of the Chamber of Peers, to appoint ministers, and to exert control over foreign policy and the army.

▼ Ministers were responsible to, and had to get bills and budgets through, the Chambers.

---

b) The restoration of the Bourbon monarchy

In April 1814 59-year-old Louis Bourbon, brother of the guillotined Louis XVI, became French King. While he lacked charisma and dynamism, he had the best legitimate claim to the throne and seemed to have some genuine support. An émigré for more than twenty years, he believed that kings were the agents of God and regarded the Revolution as one of history's great crimes. He insisted on dating his reign from 1795 – the year when Louis XVI's son died in prison – and calling himself Louis XVIII. The fact that he issued the Constitutional Charter as a 'concession' to French people, not something to which they had a natural right, was indicative of his conservative views. So was the replacement of the tricolour flag (associated with the Revolution) with the Bourbon white flag. However, Louis recognised the need to be conciliatory to those who still hankered after Napoleon or the ideals of the Revolution. Accordingly he kept his opinions about divine right hidden from public view and accepted the need to rule as a constitutional monarch. The 1814 Charter established a system more liberal than almost any other on the continent. It also confirmed most of the key legal and social changes brought about between 1789–1814. This seemed to disprove the claim that during their exile the Bourbons had learnt nothing and forgotten nothing.

The Catholic clergy and the old aristocracy hoped to reassert their former influence and regain former status. However, Louis accepted that most French people were not eager to see a restoration of the old order that had existed pre-1789.

▼ He confirmed that those who had gained from the confiscation of church and émigré lands would retain their property.

▼ Catholicism was declared the religion of the state.

▼ The Napoleonic administrative, educational and legal systems were retained.

c) The Hundred Days

In 1815 Napoleon escaped from exile in Elba, landed in France and advanced on Paris. Louis fled to Belgium. From April to June (the so-called Hundred Days) Napoleon once again controlled France. However, on 18 June 1815 he was defeated by the Allies at Waterloo and exiled to St Helena where he died in 1821. The Hundred Days dealt a serious blow to the prestige of the Bourbon monarchy. After the second restoration which followed Waterloo, Louis seemed like an Allied puppet, particularly as some 1,250,000 Allied troops now occupied France. The Hundred Days deepened French political divisions and set in motion a so-called 'White Terror'.

d) The political situation: 1816–24

In 1815 the – few – voters elected a huge Ultra majority in the Chamber of Deputies. The Ultras were extreme royalists, many of whose families had been émigrés. Returning to France in 1814–15, their concerns were the restoration of émigré (and church) land, privileges and political influence. Headed by the Comte d'Artois, the brother of the king, the Ultras were well disciplined. Had Louis wished to carry out a counter-revolution he was in a strong position to do so in 1815–16. However, he remained committed to conciliation. He worked with the Constitutionalists – moderate conservatives who saw the charter as the basis for stability. Louis's first government was deadlocked when faced with an avalanche of demands by Ultra deputies including the return of confiscated lands. Alarmed by the excesses of the Ultras, Louis dissolved the Chamber in 1816 and new elections were held. A ministerial majority was returned and Ultra representation cut to 90 in a Chamber of 238. From 1816 to 1820 French governments steered a moderate course between the Ultra and republican extremes. They had some success.

▼ French finances made an impressive recovery. By 1818 France had paid off the allied indemnity of 700 million francs and the Allied army of occupation was evacuated.

▼ Changes in the electoral laws reduced the age of voters to 25 and made one fifth of the chamber eligible for re-election each year.

▼ An 1819 Press Law relaxed censorship restrictions.

In 1820 the Duc de Berry, son of the Comte d'Artois, was murdered by a Bonapartist fanatic. The murder was portrayed by the Ultras as proof of both the radical threat and the government's weakness. Many Constitutionalists, alarmed at a swing to the left in the 1819 elections, moved right. In 1822 a government led by the more Ultra Comte de Villèle tightened censorship. A new electoral law gave some 16,000 of the wealthiest citizens a double vote. Secondary school education was placed under the supervision of bishops. The swing to the right provoked increased opposition from the left, both within the Chamber and outside. A spate of army mutinies and Carbonari-style risings in 1821–2 were easily put down. Revolutionary activity in turn strengthened the forces of reaction. After the 1824 elections the Ultras dominated the Chamber of Deputies.

e) The reign of Charles X

In 1824 Louis XVIII died and was succeeded by the 67-year-old Comte d'Artois, now Charles X. A devout Catholic and a leading Ultra, Charles disliked the 1814 Charter and seemed committed to the

REACTIONARY POLICIES OF CHARLES X

▼ In 1825 one thousand million francs was allocated as compensation for the émigrés. This enraged the middle class. However, many émigrés were similarly disenchanted: the amount they received fell well short of what they had lost.

▼ Efforts were made to muzzle the press.

▼ The elaborate religious ceremonies at Charles's coronation, the return of the Jesuits, persecution of anti-clerical critics and the re-establishment of clerical control over education were all disturbing to liberals.

ECONOMIC RECESSION: 1826–30

There was a series of poor harvests: this resulted in high food prices.

The failure of French loans to South America in 1826 led to a financial panic, resulting in a gradual decline in industrial expansion and increasing unemployment. By July 1830 more than 25 per cent of Paris's population was receiving some form of charitable help.

restoration of monarchical authority. His regime was not to be one of compromise and conciliation. His aim was to repair the damage done – as he saw it – by the Revolution. Many liberals were filled with a sense of foreboding.

It was the religious rather than the political issue which most seriously undermined Charles X's position. Most liberals feared the Church's growing influence. Opposition newspapers contained numerous reports, sometimes true but often invented, of injustices committed by Church officials and gave the (wrong) impression that the Jesuit order was slowly taking over control of the King and his ministers. In reality, a religious revival was gathering pace. There were thus growing numbers of assertive missionaries, who because they enjoyed the general support of the regime, were thought to be its agents.

There was also concern about press freedom. With half the population illiterate and with many of those who could read lacking means to purchase a paper, the daily press rarely sold more than 100,000 copies. For most French people the question of whether newspapers were or were not free to criticise the government was thus an irrelevancy. But to the people with power and influence it was a burning issue, and one which both Louis's and Charles's governments handled badly. Newspaper proprietors constantly found ways around the law. Governments alternated between a policy of energetic pursuit of lawbreakers, which made them seem dictatorial, and inactivity, which made them seem ineffectual. Attempts to muzzle the press proved counter-productive: the circulation of opposition newspapers actually increased.

The reactionary tone of Villèle's government roused increasing liberal opposition and there were anti-clerical protests in Paris and other towns. Ironically, Villèle, who insisted on working within the basic framework of the Charter, also faced growing criticism from 'ultra' Ultras, impatient at the slow pace of change. In 1827 Charles X reviewed the Paris National Guard. A minority of the 20,000 guardsmen shouted anti-clerical and anti-government slogans. Next day the government over-reacted by ordering the dissolution of the middle class institution. This was an unpopular move. Moreover, in the event of trouble in Paris, the king had no armed militia upon which he could call to restore order.

In 1827 Charles X called for new elections hoping they would restore a broad royalist base of support. This proved to be a serious miscalculation. Only 40 per cent of the new deputies were prepared to support Villèle and he resigned. For the next two years Charles relied on the ministry of the moderate Martignac. Martignac restricted clerical control in education and relaxed controls of the press, which became even more abusive. In 1829 Charles dropped Martignac, replacing him with Prince Jules de Polignac – nicknamed 'the Ultra of the Ultras'. Polignac, who lacked a majority in the Chamber, tried to halt the progress of liberalism. This was to prove a colossal blunder. What remained of moderate support for the king evaporated. When Polignac was censured by the opposition, Charles dissolved the Chamber in the spring of 1830. The subsequent election gave the opposition an even greater majority. Charles now decided to do whatever was necessary to ensure a majority for Polignac. On 25 July 1830 he issued the four Ordinances of St Cloud.

While Charles could claim that he was acting constitutionally, his opponents saw his move as an attempt to destroy the 1814 Charter. Paris was now the key. Had Charles arrested potential opposition leaders before the Ordinances were published and brought large numbers of troops into the capital, he might well have retained control of the situation. But he did nothing. Indeed in 1830 40,000 of his troops were dealing with the Barbary pirates in Algiers. Charles overestimated the degree of loyalty for his regime. Popular journalists now ignored government censorship. Adolphe Thiers, editor of the influential *Le National*, demanded a government entirely responsible to the Chamber and advocated revolt. Crowds soon assembled to denounce the government. No action was taken to disperse the mob. Charles, reassured by Polignac, went hunting.

> ### THE ORDINANCES OF ST CLOUD
> These provided for:
> ▼ virtual suppression of the liberties of the press;
> ▼ reduction of the electorate from 100,000 to 25,000;
> ▼ the dissolution of the new chamber (which had not yet met);
> ▼ the fixing of a date for new elections (to be held in September).

f) The July revolution

The Parisian troops were unable to deal with the crisis. Urged on by liberal appeals to defend the Charter, workers, students and members of the disbanded National Guard took control of Paris and demanded an end to Bourbon rule. Charles now cancelled the Ordinances and dismissed Polignac. It was too late. On 1 August Charles abdicated in favour of his young grandson the Duc de Bordeaux, and fled to Britain. A small group of powerful men now seized temporary control. Lafayette, hero of the 1789 Revolution, became commander of the new National Guard and undertook to restore order in Paris. A new system of government had to be established. There were three possible options:

▼ A temporary government (or regency) could be entrusted with power until the Duc de Bordeaux came of age.
▼ A republic could replace the monarchy.
▼ The monarchy could continue under Louis-Philippe, next in line to the throne after the family of Charles X.

The first option, which represented the wishes of Charles X, was unacceptable. So was the second: most of the middle class had no

To what extent did the events of July–August 1830 amount to a revolution?

THE 1830 CHARTER OF LIBERTIES

▼ The Chamber of Peers became an upper house of life members.
▼ The tax qualification of deputies and of electors was reduced, increasing the electorate from 94,000 to 166,000.
▼ The age at which a person could be elected to the Assembly was reduced from 40 to 30.
▼ Press censorship was abolished.
▼ Instead of being the religion of the state, the Catholic Church was recognised as the religion of only 'the majority of Frenchmen'.
▼ The Charter guaranteed freedom of worship.
▼ The king lost the power to veto legislation absolutely or to rule by decree.

wish to set up a republic which they associated with mob rule. Supported by Lafayette, Thiers and a majority of the Chamber, Louis-Philippe was proclaimed king on 9 August 1830.

g) The Orleanist Monarchy

Louis-Philippe, the so-called 'citizen king', seemed a far cry from Charles X. Son of the Duc d'Orleans, he had served as an officer in the revolutionary army in 1792. In 1793 he had fled from France to escape the excesses of the Terror. Unlike most émigrés, he had refused to support the enemies of revolutionary France. After 1815, although one of the richest men in France, he cultivated a middle-class exterior, symbolised by his top hat and umbrella. Aged 56 in 1830, he was intelligent, hard-working, and affable. The following was written in 1850 by one of his former opponents:

> He had no flaming passions, no ruinous weaknesses, no striking vices, and only one kingly virtue: courage. He was extremely polite... a politeness of a merchant rather than of a Prince. He hardly appreciated literature or art, but he passionately loved industry. His memory was prodigious and capable of keeping the minutest detail... he was enlightened, subtle, flexible...

Several of the ways in which the Orleanist regime differed from the Bourbon Monarchy were of greater symbolic significance than practical importance.
▼ Louis-Philippe retained his own name rather than becoming Louis XIX.
▼ He accepted the tricolour flag.
▼ Rather than taking the title King of France, Louis-Philippe was crowned as 'King of the French by the grace of God and the will of the people'.
▼ He accepted a new Charter.

The political changes were largely superficial. Less than 3 per cent of adult males could vote in national elections. Arguably there had been no real revolution, simply a change in the state personnel. However, the 1830 Revolution did bring some changes.
▼ A large majority of the government officials, diplomats and generals were replaced by men who were sympathetic to the new regime.
▼ Power was now clearly in the hands of the upper middle classes who had brought Louis-Philippe to power.
▼ Louis-Philippe was far less supportive of the Catholic Church. Leading churchmen no longer controlled the education system. The Jesuits were forced to leave France.
▼ Court life was much less formal than it had been under the Bourbons.
▼ The Orleanist regime presented itself as a constitutional monarchy in contrast to a legitimate monarchy established by divine right.

h) The regime consolidated 1830–40

It was by no means certain that the new regime would last more than a few months. Louis-Philippe faced fierce political opposition from several quarters.

▼ Bonapartists hoped to replace Louis-Philippe with a descendant of Napoleon. After the death of Napoleon's only legitimate son in 1832, their hopes rested with Louis Napoleon Bonaparte. Active followers of Bonapartism were small in number, yet the French masses were still able to be stirred by memories of Napoleonic glory.

▼ Legitimists were committed to restoring the Bourbons. They drew support from the landed gentry and the Catholic clergy. They helped create an atmosphere in which it was not socially acceptable to be too obviously in favour of Louis-Philippe.

▼ Republican activists were drawn mainly from the middle class. However, republicanism, which seemed to offer social justice, appealed to large sections of the poorer urban classes. The continuing economic depression in the early 1830s gave radical leaders hope of inciting revolutionary action. Republican extremists were responsible for several attempts to assassinate Louis-Philippe.

▼ Free from censorship in the early 1830s, talented political writers and artists succeeded in damaging Louis-Philippe's personal image and credibility.

▼ There were even divisions among the supporters of the regime. While the Party of Resistance opposed further change and was prepared to allow Louis-Philippe an important role in political life, the Party of Movement wanted to reduce the king's power.

Louis-Philippe, who determined to rule as well as reign, worked hard to maintain his position and showed political skills and personal courage in the first years of his reign.

▼ He made great efforts to win middle-class support, distributing rewards and jobs to erstwhile supporters, and trying to identify the state with the interests of the bourgeoisie.

▼ The National Guard was reorganised and effective membership limited to the middle class. The aim was to ensure that it would be a bulwark of the regime and the King went to great lengths to win its support.

▼ He showed good sense in his handling of day-to-day political life. While his sympathies lay with the Party of Resistance, he was prepared to tolerate ministries he did not particularly like, provided they commanded a majority in the Assembly.

▼ Given that there was no real party discipline, the Orleanist Monarchy was characterised by considerable ministerial instability. There were no less than 17 ministries in 18 years. Louis-Philippe became skilful at exploiting personal rivalries between the dozen or so main political 'players', such as de Broglie, Mole, Guizot and Thiers, in order to get his way.

Figure 4 Caricature of Louis-Philippe by Honoré Daumier

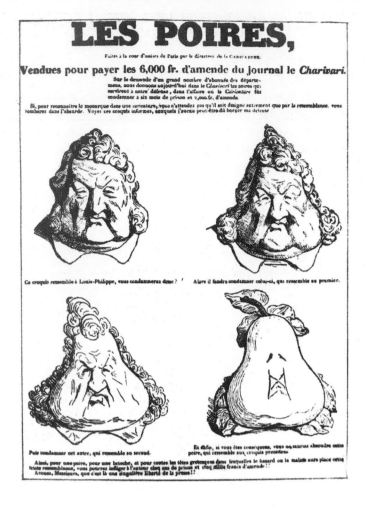

▼ He showed skill in foreign affairs. The July Revolution triggered off disturbances elsewhere in Europe. Nationalists and liberals everywhere looked forward to a French foreign policy which would support peoples struggling for freedom. However, Louis-Philippe conducted a safe and cautious foreign policy.

▼ Extremist activity discredited the opposition and brought increasing support to the regime. Risings in Lyon and Paris in 1832 and 1834 were crushed.

▼ Although the 1830 Charter supposedly put an end to censorship, new press laws were introduced which made it hard for opposition papers to operate without facing fines and confiscations.

▼ By the mid-1830s France seemed set on a course of increasing prosperity and Louis-Philippe's regime seemed firmly established. Louis Napoleon Bonaparte's ill-conceived coups of 1836 and 1840 were little short of farcical. So were the efforts of the radical leader Auguste Blanqui whose attempt to seize power in Paris in 1839 was a total failure.

FRANCE 1814–48

1814 Louis XVIII became king: Constitutional Charter 'conceded';

1815 Napoleon returned from exile: the Hundred Days;

1824 Death of Louis XVIII: accession of Charles X;

1830 Revolution: Charles X overthrown: Louis-Philippe became king;

1840 Guizot was chief minister.
–8

ACTIVITY

Examine the caricature of Louis-Philippe. Answer the following question: What were likely to have been Daumier's motives in drawing the cartoons?

i) How stable was France 1840–8?

Guizot, with Louis-Philippe's full support, dominated the government from 1840–8. The two men, both of whom were determined to preserve the *status quo*, forged an effective partnership. Guizot was convinced that economic progress, symbolised by massive investment in railway building, would rally public opinion to the dynasty. He certainly succeeded in maintaining a majority in the Chamber. In the 1846 election 291 ministerial deputies were returned against 168 for the opposition. In 1847 Guizot reported 'that for the moment there was nothing, no grave questions, nothing!' He was out of touch. By 1847 there was growing dissatisfaction.

▼ By the late 1840s Louis-Philippe, now in his mid-70s, made fewer public appearances and was less effective at creating and maintaining the personal loyalties that he had earlier established.

▼ In 1846–7 there was a widespread harvest failure. The resultant high prices and food shortages led to near starvation in both rural and urban areas. Reduced consumer demand because of high food prices led to growing unemployment in the towns. In Paris tens of thousands were left to exist in misery, depending on charity as and where they could find it. The government did little to help.

▼ Louis-Philippe's cautious foreign policy was unpopular with those who wanted to revive the glory days of Napoleon.

▼ During the 1840s numerous electoral reform bills came before the Chamber, each proposing a moderate extension of the franchise to include the urban middle class. But Louis-Philippe and Guizot were unconvinced. The stubborn refusal to consent to moderate changes in the electoral law alienated social groups which could have been the king's most loyal supporters. Frustrated by their failure to make headway within the Chamber, the reformers took to holding large meetings in banqueting halls. The idea (by no means a new one) was to demonstrate the strength of their support. The first political banquet, held in Paris in August 1847, attracted over a thousand people. A further 60–70 banquets were staged in towns across France over the next few months, their proceedings fully reported in the press. Some of the banquets were taken over by extreme republicans who urged overthrowing Louis-Philippe's regime.

ISSUE:
How successful was Metternich in maintaining stability in the Austrian Empire?

4 The Habsburg Monarchy

a) The Austrian Empire

The Austrian Empire was an accumulation of territories collected by the Habsburg family from the 13th century. It contained eleven distinct national groups. The Germans, who made up a quarter of the population, were the most powerful ethnic group. The central administration was dominated by Germans and German was the language of court, culture and government. Next to the Germans both in terms of numbers and influence came the Hungarians, or Magyars, who made up around 20 per cent of the population. Czechs, Poles and Ruthenians each made up around 10 per cent and there were also smaller numbers of Croats, Slovaks, Serbs, Slovenes, Romanians and Italians. The only real binding agent of the Empire was the Habsburg Emperor. Nationalism was a potentially destructive force.

Figure 5 Map of the Austrian Empire

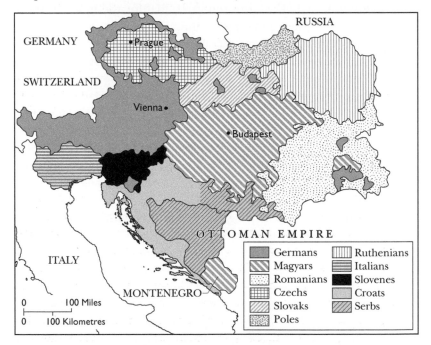

Those ruling the Empire faced other difficulties.
▼ The bureaucracy was unwieldy. Administrative reformers usually supported more centralised control, hoping that this would ensure more efficiency. However, this provoked the hostility of provincial nobles who feared losing their local powers.

▼ Austria emerged from the Napoleonic Wars financially exhausted. After 1815 expenditure continued to outstrip income.

▼ In 1845 80 per cent of the population still lived in rural districts and many peasants lived near starvation level. There was some movement to the towns. Urban housing, working and living conditions were often appalling. The growth of a prosperous middle class, ambitious to play a role in political matters, posed a threat to the established order.

b) Emperor Francis I

Francis became Emperor in 1792. He was almost immediately at war with revolutionary France. The experience of a series of wars, which had often gone disastrously wrong, left a lasting impression. By 1815 Francis hated anything which challenged stability. His motto was: 'Rule and change nothing'. After 1810 he followed a strictly personal form of government. While he possessed a strong sense of duty, his refusal to delegate trivial matters was time-consuming and inefficient.

c) The influence of Metternich

The period 1815–48 is sometimes referred to as the age of Metternich. Metternich's importance extended beyond Austria. He is often cast as the mastermind behind the restoration of the old order in Europe. (See chapter 2.) He has been depicted as a failed reactionary, as a poor policy maker, and as a selfish monster who would do anything to stay in power. Arguably, however, his influence has been exaggerated. Within Austria, he was forced to work within a given framework and set of limitations. (Metternich once remarked: 'I have sometimes held Europe in my hands but never Austria'.)

▼ Francis I played an active role in government. Whilst trusting Metternich above all other men, he did not always take his advice.

▼ After Francis's death in 1835 Francis's eldest son Ferdinand became emperor. Mentally feeble and physically weak, he was incapable of discharging his duties. Imperial power was transferred to a council of regency consisting of Francis's three brothers (Archdukes John, Charles and Ludwig), Metternich and Kolowrat, the finance minister. Metternich and Kolowrat so despised each other that on the rare occasions one wanted to change anything, the other went out of his way to sabotage the move. To some extent Kolowrat was motivated by his own ambition. But he also disliked Metternich's costly military and foreign policies. Kolowrat felt that only by balancing the books and ensuring the Empire's economic health could its survival be ensured.

THE PILLARS OF THE EMPIRE

▼ The great nobility who dominated the provinces were generally loyal to the Habsburgs.

▼ The Austrian army, raised from all parts of the empire, was loyal. The stationing of regiments far from home made it easier to use troops to crush popular demonstrations.

▼ The Empire possessed an efficient secret police force.

▼ The Catholic Church supported the Empire.

▼ The Austrian government was able to play off one national group against another.

The Metternich system

Metternich's foreign and domestic policies seem to demonstrate a large degree of common purpose: to prevent revolution and to preserve rule by monarchy and the social dominance of the aristocracy. He believed that popular challenges to legitimate authority would result in chaos, bloodshed and an end to civilisation. His single-mindedness prompted contemporaries to speak of a 'Metternich system' and historians have subsequently found this a useful concept to help analyse his actions. Some think his 'system' was based on a complex philosophy. Others, like A. J. P. Taylor, have doubted whether there was a 'system', believing that Metternich was simply a traditional conservative whose main aims were simply to maintain the Austrian Empire and to maintain himself in office.

KLEMENS METTERNICH

Metternich was a complex personality. Vain, arrogant, pompous and frivolous, he was also extremely able. He saw little point in false modesty. In 1819 he said:

> There is a wide sweep about my mind. I am always above and beyond the preoccupations of most public men; I cover a ground much vaster than they can see or wish to see. I cannot keep myself from saying about twenty times a day: 'O Lord! how right I am and how wrong they are.'

Although confident in his own abilities and ideals, he was pessimistic about the future.

> My life has coincided with a most abominable time...I have come into the world too soon or too late. I know that in these years I can accomplish nothing... I am spending my life underpinning buildings which are mouldering into decay.

-Profile-

1773	born into high German nobility in the Rhineland;
1794	his family moved to Vienna to escape a French invasion of the Rhineland;
1809	became Foreign Minister of Austria;
1814–5	played a key role at the Vienna Peace Settlement;
1821	became State Chancellor;
1848	forced to resign and flee to England;
1859	died.

d) Repression

Austria's regular police force was surprisingly small in number. In Vienna, a city with a population of 400,000, the regular force consisted of seven officers, 78 NCOs and 490 men. However, Metternich also made use of secret police, censors and swarms of informers. A close surveillance was kept of targeted individuals, including the monitoring of their private correspondence. At its most sinister the system could sanction house searches and even arrests without specific charges. The police also censored plays, poems, novels and newspapers. But imposing ideological uniformity in such a vast empire was impossible. Those who sought 'subversive' literature could easily find it and little was done to punish them. Metternich's Austria was not nearly as efficient – or violent – a police state as Nazi Germany or Stalinist Russia.

e) The German Confederation

The German Confederation, created in 1815, which allowed for a permanent Austrian presidency, was a means of maintaining Habsburg hegemony in Germany. That hegemony was threatened by liberals and nationalists. In October 1817 students of Jena University gathered at Wartburg Castle to celebrate the anniversary of the Battle of Leipzig and the start of the Reformation. The festival, which ended with the burning of reactionary books, alarmed Metternich and he sought an opportunity to take action against radical students. This came in 1819 when a student murdered the reactionary writer Kotzebue. At Metternich's insistence, a package of measures known as the Karlsbad Decrees was adopted by all the Confederation states. The decrees tightened censorship and placed universities under police surveillance. When liberals in some German states called for constitutional monarchy in 1830, Metternich persuaded the Confederation to pass the Six Acts, enabling him to limit the powers of the parliaments of the various states in the Confederation.

f) The Hungarian threat

The main nationalist threat came from Hungary. The 500,000 country gentry, united by common privileges such as exemption from the land tax, posts in local government, and their election of representatives to the diet at Budapest, identified themselves with the Hungarian nation. Their nationalism in the past had amounted to resistance to Habsburg attempts to centralise and reduce their powers. Magyar nationalism was mainly restricted to the landowning classes. The middle classes were too few in number to be significant and the peasantry were preoccupied with day-to-day subsistence. Financial problems brought Francis I into conflict with the Hungarian diet, which he ceased to summon between

> **METTERNICH'S REFORM EFFORTS**
>
> Metternich did try to reform the central administrative system and to improve the relationship between Vienna and the Empire's outlying provinces. However, his schemes met with royal indifference and his hopes of a thorough administrative overhaul were not achieved. He did not wish to impose uniformity on the various areas under Habsburg rule. He supported a federal system, respecting the different regional traditions in the Empire, in particular provincial institutions such as the local diets. These bodies, composed of the local aristocracy, had existed for many years but had little real power. Metternich was inclined to have the diets meet more frequently and to revive those which had fallen into disuse. He hoped that the appearance of local participation in imperial affairs would prevent regional discontent. Ironically he underestimated the development of regional nationalism. The diets were to become centres of opposition to imperial control and led the demands for home rule.

1812 and 1825. This only fuelled Magyar resentment. Difficulties involved in extracting money from Hungary forced Francis to recall the diet in 1825. Encouraged by this success, the Hungarian, Count Széchenyi, put forward an ambitious reform programme, including the abolition of serfdom and the establishment of Magyar as the official language. Széchenyi was not a separatist and wished his plans to be carried out gradually within the context of the Habsburg Empire.

Many minor Magyar nobles were unimpressed by Széchenyi's programme. They preferred the more radical programme of Lajos Kossuth. Kossuth supported:

▼ The creation of a separate Magyar ministry and parliamentary government.
▼ Extension of the franchise.
▼ An end to serfdom, with full compensation to the landowners.
▼ Abolition of noble exemption from taxation.
▼ Freedom of the press and association, and freedom of religion.
▼ *Magyarisation* – the promotion of Magyar culture.

A gifted writer and speaker, Kossuth lauded the Magyar squires as the embodiment of the Magyar spirit and tradition, and popularised the view that the chief cause of Hungary's problems was inefficient government from Vienna. As a result of a three year prison sentence, he became a national hero. Editor of *Pesti Hirlap*, he dramatically built up its readership by preaching a message of radical nationalism.

Metternich was not too worried by Magyar nationalism. He was confident that traditional divide and rule methods would suffice to keep it in check. 'If the Hungarian revolts,' he said, 'we should immediately set the Bohemian against him, for they hate each other, and after him the Pole, or the German, or the Italian.'

g) Conclusion

Many historians insist Metternich could and should have done more to reform the political situation. However, in fairness to Metternich he lacked the power to do much, both before and after 1835. Nor, even with the benefit of hindsight, is it clear what should have been done – not least with regard to the nationalities problem. He adopted various measures including a divide and rule approach, and the encouragement of provincial diets and local cultural traditions. It may be that his policies simply stimulated nationalist unrest. He certainly did not deal very effectively with the threat posed by Magyar nationalism. His only clear policy was rejection of reform. This drove the moderates into the Kossuth camp. His approach to Kossuth was equally unproductive: imprisonment simply made Kossuth a martyr. However, it is not clear how Magyar – or other provincial – loyalty could have been secured. Concessions for the sake of stability simply provoked new causes of instability. A. J. P. Taylor saw Metternich as 'the ablest man who ever applied himself to the Austrian problem'. If he was unable to tackle the problem, perhaps there simply was no solution.

ACTIVITY

Consider the following question: how successful was Metternich in dealing with the internal problems of the Habsburg Monarchy?

Points to consider:
▼ What were the main problems?
▼ Give details of the actions taken by Metternich in response to the problems.
▼ What were the results of his actions?
▼ Evaluate Metternich's performance.

---

5 Russia

By 1815 the Russian Empire covered almost one sixth of the world's land surface and had a population of 45 million. The Empire, made up of numerous nationalities, diverse in language and culture, was held together by the autocratic power of the Tsars.

a) Russia's Problems

> **ISSUE:**
> How successful were Tsars Alexander I and Nicholas I in tackling Russia's problems?

i) Economic backwardness
▼ Russia was essentially agrarian. Inefficient farming methods meant that crop yields were low.
▼ Russian industry was developing at a much slower rate than industry elsewhere in Europe. In 1800 Russia produced almost as much iron as England. By 1850, in contrast, England produced 12 times as much iron as Russia.
▼ Communications were a major problem. St Petersburg and Moscow were not linked by rail until 1851. By 1855 Russia had only one sixth of the length of track laid in Germany.

ii) Social backwardness
▼ Over 90 per cent of Russians were peasants. Over half were serfs, owned by hereditary nobles. As serfs they could be bought and sold, had few legal rights, and had to work for several days a week on the noble's land. Some nobles maintained a firm but benevolent paternalism. Others bullied, beat and even branded their serfs. Some 40 per cent of peasants worked land owned by the tsar.

▼ A small number of nobles owned vast amounts of land. They led the army, provided the tsar with most of his government officials, and maintained local law and order.

▼ Only 4 per cent of the population lived in towns.

▼ Russian society was hierarchical. Everyone had a place and station which was very difficult to change. This tended to stifle enterprise and initiative.

iii) Political backwardness

▼ All political power was centralised in the person of the tsar.

▼ The Orthodox Church supported and provided a firm theological basis for the tsarist autocracy. Any challenge to the tsar's position was seen as a challenge to God.

Figure 6 Portrait of Alexander I

b) Alexander I (1801–25)

Alexander became tsar in 1801 following a coup which resulted in the murder of his father. He remains something of an enigma. His critics see him as hypocritical and deceitful: his supporters stress his charm and modesty. During his formative years Alexander had been subjected to a strange mixture of liberal and military influences and throughout his reign he found it hard to reconcile the two forces. His reign has often been been characterised as a period of liberal intent followed by a period of severe repression.

i) Reform pre-1815

Alexander's reign began with a liberal flourish as he tried to distance himself from the unpopular policies of his father.

▼ In 1801 he promised an amnesty for political prisoners, the abolition of torture and repeal of the prohibition of foreign books.

▼ Some autonomy was given to Finland after its annexation in 1809.

▼ Efforts were made to improve education.

▼ Some attempts were made to reform the government.

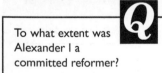

To what extent was Alexander I a committed reformer?

At war with Napoleon between 1812–14 the Tsar had to put his reforming ideas on hold.

ii) Reaction?

The years from 1815 to 1825 are usually presented as years of reaction with Alexander abandoning the liberal hopes of earlier in his reign. This is too simplistic.

▼ In 1815 Poland was guaranteed its own army, its own bureaucracy, its own legal system, and its own diet. The Polish language was recognised as was the Roman Catholic faith.

▼ Pre-1820 he had plans to introduce a constitution in Russia similar to that in Poland.

▼ Between 1816 and 1819 serfs in Estonia, Courland and Livonia were freed.

▼ The most ambitious reform of Alexander's last decade was the creation of the military colonies – an attempt to reduce the huge expenditure on Russia's army by placing soldiers on the land, alongside peasants, and making them provide for themselves.

Between 1815 and 1820 Alexander spent two thirds of his time out of Russia. What he thought of as a God-given mission to serve the greater good of mankind now occupied him more than domestic considerations. This allowed reactionary elements to dominate at home.

▼ There was little change on the serfdom front. Although Alexander disliked serfdom, he was reluctant to challenge the institution for fear of alienating the nobility.

▼ In 1817 education and religion were fused together in a new ministry of spiritual affairs and education. The new ministry tried to transform public education into a vehicle for the transmission of Christianity at the expense of practical or progressive courses. Universities were purged of staff, students, books and subjects.

▼ Alexander kept a firm grip on Poland, forbidding the diet to discuss finances, and ensuring that Russians retained command of the army and dominated the administration.

▼ Revolutions in Spain, Naples and Portugal and a mutiny by one of the crack guard regiments in St Petersburg in 1820 convinced Alexander that there was an international conspiracy against Christianity and monarchy. Abandoning whatever plans he had for constitutional reform, he adopted a more reactionary posture. The role of the secret police was expanded and censorship became tighter.

iii) Growing opposition

As Alexander became more reactionary, there was a growth of organised opposition. The two most important secret societies were the Society of the North, based in St Petersburg, and the Society of the South, based in the Ukraine. The former supported constitutional monarchy and the abolition of serfdom. The latter embraced a more extreme republican programme. Both societies were dominated by young, idealistic army officers and nobles. A full-scale military coup was scheduled for May 1826.

c) The Decembrist revolt

Alexander died in November 1825. A succession crisis followed. Alexander's next brother Constantine, governor-general of Poland, had secretly renounced his claim in favour of his younger brother Nicholas. Although Alexander had designated Nicholas his successor, he told only a few close advisers. Even Nicholas did not know of it. Thus in November 1825 each brother proclaimed the other as Tsar.

POSITIVE FEATURES OF THE MILITARY COLONIES

▼ They supported over one quarter of the peacetime army.

▼ Some colonies developed efficient farming techniques and cereal yields increased.

▼ The colonies did bring material benefits. Living conditions – housing, food, clothing – were often better than those of ordinary peasants.

NEGATIVE FEATURES OF THE MILITARY COLONIES

▼ Both the soldiers and the existing peasants resented the colonies' strict regimentation. Colonists were told when to work and at what, whom to marry and when, and even how many children to have.

▼ Many soldiers had no wish to be peasants and vice versa.

▼ Few colonies ever became self-sufficient.

▼ The colonies became the focus for the most severe criticism of the tsar. Arakcheyev, the man most associated with military colonies, brutally crushed colonist dissent.

ACTIVITY

To what extent was Alexander I a liberal autocrat?

Suggested line of response:
▼ What were Alexander's aims?
▼ What did he do that was liberal?
▼ What did he do that was autocratic?

RUSSIA

1801	Alexander I became Tsar;
1816	military colonies established;
1825	November death of Alexander I; December: Nicholas I became tsar; Decembrist Revolt
1830–1	Polish Revolt;
1855	Death of Nicholas I.

Q

To what extent was Nicholas 'a merely repressive ruler'?

Problems of communication – Constantine was in Warsaw, Nicholas in St Petersburg – compounded the problem. Not until 14 December was Nicholas finally proclaimed Tsar.

The succession debacle gave the Northern and Southern Societies a chance to act. The Northern Society spread charges among the troops in St Petersburg that Nicholas was an illegal pretender and that Constantine, depicted as a sincere constitutional reformer (which he was not), was being denied his rightful throne. On 14 December most troops took their oath of allegiance to Nicholas. But 3,000 men, answering the call of the conspirators, announced their allegiance to Constantine and marched into the Senate Square, declaring support for 'Constantine and Constitution'. Some apparently believed that Constitution was Constantine's wife! Northern Society leaders made impassioned speeches and argued over what to do next. Nicholas, in command of 10,000 loyal troops, tried to persuade the rebels to retire peacefully, hoping to avoid bloodshed. Near dusk, however, he ordered his artillery to fire at the rebels who fled. The St Petersburg rebellion was over. The Southern Society revolt in the Ukraine was quickly put down. In many ways the Decembrist revolt was a traditional attempted coup. The Decembrists counted amongst their number some of Russia's most noble families. However, it is possible to see the revolt as the forerunner of more populist movements which sought to end Tsarist autocracy. The Decembrists, although disagreeing about what changes should be made, at least agreed that fundamental change was necessary.

d) Nicholas I (1825–55)

Nicholas, who had no wish to become Tsar pre-1825, dedicated himself wholeheartedly to the task thereafter. He insisted on being in control of events and believed in firm action. He dealt sternly with the Decembrists. Five leaders were hanged and 116 others exiled to Siberia: hundreds of soldiers were flogged. Anxious to prevent a similar occurrence in the future, Nicholas made an investigation of the revolt his first priority. He then sought to remedy the problems which the investigative committee highlighted – administrative inefficiency and an antiquated legal system. He believed that change should come from him: he did not accept that there was any fault in the idea of autocracy.

i) Reforms
Nicholas's reign was by no means all reaction and repression. The Tsar desired a well-ordered society. To achieve this aim, he was prepared to implement change.
▼ The most reactionary figures from Alexander's reign, such as Arakcheyev, lost office.

▼ Nicholas reformed his own administration. The original chancery became the so-called First Section, functioning as the tsar's private secretariat. In 1826 he established the Second Section, to deal with the codification of the legal system, and the Third Section, to regulate the activities of potential opponents. A Fourth Section, to control education, and a Fifth Section, to administer the state peasants, were also created. Ironically, these reforms simply added to the bureaucracy. Nicholas, reluctant to delegate, became overloaded with work. His administration, in consequence, was slow and inefficient.

▼ In 1833 Russian law was codified and published for the first time since 1649. The legal system, while remaining corrupt, at least had a clear basis from which to work.

▼ Nicholas, convinced that serfdom was an economic and moral evil, established nine secret commissions to examine the practice. Several measures were passed to improve the lot of the serf. Laws in 1842 and 1847, for example, made it easier for serfs to buy their freedom. However, these changes did not affect the vast majority of serfs. Nicholas, fearing noble opposition, took no really decisive action.

▼ The Fifth Section aimed to make the state peasants more efficient producers, both for the benefit of the state and as an example for the landowners to follow with their serfs. Many state serfs were allowed to live as free citizens. The government purchased land from landowners for distribution among the peasants while new land in Siberia was opened up to landless peasants.

▼ Until the 1850s censorship was not as extensive as it had been in the early 1820s. Only three journals were actually closed down during the whole of Nicholas's reign. Intellectual life flourished in both the sciences and the arts. Prominent writers in this period included the poet Pushkin and novelists Gogol, Turgenev and Dostoyevsky.

▼ There was some economic progress. Russia's national debt was reduced, and the value of the rouble stabilised.

'ORTHODOXY, AUTOCRACY AND NATIONALITY'

This slogan came to represent the official ideology of the regime.

▼ Orthodoxy: the Orthodox Church, with the tsar at its head, demanded obedience. Jews and Catholics were persecuted in an effort to secure religious uniformity.

▼ Autocracy: Nicholas retained absolute authority.

▼ Nationality: non-Russian subjects were to be 'Russified' to ensure uniformity of outlook.

---

ii) The Third Section and censorship

The Third Section had the task of maintaining Russia's internal security. With a uniformed militia and a network of informers, it kept watch on potential subversive organisations and individuals. It had considerable powers of investigation and arrest and could also act as its own court of law with the authority to punish those found guilty. After 1830 it increasingly took over the maintenance of censorship. All writers were closely shadowed and were liable to be imprisoned, exiled or declared insane if found guilty of producing inappropriate material. Uvarov, minister of education from 1833–49, also had a hand in censorship. He tried to establish control over all forms of education. A large inspectorate was built up and students and teachers endured official interference in their lives and studies. Student uniforms and haircuts were introduced and professors had to have the content of their lessons officially cleared before they could be delivered.

iii) The last years of Nicholas's reign

Nicholas did all he could to limit the impact of the 1848 revolutions, both at home and abroad. Within Russia censorship was rigidly enforced. At one stage it even looked as if the universities might be closed down: they survived but were even more strictly controlled. Russia, despite a severe cholera epidemic and harvest failure, was one of the few countries to escape revolution. The country seemed stable and at the peak of its powers. However, the Crimean War (1854–6) exposed Russia's weakness. Nicholas died in 1855 with the war progressing badly. His legacy to his successor included a backward economy, an inefficient bureaucracy and an outmoded serf system.

▼ Working on Europe 1815–48: The Domestic Scene

Construct a diagram summarising the main events of this chapter. This might help you to establish connections. To what extent did France, Austria and Russia face problems arising from social and economic issues and/or nationalist, liberal and radical ideas? To what extent were their problems specifically French, Austrian or Russian? How successful were they in dealing with the problems?

Answering extended writing and essay questions on Europe 1815–48: The Domestic Scene

Consider the following question: why was France so unstable in the period 1815–48?

Make a list of the general problems facing French rulers in and after 1815. Then go on to list the specific mistakes made by the Bourbon kings (especially Charles X) and Louis-Philippe. (You will need to read chapter 3 to find more information about the events of 1848.) Now plan your essay. This should be about a thousand words in length and comprise an introduction, six to eight paragraphs, and a conclusion. Plan the content of your paragraphs. Then write an introduction of six to eight sentences. This should set the scene and give some indication of what the rest of the essay is going to say. Now write a conclusion (again of six to eight sentences) summarising your argument.

OPPOSITION

▼ There was a serious revolt in Poland in 1830–1. Following the rising (which took nine months to suppress) Poland was placed under martial law, lost its right to a national assembly and a separate army, and a process of Russification began.

▼ Opposition to the tsar in Russia was small-scale. Most opponents were forced into exile or imprisoned. Would-be reformers were further weakened by disagreements about ends and means.

Answering source-based questions on Europe 1815–48: The Domestic Scene

Source A
Liberty guiding the people, 28 July 1830, by Eugène Delacroix

Source B
Parisian rebels defend barricades at the Rue St Honoré, on the corner of Rue du Coq, by T. Higham

▼ QUESTIONS ON SOURCES

1. Comment on Source A's title. **[3 marks]**

2. Why might both sources be considered useful in providing an understanding of the 1830 Revolution? **[7 marks]**

3. Using the two sources and your own knowledge, explain the significance of the events in Paris in 1830. **[15 marks]**

Points to note about the questions

Question 1   To what extent was Delacroix trying to glorify the 1830 Revolution?

Question 2   Artists always have motives for producing a picture. While Source B provides a more realistic image of events in Paris in 1830, Source A shows us the attitude of a supporter of the Revolution. It intends to portray the idea that the spirit behind the Revolution was liberty for the people and thus the nation.

Question 3   The sources provide images of the events of 1830. But what was the significance of those events for both France and Europe?

Further Reading

Books in the Access to History series

Read *France 1814–70: Monarchy, Republic and Empire* by K. Randell, *The Habsburg Empire 1815–1918* by N. Pelling, and *Russia 1815–81* by R. Sherman.

General

Among the best books on the period as a whole are *Years of Ambition: European History 1815–1914* by D. Cooper, J. Laver and D. Williamson (Hodder and Stoughton, 2001); *The Ascendancy of Europe 1815–1914* by M.S. Anderson (Longman, 1986); *Barricades and Borders: Europe 1800–1914* by R. Gildea (OUP, 1996); and *Europe between Revolutions: 1815–48* by J. Droz (Fontana, 1967). On France try *France 1814–1914* by R. Tombs (Longman, 1996). On Austria try *The Habsburg Empire 1700–1918* by J. Berenger (Longman, 1997). On Russia read the relevant chapters in *Endurance and Endeavour: Russian History 1812–1986* by J. N. Westwood (OUP, 1987) and *Russia in the Age of Reaction and Reform 1801–81* by D. Saunders (Longman, 1992).

EUROPE 1815–48: THE INTERNATIONAL SCENE

CHAPTER 2

POINTS TO CONSIDER

In 1814-5 Europe's main statesmen assembled at Vienna to settle the fate of the continent. The task would not be easy. Europe had been at war for over 20 years. The 1815 Vienna Settlement was intended to maintain peace and stability. This chapter examines how European statesmen set about realising their aims and how successful they were in achieving them in the period between 1815 and 1848.

From 1792 until 1814 (with just a brief interlude of peace from 1802–3) Europe had been at war. French forces, first in the Revolutionary Wars and then under Napoleon, had won control of most of Europe. At its height in 1811, the French Empire covered 500,000 square miles and had a population of 44 million. In addition to the French Empire, many states in Europe (for example, Spain, much of Italy, the Grand Duchy of Warsaw, and the Confederation of the Rhine) were ruled by members of Napoleon's family or victorious marshals. In 1812 Napoleon tried to conquer Russia. His 500,000-strong grand army reached Moscow but was then forced to retreat. By December 1812 Russian troops and fierce weather had reduced the grand army to some 33,000 men. The Moscow campaign was a major factor in Napoleon's decline and fall.

In 1813 Prussia and Austria joined Russia and Britain in the Fourth Coalition against Napoleon. The decisive engagement came at Leipzig in October. Napoleon was defeated and forced to retreat into France. Thereafter he could do little more than fight a succession of rearguard actions. Meanwhile British, Spanish and Portuguese forces had recovered most of Spain and in 1814 invaded France from the south.

Napoleon's demise was brought about more by his own arrogance than by any united determination of the Fourth Coalition powers to defeat him. The disarray in the allied camp in 1813–14 was quite startling. Metternich, the Austrian Foreign Minister, for example, wanted to maintain French power – and Napoleon – as a counterweight to Russia. So serious were Metternich's concerns that he threatened to make a separate peace with Napoleon. In the end the alliance survived thanks largely to the skill of British Foreign Secretary, Castlereagh. By the Treaty of Chaumont (March 1814) the four Allied powers agreed to continue the war until Napoleon accepted their terms (he refused) and to maintain their alliance for 20 years. By late March 1814 Allied troops entered Paris and Napoleon abdicated. He was exiled to the island of Elba. Louis, brother of the last French king, was restored to the French throne. In 1814–15 representatives of Europe's major powers met at Vienna to restructure Europe's frontiers. There were ultimately three stages to the final peace settlement: the first Peace of Paris (May 1814), the Treaty of Vienna (June 1815) and the second Peace of Paris (November 1815).

ISSUE:
What were the main strengths, concerns and aims of the great powers in 1815?

Which were Europe's two main powers in 1815?

Figure 1 Europe's great powers in 1815

Castlereagh

Metternich

1   The great powers in 1815

Britain

Contribution to Napoleon's defeat
Britain had been Napoleon's chief enemy. After 1808 the British army had waged a successful war in Portugal and Spain. British money and diplomacy had played a vital role in creating and maintaining the Fourth Coalition.
Strengths and weaknesses
The basis of British power was her naval, financial and economic strength. Her army and population were only small.
Main representative at Vienna
Castlereagh: He was admired and trusted by the Allied leaders.
British aims
Britain wanted to forge an enduring peace to serve both the general interests of Europe and the particular needs of British commerce. Castlereagh had no territorial ambitions in Europe. Convinced that any future challenge to peace and stability would come from France or Russia, he was committed to the containment of France and to oppose Russian expansion. He thus hoped to create a strong central Europe which could resist aggression from both east and west.

Austria

Contribution to Napoleon's defeat
From 1792–1814 Austria had been an active member of all the coalitions formed against France. Her military contributions to the Allied war effort were substantial, if not always successful. But she had always bounced back from defeat and was in at the kill in 1814.
Strengths and weaknesses
Although the second largest state after Russia, she had limited financial and military resources. The Austrian Empire was a ramshackle collection of diverse territories.
Main representative at Vienna
Metternich: An astute and unscrupulous diplomatist, he exerted an influence that was quite out of proportion to Austria's limited resources. Some contemporaries had a low opinion of his honesty.
Austrian aims
Metternich's main priority was to re-establish Austrian power and influence in central and eastern Europe. Like Castlereagh, he wanted a settlement which would contain France and restrict Russian expansionist aims. Committed to preserving the old order, Metternich was totally opposed to the granting of concessions to nationalism and liberalism.

Prussia

Contribution to Napoleon's defeat
Although Prussia had suffered a major defeat in 1806. After 1813 the Prussian army acquitted itself with distinction and played a vital role at Waterloo in 1815.
Strengths and weaknesses
Her small territory meant that she was regarded as the weakest of the great powers.
Main representative at Vienna
Chancellor Hardenberg: Acted on behalf of King Frederick William III.
Prussian aims
Prussia hoped to increase her territory in northern Germany at Saxony's expense. King Frederick William, grateful to Alexander for liberating his country from Napoleon's grip, regarded the Tsar as his 'divine friend'. However, he also wanted to remain on good terms with Austria, a fellow-German state.

Hardenberg

Russia

Contribution to Napoleon's defeat
The failure of the invasion of Russia in 1812 had been crucial in Napoleon's defeat. After 1812 the Russian army was the most formidable military force in Europe, playing a major role in Napoleon's defeat at Leipzig and in subsequent campaigns.
Strengths and weaknesses
Russia's economy was one of the most backward in Europe. She was a great power by virtue of her size and the seemingly limitless supplies of serf conscripts for her armies.
Main representative at Vienna
Tsar Alexander I: The only sovereign among the great powers to personally represent the interests of his country at Vienna.
Russia's aims
Alexander I had one very specific goal – the take-over of Poland. With some 600,000 men in occupation, he was well placed to achieve his aim.

Tsar Alexander I

France

Strengths and weaknesses
Despite being the vanquished nation, France still ranked second only to Russia as a military power. She had a large population and a strong economy.
Main representative at Vienna
Talleyrand: A wily and able diplomat, he had survived the Revolution and for a time had been Napoleon's foreign minister.
French aims
Talleyrand was determined that French interests would be recognised and that France would be restored to an equal footing with the other European powers. He did not wish to see any nation become too strong in central or eastern Europe.

Talleyrand

ACTIVITY

In groups try to work out which powers were likely to work together to achieve their aims. Justify your conclusions.

ISSUE:

What were the main problems facing the peacemakers?

2 Peacemaking at the Congress of Vienna

a) Problems facing the peacemakers

▼ Virtually every European state had been affected by the 22-year conflict. Many parts of Europe had been occupied by French armies. Traditional values and ways of life had been attacked, rulers deposed, and frontiers altered.

▼ France had to be prevented from disturbing the peace of Europe in the future.

▼ In the late 18th century Poland had been partitioned between Prussia, Austria and Russia. Napoleon had revived part of the old Polish state, calling it the Grand Duchy of Warsaw, and turning it into a satellite of France. By 1814 it was occupied by Russian troops. Tsar Alexander's determination to create a large independent Poland with himself as king had serious implications for the balance of power. Prussia was keen to acquire Saxony, whose king had been an ally of Napoleon, as compensation for the Polish territory she would forfeit. This, in turn, had serious repercussions for Austria. An over-strong Prussia would threaten Austria's traditional dominance in Germany.

▼ From 1799 the whole of the Italian mainland had been directly or indirectly under French control. In 1814–15 there were conflicting claims to virtually every square mile of territory. The peacemakers had to decide whether to create a more unified state or to restore Italy to its pre-Napoleonic position with numerous small states.

▼ In the late 18th century there were some 300 separate German states, most of which were part of the Holy Roman Empire. In 1806 Napoleon had destroyed the Empire. Some parts of Germany had been annexed to France: some states had been truncated; others had been enlarged; and totally new states had been created.

▼ Underlying the whole process of peacemaking and exercising considerable influence over the outcome of the Congress of Vienna was the fact that a series of treaties had been concluded among some or all of the allies before 1814. For example, in the Treaty of Kalisch (1813) Russia made specific promises on Prussia's right to recover her former strength in Germany.

b) The process of peacemaking

From October 1814 to May 1815 Europe's chief statesmen met at Vienna to work out peace terms. The congress began in dispute. Under the terms of a secret article of the first Peace of Paris, the four great powers of the Quadruple Alliance had allocated to themselves the right to decide the future of Europe. This agreement excluded not only France but several significant nations which had also fought against Napoleon. Talleyrand, determined to prevent the dilution of French power, skilfully set about exploiting the disappointment of the minor powers and managed to secure a Committee of Eight consisting of the Big Four plus France, Spain, Portugal and Sweden to direct proceedings at Vienna. More importantly, he obtained the admission of France into the discussions of the Big Four, which now became the 'Big Five'. The Big Five decided most of the major territorial issues. The final peace settlement, almost inevitably, represented a series of deals and compromises between the great powers.

c) General aims and principles

While there were major differences of opinion among the Allies, there was some general agreement about fundamental principles and the nature of the final settlement. These included:

▼ *The need to provide for the maintenance of lasting peace, security and order in Europe.*

▼ *Restoration of rulers and states on the basis of the principle of legitimacy:* The main supporter of the principle was Talleyrand. Given the opposition to republicanism, there was often little alternative to the restoration of hereditary rulers. However, the application of the principle of legitimacy was haphazard in practice. Former dynasties were restored when it suited the convenience of one or more of the great powers. In central Italy, for example, restoring Habsburg dukes and princes was part of Metternich's design to create an Austrian paramountcy over Italy. However, the rights of legitimate rulers were often ignored.

▼ *The balance of power:* At its most basic level this concept held that the ideal state system was one where no single power was able to exercise control over the others. Napoleon had upset this balance and, in Castlereagh and Metternich's view, it was the peacemakers' task to restore Europe's 'equilibrium'. This was no easy matter. Different states interpreted the balance of power concept to suit their own interests.

▼ *Rewards for the victors:* It was agreed that the victors should benefit at the expense of Napoleon's allies.

▼ *Containment of France:* Most of the states bordering France in 1789 had been too weak to offer effective resistance to French armies. All the victorious powers agreed on the need to contain France by creating a chain of buffer states along the French frontier.

ISSUE:
What were the main terms of the Vienna peace settlement?

3 The Vienna Settlement

a) The settlement of France

The first Peace of Paris (May 1814) was exceptionally lenient to France. Leniency seemed the best guarantee for stability in Europe. A harsh settlement would only serve to increase French resentment.

▼ France was restored to her 1792 frontiers.

▼ Britain received several former French West Indian colonies.

▼ There was to be no occupying army in France and France did not have to pay compensation for the damage she had caused.

The first Peace of Paris was soon amended. In March 1815 Napoleon escaped from Elba and restored his position in Paris. Napoleon's 'Hundred Days' ended decisively when he was defeated by British and Prussian forces at Waterloo in June 1815. The second Peace of Paris (November 1815) was a harsher settlement than the first.

▼ An Allied army of occupation was imposed. This would remain until France had paid an indemnity of 700 million francs.

▼ French frontiers were reduced to those of 1790.

Even so the victorious powers were remarkably lenient towards the state which had created such upheavals in Europe since 1792.

b) The 'cordon sanitaire'

France found herself contained by an arc of buffer states. The aim of this 'cordon sanitaire' was to restrict French opportunites to expand in future.

c) Poland and Saxony

The Polish-Saxon issue dominated the early work of the Congress of Vienna. Tsar Alexander was determined to establish a large Polish state as a Russian satellite. In return for accepting the loss of her former Polish territories, Prussia was to receive the whole of Saxony. Both Castlereagh and Metternich opposed this plan. Metternich feared an enlarged Russia so close to Austria's frontier and was also opposed to any extension of Prussian power in Germany. Castlereagh opposed Russian expansion on the grounds that this would endanger the balance of power. With the former allies split, Talleyrand was able to play a key role in helping to settle the dispute. Worried by the consolidation of Prussian power, he was ready to work with Britain and Austria. In January 1815 the three powers signed a secret military convention which was designed to deal with possible Russian aggression should a solution not be found. The final settlement was a compromise. Prussia received about half of Saxony and a larger area of Polish land. Poland became an independent kingdom with its own constitution but was ruled over by the Tsar. Austria retained more of her former Polish territory. The Polish issue was thus settled with Alexander gaining most but not all of his demands.

d) The reshaping of Germany

▼ The peacemakers accepted the logic of Napoleon's drastic reduction in the number of states of the old Holy Roman Empire but they failed to provide Germany with a coherent structure. Prussian proposals for a north/south division of influence between Prussia and Austria were successfully opposed by Metternich. Instead a 39-state German Confederation was created which included Austria and Prussia. The kingdoms, dukedoms and free cities which made up the Confederation sent representatives to a diet at Frankfurt, dominated by Austria whose chief minister presided over the diet.

▼ Prussia was strengthened. As well as taking half of Saxony, she also gained the Duchy of Westphalia, Swedish Pomerania and most of the Rhineland.

▼ Bavaria gained additional territory, strengthening the Rhine frontier.

Figure 2 Central Europe in 1815

THE WINNERS

▼ By 1815 Russia had advanced her western frontier several hundred miles, gaining large amounts of Polish territory, Finland and Bessarabia.

▼ Prussia obtained valuable additions of territory, consolidating her previously scattered possessions in the Rhineland and Westphalia.

▼ Austria was now in a strong position in Italy.

▼ Britain took a number of naval/trading bases including Malta, the Ionian Islands, Tobago, St Lucia, Mauritius, and Ceylon and Cape Colony (both taken from Holland).

e) Italy

The Italian settlement was designed to serve Austrian interests. She secured Lombardy and acquired Venetia as compensation for the loss of the Austrian Netherlands. Austrian influence was further increased by the restoration of Habsburg rulers to the central duchies of Parma, Modena and Tuscany. The restoration of the old regime in Italy was symbolised by the return of the Pope to rule the Papal States. Ferdinand I's recovery of Naples, demanded by Talleyrand in the name of legitimacy, was made possible by King Murat's ill-judged decision to side with Napoleon in 1815. This enabled Metternich to ignore his treaty obligations to Murat.

f) Assessment of the Vienna Settlement: success or failure?

For much of the 19th century the Vienna Settlement attracted more criticism than praise. It continues to have its critics.

▼ The peacemakers have often been viewed as reactionaries, setting their faces against the new forces of the age – liberalism and nationalism. Millions of people, entire national groups, were transferred into the possession of remote kings, without the slightest regard for their wishes.

▼ The Settlement failed to achieve its aim of re-establishing order within states. Arguably the return of discredited and despotic dynasties simply provoked revolutions.

▼ There was no real balance of power. Austria's financial and military resources were not adequate for her new role as defender of the status quo against likely challenges from France and Russia.

However, historians today tend to view the 1815 Settlement more positively than they do the settlements which ended the First and Second World Wars.

▼ The Settlement was a reasonable compromise between the interests of the leading states.

▼ The statesmen did not make the mistake of enforcing a dictated peace on the defeated nation like the peacemakers of 1919.

▼ The statesmen cannot be fairly criticised for ignoring the national aspirations of the masses which scarcely existed in 1815.

▼ Some concessions were made to the new forces of liberalism and nationalism.

▼ The new Germany was a good deal less divided than the old one. All the German rulers were supposed to establish constitutions.

▼ The Vienna statesmen were far from repressive reactionaries. They were a typical sample of European royalty and aristocracy, men whose formative years had been influenced by the Enlightenment, the rationalist philosophical movement of the 18th century. Their 'enlightened' ideals had been betrayed by the French Revolution. The statesmen associated that Revolution with the Reign of Terror, with continual warfare, and with Napoleon's dictatorship. It was only natural that they should want to re-establish order.

▼ The Settlement was necessarily concerned with re-establishing order within states as well as between states. Although there were a number of revolutions in the following decades, there was more stability than instability.

▼ The Settlement produced stability because all the powers were willing to try to resolve problems that arose within the new framework rather than attempt to destroy it in order to achieve their individual ambitions. There was no war between the great powers for some forty years. There was to be no world war for nearly one hundred years.

ACTIVITY

Consider the following question: 'What were the aims of the peacemakers at Vienna? How far were they achieved?' Devise a plan of seven or eight paragraphs. Then write a conclusion of no more than eight sentences.

THE MAIN EVENTS 1814–15

1814 March Treaty of Chaumont; April Napoleon abdicated; May First Peace of Paris; October Congress of Vienna opened;

1815 April Napoleon re-established himself in Paris; June Treaty of Vienna; June Battle of Waterloo; September Holy Alliance; November Quadruple Alliance; November Second Peace of Paris.

---

4 The 'Concert of Europe' 1815–23

ISSUE:
How successful was the Congress System?

a) The Congress System

The term 'Concert of Europe' is used to describe various attempts by the great powers to cooperate in settling possible causes of conflict between themselves in order to maintain peace. Initially the collaborative effort was conducted through the medium of periodic meetings known as congresses. The congresses were an attempt to continue the great power alliance which had maintained a sense of common purpose in the final stages of the war against Napoleon. This sense of common purpose derived from the almost unique personal contact between the statesmen of the period. For example, both Alexander I and Castlereagh spent well over a year away from home between 1813 and 1815, attending a series of meetings to coordinate Allied policy towards France.

Most historians use the term 'Congress System' when discussing the style of great power diplomacy between 1815–23. The term can be misleading. Indeed, it is possible to argue that there was no Congress System as such. There were congresses after 1815 but there was little that was systematic about them. Congresses took place because all the great powers agreed to hold them. They were conducted without any rules of procedure. There was no permanent organisation for international cooperation. The congresses themselves were simply the tip of the iceberg of diplomatic activity of these years.

The Congress System was little more than an attempt to ensure that the conflicting ambitions of the great powers did not lead to conflict. As such its effectiveness was dependent on the willingness of all five powers to show restraint in the pursuit of their individual interests. A major obstacle to the successful working of the system turned out to be that the great powers did not agree on the fundamental question of the purpose of the alliance in peacetime. Moreover, although the issues discussed at a congress were certainly matters of common concern, it did not follow that all would agree on what action was appropriate to a particular situation. Indeed, international relations were soon marked by mutual suspicion, competition and rivalry.

b) The Holy Alliance

In September 1815 Tsar Alexander produced the so-called Holy Alliance. The signatories, who included virtually all of Europe's rulers with the exception of the Pope, the Ottoman Sultan and the British King, pledged that:

Source A Extract from the Holy Alliance

> ... they will remain united by the bonds of a true and indissoluble fraternity, and considering each other as fellow countrymen, they will on all occasions, and in all places, lend each other aid and assistance; and regarding themselves towards their subjects and armies as fathers of families, they will lead them in the same spirit of fraternity with which they are animated to protect religion, peace and justice.

Why were Britain and Russia increasingly hostile?

At first only Alexander took the Holy Alliance seriously. Castlereagh regarded it as 'a piece of sublime mysticism and nonsense'. Even Metternich called it a 'loud-sounding nothing'. However, as revolutionary outbreaks disturbed European peace after 1820, the Holy Alliance was redefined and directed against those who would dare to challenge the existing political order. It came to be associated in the minds of liberals with the repressive actions of Russia, Austria and Prussia.

c) The Quadruple Alliance

The 'Hundred Days' proved the need to make some permanent arrangements to safeguard the peace settlement. Thanks largely to the efforts of Castlereagh it was agreed that the Quadruple Alliance of

Austria, Russia, Britain and Prussia should continue for another 20 years to exclude the Bonaparte dynasty from France. Castlereagh never doubted that the Quadruple Alliance should be the foundation upon which all the other arrangements should rest. Article VI of the Alliance provided that congresses would be held so that the Allies could discuss 'great common interest' and measures necessary 'for the repose and prosperity of the peoples and for the maintenance of the peace of Europe'. This provided the basis for the Congress System.

d) The Congress of Aix-la-Chapelle (September–November 1818)

In 1818 the Allies met at Aix-la-Chapelle to review their relationship with France. The congress, attended by the rulers of Russia, Austria and Prussia as well as the leading ministers of the four Allied powers, settled the issues of payment of the indemnity and withdrawal of the army of occupation from France. Beneath the cooperative surface, however, there lurked steadily deepening divisions. Alexander hoped to use the congress to obtain the admission of France into the alliance. This would allow the French monarchy to take its place as another bastion of order against possible unrest in Europe. It would also help bring about a Franco-Russian alignment directed against Britain and Austria. Metternich and Castlereagh recognised the danger and opposed the proposal. In the end a compromise was arranged. The Quadruple Alliance was renewed to ensure continued vigilance against possible French aggression. However, France was now admitted to the conferences on an equal basis. There seemed little prospect for further agreement. Alexander's proposals for a 'universal league of sovereigns', which would guarantee all sovereigns their thrones, fell on deaf (British and Austrian) ears.

e) The 1820–1 revolutions

In 1820–1 revolts broke out in Spain, Portugal, Naples and Piedmont against despotic rule. The differing response of the Allies to these revolutions had profound effects on congress diplomacy and led to the reshaping of great power alignments. The revolutions, plus an attempt to kill the British Cabinet and the assassination of the French king's nephew, alarmed Metternich. He feared that there was a central committee in Paris coordinating revolutionary activity, and that if the infection was not halted it could spread into the Austrian Empire. He thus proposed that the power of the alliance should be harnessed and directed in a united effort against the forces of revolution.

Castlereagh, echoing the views of British public opinion, objected

---

EUROPEAN RIVALRIES: 1815–20

Divisions between the great powers – particularly between Britain and Russia – were becoming apparent even as the ink dried on the peace treaties of 1815.

▼ Britain was determined to restrain France and to oppose further Russian expansion. Austria seemed a natural ally.

▼ Austria feared both France and Russia. Metternich, while favouring close relations with Britain, hoped to remain on good terms with Russia.

▼ Russia resented Britain's attempts to keep a check on her ambitions. Aware of Anglo-Austrian cooperation, she was prepared to align with France.

▼ France was acutely aware of her isolation in Europe. She looked for an ally. The prospect of cooperating with Russia against Britain was attractive.

▼ Prussia, fearful of a French attack on her new Rhine territories, looked to both Russia and Austria for protection.

strongly to the suggestion that the alliance should be used in this way. In May 1820 he made his position clear. In his view revolutions were internal matters, to be dealt with by the governments of the states concerned. Each great power ought to act within its own sphere of influence according to its own interests. He refused to associate Britain with the 'moral responsibility of administering a general European peace'. Castlereagh did not favour revolutionary upheavals. Even so, the British government was sympathetic to movements seeking constitutional change in a reasonably ordered fashion.

Metternich's main concern was the Neapolitan revolt – a direct threat to Austrian interests in Italy. He was suspicious of France's efforts to call a congress to discuss the revolt. France's aim was to use collective intervention by the alliance to press the Neapolitans into adapting a system of government modelled on the 1814 French Charter. If successful, France would become the champion of constitutional government in Italy and a rival focus of influence to Austria within the Italian peninsula. Metternich, by contrast, wanted to secure an outright condemnation of the Neapolitan revolt by all the powers and moral backing of the alliance for Austrian military intervention.

f) The Congress of Troppau (October–November 1820)

When the Tsar arrived at the Congress of Troppau, he was still undecided as to whether he would support France or Austria. He shared Metternich's alarm at the challenge to monarchical authority posed by the revolutions but realised the benefits of cooperation with France. Castlereagh had made Britain's position clear before the congress met. He opposed intervention by the powers collectively while conceding that Austria had a right to act under the terms of the Austro-Neapolitan Treaty of 1815 and in order to maintain her influence over Italy. The fact that both Britain and France only sent observers to the congress made it easier for Metternich to hold talks with Alexander. Since Metternich now gave priority to the battle against revolution, he was ready to abandon his policy of cooperation with Britain for the sake of closer ties with Russia. Alexander, in turn, was willing to be persuaded that Europe was threatened by revolutionary conspiracies and that he must support Austria and suppress revolution. Prussia readily fell into line. In November 1820 the three states signed the Troppau Protocol, agreeing that:

States which have undergone a change of Government due to revolution, the results of which threaten other states, ipso facto cease to be members of the European Alliance, and remain excluded from it until their situation gives guarantees for legal order and stability. If, owing to such situations, immediate danger threatened other states, the Powers bind themselves, by peaceful means, or if needs be by arms, to bring back the guilty state into the bosom of the Great Alliance.

g) The Congress of Laibach (January–April 1821)

The Troppau meeting was adjourned to Laibach. The main purpose of the congress was supposedly to attempt some sort of mediation by the great powers between King Ferdinand of Naples and his subjects. However, at the congress there was little attempt at mediation. Instead, the congress gave Austria a mandate to intervene by force to suppress the revolution. During March 1821 Austrian troops stamped out the last remains of the rebellion and restored Ferdinand to the throne. Although Castlereagh agreed that Austria had the right to intervene in Naples, he objected to her doing so in the name of the Alliance. This was the real reason for the collapse of the Congress System. The Holy Alliance powers claimed the right to support any established government against internal revolt. Britain and France objected to this.

The Congress at Laibach was a triumph for Metternich. France's attempt to support the cause of moderate revolution had been a failure, serving only to annoy the Tsar, now committed (like Metternich) to opposing all revolutions. While Austria was no longer so closely linked to Britain, there was still some common ground between them, especially in the Near East and Spain where the revolution had developed into a civil war. France looked set to intervene and Alexander was also keen to send Russian troops to restore Spanish King Ferdinand. Neither prospect appealed to Metternich and Castlereagh. The first might result in Spain falling under French influence while the prospect of a Russian army marching across Europe was nightmarish. Both men agreed that a congress be held in Italy in 1822 to discuss the issue.

h) The Congress of Verona (October–December 1822)

Before the Verona congress assembled, Castlereagh committed suicide. The new British Foreign Secretary was George Canning. Unlike Castlereagh, Canning had no commitment to the collective diplomacy of the Congress System and believed in the simple rule: 'every nation for itself'. Moreover, Canning was not well disposed to Metternich, calling him the 'greatest rogue and liar in Europe, perhaps in the civilised world'. Metternich thus found it impossible to work with Canning as he had with Castlereagh.

To what extent the Congress System a praiseworthy effort to maintain peace?

THE GREEK REVOLT

Spain was not the only issue threatening the Concert of Europe. By 1821 there was a full-scale Greek revolt against the Sultan of Turkey (see section 6). Metternich feared that Alexander, who sympathised with his fellow Orthodox Christians in their struggle against the Muslim Turks, would damage the anti-revolutionary stance of the eastern powers by supporting the Greeks. He also feared that Russia might expand at Turkey's expense, threatening Austria. Alexander was persuaded by Metternich to support the principles of the Troppau Protocol and not to lend assistance to the rebellious Greeks.

Alexander remained certain that the only aim of the alliance was to combat revolution. Since he had agreed not to destroy the unity of the alliance by siding with the Greek rebels, he demanded that the alliance now prove its worth by suppressing the Spanish revolt. Britain remained opposed to any interference in the domestic affairs of another state. The French government was undecided about the best course of action but at least decided that if a French army did enter Spain, it would not be as an agent of the alliance but as a demonstration that France could act independently. This difference of view put Metternich in a quandary. He did not want to give Russia an excuse for marching an army across Europe but feared that a French army might set up a constitutional monarchy in Spain which would set a bad example to the Italian states. But any intervention in the name of the alliance would alienate Britain whose support Austria needed to keep Russia in check in the Near East. Metternich's solution to this dilemma was to persuade France to join the other three powers in sending protest notes simultaneously to Madrid. The notes were to be so threatening that it was assumed the Spanish government would react in a way that would justify allied intervention. This scheme enabled Metternich to preserve an appearance of solidarity among the four powers. It also went sufficiently far towards satisfying the Tsar's demand for action against the revolution in Spain to enable Metternich to persuade him to maintain a united front towards the Greek revolt. Much to Metternich's satisfaction, the congress concluded with a general condemnation of the Greek revolt as 'a rash and criminal enterprise'.

i) The breakdown of the Congress System

Canning's opposition to the alliance interfering in Spain marked Britain's final withdrawal from the Congress System. In many respects, Canning was not pursuing a new policy: he was following the pattern of separation from the alliance which Castlereagh had begun in 1820. The key difference was that Canning felt relief rather than regret at the collapse of the system. At the time many believed that Canning was a champion of liberal causes. However, this was not the case: he objected equally to the excesses of revolution and the unrestrained power of despotism. His association with liberal causes was not so much due to commitment to liberalism but to the calculation that such a policy best suited British commercial interests. Canning regarded the split in the alliance at Verona as a return to 'a wholesome state again', rejoicing that it was once more a case of 'Every nation for itself and God for us all'.

In 1823, French policy became more decisive. France did not abide by the agreement to deliver a severe note to Madrid (simultaneously) with the three eastern powers. Instead a French army of 100,000 men marched into Spain in April 1823. Metternich's attempt to persuade the other powers to join Austria in stopping the French move was in vain. The Tsar approved of the French intervention. Canning disapproved but would not cooperate with Metternich to oppose it. By September French forces had restored the authority of Ferdinand who, to French embarrassment, brutally punished the former rebels. The French invasion, without the backing of the alliance, was an assertion of France's right to pursue an independent foreign policy. The Congress System was clearly in ruins by 1823.

j) The Congress System (1815–23): success or failure?

As an experiment, the Congress System was not so much a forerunner of the United Nations as an early form of 'summit diplomacy'. Arguably a few periodic meetings was an insufficient basis for a successful experiment in international cooperation. Without a permanent organisation to prepare an agenda and to establish agreed rules of procedure, the congresses were incapable of operating in anything but an improvised way. Perhaps the greatest flaw in the system was the failure to establish agreed principles on which the alliance of the powers was supposed to operate. What was constituted in 1815 was an alliance, directed in Britain's view at least, against a revival of French militarism. This was confused with the Tsar's Holy Alliance scheme. By 1820 there was a clear divergence of views about the purpose of the alliance and about what was a serious danger to the peace of Europe. The system was unable to accommodate the different opinions. Once it became clear that there were popular pressures for liberal government, the Congress System might have helped bring about modifications to the Vienna Settlement. Instead, the three eastern powers tried to preserve peace and stability by repressing popular movements.

However, even if the Congress System did not work particularly effectively, European statesmen did have some success in the period 1815–23. The four congresses were each preceded by intense diplomatic activity and followed by searching examination of their consequences. This diplomatic activity was as important and as useful as the congresses themselves. The basis for a stable international order was created. France was brought back into the diplomatic community in 1818. Anglo-Austrian cooperation until 1820 helped to maintain stability by keeping both France and Russia in check. When this cooperation broke down, Austria looked to Russia for aid in defending the established order. The protection she gave to Austria and Prussia helped to preserve the territorial system created in 1815. For Britain, the collapse of the Congress System and the Anglo-Austrian entente were not serious blows. Austria's weakness did not make her an ideal partner for Britain and the cooperation of the two powers had tended to push Russia and France together. The fact that the Congress System had collapsed did not mean that the four powers of the Quadruple Alliance ceased to work together to contain France. The concert of Europe, more important than the Congress System, continued to function.

THE MAIN EVENTS

1818 Congress of Aix-la-Chapelle;
1820 Congress of Troppau;
1821 Congress of Laibach;
1822 Congress of Verona;
1823 French intervention in Spain.

ACTIVITY

Examine Source A – The Holy Alliance (page 42).

1. Explain what was meant by the term Holy Alliance in relation to international relations after 1815.
2. Why were some European leaders heavily critical of the Holy Alliance?

---

5 The impact of Canning 1823–7

Although congress diplomacy ended at Verona, there were continued attempts to organise international responses to events which seemed to threaten European stability. After 1823 conferences replaced congresses as the forum for great power discussions. However, Canning preferred to defend British interests, which he defined similarly to Castlereagh, by unilateral action. He was helped by the fact that crises were often in areas where the Royal Navy could be brought into action.

a) Spain and the Spanish American colonies

The French invasion of Spain in 1823 was seen as a potential threat to British interests. Canning secured French assurances on three points in April 1823:

▼ the occupation of Spain would be temporary;
▼ French forces would not go on to invade Portugal, seen as a British satellite;
▼ force would not be used against the rebellious Spanish colonies, with whom Britain had established important commercial links.

The advance of the French army to Cadiz in September 1823 led Canning to threaten war with France if she broke her word. Direct negotiations proved effective. In October 1823, France again declared she had no intention of helping Spain recover her colonies. Prior to this Canning had approached the USA for a joint declaration against European interference in Latin America but with no success. The declaration by US President Monroe in December 1823 that European interference in the affairs of the Americas would be regarded as an 'unfriendly act' was of little importance at the time and depended on British sea power to be effective.

By 1825 Canning had officially recognised the independence of the new South American states. In a speech to the House of Commons in December 1824, he declared:

> I will admit, for argument's sake, that the occupation of Spain by France was a disparagement to the character of this country; I will admit even that it was a blow to the policy which ought to be maintained in the regulation of the balance of power. What, then, was to be done? There were two means to be adopted in our resistance to it, one of them was to attack the French troops which entered Spain; the other was to render the conquest harmless as far as regarded us, and valueless, or something worse, actually injurious, to the possessor... Was it necessary to blockade Cadiz ... to restore the situation of England? No. I look at the possessions of Spain on the other side of the Atlantic; I look at the Indies and I call in the New World to redress the balance of the old.

ACTIVITY

1. Explain the term 'the regulation of the balance of power'.

2. Using the source and your own knowledge, explain a) why French forces had been sent into Spain and b) Canning's response to the French invasion.

Canning exaggerated what he had done. The facts of geography virtually guaranteed the independence of the new Latin American states. Given the strength of the Royal Navy, European intervention was impossible. Spain and the Holy Alliance powers strongly protested against the recognition of rebel regimes and held a conference in Paris in 1826 to discuss the affairs of Spain and her colonies. Canning declined the invitation to attend.

b) Portugal

Canning also acted independently in Portugal. On the death of King John in 1826, his successor granted a charter of liberties before abdicating in favour of his infant daughter. The three eastern powers expressed alarm at this encouragement of liberalism, fearing its effect on Spanish politics. They encouraged Spain to provide unofficial military aid to the absolutist forces in Portugal to enable Miguel (King John's second son) to overthrow the regency and establish an absolutist regime. In 1826 Canning responded to Portuguese appeals for aid, sending naval and military forces to support the legal government. Faced with this display of British determination, Spain ceased its aid to the Miguelites, temporarily at least.

THE EASTERN QUESTION

The Eastern Question – the problem of what to do about the decline and possible collapse of the Ottoman Empire – was a recurring issue in international affairs throughout the nineteenth century. Turkey's decline had important implications for most of the great powers and posed a major challenge to the Concert of Europe.

6   The Eastern Question: 1823–33

a) The Ottoman Empire

By the early 19th century, the Ottoman Empire extended through the Balkans and Asia Minor to Persia, through Syria and Palestine to parts of Arabia, and included Egypt and the coast of North Africa. Governing such a vast, ramshackle empire, which contained so many different nationalities and religions, was a daunting task. Effective government depended on strong leadership from Constantinople (modern Istanbul), which most of the sultans of this period were incapable of providing.

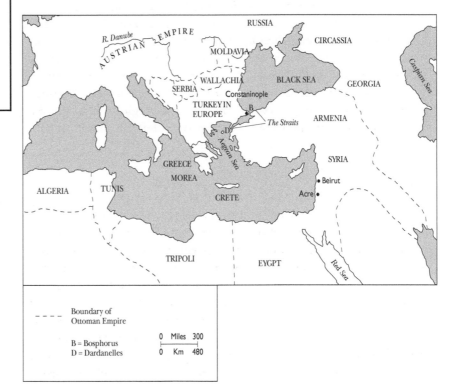

Figure 3 The Ottoman Empire

b) The interests of the great powers

▼ As a result of a series of successful wars against the Turks from 1768 to 1812, Russia had pushed her boundaries southwards. She was suspected of having designs on Constantinople and the Straits (the Bosphorus and Dardanelles), enabling her to obtain naval access from the Black Sea to the Mediterranean. However, after 1815, Russia did not always aim to expand at the Ottoman Empire's expense, as the other powers feared. Indeed, Russia saw advantages in preserving a weak Turkey rather than risk the prospect of a stronger alternative.

▼ Austria was the only other great power whose territory bordered on Turkey in Europe. She had no serious designs on Turkish territory. The Austrians tended to regard the Ottoman Empire as a useful barrier against further Russian expansion and therefore sought to preserve, not weaken it.

▼ In the early 19th century Britain was not committed to the preservation of the Ottoman Empire, described by a British minister in 1830 as 'this clumsy fabric of barbarous power'. However, she was deeply suspicious of Russia's aims, fearing that Russian control of Constantinople would threaten British commercial and strategic interests in the Near East. British policy towards Turkey fluctuated. A complicating factor was British public opinion. This could, on occasion, be aroused by the press to a frenzy of either anti-Russian or anti-Turkish feeling.

▼ France's political and commercial links with Turkey went back over several centuries. By the 1830s France viewed the Pasha of Egypt, Mehemet Ali, as her protégé. France hoped to extend her influence in the eastern Mediterranean – through trade, finance, and technical assistance – regardless of the resultant rivalry with Britain.

c) The Greek revolt

The Greek revolt against Turkish rule broke out in 1821. It hardly lived up to the Romantics' ideal of a heroic struggle for independence, personified by the tragic death of the poet Byron in 1824. Instead, it was a bloody affair in which both sides slaughtered each other mercilessly. The revolt drew on peasant unrest, middle-class demands for a liberal nation state, and religious discontent: Turkey's treatment of her Christian subjects was barbarous. By 1824 the Greeks seemed to have gained the upper hand. Their success prompted the Sultan to appeal for aid from his vassal Mehemet Ali, Pasha of Egypt. Egyptian intervention tipped the scales. By 1825–6 it was clear that unless the European powers intervened the Greek revolt would be suppressed.

European public opinion in general was on the side of the Greeks who were regarded as the heirs of the glories of Ancient Greece. In Russia, opinion focused more on the fate of their co-religionists, the Greek branch of the Orthodox Church. Despite this, until 1825 European intervention seemed unlikely. Metternich attacked the Greek uprising as another manifestation of the revolutionary spirit that threatened monarchical rule in Europe and sought to persuade Tsar Alexander that he should not aid these rebels against their legitimate ruler. However in November 1825 Alexander died and was succeeded by Nicholas I. The new Tsar favoured supporting the Greek rebels.

Britain faced a dilemma. A Russian victory over Turkey could increase her power in the Near East, threatening British interests. On the other hand Canning was aware of British enthusiasm for the Greek cause and of the prospect of trade opportunities if Greece won independence. He decided that it was better to cooperate with Russia in order to restrain her than to persist in opposing her and risk unilateral Russian action. Accordingly, the St Petersburg Protocol of 1826 was arranged between Russia and Britain. This called for the establishment of self-government in Greece and made vague threats about joint intervention if this was not achieved. When the Sultan rejected offers of mediation, Russia, Britain and France (who signed the Treaty of London with Britain and Russia in 1827) were left with no clearly agreed policy on what to do next. Canning's death in August 1827 did not help matters. Fate intervened in the person of Admiral Codrington, commander of the British naval squadron blockading the Morea to prevent supplies reaching the Turko-Egyptian forces. On entering Navarino Bay in October 1827, British ships were fired upon. Codrington promptly sank the Turko-Egyptian fleet.

d) The Russo-Turkish War and Greek independence

Navarino had important effects on the situation. The Sultan was incensed and proclaimed a 'holy war' against Russia, regarded as the instigator of the hostile blockade. All Christians were expelled from Constantinople and the Turks became even more determined to ignore the efforts of the three powers to mediate. The British government, embarrassed by Codrington's action, became reluctant to approve any further measures against the Turks and withdrew from cooperation with Russia. Consequently, it was left to France to send troops to evict the Egyptians from the Morea, while Russia provided supplies for the Greek forces. Then in April 1828 Russia declared war on Turkey. After a sluggish campaign, a Russian army reached Adrianople, less than 150 miles from Constantinople, in August 1829. The Sultan sued for peace. In the Treaty of Adrianople (September 1829), Russia made substantial gains in Armenia and Georgia but sought only modest rewards in Europe, establishing a protectorate over Moldavia and Wallachia. Tsar Nicholas judged that greater demands might lead to the complete collapse of Turkey which might in turn lead to a wider European conflict which he did not want.

Turkey's defeat by Russia severely weakened her ability to resist pressure to discuss terms for a settlement of the Greek revolt. After prolonged negotiations in London the frontiers of Greece and its status as an independent constitutional monarchy were agreed in 1830. The new state was guaranteed by Britain, Russia and France.

THE MAIN EVENTS

1821	Greek revolt began;
1825	Death of Alexander I; succeeded by Tsar Nicholas I;
1827	July Treaty of London; October Battle of Navarino;
1828	Russia declared war on Turkey;
1829	Treaty of Adrianople;
1830	Greece won independence.

7   The revolutions of 1830–1

ISSUE:
What impact did the 1830–1 revolutions have on international relations?

a) The July revolution in France

The July 1830 revolution in France ended the rule of Charles X and brought Louis-Philippe to power. This had a significant impact on international relations. Alarmed at the outbreak of revolution in France, the three eastern powers renewed their pledges to sustain the 1815 treaties. However, they reluctantly accepted the situation and merely warned France against any attempt to disturb the *status quo*. In Austria's case, the decision to recognise the new French regime stemmed from the realisation that the Austrian army was in no fit state for a war. The Tsar, however, refused to recognise the 'vile usurper' Louis-Philippe until 1831, souring relations to such an extent that a Franco-Russian alignment ceased to be regarded as a serious possibility for nearly two decades. In Britain, the change of regime in France was welcomed by the new Whig government. Foreign Secretary Palmerston was eager to promote an Anglo-French entente, committed to the defence of liberalism. However, his willingness to maintain friendly relations with France was conditional on her respect for the 1815 settlement and on French support for British policy in the Near East. This 'Liberal Alliance' had some impact on international affairs in the early 1830s, counter-balancing the conservative alliance of the three eastern empires. Louis-Philippe was anxious to remain on good terms with Britain to avoid French isolation. French governments, however, soon found the role of junior partner to Britain irksome.

b) The Belgian Revolt of 1830

The union of the former Austrian Netherlands with the Kingdom of Holland had been established in 1815 on military and strategic grounds. It was never popular in the Catholic provinces of Belgium. Grievances over religion, taxation and the predominance of Dutch officials soured relations between Belgium and Holland. A riot in Brussels in August 1830, following the July Revolution in Paris, escalated into a full-scale revolt. By September a provisional Belgian government had been set up which proclaimed independence from Holland. An appeal by the Dutch king to Prussia for aid against his rebellious subjects could not be ignored by the great powers. The revolt directly challenged the 1815 peace settlement. The Dutch appeal produced a sympathetic response from the three eastern powers – staunch supporters of monarchical rights and enemies of revolution. However, if Prussian troops went to the aid of Holland, popular pressure in France might force Louis-Philippe to send an army to assist the Belgians and the great powers would then find themselves at war. Britain, meanwhile, sought to defend Belgian independence. This seemed preferable to any one major power, especially France, controlling the coastline facing her across the Channel.

Although sorely tempted, Louis-Philippe chose not to annex Belgium. Instead he worked as closely as possible with Britain to ensure that Belgium became independent. He even refused the throne of Belgium for his son despite great pressure in France to accept. He realised that this would spell the end of the partnership with Britain and was not prepared to sacrifice this for dynastic ambition. The immediate danger of a great power conflict was avoided when Prussia accepted a French proposal for non-intervention in October 1830. In November, the Dutch king and the other powers agreed to an Anglo-French proposal for a conference of ambassadors in London. The conference's initial success owed much to the cooperation of Talleyrand, the new French ambassador to London, and Palmerston, and to the fact that the outbreak of a revolt in Poland diverted Russia's attention from the Netherlands. Since Prussia and Austria were unwilling to act without Russia, agreement was secured on the basic issue of seeking a negotiated settlement.

In December 1830 the London Conference accepted the fact of Belgian independence – a remarkable display of collective responsibility on the part of the great powers. There then followed endless economic and frontier-related difficulties over the terms of Belgian-Dutch separation. After the Belgians accepted the terms of the settlement in June 1831, it was the turn of the Dutch to cause trouble. When their troops marched on Brussels in August, the great powers gave approval to the despatch of a French army and a British naval squadron to force the Dutch to retreat. The presence of French troops in Belgium encouraged French aspirations for territorial gains until a British threat of war persuaded them to withdraw. Dutch obstinacy persisted, however, so that another Anglo-French operation was needed in 1832 to evict the Dutch from Antwerp. Not until 1839 did the Dutch king finally accept Belgium's independence. The great powers were then able to guarantee Belgium's permanent neutrality. (France thus committed herself to her own containment.) Much of the credit for this successful outcome belongs to the skill displayed by Palmerston.

c) The Polish Revolt of 1830–1

In November 1830 the Warsaw garrison rose in revolt against Russian rule. The rising was inspired by a sort of romantic nationalism, promoted by secret societies to which young officers and students belonged. The strength of the revolt lay in the backing of the Polish army which initially outnumbered Russian forces in Poland. Its weaknesses resulted from the lack of mass support: the Polish peasantry suffered less from Russian repression and more from the burdens imposed on them by Polish landowners – the leaders of the revolt. By 1831 Russian forces had put down the revolt. Harsh retribution followed. Poland was placed under military rule. The Polish Diet, Polish universities and the separate Polish army were abolished. A policy of Russification, including the use of the Russian language in schools, was vigorously applied to weaken Polish nationalism.

The Poles had assumed that the western powers would come to their aid. However, they ignored the harsh realities of political life. Poland lay in Russia's sphere of influence and there was little that Britain or France could do to help her even if they so wished. While there was some British sympathy for the Poles, Palmerston had no wish to challenge Russia's right to rule over Poland which was founded on the treaties of 1815. France, the benefactor of Poland in the Napoleonic era, felt a stronger obligation towards the Poles, but Louis-Philippe was not prepared to risk a crusade to liberate Poland. France thus had to content itself with diplomatic gestures and verbal condemnations of Russian action in Poland. This had no effect except to worsen Franco-Russian relations.

d) The Italian Revolt of 1831–2

In 1831 there were risings in the duchies of Parma and Modena. The rebels, hopeful of French support, campaigned for a union of central Italy. The risings, ill-coordinated and weakened by local rivalries, were quickly suppressed by Austrian troops. Austrian forces also dealt with an uprising in the Papal States. This provoked the despatch of a French force to the papal port of Ancona in 1832. France's action, however, was a symbolic gesture: it was not meant to challenge Austria to the point of war. The main result of the action was the strengthening of the conservative alliance against her.

THE MAIN EVENTS

1830 July: Revolution in France;
August–October: Belgian revolt;
November: Polish revolt;
November: London Conference on Belgium began;
1831 Austrian intervention in Italy.

ACTIVITY

Plan a brief answer to the following question. Why was there no war between the great powers in the 1830s over the Belgian, Polish and Italian revolts?

ISSUE:
Why did events in the Near East threaten the Concert of Europe?

8 Near Eastern crises 1831–41

a) The 1831–3 crisis

In 1831 Mehemet Ali invaded Syria which he claimed as the reward promised him by the Sultan for the assistance which the Egyptians had given the Turks in Greece. In 1832 the Sultan declared war on his vassal. By the winter of 1832–3 the Turks had been decisively defeated and Constantinople was threatened by Ali's forces. The Sultan turned to Britain to save the Ottoman Empire from disaster. Palmerston favoured providing support but was overruled by a Cabinet not anxious to increase naval spending. Reluctant to follow an Austrian lead and allow the crisis to be settled by conference diplomacy at Vienna, Palmerston unwittingly paved the way for a Russian triumph.

Of all the great powers, Russia was the most alarmed by the situation. Russia had no wish to see the Sultan's rule overthrown and replaced by the more vigorous regime of Mehemet Ali. Moreover, since Ali was regarded as a protégé of France, his triumph would serve to increase French influence in the Near East. There were sound reasons, therefore, why Russia – Turkey's traditional adversary – should offer the Sultan military assistance. It was gratefully accepted. Consequently, in February 1833, a Russian squadron arrived off the Bosphorus, followed some weeks later by several thousand Russian troops. This show of force, combined with pressure from the other powers, induced Mehemet Ali to come to terms with the Sultan. By May 1833 he had secured recognition of his claim to rule Syria. Russia's reward for her aid to Turkey was the Treaty of Unkiar-Skelessi (July 1833). This was essentially a mutual defence pact. Russia would come to Turkey's aid if called upon and vice versa. In a (not so) secret clause, Russia waived her right to Turkish aid in return for the closure of the Straits to all warships, Russian included, reaffirming what had long been Turkish policy.

The main effect of the crisis of 1831–3 on international relations was to deepen British and French mistrust of Russian policy in the Near East. The quite mistaken belief that Russia had secured an exclusive right of passage for her warships through the Straits created great alarm. Moreover, Unkiar-Skelessi was regarded as reducing Turkey to the status of a Russian satellite. Britain and France's ambassadors did all in their power to limit Russian influence with the Sultan. Britain saw Russia as its main rival for much of the 1830s. Russophobia became an important element shaping Britain's attitude towards Europe. It combined a hatred of absolutism with a deep-rooted belief that Russia was an expansionist and aggressive power. Russia, by contrast, was never as overtly anti-British as Britain was anti-Russian. Nicholas regarded France, the principal source of all revolutionary excitement which he deplored, as Russia's main enemy.

b) The crisis of 1839–41

In 1839 the Sultan, desirous for revenge against Mehemet Ali, ordered an invasion of Syria. However, his forces were routed by the Egyptians, leaving Constantinople open to attack, especially after the desertion of the Turkish fleet to Ali's side. Once again Turkey was saved by European intervention but with some important differences from 1833. Tsar Nicholas, fearing the Anglo-French entente, declined to come directly to Turkey's aid, as might have been expected by the terms of the Treaty of Unkiar-Skelessi. Instead he supported a meeting of the powers to decide the issue. This was an astute move. The French premier, Thiers, sided with Mehemet Ali while Britain joined Russia in siding with Turkey. Nicholas thus found a way of driving a wedge between Britain and France and improving relations with Britain. Palmerston, who was opposed to French ambition in the Mediterranean, appreciated that no lasting settlement could be achieved in the Near East without some agreement between Britain and Russia.

Anglo-Russian cooperation enabled Palmerston to ride roughshod over France. The fate of Mehemet Ali, and of Thiers' policy, was virtually sealed by the Treaty of London in July 1840. By this treaty, all the great powers, except France, guaranteed the 'integrity and independence of the Ottoman Empire in the interests of cementing the peace of Europe'. They agreed on an ultimatum to Ali and authorised military action to coerce him, if he rejected the terms offered. France, totally isolated, reacted to this treaty by threatening to unleash a war on the Rhine. This simply united Prussia and Austria against France. The diplomatic tension ended in October with the dismissal of Thiers by Louis-Philippe. Mehemet Ali's rejection of the Treaty of London obliged the powers to enforce his submission to the Sultan. A British squadron bombarded Beirut and helped capture Acre. By February 1841, Syria was cleared of Egyptian troops.

France's return to the European concert was formalised in July 1841 by her participation in the Straits Convention, signed by all five great powers. The Convention raised to the status of international law the so-called 'ancient rule of the Straits', which prohibited all foreign warships from passing through the Straits while Turkey was at peace.

The crisis of 1839–41 was a triumph for Palmerston's diplomacy which lessened both Russian and French influence in the Near East. It also had a significant effect on international relations. Anglo-Russian cooperation became so cordial that the Tsar even proposed a secret alliance with Britain, which Palmerston rejected. Anglo-French relations, on the other hand, were seriously embittered. The crisis thus contributed to the ending of the alignment of the powers along ideological lines, a feature of the early 1830s. Lord Aberdeen,

THE MAIN EVENTS

1831 Mehemet Ali invaded Syria;
1832 Ottoman Empire went to war with Mehemet Ali;
1833 Treaty of Unkiar Skelessi;
1839 Sultan attacked Mehemet Ali;
1840 July: Four-power Treaty of London;
1841 Straits Convention.

Palmerston's successor as Foreign Secretary in 1841, while hoping to restore the Anglo-French entente, still sought to maintain good relations with Russia. Tsar Nicholas visited Britain in 1844 and had talks with Prime Minister Robert Peel. Both agreed that joint action in the Near East was the best hope of maintaining peace. 1844–5 was the high point of Anglo-Russian cooperation.

ISSUE:
To what extent was Europe divided into two opposing camps in the period 1830–48?

9 The Concert and diplomatic alignments 1830–48

The apparent division of the great powers after 1830 into two opposing ideological camps – the Liberal Alliance and the Holy Alliance – was a potential threat to the working of the Concert of Europe. The re-emergence of revolutionary tendencies in the early 1830s served to consolidate the grouping of the three eastern powers, which had been weakened by disagreements over the Eastern Question in the late 1820s. Tsar Nicholas felt it to be his personal duty to defend Europe from the threat of revolution and worked hard to preserve the Holy Alliance. By the Convention of Berlin (October 1833) Austria, Prussia and Russia promised to assist each other in the suppression of revolution. However, the 'ideological divide' almost ceased to have any significance in foreign affairs by the 1840s. Cooperation in the 1839–41 Near East crisis led to a dramatic improvement in Anglo-Russian relations. Anglo-French cordiality, by contrast, fluctuated alarmingly.

The end of the Congress System did not see the end of European cooperation. After 1822 there was still a widespread feeling that important territorial changes should only be made with the general consent of the great powers. Several major issues in international affairs, not least the Belgian revolt and the 1839–41 Near Eastern crisis, were settled by means of 'Conference Diplomacy'. Conferences were held in one of the European capitals with the resident ambassadors acting as representatives for their countries, under the chairmanship of the host foreign minister. Unlike congresses, conferences did not need the participation of all the powers and they dealt with specific issues of pressing concern rather than ranging over a wide variety of topics. They thus tended to be more effective than congresses. This form of diplomatic cooperation enabled the great powers to preserve peace. This is not to suggest that international relations were characterised by sweetness and light. Serious disagreements existed, crises verging on war arose and personal animosities abounded. Nevertheless, a degree of flexibility developed in the alignment of the powers, despite their ideological differences. This contributed to the continuing vitality of the Concert of Europe.

▼ Working on Europe 1815–48: The International Scene

The 'Points to Consider' at the start of the chapter suggested that European statesmen's main aim in the period was to ensure peace and stability. How successful were they in achieving this aim? The following questions might help you reach an answer.

▼ What were the main problems facing Europe's statesmen in and after 1815?

▼ How were the problems resolved?

▼ Do the statesmen deserve praise or criticism for their conduct of foreign policy? (They did succeed in resolving the various disputes without a major war.)

▼ Do some countries – and some statesmen – deserve more credit than others?

Answering extended writing and essay questions on Europe 1815–48: The International Scene

Consider the following question: How successful was Metternich in terms of imposing his 'system' on Europe in the period 1815–48?

You will need to plan an introduction, seven or eight paragraphs and a conclusion. Introductions and conclusions are the most important parts of an essay – and the hardest to write. The following ideas are the kinds of points you might make in either your introduction or your conclusion.

▼ The period from 1815–48 is sometimes described as the 'Age of Metternich'. Some historians believe that the Austrian minister imposed his 'system' on Europe. However, Britain and Russia – not Austria – were Europe's great powers in the decades after 1815. For much of this period they were engaged in rivalry for the diplomatic leadership of Europe. They were also, on occasions, willing to act together to resolve matters of mutual concern. Metternich, therefore, was not in a position to dictate to Europe.

▼ Did Metternich operate according to a 'system'? Perhaps there was sufficient coherence to his ideas and consistency in their application to merit the use of the term. His chief objective was to maintain the existing international, political and social order. His task was facilitated by the 1815 Settlement and his ability to appeal to the sanctity of treaties when events threatened it. The congresses held between 1815 and 1822 also provided him with opportunities to convince other leaders that there really was a revolutionary conspiracy in Europe. For most of the period Austria, Prussia and Russia acted in concert to check those forces which Metternich believed threatened Europe's stability.

▼ The merits of Metternich's strategy and his degree of success in pursuing it have long been matters of debate. His critics believe that by inhibiting gradual, orderly change he contributed to the very explosion he sought to prevent – the revolutionary upheavals of 1848. However, it is hard to deny that for much of the period most of Europe more closely resembled Metternich's ideals than those of his opponents. The solidarity of the three eastern powers, which he did much to create, was a significant factor from 1815–48.

Answering source-based questions on Europe 1815–48: The International Scene

Source A Extract from Castlereagh's confidential State Paper, 5 May 1820

The principle of one state interfering by force in the internal affairs of another, in order to enforce obedience to the governing authority, is always a question of the greatest moral as well as political delicacy... It is important to observe that to generalise such a principle and to think of reducing it to a system, or to impose it as an obligation, is a scheme utterly impracticable and objectionable... This principle is perfectly clear and intelligible in the case of Spain. We may all agree that nothing can be more lamentable, or of more dangerous example, than the recent revolt of the Spanish army... but it does not follow that we have therefore equal means of acting upon this opinion.

Source B A secret memorandum to Tsar Alexander from Metternich, 15 December 1820.

Kings have to calculate the chances of their very existence in the immediate future; passions are let loose, and join together to overthrow everything which society respects as the basis of its existence; religion, public morality, laws, customs, rights, and duties, all are attacked, confounded, overthrown, or called into question... The first principle to be followed by the monarchs... should be that of maintaining the stability of political institutions against the disorganised excitement which has take possession of men's minds... In short, let the great monarchs strengthen their union, and prove to the world that if it exists, it is beneficent, and ensures the political peace of Europe; that it is powerful only for the maintenance of tranquillity at a time when so many attacks are directed against it.

▼ QUESTIONS ON SOURCES

1. Study Source A. Comment on Castlereagh's view that 'It is important to observe that to generalise such a principle and to think of reducing it to a system, or to impose it as an obligation, is a scheme utterly impracticable and objectionable'. **[3 marks]**
2. Using your own knowledge and the evidence in the sources explain why Castlereagh and Metternich disagreed in 1820. **[7 marks]**
3. Using your own knowledge and the two sources, explain why the disagreement between Castlereagh and Metternich was so important to European diplomacy. **[15 marks]**

Points to note about the questions

Question 1 What was 'utterly impracticable and objectionable'?
Question 2 The two extracts suggest that Castlereagh and Metternich disagreed about the principle of intervention in states which had had revolutions. Why was this?
Question 3 What had been the state of affairs from 1815–20? What was the state of affairs after 1820?

Further Reading

Books in the Access to History series

Try *The Concert of Europe: International Relations 1814–70* by J. Lowe.

General

Two excellent texts are *Peace, War and the European Powers, 1814–1914* by C. J. Bartlett (Macmillan, 1996) and *The Great Powers and the European States System 1815–1914* by F. R. Bridge and R. Bullen (Longman, 1980). Useful information can also be found in *The Ascendancy of Europe 1815–1914* by M. S. Anderson (Longman, 1986) and *Barricades and Borders: Europe 1800–1914* by R. Gildea (OUP, 1996).

3

THE 1848 REVOLUTIONS

POINTS TO CONSIDER

In 1848 many European countries, with the important exceptions of Russia and Britain, experienced revolution. A striking feature of the 1848 revolutions was the rapidity of the success they enjoyed. Another striking feature was the fact that they all – equally rapidly – failed. This chapter will examine the general – European-wide – factors which helped spark revolution and which then ensured defeat. Despite apparent unity, the reality was that across Europe the revolutionaries had different grievances and demands. Even within specific countries, there was often little cohesion among the revolutionaries and what there was soon collapsed. Thus, in order to understand the 1848 revolutions it is necessary to carry out a state–by–state examination.

Historians debate many aspects of the 1848 revolutions. You need to keep the following contentious issues in mind as you tackle this chapter.

To what extent did France sneeze and Europe catch a cold?

On 24 February 1848 King Louis-Philippe was overthrown and a republic was established. Within three weeks revolutions had flared up in many German and Italian states and throughout the Habsburg Empire. It has often been claimed that the French example sparked off revolution elsewhere. Certainly there was an element of contagion. French revolutionaries' proclamation of the idea of the sovereignty of the people called in question all established authority. It was now up to the people of Europe to set themselves free. However, the notion that France sneezed and the rest of Europe caught a cold is far too simplistic. Most of the revolutions in 1848 were not just slavish imitations of the French example. Moreover, it is arguable that the revolutions did not even start in France. There were food riots among the poorer classes across much of central Europe in 1846–7. In January 1848 there was an insurrection in Sicily against misrule from Naples.

Did the revolutions have common causes?

Another generally accepted view is that the spate of revolutions took place at about the same time because conditions in France, Germany, Italy and the Austrian Empire were all very similar. Certainly the poorer classes were suffering from high food prices and high unemployment. Coupled with this was the growing strength of liberal and nationalist ideas. These ideas, as Metternich had long realised, were a particular threat to the multi-national Habsburg Empire. In 1848 the Hungarians, Czechs and Italians all pressed their claims for a greater measure of self-determination or full independence. However, in many respects the nationalist revolutions, far from being general, were merely a revolt within the Austrian Empire. Revolution did not spread to the other great multi-national empire Russia. Nor were the revolutions simply the fruit of agrarian and urban tensions. Interestingly, 1846 and 1847 were the years of real hardship – not 1848. Arguably unrest among workers was as much an effect as a cause of the political revolutions of 1848.

Why did the revolutions fail? Did they fail?

To radical idealists March 1848 was 'the springtime of Europe'. The spate of revolutions seemed to promise new constitutions, new societies and a new world. However, the high hopes of the revolutionaries were soon to be dashed. Whether there were common causes of failure or whether the causes of failure were specific to particular areas is debatable. Whether indeed all the 1848 revolutions failed is another contentious area.

1 Economic and social problems

ISSUE:
Why did revolutions occur across most of Europe in 1848?

Most historians are agreed that the revolutions sprang, at least in part, from social and economic crisis. However, the precise nature of this crisis, and its effects on different classes of the population, has generated much debate.

a) Long-term problems

i) Overpopulation in the countryside
The number of people working on the land was increasing – so much so that by the 1840s many areas found it difficult to sustain their populations.

ii) Urbanisation

Given the shortage of land, many peasants migrated to towns hoping to find work. In most towns there were insufficient jobs and housing to cope. Living and working conditions (while possibly improving!) were atrocious. Inadequate sanitation encouraged diseases like typhoid and cholera. Many newcomers, unable to find work, depended on charity or turned to crime. The cities had concentrations of discontented people who were far more likely to act together than their rural counterparts. The 1848 revolutions were overwhelmingly urban, particularly occurring in capital cities rather than factory towns, which were few and far between. Indeed, the 1848 French revolution was essentially a Parisian revolt, the Prussian revolution a Berlin revolt, etc.. Except in Hungary none of the revolutions had real roots in the countryside.

iii) Growing class consciousness

Historians remain divided about whether 'class consciousness' was developing among industrial workers. This was a key issue for Marxist historians who believed that historical change grew out of conflicts between classes. Karl Marx argued that as industrialisation developed so each class evolved its own consciousness. He believed that the proletariat was inevitably opposed to the bourgeoisie who owned the means of production. Marxist historians have argued that the 1848 revolutions were caused by the effect of industrialisation on the working class. However, they find it hard to explain why revolution occurred in parts of Europe where there was no strong proletariat and not in Britain where working class consciousness was strongest.

iv) Disaffection among skilled artisans

Across Europe large-scale factories were still uncommon. Nevertheless, skilled artisans felt threatened by the advance of mechanisation which forced down the costs of production and made hand-produced goods relatively expensive.

b) The economic crisis: 1845–8

i) The food crisis

In 1845–6 there was an agricultural crisis across most of Europe due to failures in the cereal and potato harvests. Poor communications, panic buying by consumers, and speculation by merchants accentuated the impact of the harvest failures. Cereal and potato yields remained low during 1847, drastically affecting the living standards of peasants and the urban masses. Food prices rose dramatically. The impact of the crisis varied between countries and regions. Conditions were probably worst in Ireland where over 500,000 people died.

ii) Industrial crisis

The rise in food prices in 1846–7 led to a sharp reduction in consumer spending on items other than foodstuffs. Consequently, craft and industrial production suffered a steep fall in demand. There was thus a rapid increase in unemployment, particularly in the textile industry. At the same time, a financial crisis developed as British capital, the mainstay of European railway and industrial investment, was withdrawn. The result was a credit squeeze which forced many businessmen into bankruptcy and which led to a decline in railway building. This had a knock-on effect on the coal, iron and metallurgical industries. Share prices fell sharply. By 1847–8 the urban middle and working classes constituted a huge body of discontent, particularly in France.

The economic crisis helped to shake the prestige and self-confidence of existing regimes which lacked the financial and bureaucratic resources – and also possibly the will – to intervene effectively to alleviate the social distress and reverse the economic collapse. It also made it easier to mobilise the masses. However, there was no clear correlation, either in time or space, between extreme economic suffering and revolutionary activity. The 1847 harvest was reasonably good. Food prices fell and peasants were able to feed themselves again. The 1848 revolutions thus took place against a background of generally improving economic conditions. Moreover, those areas which suffered most in 1845–7 were not necessarily those in which revolutionary activity was strongest in 1848.

> **Q** Does economic and social crisis inevitably lead to revolution?

2 Political problems

a) Authoritarian rule

By 1848 virtually all of Europe was still ruled by conservative regimes, which favoured the interests of privileged and wealthy elites. The calibre of rulers was not high. Many monarchs and their ministers attracted a great deal of personal unpopularity.

b) Liberalism

The growing number of educated middle class – lawyers, teachers, doctors, journalists – were critical of systems which largely excluded them from participation in the political process, and in which they were restrained from free expression of their grievances by the censor and the secret police. The middle classes wanted the elimination of arbitrary government, the establishment of some form of parliamentary system and the guarantee of basic civil rights.

c) Nationalism

Nationalism was growing, especially among the educated elite in Germany, Italy and Hungary.

d) Socialism

Against the grim background of developing industrialisation there developed socialist proposals, mainly emanating from France, for a more rational organisation of society.

▼ Saint-Simon looked to a more equal society based on increased productivity (by eliminating wasteful competition) and a greater valuation upon the status of labour.

▼ Charles Fourier and Pierre Proudhon looked towards the establishment of small-scale cooperative units of workers in which there would be no need for private property.

▼ Louis Blanc argued that state power should be used to end capitalism by creating cooperative national workshops and nationalising railways, banks and mines.

However, socialist ideas had little mass appeal in the early 19th century. Few workers felt any real sense of class solidarity or unity.

e) Karl Marx and Communism

Karl Marx, the son of a German Jewish lawyer, produced a theory of socialism more adapted to the circumstances of advanced industrialisation. The essentials were expressed in the *Communist Manifesto* (1848), which argued:

▼ Economic production is the main determinant of the nature of society.

▼ The dominant class always controls the state in its own interests. With economic development new classes emerge and struggle with the old to win control of the state.

▼ The capitalist industrialist phase would prove to be the last great change in economic development. The force of the factory workers (proletariat) would overthrow the bourgeoisie. The new society would be classless, egalitarian and democratic.

The main aims of Communism, as expressed in the Manifesto, were as follows:

Source A K. Marx and F. Engels, *The Communist Manifesto* (1848)

1. Abolition of property in land and application of all rents of land to public purposes.

2. A heavy progressive or graduated income tax.

3. Abolition of all right of inheritance.

5. Centralisation of credit in the hands of the State, by means of a national bank with State capital and an exclusive monopoly.

6. Centralisation of the means of communication and transport in the hands of the State.

7. Extension of factories and instruments of production owned by the State.

8. Equal liability of all to labour. Establishment of industrial armies, especially for agriculture.

10. Free education for all children in public schools. Abolition of children's factory labour in its present form.

f) The situation in 1848

In 1848 few people actually expected revolution. Across Europe there was still widespread loyalty to the established dynasties. Moreover, the economic situation was beginning to improve slightly. Nevertheless, economic distress in the major cities, which continued over the winter of 1847–8, helped foment revolution, encouraging subversive propaganda, undermining the credit of the state, and unifying the discontented. Across Europe a common pattern of events was to occur. Massive anti-regime demonstrations took place in major cities – Paris, Vienna, Prague, Venice, Milan and Berlin. Soldiers or police failed to clear the streets and those in power lost their nerve – and capitulated. 'There is no more astonishing series of events in the history of modern Europe than this collective and cumulative failure of nerve on the part of the monarchies and governments which were, in a physical sense, fully able to control events and repress the often almost trivial movements before which they hastened to abase themselves,' wrote historian M. S. Anderson. The old regimes granted concessions: new liberal governments were appointed; and constitutional reforms were promised. For a time the revolutionary tide seemed irresistable, merely because no one was resisting it. The speed with which most of the 1848 movements collapsed once the conservative forces recovered their nerve suggests that the revolutions were in many cases a kind of confidence trick.

ACTIVITY

Having studied sections 1 and 2 make a list of the five factors – in order one to five – which you think might have been most influential in sparking revolution in 1848. Compare your choice with others in the group.

ISSUE:
What caused the 1848
revolution in France?

3 The 1848 revolution in France

a) The causes of the revolution

In France, an active liberal opposition, angry that the bulk of the middle class was disenfranchised, had emerged (see pages 16–19). Demands for changes in the electoral law fell on deaf ears: no changes were forthcoming from King Louis-Philippe and his premier Guizot. However, liberal grievances – the narrow franchise, a series of government scandals, an uninspiring foreign policy – were unlikely to generate deep and sustained popular hostility. It was the 1847–8 economic and financial crisis which heightened the calls for change.

In 1847–8 the liberal opposition reverted to holding 'reform banquets' where the after-dinner speeches focused on demands for constitutional reform. Alert to the propaganda value of such meetings, the government banned a dinner planned for 20 February 1848. Radicals used the banning of the banquet to call for a protest demonstration in Paris on 22 February. The demonstration was well attended and the police had difficulty controlling the crowd. There still seemed no reason for the king to panic: there were 80,000 National Guardsmen and some 30,000 garrison troops in or near Paris. However, on 23 February excited crowds again assembled and the situation seemed to be deteriorating. Losing his nerve, Louis-Philippe dismissed Guizot, hoping to appease the opposition. Both the King and the opposition in the assembly now assumed – mistakenly – that the crisis was over. Instead of weakening the appeal of the agitators, Louis-Philippe's action gave them increased hope. That evening a crowd advancing on the Foreign Ministry was fired upon by nervous troops. Some 40 protestors were killed and within hours Paris was in open revolt. Barricades were set up in the streets and gunsmiths and barracks looted for weapons. Some National Guardsmen, called out to restore order, defected. Regular troops failed to break the barricades and retreated in disarray. Unwilling to call up more troops to suppress the revolutionaries, as he had done in Paris in 1832 and 1834, Louis-Philippe chose to abdicate. On 24 February he fled to England.

The events of 22–24 February should not have toppled Louis-Philippe's regime. The opposition in the assembly simply wished to replace Guizot: they had no wish to spark a revolution. A resolute government could have imposed its will on Paris. But Louis-Philippe, conscious that he had lost a great deal of support, lacked the resolve. The writer and politician Alexis de Tocqueville tried (in 1850) to make sense of what had happened. He saw some long-term causes for the revolution: the impact of industrialisation; 'a disease of envy';

new economic and political theories; the fact that France had, in less than 60 years, undergone the shock of seven revolutions. But de Tocqueville blamed 'above all, the senile imbecility of Louis-Philippe, his weakness, which no one could have foreseen and which still remains almost incredible, after the event has proved it'.

b) Events: 24 February to the April elections

Louis-Philippe's abdication left a vacuum of power. The Chamber of Deputies, in session at the time, would probably have declared a regency for the ex-king's grandson had not an armed mob burst in, causing most of the deputies to flee. To those who remained it was clear that only the declaration of a republic would calm things down. Lamartine, a popular poet and the leading republican in the chamber, announced the formation of a provisional republican government. However, radicals demanded a right to be represented in the new, essentially moderate, government. Accordingly four radicals, suggested by the chief republican newspapers, and including the socialist Louis Blanc and a solitary worker Albert, joined the government. In Paris there was remarkably little violence. Despite the poverty, no general uprising of the 'lower orders' took place. Instead there was a brief period of euphoria. Lamartine declared: 'We are making together the most sublime of poems.' From the start, however, the alliance between moderate middle-class politicians and the discontented labouring masses was a marriage of convenience. The mutual suspicion felt by the partners in the flimsy alliance soon provoked hostility.

> **Q** Why did Louis-Philippe face opposition from both the middle class and the Parisian workers?

The radicals, or 'red republicans', who claimed to articulate the hopes of the urban masses, were far from united. Their leaders, for example Ledru-Rollin and Blanqui, hated each other. However, they had some things in common. Most wished to establish a republic based on universal manhood suffrage. They were also committed to extensive social reform and hoped to see the revolution exported abroad. By contrast, moderates, like the middle class generally, wished only to establish constitutional parliamentary government, tended to have little sympathy for the poor, and were alarmed at the prospect of war. Lamartine, anxious to allay the fears of the other great powers, made it clear that the France of 1848 was not the France of 1792: French republican armies were not going to make war on the rest of Europe. Republican ideals would be spread by words not by deeds. The Second Republic held to this peaceful policy.

The provisional government, radicals and moderates alike, agreed on the need to hold elections to choose a constituent assembly whose duty it would be to draw up a constitution. These elections were scheduled for April. In the meantime, under pressure from the Parisian masses, the provisional government introduced a number of measures.

THE APRIL 1848 ELECTIONS

The 1848 revolution, based in Paris, had largely ignored the peasants. However, the introduction of universal manhood suffrage meant that peasants now comprised the majority of voters. Most resented the tax increases, were suspicious of socialism which seemed to imply the nationalisation of their lands, and wished to see a restoration of order. They were also swayed by the influence of the Catholic Church which opposed republicanism. Bishops prepared lists of acceptable candidates which priests then made known to the peasants. The final reminders came at morning Mass on Easter Sunday, the day chosen for the elections. Having preached against the evils of red republicanism, the priest led the faithful to vote. The vast majority of the 900 deputies were monarchists or moderate republicans. Socialists and radicals won only 70–80 seats. The new assembly elected a five-man executive directory: it included only one radical – Ledru–Rollin.

▼ The National Guard was opened to all classes.

▼ Press freedom and individual liberties were granted.

▼ The principle of universal male suffrage was recognised. The electorate thus increased from 250,000 to over 8 million.

▼ The government declared that every man had the right to work. A supplementary tax, mainly falling on the landowning classes, was levied to pay for this right. The red republicans in the government then spent weeks trying to organise jobs via national workshops for the unemployed. Without any experience of organising on such a scale and without a large supportive bureaucracy, only a few ventures actually commenced. Most of those on the unemployed lists were merely given a small weekly payment, for there was no work for them to do. Even extreme radicals recognised that there was not an endless supply of money to hand out to the poor and it was decided that once the lists were full no further names would be added. Thus 120,000 received the 'dole' with an unknown number – perhaps 50,000 – left unprovided for.

These measures raised the expectations of the labouring classes who saw them as the first steps towards social justice. However, the moderates had no intention of moving further in the direction of social reform. Their main concern was the deteriorating financial situation. In the three weeks after the fall of the monarchy the reserves of the Bank of France fell by 70 per cent and share values fell by 55 per cent. Industrial output slumped. In March the government tried to fill the budgetary deficit by imposing a 45 per cent increase in direct taxation. Crucially the bulk of this new burden fell on the peasants.

c) Counter-revolution

The April 1848 election results frustrated the left. On 15 May an attempted coup by Parisian radicals gave the new government an excuse to arrest prominent left-wingers such as Blanqui. The real body-blow to the radical movement came on 21 June with the announcement that the national workshops were to be closed down. Conservatives associated the workshops with revolution and saw them as an unnecessary financial burden. The 120,000 men registered with the workshops were given the option of military service or removal to the provinces to labour on public works schemes. Although the workshops had achieved little, many workers saw them as symbolic of a commitment to social justice. On 22 June barricades were erected in the poorer districts of Paris and an attempt was made to restart the revolution. Many of the 50,000 or so rioters were armed and this was a more determined resistance than had caused the downfall of Louis-Philippe.

In that city [Paris] there were a hundred thousand armed workmen formed into regiments, without work and dying of hunger. Society was cut in two: those who had nothing united in common envy; those who had anything united in common terror. There were no longer ties of sympathy linking these two great classes, and a struggle was everywhere assumed to be inevitable soon...

A dull despair had descended on the oppressed and threatened middle classes, but imperceptibly that despair was turning into courage. I had always thought that there was no hope of gradually and peacefully controlling the impetus of the February revolution and that it could only be stopped suddenly by a great battle taking place in Paris... What I now saw persuaded me that the battle was not only inevitable but imminent, and that it would be desirable to seize the first opportunity to start it...

In truth it was not a political struggle... but a class struggle, a sort of 'Servile War'.

Source B Alexis de Tocqueville's view of the events of June 1848

ACTIVITY

1. Explain de Tocqueville's view that 'In truth it was not a political struggle...but a class struggle, a sort of 'Servile War''.
2. How reliable is de Tocqueville as a source for the 'June Days'?
3. Explain the differences between the events in February 1848 and June 1848.

The government stood firm. 30,000 troops, led by General Cavaignac, were moved into Paris to support the National Guard. For the next six 'June Days', Cavaignac's men cleared the streets of barricades and protestors. Over 1,000 troops were killed along with some 500 insurgents. In the mopping up operations that followed, troops killed some 3,000 suspected rioters: a further 12,000 suspects were arrested. Of those brought to trial 4,000 were deported to penal settlements abroad.

Had Cavaignac wished to become a dictator he could well have done so in the summer of 1848. Cavaignac, however, still had faith in republican government based on the will of the people. Appointed chief of the executive power by the assembly, he ensured that order was maintained while the assembly carried on with the work of drawing up a constitution. That a republican constitution emerged in November was the result of a split between the monarchists. The Legitimists wanted a restoration of the Bourbons while the Orleanists championed the grandson of Louis-Philippe.

THE 1848 FRENCH REVOLUTION

1848 22 February:
demonstrations in Paris;
23 February: Louis-Philippe
dismissed Guizot;
24 February: Louis-Philippe
abdicated: provisional
republican government
declared;
March: national workshops
established;
April: elections for
constituent assembly;
June: end of national
workshops: 'June Days';
November: Constitution of
the Second Republic
introduced;
December: Louis
Napoleon elected
President.

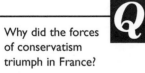

Why did the forces
of conservatism
triumph in France?

> ### The constitution of the Second Republic
>
> ▼ The principle of universal manhood suffrage was accepted.
> ▼ Power was divided between a single legislative assembly of 750 members, elected every three years, which would make the laws, and a president – directly elected by popular vote – who would carry them out. Presidents were to serve a single four-year term, a measure intended to ensure that no leader would develop dictatorial ambitions.

In December Louis Napoleon, the 40-year-old nephew of the great Emperor, was elected as president. He received 5,400,000 votes. General Cavaignac obtained only 1,500,000. Red republican Ledru-Rollin received 370,119 votes while Lamartine obtained just 17,000 votes. The myth of Bonapartism – and its association with national glory and the restoration of order – was powerful among all classes of society but particularly with the peasantry and working class. Louis Napoleon, an excellent propagandist, was seen as a man who had the people's interests at heart. He also had the support of veteran politicians who believed that he would keep radicalism at bay and that they could control him. Time would prove them right in one respect and wrong in the other.

Louis Napoleon accepted a ministry dominated by conservatives and purged both central and local government of its republican personnel. In the elections for the new legislative assembly held in May 1849 conservatives were easily in the majority, winning about 500 seats. An attempted republican insurrection in June 1849, in protest at French troops being sent to Rome to restore the papacy, failed. Ironically, the main threat to the conservative assembly came not from the radicals but from Louis Napoleon who had no intention of being president for just one four-year term. In December 1851 he overthrew the Second Republic, proclaiming himself emperor in 1852. (See pages 218–28.) The constitution designed to prevent dictatorship had effectively ended in dictatorship.

4 The revolutions in the Habsburg Empire

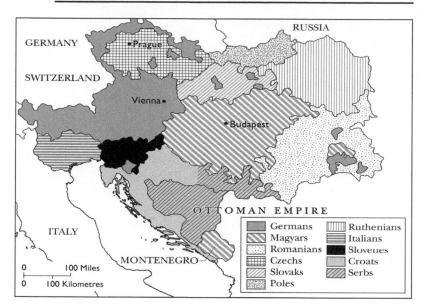

Figure 1 The Habsburg Empire

a) The causes of the revolutions

▼ *Population growth and the agricultural crisis*: 75 per cent of the Empire's inhabitants lived in the countryside where rapid population growth led to increasing problems. Bad harvests between 1845–7 exacerbated the situation. Hungry peasants made their way into the towns hoping to find work.

▼ *Urban problems*: There was simply not enough work in the towns to absorb the rapid influx of labour.

▼ *The influence of nationalism*: The Empire was threatened by the rise of nationalism. Nationalist movements were especially strong among Italians, Hungarians and Czechs. However, these movements were very different in terms of their political aims. While many Italians wanted full independence, most Czechs wanted self-rule within the framework of the Empire. Hungarians were divided: some wanted independence: most wanted only self-government. A further major complication was that national groups did not reside in neatly separated geographical areas. Croats, Serbs and Romanians had no more wish to be ruled by Hungarians than Hungarians had to be ruled by Austrians. This enabled the Empire's rulers to play off one nationality against another. Nevertheless, nationalism proved a potent vehicle for opposition to Habsburg rule.

▼ *The influence of liberalism*: Liberals wanted to create a new constitution which guaranteed civil rights and which set up an elected assembly, limiting the power of the emperor. However, most liberals were propertied middle-class men who had no wish to allow the masses to acquire power. There was thus a paradox about liberalism: in some ways it was a threat to the autocratic Habsburg system; but in other ways it was a support, acting as a buffer against violent or far-reaching change.

b) The fall of Metternich

The revolutions in the Habsburg Empire began in France. The news that Louis-Philippe had been overthrown created huge excitement in Vienna. Some hoped that change would now take place in the Empire: others feared that events in France might lead the Austrian authorities to clamp down even more severely. Chancellor Metternich was worried by the turn of events. The removal of a king and the establishment of a republic was, in his eyes, a threat to the old order which he had worked to preserve throughout his public life. He knew that revolutions which began in France had a habit of spreading to the rest of Europe. He toyed with the idea of military intervention to restore Louis-Philippe but soon realised that Austria lacked the funds needed to embark on such a risky venture.

The first sign that a storm was about to break came in Hungary. On 3 March, Lajos Kossuth made a powerful speech in the Hungarian Diet, in which he called for self-government for Hungary. Kossuth went on to claim that this was the 'right' of all the historic nations within the Empire. In effect he called for the complete dismantling of the old system. Copies of his speech were soon circulating in Vienna and led to speculation that when the Austrian Diet met on 13 March there would be similar calls for reform. On 12 March university students drafted a petition calling for numerous liberal reforms – press freedom, jury trials, emancipation of the serfs, and constitutional government. The petition was presented to the Emperor's uncle, Archduke Ludwig. No promise was made but the students felt that they had had a sympathetic hearing and this encouraged them to think that the court might be prepared to accept change. On 13 March the Austrian Diet duly met to debate reform proposals. A large expectant crowd gathered. Attempts by students to burst into the building and the general noise and disturbance eventually led to the Diet breaking up. The mob, sensing victory, moved on to the imperial palace.

Emperor Ferdinand, weak and mentally deficient, was not blamed for imperial policies. Metternich was seen as the real ruler and as such he was the target of the crowd's hostility. Troops panicked and opened fire, killing four people. The protest turned instantly into a riot. The Emperor was left with two alternatives: give in to the people's demands or use force to suppress the rioters. The role of Ferdinand's advisers now became crucial. Metternich could usually rely on the support of Archduke Ludwig. But within the court there was also a strong anti-

Metternich faction, led by Archduke John and Kolowrat. The latter, long Metternich's bitter rival, sought to exploit the moment and persuaded the Emperor, and more importantly Archduke Ludwig, that the time was right for dropping the Chancellor.

Thus on 13 March, Metternich resigned. The next day he fled in a laundry wagon to seek refuge in England. His fall – as much the result of behind-the-scenes court rivalries as it was the product of social unrest and demands for political reform – had major results. It seemed to promise the dawn of a new era. The monarchy, thrown onto the defensive, made other concessions. On 15 March the Emperor promised a new constitution and appointed a new ministry, led by Kolowrat, with the specific task of producing it.

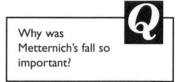

Why was Metternich's fall so important?

c) The April Laws

After Metternich's fall, the Hungarians immediately began demanding concessions, not least a parliament with far greater powers.

1. Freedom of the press; abolition of censorship.
2. A responsible ministry with its seat in the capital Budapest.
3. An annual parliament in Budapest.
4. Political and religious equality before the law.
5. A national guard.
6. Taxes to be paid by all.
7. Abolition of serfdom.
8. A jury system with equality of representation.
9. A national bank.
10. The military to take an oath to the constitution; Hungarian soldiers not to be stationed abroad; foreign soldiers to be removed.
11. Political prisoners to be freed.

Source C Demands of the Hungarian people, 15 March 1848

Kossuth pressed to alter the constitutional relationship between Hungary and the crown. Although Hungarians would still swear loyalty to the emperor, Ferdinand would be unable to introduce any legislation affecting Hungary without the approval of its new parliament. Ferdinand and his advisers, fearing that obstruction would only result in the demise of the Empire, ratified Hungarian demands on 11 April. The 'April Laws' were nothing short of a constitutional revolution. The emperor's authority over Hungary was effectively terminated and power passed to a Magyar government headed by Count Batthyany. Kossuth became Minister of Finance.

However, the April Laws, which introduced national 'rights' for Hungarians only, sowed the seeds of future Magyar defeat. Non-Magyars who made up over half of 'Hungary's' population, resented Magyar domination, for example, the fact that the speaking of Magyar was necessary in order to vote or be a member of the parliament. The Croatian governor, Jelačič, a passionate patriot who preferred Austrian to Magyar rule, was bitterly opposed to the April Laws and advocated Croat autonomy. Serbs, Slovaks and Romanians also set out to create their own assemblies. Meanwhile there were problems between Austria and Hungary over control of the Hungarian army and over the extent of Hungarian jurisdiction. In July 1848 the newly elected Hungarian parliament voted in favour of mass levy of troops to defend Hungary: this was a signal for conflict.

d) The second Viennese revolution

On 25 April Austria's promised and eagerly awaited constitution was published. Its main author, Count Pillersdorf, offered a central imperial parliament to which each national group would send representatives. This parliament would be elected on a narrow franchise and the emperor would retain the right to veto any legislation. In most people's eyes Pillersdorf's proposals did not go far enough. On 15 May a crowd gathered outside the imperial palace, demanding a different constitution. Ferdinand – or his advisers – once more gave way. Given the problems elsewhere in the Empire, it made sense to make concessions. A new constitution, based upon universal manhood suffrage, was promised. Riotous celebrations followed. It seemed that the mob now controlled the capital. Fearing for their lives, Ferdinand and his court fled from Vienna to Innsbruck on 17 May. The Emperor's flight seemed to clarify the political issues. Whereas before it was possible to claim loyalty to the monarchy and still demand change, now it seemed that one was either for or against the Empire. Divisions opened up between radicals and moderates. Middle-class liberals, suspicious of social reform and wanting only a limited extension of the franchise, affirmed their loyalty to the monarchy. Radicals, urged on by workers' demands for social improvements, were keen to move towards a republic.

e) Events in Italy

The news of Metternich's fall sparked nationalist uprisings in Lombardy and Venetia. On 18 March in Milan 10,000 protestors presented a petition calling for freedom of the press and elections to a parliament. Trouble soon flared. Street battles between Austrian troops and the people of Milan raged for five days before the 81-year-old Austrian commander Radetzky was forced to withdraw from the city. In Venice a rising, begun by artisans and fishermen and then taken over by the middle class, led to the creation of an independent Venetian republic. Lombardy looked to Charles Albert, King of Piedmont, for support. Hoping to transform Piedmont into a major power, he was ready to free Lombardy and Venetia from Habsburg control in the name of Italian nationalism and annex them to his own kingdom. On 23 March a 60,000-strong Piedmontese army marched into Lombardy. Heavily outnumbered, Radetzky retreated to the Quadrilateral fortresses, the key to the security of northern Italy, and awaited reinforcements. Fortunately for Austria, Italians as a whole did not rally to the flag of Charles Albert.

f) Prague: the turning point

In March the Czechs, inspired by the Hungarians, pressed their claim for autonomy. A delegation, headed by history professor Francis Palacky, was sent to Vienna to present the Czech demands – a package of liberal reforms and the unity and independence of Bohemia, Moravia and Silesia. In April Vienna agreed to some of the demands including abolishing the laws which made it illegal for Czech speakers to occupy high office. It also agreed to establish a parliament in Prague.

In June the first Slav congress opened in Prague. In some ways this was a defensive response to the Frankfurt Parliament (see section 5) which seemed to want to subsume the Czechs into a new German empire. Palacky was opposed to this, just as he was hostile to Russian ambitions to lead a federation of Slav states. He felt that the Habsburg Empire was the best guarantee of security the Czechs had, admitting that 'if the Austrian Empire did not exist it would be necessary for us to create it'. In essence, he wanted a federal constitution which would give the Czechs a greater measure of home rule whilst remaining under the protective cloak of the Empire. Palacky's chances of success were slight. Bohemia, Moravia and Silesia had a significant German-speaking community who had no wish to be ruled by Czechs. Nor did the Slav Congress inspire confidence. The Czechs were just one Slav group within the Austrian Empire. Mutual rivalries divided Czechs, Poles, Slovaks and Serbs – all of whom were represented at Prague. Unable to agree on a common purpose, the Congress achieved nothing and served merely to reveal the divisions within Slav nationalism.

On 12 June riots broke out in Prague. They had almost nothing to do with the Congress, being essentially a protest by unemployed workers who were joined by radical students. The Prague revolution was in a real sense the revolution that never was. As few as 1,200 people out of a population of some 100,000 were involved. General Windischgraetz, commander of the imperial army in Prague and fierce opponent of the revolution, seized the opportunity to take action. Within five days the rising was subdued. The severity of the consequent trials for treason was clearly meant as a lesson for the rest of the Empire's unruly subjects. Most Austrian Germans felt little sympathy for the Czech rebels and were pleased that Prague was once more under imperial control. The failure of the Prague revolt and the forcible closure of the Slav Congress proved to be a decisive turning point in the history of the 1848 revolutions in the Habsburg Empire.

Windischgraetz's triumph gave heart to the Emperor's supporters. Radetzky now determined to try and defeat the Italians. The result was a brilliant victory over Charles Albert's force at Custoza on 25 July. An armistice was arranged on 9 August and Radetzky re-established control over Milan and laid siege to Venice. Given that the Italian revolt, unlike that in Prague, had posed a genuine threat to imperial unity, Radetzky, not Windischgraetz, was the real saviour of the Empire and Custoza the real turning point. By August the monarchy felt strong enough to seek to undo all the constitutional concessions made since March.

g) The October Days in Vienna

The summer in Vienna was tense. There were several rival centres of power. Oddly, government ministers, though claiming control over other nationalities, had limited influence. A Committee of Public Safety, set up in May, had more authority: it aimed to safeguard the reforms so far secured and to maintain order. Emulating France, it set up national workshops which were supposed to provide useful work with pay. Radical groups, while always in a minority and with more ideas than discipline, attracted support from students and some of the working class, enabling them to put the force of the mob behind their arguments. Worker protests in June and August were suppressed by the middle-class National Guard. To complicate matters further an imperial parliament met in July. The deputies, representing various nationalities (there were no Magyars) found it difficult to work together and rivalries between the majority moderates and minority radicals did not help matters. A commission, charged with devising a constitution, was soon lost in discussion. The parliament's main achievement was the abolition of the last vestiges of serfdom in the Empire. However, real power lay not with the parliament but with the army, loyal to the emperor and no longer tied down in Italy or Bohemia. In August Emperor Ferdinand returned to Vienna feeling that the worst excesses of the revolution were over. He had miscalculated.

In September 1848, Jelačič, Governor of Croatia, inspired by the success of Windischgraetz and Radetzky, invaded Hungary with a Croat army. On 3 October the Emperor pronounced the April Laws illegal and the Hungarian Diet dissolved. Kossuth, declaring the revolution in danger, broke with the Hungarian moderates. Taking (effectively dictatorial) power, he called on all opponents of reaction to act together to save the cause. Most Austrians had little sympathy with the Hungarians. However, radicals in Vienna saw a link between Hungarian success and their own position: if the Hungarians were crushed – so would they be. On 6 October Viennese crowds sought to prevent soldiers being sent to Hungary to aid Jelačič. Fighting broke out and there were some casualties. Workers and students seized control of the inner city. An angry mob marched on the Ministry of War, brutally murdering the minister Count Latour. The court once again fled the capital, this time to Olmutz, while the parliament – a few radicals excepted – moved to nearby Kremsier. Windischgraetz and his 100,000 troops were sent to deal with Vienna. In late October Windischgraetz's men finally 'liberated' the city. Over 2,000 people were killed during the 'October Days'. The rebel leaders were rounded up and shot. The revolution in Vienna was over. Only the Magyars remained defiant.

h) The end of revolution

In November Prince Schwarzenberg, brother-in-law of Windischgraetz, was placed in control of the government. The half-witted Emperor Ferdinand was now persuaded to abdicate. This he did in December in favour of his 18-year-old nephew, Francis Joseph. The new Emperor was determined to follow a policy of monarchical absolutism. When the imperial parliament finally presented a constitution in March 1849 it was ignored.

The loose ends were finally tied up in 1849. A fresh effort by Charles Albert of Piedmont to stir up trouble in Lombardy was defeated at Novara in March 1849. Hungary proved to be the most difficult region to subdue. In April 1849 Kossuth proclaimed the Habsburg dynasty deposed and Hungary totally independent. Military reverses led the Austrian government to request Russian military assistance in May. Tsar Nicholas I, acting partly in the broad interests of monarchical solidarity and partly because he thought Hungarian success might lead the Poles to seek independence from Russia, agreed to help. In the event Russian intervention was not decisive and the main engagements took place between Hungarian and Austrian troops. The Magyars were finally crushed at Világos in August 1849. Kossuth escaped into permanent exile but some 100 Hungarians were executed and 2,000

THE HABSBURG REVOLUTIONS

1848 13 March: first Vienna revolution: Metternich resigned;
18–22 March: street battles in Milan;
23 March: Piedmontese army invaded Lombardy;
11 April: April Laws;
25 April: new constitution introduced;
15 May: second Vienna revolution;
17 May: Emperor fled to Innsbruck;
2 June: Slav Congress opened;
Late June: Prague revolt crushed;
July: Austrian victory over Piedmontese at Custoza;
6 October: third Vienna revolution;
Late October: Vienna revolt crushed;
December: Francis Joseph became Emperor;
1849 April: Kossuth proclaimed Hungarian independence;
August: Hungarian surrender.

imprisoned. The Austrians were criticised by many at the time for this savagery but by 20th-century standards it was positively humane! Venice capitulated later the same month. By 1849 the Austrian Empire had emerged from the months of turmoil with a strengthened political leadership and all its territory intact.

WHAT WERE THE MAIN CONSE-QUENCES OF THE HABSBURG REVOLUTIONS?

▼ The traditional forces of conservatism – the Church, the nobility and the army – remained in control.

▼ The forces of liberalism and nationalism received a serious blow. But the desire of Magyars for self-government and Italians for independence had not been broken.

▼ The last remnants of serfdom in the Empire had been swept away.

i) Why did so much revolutionary activity achieve so little?

▼ The restoration of imperial authority owed much to the loyalty of the army. The officer class tended to be of noble origin and was generally conservative. Regular, mainly peasant, troops obeyed orders.

▼ The fact that the revolutionaries were not united weakened their efforts considerably. Moderate 'revolutionaries' retained a faith in the monarchy and a respect for legality. They wanted, and for a time seemed to secure, imperial consent for their revolution. They had little in common with the radical revolutionaries in Vienna. Middle-class reformers had an ambivalent attitude to the working class as allies: they were seen as a useful means of intimidating the authorities but they were also regarded as politically dangerous. Mob violence, like the lynching of Latour, resulted in many of the middle class actively opposing the revolution. The workers, mainly concerned with their deteriorating economic condition, had little in common with the radical students.

▼ Tensions between the differing sorts of nationalism precluded the emergence of any form of cooperation between non-German opponents of the regime. National rivalries aided the recovery of imperial authority. The Austrian government, for example, was able to play off other nationalities, particularly the Croats, against the Magyars.

▼ Hungary apart, few peasants showed much interest in revolutions which seemed to do little to address their needs. In Lombardy and Venetia, for example, middle-class revolutionaries refused to concede much-needed agrarian reforms to the peasants. The potential of mass support withered away and the cities were left isolated: easy pickings for Radetsky. Abolition of feudal labour in September 1848 ensured the acceptance of Habsburg rule by peasants throughout the Empire. Revolution was thus largely confined to the ruling classes (in Hungary and Italy) and to the large cities.

▼ In Italy only Piedmont rallied to the support of Lombardy. This turned the Lombard revolt into an Austro-Piedmont war which aroused the patriotism of most Austrians. The fact that Pope Pius IX condemned the anti-Habsburg rising in northern Italy had considerable influence, particularly for the peasantry.

▼ External factors helped change the situation. News of the defeat of the French radicals during the June Days gave Windischgraetz the confidence to crush the Prague revolution.

5 Revolution in Germany: 1848–9

ISSUE:
What were the main causes of the German (and Prussian) revolutions? Why did they fail?

In 1848 it is not possible to talk of 'Germany' in any coherent sense as a nation. Although there was a growing sense of national identity, there was no German administration or army. The German Confederation, comprising 39 independent states, was simply a loose alliance of rulers: its diet had little influence. If there was a common theme to the 'German revolution', it was the emergence of liberalism and the search for national unity.

a) What caused the revolutionary movements?

▼ The German population doubled in the century up to 1848. Some people left the land and drifted to the towns in search of work.

▼ In 1846–7 the corn and potato harvests were disastrous. This caused distress and unrest. Peasants demanded the abolition of feudal dues.

▼ Artisans, threatened by mechanisation, turned to machine-breaking in 1847–8.

▼ The middle classes were frustrated. Power lay where it always had, with the nobility.

▼ The political ideas of liberalism and nationalism proved increasingly attractive to the middle classes. The impetus for a united Germany came from south-western states, especially Baden which had a parliament elected on a wider franchise than in any other German state. In October 1847 an assembly of liberals from south-western states agreed on the urgent need for an independent German parliament.

▼ The revolution in France had a major impact in Germany. Lamartine, speaking for the new French republic, declared in March that France would protect 'legitimate movements for the growth of people's nationalities'. This gave encouragement to German nationalists.

b) The impact of revolution

In 1848, following the February Revolution in France, revolution spread to many small south-west German states. In some places, peasants attacked their landlords, stormed castles and destroyed feudal records. In Baden radical republicans tried to lead a peasant and worker rising.

The revolution attracted little support and was quickly suppressed by the liberal government. Meetings, demonstrations and petitions, not armed risings, were the chief weapons of the – middle-class – revolutionaries who hoped to work with and not destroy the princes. Most rulers gave in easily, if temporarily, to demands for more representative government. Although the eccentric King Ludwig I of Bavaria was forced to abdicate, in most states the old rulers survived and watched developments.

c) The Frankfurt Parliament

In March 1848, at a meeting in Heidelberg, 51 representatives from six states discussed changes to Germany's political institutions. They did so before revolutions had made an impact on the individual German states. On 5 March their decisions were published in the Declaration of Heidelberg. They agreed:

> that as soon as possible a more complete assembly of men of trust from all German peoples should come together in order to continue deliberation of this most important matter and to offer its co-operation to the Fatherland as well as to the Governments.

Invitations for the proposed assembly were quickly issued. This move, which looked directly to the German people for support, was unexpectedly successful. On 31 March 574 representatives, from almost all the states of the Confederation, assembled in St Paul's Church in Frankfurt. This assembly, a kind of 'preparatory parliament' with the task of preparing the way for the real parliament, is known as the *Vorparlament*. After five days of debate, it reached agreement on how to elect a national parliament. This should consist of one representative for every 50,000 inhabitants and be elected by citizens, who were of age and 'economically independent'.

The fact that a national parliament met in Frankfurt in May was a triumph. The elections, arranged at short notice in all 39 states, were carried out peacefully and successfully. Most states decided on residence and property qualifications. All women and most servants, farm labourers and anyone receiving poor relief were denied the vote. The last category alone excluded large numbers: in Cologne, for example, nearly a third of the population was on poor relief. In most states the voters elected 'electors', who in their turn chose representatives. The Frankfurt Parliament, while elected by a wider franchise than that operating in Britain at the time, was not very representative of the population as a whole. The vast majority of the 596 members were middle class and over 80 per cent held university degrees. There were some 60 teachers, 50 professors and even more lawyers and government officials. There were just four craftsmen and one peasant. The Parliament was essentially moderate and liberal. It started with the advantage that the old Diet of the Confederation had agreed to its own demise and nominated the Parliament as its legal successor. The key issue was whether it would be able to draw up a national constitution which would be accepted by all Germans.

The Frankfurt Parliament started by considering the relationship between itself and the individual states. Its intention was that the new 'Germany' should have much stronger central government than the old Confederation. It quickly decided that any national constitution which it framed would be sovereign, and that while state parliaments would be free to make state laws, they would only be valid if they did not conflict with the constitution, whatever that was. Drawing up a constitution and organising a government, however, proved far more difficult. Without the discipline imposed by well-organized political parties, the Parliament became a 'talking shop' in which it was difficult to reach agreement. While the debates continued, steps were taken to establish a provisional government. An elderly Austrian Archduke John, with known liberal views and German nationalist sympathies, was elected as Imperial Regent. He appointed a number of ministers who were responsible to the Parliament. As they did not have any staff or offices or money, and their duties were not clearly defined, they could do little.

In fairness to the Frankfurt delegates, there seemed no great need for speed in working out a new constitution. The important thing was to get it right. This would not be easy. The Parliament was divided between a majority who wanted a constitutional monarchy, and a small but vocal minority who wanted to establish a republic. But if Germany was to be a monarchy, who should be monarch and how much power should he have? And what should be the relationship between the central and the state governments? While there was attachment to the idea of a united Germany, most Germans wished to preserve the identity and self-government of their own states.

Another problem concerned the territorial extent of 'Germany'. The Confederation's existing boundaries did not conform to any logical definition of 'Germany'. Parts of Prussia and the Austrian Empire were included while others were not. Some parts within the Confederation contained Czechs and Poles while some of the excluded provinces had large German-speaking populations. The Austrian Empire, which comprised a host of different nationalities, was a major problem. Should all the Austrian Empire be admitted into the new Germany? Should only the German part of it be admitted? Should none of it be admitted? The Parliament was divided between the members who wanted a *Grossdeutschland* (Great Germany) which would include the predominantly German-speaking provinces of the Austrian Empire, and those who favoured a *Kleindeutschland* (Little Germany) which would exclude Austria but include the whole of Prussia. The *Grossdeutschland* plan would ensure the leadership of Germany by Catholic Austria, while the *Kleindeutschland* plan would give dominance to Protestant Prussia. The Parliament was unable to decide between the two proposals. It did not seriously consider that the non-German territories of the Austrian Empire should be forced into a united Germany.

In general, the Parliament had little sympathy for non-Germans within Germany. Having no wish to see a diminution of German power, it opposed the claims of Poles, Czechs and Danes for territory seen as part of Germany, namely Posen, Bohemia and Schleswig-Holstein. The Parliament applauded many of the actions of Austria in re-establishing control in Prague and Italy. It also supported Prussia's war against Denmark over the disputed provinces of Schleswig-Holstein.

In December 1848 the Parliament approved the Fifty Articles of the fundamental rights of the German citizen. These included equality before the law, freedom of worship, freedom of the press, and an end to discrimination because of class. Not until March 1849 did the Parliament finally agree to a constitution. Germany was to be a constitutional monarchy. There were to be two houses: a lower house elected by men 'of good reputation' over the age of 25; and an upper house made up of the reigning monarchs and princes of the Confederation. The two houses would have control over legislation and finance. Although the emperor would have considerable powers, he would only be able to hold up legislation for a limited time. The Parliament voted, half-heartedly – 290 votes in favour, 240 abstentions – to elect Prussian King Frederick William as Emperor of Germany.

d) The 1848 revolution in Prussia

In 1848–9 the hopes of the Frankfurt Parliament lay with Prussia, and her King Frederick William IV, a strange and complex character – sensitive, cultured, charming, but moody and unpredictable. Although a fervent believer in the divine right of kings, Frederick William was far from a total reactionary. At the start of his reign in 1840 he released political prisoners, abolished censorship and gave greater power to Prussia's eight provincial diets. These concessions, however, served only to encourage liberal agitation for more reform. Angered by this opposition, Frederick William imposed more restrictive policies. For most of the 1840s, he was a friend and ally of Metternich and dedicated to maintaining the old order in Europe. Then in 1847 he swung back to what seemed a more liberal policy and called a united diet – which included representatives from all the provincial diets. Having called the diet, the King made few concessions to its demands for liberal reforms and a written constitution.

When news of the revolution in Paris reached Berlin, a demonstration by workers took place on 13 March 1848. Troops were needed to preserve order. As rioting continued, deputations of citizens called on the king and asked him to make political concessions. On 18 March Frederick William accepted the idea of a new German constitution. A large crowd gathered outside the royal palace to cheer the king. However, attempts by troops to clear the crowd led to shots being fired. Students and workers immediately set up barricades and fighting erupted. At least 300 rioters were killed as troops won control of the city.

The King, who hated bloodshed, decided to make a personal appeal for peace. Copies of his letter 'To my dear Berliners' were distributed, promising that the troops would be withdrawn if the street barricades were demolished. Troops were indeed withdrawn, largely due to a misunderstanding, so that the King was left in his palace guarded only by Berlin citizens who formed a civic guard. On 19 March he had little option but to appear on the balcony and salute the bodies of the dead rioters. Berliners hoped that Frederick William might become a constitutional monarch and that he might also support the German national revolution. On 21 March he appeared in the streets with the German colours, black, red and gold, round his arm. He was greeted with tumultuous applause and declared: 'I want liberty: I will have unity in Germany.' He proceded to grant a series of reforms, agreeing to the election of an assembly to draw up a new constitution and appointing a liberal ministry.

The King's apparent liberalism did not last long. As soon as he rejoined his loyal army at Potsdam, he expressed very different feelings. He spoke of humiliation at the way he had been forced to make concessions to the people and made it clear that he had no wish to be a 'citizen' king. However, he took no immediate revenge on Berlin and allowed decision-making for a time to pass from his hands to that of the liberal ministry. The ministry was hardly revolutionary. Its members were loyal to the crown and determined to oppose social revolution. Riots and demonstrations by workers were quickly brought under control. Meanwhile the ministry, supporting German claims to the Duchies of Schleswig-Holstein, declared war on Denmark. It also supervised elections to a Prussian Parliament on the basis of manhood suffrage. The new Parliament met in May. Although it was dominated by liberals, some 30 per cent of its members were radicals and there was no agreement about the nature of a new constitution. Its main achievement was to abolish the feudal and other legal and financial privileges of the Junker class.

In Potsdam Frederick William was surrounded by conservative advisers who urged him to win back power. The conservatives – Junkers, army officers and government officials – were not total reactionaries. Most hoped to modernise Prussia but insisted that reform should come from the king. They were totally opposed to the notion of popular sovereignty. The tide seemed to be flowing in their favour. By the summer most Prussians seemed to have lost their enthusiasm for revolution and for German unity. The liberal ministry was increasingly isolated. In August the King resumed control over foreign policy and concluded an armistice with the Danes to the disgust of the Frankfurt Parliament. Riots by workers in Berlin in October ensured that the middle classes drew closer to the traditional ruling class. Habsburg success in Vienna in October encouraged the King to put an end to the Prussian parliament and to dismiss the liberal ministers.

In November 1848 Frederick William appointed his uncle Count Brandenburg to head a new ministry. Brandenburg proceeded to prorogue the Prussian Parliament and exile it from the capital. The civic guard was dissolved and thousands of troops moved into Berlin. There was virtually no resistance to the counter-revolution. In provincial towns in Rhineland and Silesia the army made short work of industrial unrest. The Prussian Parliament, still unable to agree to a constitution, was dissolved by royal decree in December. Frederick William now proclaimed a constitution of his own. This was a mixture of liberalism and absolutism. It guaranteed his subjects freedom of religion, of assembly and of association, and provided for an independent judiciary. There was to be a parliament with two houses – an upper house elected by older property owners and a lower one by manhood suffrage. Ministers, however, were to be appointed and dismissed by the king, and were to be responsible only to him. The king could also alter the constitution at any time it suited him to do so. He also retained total control of the army. The constitution thus confirmed the monarch's divine right to rule whilst limiting his freedom to act in practice. A genuine parliament, albeit subservient to the crown, had been created – from above. While Frederick William would not accept limitation of his power imposed by any of his subjects, he was prepared to limit his own powers. The new constitution, while bitterly opposed in Frankfurt, which was still debating the German constitution, was well received in Prussia.

Why did Frederick William launch a counter-revolution in the autumn of 1848? *Q*

e) The failure of the revolution(s)

The Frankfurt Parliament had little option but to pin its hopes on the Prussian king to provide the leadership necessary to create a constitutional modern Germany. By the spring of 1849, however, these hopes were illusory. When a deputation from Frankfurt offered Frederick William the German crown in April 1849 he refused it on the grounds that it was not the Parliament's to offer. He would only accept it if the offer came from his fellow princes. He was not prepared to be German Emperor if it meant putting himself and Prussia under the control of the Frankfurt Parliament. The refusal of Frederick William to accept the German crown was the death knell of the Frankfurt Parliament. The rulers of Bavaria, Saxony and Hanover together with Prussia rejected the German constitution. Many members of the Parliament lost heart and, like the Austrian and Prussian representatives, went home. The remnants, about 130 of them, made a last attempt to recover the situation, calling for elections for the first new German Parliament in August. The call fell on deaf ears. Meanwhile, the Parliament, driven out of Frankfurt by the city government, moved to Stuttgart, the capital of the Kingdom of Württemberg. There it was forcibly dispersed by the King's soldiers in June 1849. Popular uprisings in Saxony, Baden, Bavaria and some Rhineland towns were put down by Prussian troops. Constitutional changes obtained from their rulers in Saxony, Hanover and several smaller states were revoked. Thus little had changed in most German states.

f) Why did the German revolution fail?

The Frankfurt Parliament has been harshly treated, particularly by Marxist historians. Marx's collaborator, Engels, described it as 'an assembly of old women' and blamed it for not overthrowing the existing power structures. However, it is perhaps unfair to condemn the Parliament for failing to do something that it did not want to do. Most of its members had no wish to be violent revolutionaries and had little interest in social reform. Another charge levied against the Parliament is that, unable to agree on a new constitution, it failed to grasp the opportunity of filling the power vacuum in Germany in 1848. In reality, however, and despite the early successes of the 1848 revolution in Prussia and Germany, there probably never was a real possibility of creating a unified German nation ruled by a German government. Had the members of the Frankfurt Parliament acted as decisively and quickly as their critics would have them act, they would probably have been dispersed far earlier than they were. Dependent on the willing cooperation of the individual states, the Parliament lacked the power to enforce its decrees. The Schleswig and Holstein episode showed its ineffectiveness. Denmark's decision to absorb the two provinces brought a noisy protest from Frankfurt. Not having an army of its own, it looked to Prussia to defend German interests.

THE GERMAN AND PRUSSIAN REVOLUTIONS

1848 5 March: Declaration of Heidelberg;
Mid-March: Riots in Berlin;
Late March: King Frederick William made concessions to liberal opposition;
31 March: meeting of Vorparlament;
May: meeting of Prussian and Frankfurt Parliaments;
November: Frederick William re-established control in Berlin;
December: new Prussian constitution;
1849 March: Frankfurt Parliament agreed on a constitution;
April: Frederick William rejected the offer of the German crown;
June: Frankfurt Parliament finally dispersed.

Prussia occupied the two duchies in April–May 1848 but King Frederick William, aware of Russian and British opposition and doubting the wisdom of war with Denmark, agreed in August to the armistice of Malmö. The Frankfurt deputies regarded the Prussian withdrawal from Schleswig-Holstein as a betrayal of the German national cause but could do nothing about it.

Austrian and Prussian attitudes were crucial. Constitutional government and national unity could only be achieved on their terms. Austria had no wish to see a more united or democratic Germany: she hoped to dominate Germany by keeping her weak and divided. The best, perhaps the only, chance of the Frankfurt liberals lay in working out an agreement with Prussia. The chaos in Austria in 1848 gave Prussia a unique chance to play a dominant role in German affairs. She did not grasp this opportunity. This was a failure not just on the part of the King but also on the part of the Prussian liberal ministry. They failed because in the final analysis they were not at all anxious to succeed. King Frederick William, like most of his subjects, was unwilling to see Prussia merged in a united Germany at least in the way envisaged by the Frankfurt Parliament.

In fact, the authority of the Frankfurt Parliament was never accepted wholeheartedly by most of the individual states or their rulers. When the ruling princes feared that they were about to lose many of their powers or even their thrones because of revolutions within their territories, they were prepared to appear to support the Parliament. By opposing it, they feared stirring up even more opposition. But once the rulers had re-established their authority, their enthusiasm waned. Attractive as might be the idea of a strong and united Germany in theoretical terms, they had no wish to see their powers limited by liberal constitutions and a strong central authority.

6 The revolutions in Italy

Revolutions occurred in most Italian states in 1848–9. (See Figure 2 and pages 118–21). They were inspired by a number of forces:

▼ Italian nationalists dreamed of a united Italy and opposed Austria's presence in Italy.

▼ There was a general demand for more liberal forms of government.

▼ Grave economic difficulties resulted in social conflict in both towns and the countryside.

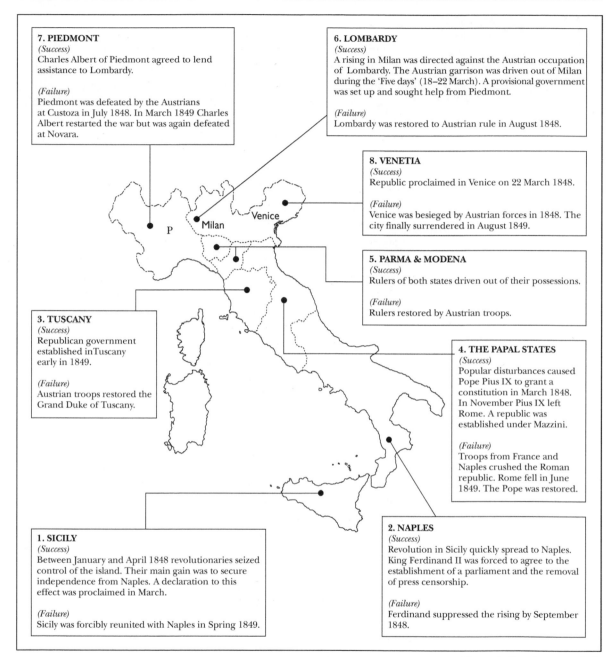

7. PIEDMONT
(Success)
Charles Albert of Piedmont agreed to lend assistance to Lombardy.

(Failure)
Piedmont was defeated by the Austrians at Custoza in July 1848. In March 1849 Charles Albert restarted the war but was again defeated at Novara.

6. LOMBARDY
(Success)
A rising in Milan was directed against the Austrian occupation of Lombardy. The Austrian garrison was driven out of Milan during the 'Five days' (18–22 March). A provisional government was set up and sought help from Piedmont.

(Failure)
Lombardy was restored to Austrian rule in August 1848.

8. VENETIA
(Success)
Republic proclaimed in Venice on 22 March 1848.

(Failure)
Venice was besieged by Austrian forces in 1848. The city finally surrendered in August 1849.

5. PARMA & MODENA
(Success)
Rulers of both states driven out of their possessions.

(Failure)
Rulers restored by Austrian troops.

3. TUSCANY
(Success)
Republican government established inTuscany early in 1849.

(Failure)
Austrian troops restored the Grand Duke of Tuscany.

4. THE PAPAL STATES
(Success)
Popular disturbances caused Pope Pius IX to grant a constitution in March 1848. In November Pius IX left Rome. A republic was established under Mazzini.

(Failure)
Troops from France and Naples crushed the Roman republic. Rome fell in June 1849. The Pope was restored.

1. SICILY
(Success)
Between January and April 1848 revolutionaries seized control of the island. Their main gain was to secure independence from Naples. A declaration to this effect was proclaimed in March.

(Failure)
Sicily was forcibly reunited with Naples in Spring 1849.

2. NAPLES
(Success)
Revolution in Sicily quickly spread to Naples. King Ferdinand II was forced to agree to the establishment of a parliament and the removal of press censorship.

(Failure)
Ferdinand suppressed the rising by September 1848.

P
Milan
Venice

Figure 2 Revolutions in Italy

All the revolutions were ultimately put down. Everywhere, with the exception of Piedmont, constitutions were abolished and the old order re-established. In 1848–9 Italian nationalism was not strong enough, nationalists not united enough, and Piedmont not strong enough to secure success.

ISSUE:
Why were conservative regimes able to reassert themselves?

7 Conclusion

The 1848 revolutions are usually seen as having failed. According to historian G. M. Trevelyan, 1848 was a potential 'turning point when Europe failed to turn'. By 1849 the forces of reaction were once again in the ascendant. The three dynastic empires of Austria, Prussia and Russia continued to dominate central and eastern Europe. No single new nation state had emerged, and radical revolutionaries had been rejected across Europe. Historians have sought general as well as specific explanations for the revolutions' failure.

▼ The revolutionaries were deeply divided. Different social groups had very different interests. While popular movements were at the root of the revolutions, it was the propertied classes who seized power. Once middle-class liberals secured the election of their own assemblies, most were as afraid of social revolution as the conservatives. Working-class movements and the organisations of the radical left were not sufficiently well-developed to force social change in their favour. Most workers had a purely practical revolutionary aim: the removal of the intolerable pressures on their lives. Unlike their 'intellectual', often self-appointed, leaders, they were not concerned with – or even aware of – political ideologies which supposedly espoused their cause. Workers were also divided: master craftsmen and the mass of unskilled workers had little in common.

▼ Europe was still essentially agrarian in 1848. The 1847 and 1848 harvests were reasonably good. The rural populations were thus not generally in a desperate economic situation in 1848–9. This may explain the unenthusiastic support for revolutionary movements among peasants and even their role in suppressing revolution by voting for conservatives, for example, in France, and by serving as military conscripts virtually everywhere. In central and eastern Europe the peasantry lost interest in the revolution once the last remnants of the feudal system had been removed. While the peasants were not necessarily conservative, many felt hostility rather than affinity to the urban revolutionaries. The failure of the peasantry to support revolutionary and nationalist movements – except in Hungary and the Roman Republic – was of crucial importance.

▼ The strongest force in 1848 was nationalism. However, it also proved to be as divisive as it was unificatory. Ironically, the very nationalism which inspired the revolutions was also to destroy their chances of success. Austria was able to play on the antipathy between various national groups to maintain imperial unity. The Hungarians, strongly nationalistic themselves, were strangely blind to the strength of nationalism within their own borders. National consciousness failed in most areas to affect the masses. Moreover, local loyalties remained strong and proved an important obstacle in the way of national unity.

WHAT WAS RUSSIA'S ROLE IN 1848–9?
Russia, seen as the chief supporter of autocracy and the 'gendarme of Europe', did little to bolster the conservatives. Tsar Nicholas was more concerned with preventing liberalism from infecting his own domains, particularly Poland, than filled with zeal to stamp out revolution elsewhere. He largely confined himself to sending advice to his fellow monarchs – although he did send troops to assist Austria against the Hungarians in 1849.

▼ Liberals and nationalists soon found that they were not necessarily on the same side. Until 1848 it was possible for some nationalists, like the Italian, Mazzini, to believe that the triumph of nationalism would, by some never explained alchemy, usher in an age of international peace and harmony. Events in 1848–9 showed how hollow such expectations were. In both Vienna and Frankfurt, German liberals backed German interests and supported the crushing of 'liberal' revolts in Prague, Italy and Hungary.

▼ Across Europe, the army's role was crucial. Everywhere armies remained loyal to the established rulers. Nowhere did any army declare for a constitution. Except in Hungary and the Roman Republic, capable revolutionary armies were not created.

▼ The revolutionaries drew little support from Britain or France. The British Foreign Secretary Palmerston, regarded as the champion of liberalism before 1848, had no intention of risking war to further ideological causes on the continent. Expectations of French intervention on the side of revolutionaries also failed to materialise. Ironically, the only French intervention came in 1849 when French troops overthrew the Roman Republic.

The 'failure' of the 1848 revolutions helped ensure that a conservative political and social order maintained its hold on Europe until the First World War; that the unification of Germany and Italy occurred within a conservative rather than a liberal framework; and that violent revolutionary movements, though not anarchism and terrorism, virtually disappeared in Europe (except in France in 1871 and in Russia in 1905) before 1914. The old order was helped by the return of general economic growth and prosperity post-1848.

> ### DID THE REVOLUTIONS FAIL?
>
> Arguably the revolutions were not a total failure.
>
> ▼ The remnants of feudalism in central Europe were abolished.
>
> ▼ Manhood suffrage was introduced in France.
>
> ▼ Parliamentary government (of sorts) was introduced in Prussia and Austria.
>
> ▼ After 1848 virtually every monarchical regime accepted the need to modernise, even if it was not prepared to accept a dilution of traditional forms of power.
>
> ▼ The revolutions had helped stir national consciousness across a wide swathe of Europe.

▼ Working on The 1848 Revolutions

To help draw your thoughts together, try to construct diagrams to explain the main points made in each section. A diagram summarising the main points made in section 1 is done for you. (Figure 3)

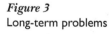

Figure 3
Long-term problems

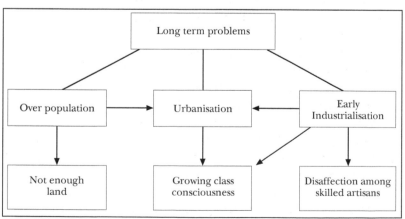

Figure 3b The situation
in 1845–8

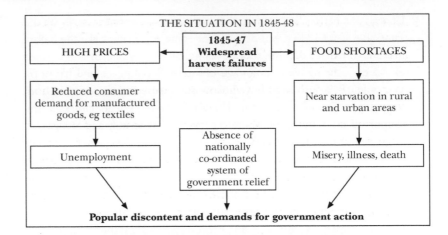

Answering extended writing and essay questions on The 1848 Revolutions

Consider the question: to what extent were the revolutionaries in France and Austria responsible for their own failure?

Start by simply listing – in rough – all the reasons why both revolutions failed. What, if anything, was common to both revolutions? You might come up with the following mistakes made by both French and Austrian revolutionaries.

▼ Failure to maintain unity.

▼ Raising of expectations by revolutionaries which they were unable/ unwilling to satisfy.

▼ Introduction of new measures which undermined the revolutionaries' position.

However, the revolutionaries clearly faced huge problems. These included:

▼ The nature and role of the rural peasantry.

▼ The role of the armed forces.

You will also need to consider the specific situations in both France and Austria which led to the defeat of the revolutions. Try drawing up an essay plan.

Answering source-based questions on The 1848 Revolutions

Read Sources A and C on pages 66–7 and 75 and answer the following questions.

1. Study Source A. Why would Marx favour 'A heavy progressive or graduated income tax'? **[3 marks]**
2. How useful is source C in helping historians understand the mood in Hungary in 1848? **[7 marks]**
3. Using your own knowledge and the evidence in the sources, explain why the 1848–9 European revolutions failed. **[15 marks]**

Points to note about the questions

Question 1 Marx sympathised with the underdog. His proposals had to be paid for.

Question 2 The source is primary. But to what extent did all Hungarians agree with the 'demands'? To what extent did Hungarian views change during the course of 1848?

Question 3 You are required both to analyse the sources and to bring in your own knowledge. As a rule of thumb it is best to give each a roughly equal treatment. You might start by emphasising the difference between the sources and the fact that the authors had very different aims and were appealing to very different 'audiences'. By doing this you make the point that the revolutionaries were very divided. Lack of unity was one problem. What other factors led to the defeat of the revolutions?

Further Reading

Books in the Access to History series

The key texts are *France: Monarchy, Republic and Empire 1814–70* by K. Randell; *The Habsburg Empire* by N. Pelling; and *The Unification of Germany 1815–90* by A. Stiles.

General

Specific books on the 1848 revolutions include: *The 1848 Revolutions* by P. Jones (Longman, 1991) and *1848: A European Revolution?* edited by A. Korner (Macmillan, 2000) On events in France try *France 1814–1914* by R. Tombs (Longman, 1996); on Austria try *The Decline and Fall of the Habsburg Empire 1815–1918* by A. Sked (Longman, 1989); and on Germany try *The Struggle for Mastery in Germany, 1779–1850* by B. Simms (Macmillan, 1998).

4 The Impact of the Crimean War

POINTS TO CONSIDER

The Crimean War, in which over 500,000 men died, was easily the costliest war fought in Europe between 1815 and 1914. It began as a conflict between the Ottoman Empire and Russia in 1853. In 1854 Britain and France declared war on Russia: Piedmont did the same in 1855. Why did the war start? What were its main results?

KEY ISSUE:
What were the main causes and results of the Crimean War?

Historian M. S. Anderson thought the Crimean War 'was the outcome of a series of misjudgements, misunderstandings and blunders, of stupidity, pride and obstinacy rather than of ill will'. However, this traditional interpretation of the origins of the Crimean War has been challenged. It is possible to argue that the war occurred because certain groups and individuals actually wanted a conflict. To what extent was the war an accident? To what extent was it deliberately intended? Who was most responsible?

Historian Andrew Lambert has argued – persuasively – that the very term 'Crimean War' has no historical reality. The war did not begin or end in the Crimea. Nor was it decided there. Lambert points out that the campaign in the Crimea was only one part of a much wider struggle against Russia which involved other campaigns in Asia Minor, the White Sea, and the Baltic Sea. The British naval threat in the Baltic in the spring of 1856 was more important in persuading Russia to make peace than events in the Black Sea. The war, whatever it is called, tends to be remembered in Britain for the Charge of the Light Brigade, Florence Nightingale and for popularising the cardigan and the balaclava. In some respects this trivialises a major war, the only major military conflict involving more than two of the great powers between 1815 and 1914.

1 The causes of the Crimean War

ISSUE:
Was the Crimean War an accident or an accident waiting to happen?

a) The Ottoman Empire

By the mid-19th century, the Ottoman Empire was in a ramshackle state. The Turkish government at Constantinople (modern Istanbul) claimed authority over territories which included much of the Balkans, Asia Minor, the Middle East, Egypt and the coast of North

Africa (see map on page 50). Governing such a vast empire, which contained so many different nationalities, was a daunting task. Effective government ultimately depended on energetic and resourceful direction from Constantinople, which few of the Sultans of this period were capable of providing. Some reforms did take place, including military and naval modernisation. Such measures, albeit sporadic and incomplete, contributed to the ability of the Ottoman Empire to survive. Nevertheless, that survival depended less on her own efforts than on the attitude of the European powers towards her. Several of the great powers saw some advantage to themselves in the preservation of the Ottoman Empire.

b) The interests of the great powers

Russia was the great power most directly involved in the fate of the Ottoman Empire. Military success against Turkey in the late 18th century had brought Russian gains around the Black Sea and in the northern Caucasus. This success brought Russia more than territorial gain. By the Treaty of Kutchuk-Kainardji (1774), she acquired three important rights: freedom of navigation for Russian merchant shipping in the Black Sea; the right of passage for merchantmen through the Straits (the Bosphorus and Dardanelles) which form the outlet from the Black Sea into the Mediterranean; and an ill-defined right of protection over the Orthodox Church in the Ottoman Empire. The maritime rights granted by this treaty were of great importance to Russia's development. Russia was handicapped militarily and commercially by the fact that most of her ports were ice-bound for much of the year. After 1815, Russia had several options with regard to Turkey. One option was to seek further territorial gains at Turkey's expense. Another was to support the efforts of her fellow Slavs in the Balkans to throw off Turkish rule. A third option, and one favoured in the 1830s and 1840s, was to seek to preserve Turkey in her existing condition of gradual decline. It was preferable having a weak Ottoman Empire to having a stronger state bordering on Russia in its place.

Austria regarded the Ottoman Empire as a useful bulwark against Russian expansion and thus sought to preserve, not weaken it. Moreover, she did not share Russia's sympathy for the stirrings of Slav nationalist feeling in the Balkans, for fear of its effects on her own Slav peoples.

By the mid-19th century, Britain had committed herself to the preservation of the Ottoman Empire. In the early 1800s there had been little to suggest that Britain would adopt such a role. In the 1820s she had supported the Greeks in their struggle for independence from Turkey. The key factor in the change of British policy was an exaggerated suspicion of Russia's aims. Britain's main fear was that Russia planned to dismantle the Ottoman Empire and control Constantinople. This would lead to a marked growth in Russian power throughout the Near and Middle East. This might threaten Britain's position in India and damage Britain's growing trade and investments in Turkey. Nevertheless, an influential body of British opinion deplored the idea of supporting the despotic and Muslim Ottoman Empire. Another complicating factor was British public opinion. This could, on occasion, be aroused by the press to a frenzy of either anti-Russian or anti-Turkish feeling. Consequently, British policy towards Turkey and Russia was liable to fluctuate, often according to which party was in power.

In the 18th century French kings had been recognised as protectors of the interests of the Catholic Church in the Sultan's dominions. While French influence at Constantinople declined in the early 19th century, she extended her influence in the eastern Mediterranean where her commercial interests often clashed with those of Britain.

c) The situation c.1840–50

After the 1839–41 crisis (see pages 57–58), the Eastern Question – the problem of what to do about the decline of the Ottoman Empire – played only a minor role in European affairs for the next ten years. Britain and Russia, the two main players in the Near East 'game', remained on reasonably friendly terms for most of the 1840s. In 1844 they agreed that joint action in the Near East was the best way of maintaining peace.

In 1848 Louis Napoleon became French President. In 1852 he proclaimed himself Emperor Napoleon III. Napoleon III hoped to restore French influence in Europe and overthrow the 1815 settlement which endeavoured to contain France. He was determined to pursue an active role in foreign policy, partly for personal reasons and partly because he realised he had to meet the expectations of his supporters who associated the name Napoleon with glory. He was thus keen for a major success in foreign affairs. He was particularly keen to challenge Russia, the country most associated with containing France. This would not be easy. Russia's power and prestige had been increased by the defeat of the 1848–9 revolutions.

Tsar Nicholas I viewed Napoleon III with great suspicion. Alarmed by the revival of Bonapartism in France, he feared that Napoleon III would try to emulate his uncle. The fact that he espoused national causes, not least those of the Poles, was a further concern. Britain too was worried about the new threat from Bonapartism. The possibilty of a French attack on Britain was taken very seriously in the years 1851–3. As a result Britain looked to cooperate with the eastern powers and also increased her military spending. Even in late 1853 when Britain was preparing for possible war with Russia, French naval activities were still closely monitored. It was ironic that the British navy, strengthened to protect Britain from French attack, was to find itself allied in 1854 with the power it was primarily designed to fight!

d) The Holy Places dispute

Napoleon III decided that the best area in which to challenge Russia was the Near East. In 1740 French Catholic monks had been granted the right to look after the holy places in Palestine. In the early 19th century, however, Greek Orthodox monks had taken over control of them. They had the support of Russia. Since the 1774 Treaty of Kutchuk-Kainardji, Russian tsars had seen themselves as the protector of the religious freedom of the Sultan's Christian subjects. This situation gave Napoleon III his chance to interfere. The dispute over the guardianship of the holy places, which included such issues as which monks should hold the keys to the Church of the Nativity at Bethlehem, has been called a 'churchwardens' quarrel'. Nevertheless, it had serious implications. At root it was a question of whose influence prevailed at Constantinople – French or Russian. In 1850 the Sultan was presented with a French demand for the reinstatement of the full rights of the Latin monks as granted in 1740. This was a good issue for Napoleon III. It was likely to win him the approval of Catholic opinion in France, and was also likely to have the sympathy of Catholic Austria, thus undermining the Holy Alliance. By challenging Russia's vague religious rights, Napoleon III had no wish to provoke war with Russia. He simply wanted to win some prestige. A two-year struggle ensued between French and Russian diplomats at Constantinople. The Sultan resorted to duplicity, which only served to aggravate the crisis. In December 1852, after a series of overt French threats, the Sultan handed over the keys to the Holy Places to Catholic priests.

e) The Menshikov mission

Tsar Nicholas was outraged by this triumph for French diplomacy. With his prestige at stake, Nicholas believed that he had to take firm action. He needed to show that Russian influence at Constantinople was greater than that of France. The only way to do this was to force the Sultan to revoke his decision in favour of the Catholic monks. In his determination to put pressure on the Turks, Nicholas seriously misread the international situation. Confident that he could rely on Austria, he also assumed that he could count on British support, an attitude encouraged by the fact that the anti-Turkish Lord Aberdeen became head of a coalition government in December 1852.

Palmerston was shunted off to the Home Office while Lord John
Russell became Foreign Secretary. Tsar Nicholas had established
good relations with Aberdeen in the 1840s and hoped to revive the
good rapport. In January 1853, the Tsar initiated a series of
conversations with Sir Hamilton Seymour, the British Ambassador to
Russia. Reviving proposals he had made in 1844 in the course of a
state visit to Britain, the Tsar suggested a 'gentleman's agreement'
between Russia and Britain for dealing with the supposedly
imminent collapse of the Ottoman Empire.

Lord John Russell's polite response to the Seymour conversations
was misunderstood by Nicholas who thought he had British
sympathy. In fact, Aberdeen's cabinet was divided. Some, like
Aberdeen, hoped to maintain good relations with Russia, disliked
Turkey, and distrusted Napoleon III; others, like Palmerston, were
mistrustful of Nicholas's intentions, suspecting that he was aiming to
destroy the Turkish Empire.

Such suspicions were increased by the Tsar's actions in 1853. The
Russian Foreign Minister argued, that if it was fear that had induced
the Sultan to give way to France's demands, then fear of Russia was the
weapon that had to be applied at Constantinople to reassert Russian
influence. Thus in January 1853 Russian troops were concentrated on
the borders of Moldavia and Wallachia. The Tsar also sent a high-
powered mission, headed by Prince Menshikov, to Constantinople in
February. Menshikov demanded that the keys be given back to the
Orthodox priests and that the minister who bowed to French pressure
over the Holy Places be dismissed. More importantly, he also
demanded that the tsar should be recognised as the protector of all
Christians living in the Turkish Empire. Since Orthodox Christians
amounted to over one third of the Sultan's subjects, such a right, if
conceded, would reduce Turkey to the status of a Russian protectorate.
Menshikov's overbearing manner was intended to intimidate the
Turks. From the outset he attempted to dictate to the Turkish
government, not negotiate with them. Nicholas was strangely blind to
the effect that diplomatic pressure on the Turks might have on Britain.

Palmerston and Russell both wanted to support Turkey.
Palmerston argued that Russia would back down if firmly opposed.
Aberdeen remained cautious. Disliking the idea of supporting the
Turks, he believed that the problem could best be solved by
negotiations. He was not convinced that Russia was plotting the
destruction of the Ottoman Empire but was concerned that she
might try to win control over Constantinople with the dire prospect
of Russian warships coming and going through the Straits as they
pleased. However, Aberdeen's efforts to find a peaceful solution were
hampered by divisions within his cabinet and by a great surge of
Russophobia among the British public. Liberals and radicals became
excited at the prospect of taking on Russian autocracy.

Meanwhile the pro-Turkish British Ambassador in Constantinople, Lord Stratford de Redcliffe, encouraged the Sultan to resist Menshikov's demands. These had offended the Turks and aroused genuine anger and nationalist fervour in Constantinople. The Sultan was prepared to restore the privileges to Orthodox monks in Palestine but rejected the demand that Russia be recognised as protector of all Christians living in the Turkish Empire. Nicholas now scaled down the substance of the demands to a more modest level – ultimately to little more than a face-saving formula. When these more limited demands were also rejected by the Turks in May, the infuriated Tsar broke off diplomatic relations with Turkey. Aberdeen, influenced by Palmerston, Russell and by the British press, agreed to send a naval force to Besika Bay just outside the Dardanelles in June as a gesture of support for Turkey. (Palmerston wanted the fleet to sail into the Black Sea as a real warning to Russia.) It was soon joined by a French fleet. By opposing Russia, Britain could not escape cooperation with France.

> **Q** Did Russophobes in Britain (such as Palmerston) aim to provoke a war with Russia?

f) The coming of war: 1853–4

Confident of the support of Austria and Prussia, Nicholas was not impressed by the British-French action. Russian prestige and her influence in Turkey were at stake. Faced with the choice of a humiliating climb-down or an increase in pressure on Turkey, Nicholas chose the latter course. In July Russian troops occupied the Danubian Principalities of Moldavia and Wallachia which acknowledged the Sultan's suzerainty. Nicholas specifically stated that he did not seek war. Russian forces would withdraw when the Turks conceded to the demands which Menshikov had made. Turkey, confident of British and French support, was not ready to give way. Suddenly war seemed imminent. Britain and Austria were now concerned. Count Buol, the Austrian Foreign Minister, was alarmed by the occupation of the Principalities which gave Russia control of the mouth of the Danube. The British government feared that Russia now sought the complete domination or destruction of the Ottoman Empire.

In an attempt to defuse the crisis Austria organised a conference in Vienna in July, attended by Austrian, Prussian, French and British diplomats, hoping to find a formula that would satisfy the Tsar's honour while safeguarding Turkey's integrity. The diplomats proposed that the Sultan should make a few concessions to the Tsar and should consult both Russia and France about his policy towards the Christians. In return Russia should leave the Principalities. Nicholas, now aware that help from Prussia and Austria was unlikely, accepted the so-called Vienna Note. The Sultan, however, with the support of British Ambassador Stratford de Redcliffe, insisted on some amendments to the note. The Turkish amendments were rejected by the Tsar in

September. Attempts to find a diplomatic solution to the dispute had thus suffered a major setback. Nicholas now met Austrian Emperor Francis Joseph and Prussian King Frederick William IV in an attempt to win support but the most they would agree was to remain neutral if war broke out. Britain and France, who knew of the meetings but not what been decided, feared that the three rulers had hatched a plot to divide the Turkish Empire. Thus in October the British government ordered the fleet to Constantinople where it was soon joined by French warships.

Turkish nationalist resentment at Russia's occupation of the Principalities put the war party in the ascendant at Constantinople. In late October, Turkey declared war on Russia. Turkish troops crossed the Danube and attacked the Russians in Wallachia. The Russians replied by attacking and sinking part of the Turkish fleet at Sinope in the Black Sea in November 1853. This engagement, in which 4,000 Turks lost their lives, created a storm of protest in Britain and France. It was depicted, wrongly, by the press as an illegitimate action by Russia. The British and French governments were subjected to increasing pressure from liberal public opinion to stand firm against Russia. Lord Aberdeen's government dithered. While Aberdeen was still opposed to war, Palmerston urged the need to put paid to Russian arrogance once and for all. His resignation in December increased the popular pressure on Aberdeen's government. Napoleon now took the lead, ordering the French fleet into the Black Sea, although still appealing to Russia for peace. In January 1854 the British fleet followed the French example. The western allies declared that their fleets' job was to protect Turkish shipping (by confining the Russian fleet to its base in Sevastopol). The Tsar's rejection of a proposal for a six-power peace conference was a further setback to efforts to avoid war. Nicholas now sent Prince Orlov on a special mission to Vienna and Berlin to ask the two German powers for their armed neutrality. Both refused. The failure of the Orlov mission was a turning point in the history of Europe. It confirmed the collapse of the Holy Alliance which for nearly four decades had been the great bulwark of order in central and eastern Europe. In February Britain and France sent Nicholas an ultimatum demanding the withdrawal of Russian troops from the Principalities. The ultimatum was ignored. Thus on 28 March 1854, Britain and France declared war on Russia.

g) Responsibility for the war

Tsar Nicholas was torn between the possibility of dividing the Turkish Empire or trying to preserve it in its weak state. His indecision possibly explains why there was – and has been – disagreement about Russia's real intentions. At the time many believed Russia did intend to destroy the Ottoman Empire. Nicholas was also responsible for a series of

Q

Which state or statesman bore most responsibility for the outbreak of war?

miscalculations and errors of judgement which resulted in a confrontation with Turkey from which it was difficult to extricate himself with honour. His conviction that Turkey was in a state of imminent collapse was also wishful thinking, leading to the assumption that the Turks could be bullied into accepting Russia's demands. The Menshikov mission was thus a crucial step towards war. It generated a powerful current of anti-Russian feeling in Turkey which reached fever pitch after the Russian occupation of the Principalities. This military action raised the stakes in an already tense diplomatic crisis. Finally, Nicholas's exaggerated sense of honour led him to reject several diplomatic attempts to resolve the crisis over the winter of 1853–4.

The Tsar's blunders were almost equalled by those of the British government. Lord Aberdeen's coalition government was sharply divided between the pacific and anti-Turkish Aberdeen, and the aggressive and anti-Russian Palmerston. As a result the government frequently resorted to half-measures. For example, the despatch of the fleet to Besika Bay in June 1853, instead of to the Black Sea, encouraged the Turks more than it deterred the Russians. Furthermore Aberdeen's government came under increasing pressure from the press, which gave full expression to the violent Russophobia that characterised public opinion after 1848–9. Almost irrespective of the issues involved, British public opinion regarded Russia as a dangerous reactionary force whose supposed expansionist designs had to be resisted at all costs. Hence the popularity of Palmerston. The role of Stratford de Redcliffe, ambassador at Constantinople, in encouraging Turkey to reject both Menshikov's demands and the Vienna Note, remains highly controversial.

> **Q** Would a tougher British stand earlier in 1853 have deterred Russia and averted war?

France's culpability lay mainly in initiating the crisis in the Near East by raising the issue of the holy places. Napoleon III can be accused of playing to the gallery at home, regardless of the likely repercussions on Russo-Turkish relations. His aim was to weaken if not destroy the Holy Alliance – a necessary prelude to the reassertion of French influence in Europe. While Napoleon made several proposals designed to facilitate an honourable retreat by the Tsar in 1853–4, French naval action mirrored that of Britain.

The indecisiveness of Austrian policy in 1853–4 can be seen as contributing to the outbreak of war. For too long she allowed the Tsar to persist in his belief that he could rely on Austrian support. Had Austria come out openly against Russia at an earlier date, the Tsar might have realised the need to tread more warily in his dealings with Turkey.

Although the Turks may appear to be the hapless victims of great power politics, they were by no means innocent of warlike intentions. Western support in the mounting crisis presented them with a unique opportunity to take revenge on their traditional enemy

EVENTS LEADING TO THE CRIMEAN WAR

1852 Sultan accepted French demands for restoration of rights of Catholic monks in the Holy Land;

1853 March: Menshikov mission arrived in Constantinople; May: Russia broke off diplomatic relations with Turkey; July: Russian forces occupied the Principalities; October: Turkey declared war on Russia;

1854 January: Allied fleet entered Black Sea; March: Britain and France declared war on Russia.

Russia. The Sultan's rejection of the Vienna Note sabotaged the best hope of a peaceful solution. Whether the amendments insisted on by the Turks were justified by legitimate concern, or whether they were intended to make war more likely, is a matter of dispute.

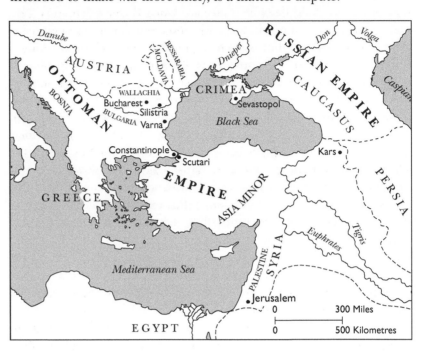

Figure 1 Map of the Near East

ISSUE:
How and why did the allies win the Crimean War?

2 The war: 1854–6

a) Diplomacy 1854–5

In the spring of 1854 Britain, France, Austria and Prussia were in basic agreement on the need to defend the integrity of the Ottoman Empire, but only Britain and France had declared war on Russia for the sake of protecting it. Moreover British and French war aims were far from identical. Although at times Napoleon III dreamed of extending the scope of the war with the aim of liberating Poland and Finland, essentially he wanted a quick victory to raise his prestige both at home and in Europe. In Britain, Palmerston wanted the widest possible campaign to reduce Russian power and set her back a generation or more. In a memorandum which he drew up for the cabinet in March 1854 Palmerston proposed carving up Russia. Finland was to be returned to Sweden, the Baltic provinces given to Prussia, Poland would become independent, Austria would gain Wallachia and Moldavia, but lose her Italian possessions, while the Ottoman Empire would regain the Crimea and Georgia. Aberdeen dismissed this as unrealistic daydreaming, a view shared by most of the cabinet at the time and by most historians since.

Aberdeen's main concern was to bring Austria and Prussia into the war. In Prussia some liberals favoured an alliance with Britain and France. So did Minister President Manteuffel. However, Prussian army leaders had little difficulty persuading the Prussian King to maintain a position of armed neutrality. Austria's position was more complicated. Both her economic interests and her military security were threatened by the Russian occupation of the Principalities. While Austrian Foreign Minister Buol was keen to support Britain and France, Emperor Francis Joseph and his generals were opposed to war with Russia on the grounds that Austria would do most of the fighting and that war would endanger the stability of the Habsburg Empire. Austrian policy was thus to keep out of war but to put pressure on Russia to evacuate the Principalities. In June, Austria, with Prussia's backing, demanded Russia's evacuation of the Principalities. In August Russia withdrew and the area, with Turkish agreement, was occupied by Austrian troops. Austria now saw no reason to fight. The Balkan issue had been solved entirely to her satisfaction without a single Austrian shot being fired.

Austria now took the lead in promoting diplomatic moves to end the war. The 'Four Points', accepted by the western powers in August 1854, became the basis of peace proposals – and thus allied war aims – for the rest of the conflict.

The Tsar's rejection of the Four Points in September left Britain and France with two courses of action: to persuade Austria to side openly with them against Russia; and to force Russia to negotiate by inflicting military defeats on her forces. Both were pursued, with varying degrees of success. For example, military setbacks induced the Tsar to accept the Four Points in late November 1854. The war ought now to have ended in a negotiated peace but by this time Britain had decided to insist on stiffer terms regarding the Black Sea. Negotiations in the spring of 1855 also broke down over this point, so that renewed peace talks had to await further victories. More rapid success seemed to reward allied efforts to include Austria within the anti-Russian coalition. Foreign Minister Buol, dreaming of a greater Austrian Empire dominating the Balkans, was enthusiastic. In December 1854 he persuaded a reluctant Francis Joseph to sign a treaty with Britain and France. Although called an alliance, the treaty did not mean that Austria had to fight. (In January 1855 Piedmont, anxious to gain support for her ambitions in northern Italy, agreed to join Britain and France.)

b) Military action: 1854–5

The first phase of the war, from October 1853 – August 1854, involved Turkish and Russian forces fighting on the Danube and in the Trans-

> ### THE FOUR POINTS
> ▼ Russian guarantees of the Principalities were to be replaced by a European guarantee.
> ▼ The Danube was to be a free river.
> ▼ The 1841 Straits Convention was to be revised 'in the interests of the balance of power'.
> ▼ The Sultan's Christian subjects were to be placed under European and not just Russian protection.

What were the allies fighting for once the Russians evacuated the Principalities?

Caucasus. A Turkish offensive on the Danube front was driven back after fierce fighting. In the Caucasus region Russian troops held their own against Muslim tribesmen and a large Turkish army. In the spring of 1854 Russian forces, trying to push south from the Principalities, encountered valiant Turkish resistance at Silistria. The Russian attack quickly ran out of steam.

For Britain and France, the war was initially something of an anti-climax. Allied troops landed at Gallipoli expecting the Russians to be advancing on Constantinople. In fact Constantinople was under no threat. Allied soldiers were then sent to Varna on the Black Sea coast. However, as a result of Austrian rather than allied pressure, the Russians pulled out of the Principalities before the allied troops fired a shot in anger. Britain and France now agreed to strike against the Crimean port of Sevastopol. This seemed a sensible option. The capture of Sevastopol would destroy Russian naval power in the Black Sea, thereby eliminating a major threat to Turkey's security. In September 1854 allied troops arrived in the Crimea. The attack, one of the worst-kept secrets of war, still took the Russians by surprise. Badly organised and ill-equipped, the 60,000-strong allied forces (30,000 French, 26,000 British and 4,000 Turks) made heavy weather of the campaign. The failure to follow up initial successes with a rapid assault on Sevastopol proved a costly error. It enabled the Russians to strengthen Sevastopol's fortifications. The allies had little option but to lay siege to the town: to have evacuated the Crimea without its capture would have a been a serious blow to their prestige.

After the Russians failed to dislodge the allied armies from the Crimea in the battles of Balaclava and Inkerman, military deadlock ensued. British forces, short of food, clothing, ammunition, and medical supplies, were ill-prepared for a long campaign and the winter of 1854–5 brought dreadful suffering, aggravated by medical and administrative incompetence. Newspaper correspondents (for example, W. H. Russell of *The Times*) sent back detailed and uncensored reports so that the British public was reasonably well informed about what was happening. From the British point of view there was probably no greater incompetence than at the start of most wars: it just appeared as though there was. Partly because of Russell's vivid accounts, Florence Nightingale and her team of nurses went out to try to bring some order to the chaos in the hospitals. By the spring of 1855 there were over 200,000 allied troops in the Crimea (including 17,000 Piedmontese), only 32,000 of which were British.

If the allies had problems in the Crimea, the Russians had greater problems. Given that there was not a single railway line south of Moscow, it took three months for men and supplies to get to the Crimea. (It took the allies three weeks.) The corrupt Russian administrative system made the supply system something of a lottery.

The huge but ill-equipped Russian army was thus unable to defeat the smaller invading force. Fearing and facing attacks on a number of fronts, the Russians failed to concentrate their military effort in the Crimea: instead they dissipated their strength trying to guard all possible points of attack. They were already fighting a major war in the Caucasus area. Given that Austria mustered a 100,000-strong army of 'observation', Nicholas was forced to station much-needed troops on the Austrian border to guard against the threat.

c) The end of the war

In Britain mounting criticism of Aberdeen led to the fall of his government early in 1855. Palmerston became Prime Minister, ensuring the British war effort was waged with more vigour and efficiency. However, he was unable to persuade his cabinet to enlarge on the Four Points or to wage a more ambitious war against Russia. Given the weakness of the British army, he also had to accept an increasing degree of French direction of the war in the Crimea. The death of Nicholas I in March 1855 and the succession of Alexander II, who did not have the same personal commitment to the war, seemed to offer some hope of peace. An Austrian-sponsored peace conference met at Vienna from March–June 1855. It collapsed when Russia refused to agree to the neutralisation of the Black Sea.

The fall of Sevastopol in September 1855, largely the result of French military action, was a serious setback for Russia but by no means amounted to a total defeat. Russian guns to the north still dominated the city, preventing the allies from occupying it in safety. For the remainder of the war the two armies in the Crimea sat and watched one another. French public opinion, never as pro-war as that in Britain, felt that the capture of Sevastopol satisfied France's honour and wanted an end to the war. Napoleon agreed. Palmerston, however, was still in a belligerent mood. Determined to 'confine the future extension of Russia', he advocated campaigns in the Baltic and the Caucasus. His aggressive stance, although supported by British public opinion, struck no responsive chord in Europe. In November 1855 the Russians broke through on the Caucasus front, capturing the fortress of Kars. Undeterred, Palmerston planned a major new campaign in the Baltic. The British fleet had already had considerable success, blockading Russia and destroying the Russian dockyard at Sweaborg in Finland. Some 250 British ships – the 'Great Armament' – prepared for inshore and amphibious operations in April 1856 which it was hoped would lead to the capture of the main Russian naval base at Kronstadt.

Palmerston's main fear, that war-weary France would begin secret peace talks with Russia, came to pass. In December 1855 Austria, after

Q

Why did Russia agree to the Austrian ultimatum?

THE CRIMEAN WAR

1854	July: Russian troops left the Principalities; September: Allied troops landed in Crimea: battle of the Alma; October: Battle of Balaclava; November Battle of Inkerman;
1855	January: Piedmont joined the Allies; February: Palmerston formed a new British government; March: Death of Nicholas I: Alexander II became Tsar; September: capture of Sevastopol;
1856	March: Treaty of Paris signed.

THE CASUALTIES

The Crimean War involved far heavier casualties than any other European war fought between 1815 and 1914. Between 650,000 and 750,000 are thought to have died. Britain lost 22,000, France 90,000, Russia (at least) 450,000 and Turkey some 150,000. Only one in five lost their lives in battle: most died of disease.

discussions with France, but not Britain, issued an ultimatum threatening Russia with war if she did not negotiate on the basis of the Four Points. In January 1856 the Russian Council of Ministers discussed the Austrian ultimatum which they realised was merely a gesture. The Austrian army was actually in the process of demobilising and posed no serious threat. Russia's main concern was the Baltic. The British naval blockade was ruining Russia's economy and endangering domestic stability. The threat from the 'Great Armament' to Kronstadt and St Petersburg – and the rumour of Swedish intervention – was also a major worry. In mid-January Tsar Alexander II accepted the Austrian ultimatum as the basis of peace talks. Palmerston had no choice but to agree: Britain could not fight Russia alone. An armistice was soon agreed. The opening of a peace conference in Paris in late February marked the end of the Crimean War.

d) The Treaty of Paris, March 1856

The Paris peace conference was a major European event – the greatest congress since that at Vienna in 1814–15. At the conference, the western allies were divided. Napoleon III desired to improve relations with Russia, even at the expense of his entente with Britain. The British consequently found themselves alone in pressing for severe terms on Russia – the loss of Finland, the Caucasus and the Crimea. Indeed, Palmerston wanted the peace conference to fail, to justify extending the war against Russia. The desire of the other states for peace, however, ensured the defeat of this strategem.

In general, the terms of the Treaty of Paris were an elaboration of the Four Points, proposed in August 1854.

▼ Russia's protectorship over the Principalities was replaced by a collective European one, while the existing rights and privileges of the Balkan Christians were guaranteed by a new reform edict issued by the Sultan.

▼ Turkey's territorial integrity and independence were agreed.

▼ The fortress of Kars was returned to Turkey.

▼ An international commission was set up to ensure freedom of navigation on the Danube.

▼ Southern Bessarabia, ceded to Russia in 1812, was restored to Turkey and incorporated into Moldavia.

▼ The administration of the two Danubian Principalities was to be reformed so as to create an 'independent national administration' under Turkish suzerainty.

▼ The Black Sea was neutralised. Russia and Turkey were prohibited from maintaining warships or naval arsenals there.

There was thus no major redrawing of the map of Europe. Britain and France hoped that Moldavia and Wallachia might be given to Austria, in return for which she would hand over Lombardy and Venetia to Piedmont. Austria, however, would not accept this.

Although the neutralisation of the Black Sea terms were a major blow to Russian pride and prestige, the Paris Treaty was, in general, a lenient peace settlement. This was not too surprising: Russia had come to Paris not on the basis of unconditional surrender but because she accepted Austria's 'ultimatum'. In the British government's view, the treaty did not go far enough to weaken Russia. In the event relatively few of the terms had much permanence. Nevertheless, the allies could claim that they had achieved most of their objectives: Russia was considerably weakened, her Balkan ambitions checked and her navy kept out of the Mediterranean. Moreover, the Turkish Empire had survived and the Eastern Question was put on hold for two decades.

> **Q** Did the results of the war justify the cost in money and lives?

3 The effects of the Crimean War on international relations

> **ISSUE:**
> What were the main effects of the Crimean War?

The Crimean War marked the demise of the 'Concert of Europe' established in 1815. The period from 1856 to 1870 was a chaotic period of diplomacy. There were no stable alignments between the great powers: each sought to further their own interests rather than acting in the interests of Europe as a whole. The war, preceded by almost 40 years of peace, was followed by 14 years of intermittent warfare. Two major territorial changes took place during this period: the unification of Italy under Piedmont and the creation of the German Empire under Prussia.

The war ended the generally accepted view of Russia as Europe's dominant power. After 1856 Russia's main diplomatic aim in Europe was to remove the humiliating restrictions imposed on her naval power in the Black Sea. (This was not achieved until 1870–1.) No longer committed to maintaining the *status quo*, she was prepared to countenance changes to the 1815 Settlement if her own interests were not directly threatened. Russia continued to play a major role in European diplomacy after 1856, seeking initially to win over the French and to encourage Franco-Austrian rivalry. French desire for revisionism of the 1815 settlement, rather than being opposed, was now a force to be exploited to achieve Russian revision of the 1856 treaty. While pursuing a cautious policy in Europe, Russia followed an expansionist policy in Asia where it was possible to win prestige, as well as land, markets and sources of raw materials, without the risk of a major war. Between 1857 and 1864 Russian forces pacified the Caucasus and then won control over a large area of central Asia. This brought her into rivalry with Britain – ruler of the Indian sub-continent. Finally, Russia's defeat made it clear to all but the most

> **Q** Why did Russia see Austria's role in the Crimean War as a betrayal?

reactionary that a radical overhaul of Russian society, especially the abolition of serfdom, was essential. While change would no doubt have occurred eventually, the war speeded things up.

After 1856 Austria, the only great power still committed to the defence of the *status quo* in Europe, found herself in a vulnerable position. Financial weakness and military backwardness seriously undermined her position as a great power. Moreover, her hesitant policies had succeeded in alienating Britain, France and Russia. Austria's role in the war, not least the fact that she joined the 'Crimea Coalition', ended the previous three decades of friendship and cooperation with Russia and began an era of hostility that lasted until 1918. Austria's 'betrayal', as the Russians saw it, was to have important consequences. In the period 1856–63 Russia aligned herself first with France and then from 1863–70 with Prussia, both of whom were pursuing anti-Austrian policies. Unable to rely on Russian help, Austria could not prevent the unification of Italy and Germany, both of which were disastrous from an Austrian perspective.

France was seen as the real victor of the Crimean War since she seemed to have played a larger and more glorious military role than Britain. The 1856 congress made Paris the centre of European diplomacy as Napoleon III had hoped. Seen as the 'Arbiter of Europe'

Other results of the war

▽ Although emerging victorious, Britain's military reputation had been damaged by the war. Many Britons felt that the sacrifices of men and money had achieved little. Disenchanted with active involvement in European affairs, Britain stood aside from playing a major role in continental diplomacy for a generation after 1856.

▽ Although Piedmont came away from Paris empty-handed, the fact that she was on good terms with France and Britain was to help her considerably in the years ahead.

▽ After Austria evacuated Moldavia and Wallachia in 1857, the two provinces were consolidated, became virtually independent and assumed the name of Romania in 1862.

▽ Prussia emerged with little glory from the war and suffered the humiliation of being excluded from most of the sessions of the Congress of Paris. However, her passive role during the war meant that, unlike Austria, she had avoided alienating Russia. As it turned out, the war created favourable conditions for Prussian expansion in the 1860s.

▽ Although no major crisis arose in the Near East for two decades, the war resulted in no lasting solution to the Eastern Question. Turkish maladministration continued.

in the period 1856–63, Napoleon III seemed able to pursue his own agenda, not least the cause of Italian nationalism. In reality, his position was not as strong as it appeared. Although Franco-Russian relations were quite cordial after 1856, France failed to secure a firm alliance with Russia. The two countries' interests did not really coincide.

▼ Working on The Impact of the Crimean War

Much of this chapter is concerned with the causes of the Crimean War. Causation is a vital historical concept. It helps to think in terms of long-term causes (preconditions), medium-term causes (precipitants) and short-term causes (triggers). The Eastern Question was an essential precondition of the Crimean War. Can you think of any other long-term causes of the war? What were the main events between 1850–3 which helped precipitate the war? What were the main triggers which finally brought about war? Historian M. S. Anderson claimed that: 'No state or statesman had wanted the war. All bore some responsibility for it'. Do you agree?

Answering extended writing and essay questions on The Impact of the Crimean War

The Crimean War has been described as 'the most important European war fought between 1815 and 1914'. Discuss this view.

Just how important was the Crimean War? It will obviously help your cause if you know what other major wars were fought in the period. This will involve some – but not a great deal of – research on your part. The good news, in every sense, is that there were not many other major European wars in the period 1815–1914. You will need to say something about the reasons why the Crimean War was fought. What were British, French, Russian and Turkish aims? You will also need to say something about the nature of the war. Was the Crimean War the first 'modern' war? However, essentially you will need to focus on the outcomes of the war. What were the main terms of the Treaty of Paris? What implications did the war have on Europe after 1856?

A TURNING POINT IN WARFARE?

The Crimean War gave some indication of the way in which future wars would be fought. It saw the first use of iron-clad ships, the first military railway and the production of the breech-loading Armstrong gun. It also made obvious the interdependence of military and industrial strength. However, it was probably not a turning point in the history of warfare. It was by no means a 'total war': it was not fought by mass armies; nor did it cause much disruption to normal civilian life in Britain and France.

Answering source-based questions on The Impact of the Crimean War

Source A Punch cartoon: 1853

TURKEY IN DANGER.

Source B Extracts from a House of Commons Debate: August 1853

Lord John Russell: …Sir, I will only further say that this question of the maintenance of Turkey is one that must always require the attention – the vigilant attention – of any person entrusted with the conduct of the foreign affairs of this country; and further, that I think it can only be secured by a constant union subsisting between England and France, and by a thorough concert and cordial communication between the two Powers…

Cobden: I do not exactly see, Sir, that there is any difference of opinion on the question that is before us. I find everybody is agreed that Russia has acted in a manner that is treacherous, overbearing, and violent. I find that, in and out of this House, everybody entertains the opinion that the most fortunate result of the late proceedings in the East is, that it has brought about a firm alliance, not only between the people of England and France, but between the Governments of England and France.…But though evidently there is a great acquiescence of opinion amongst us all, there is still a great deal of uneasiness on the subject of Turkey…Disguise it as you will, we are not in earnest in the belief that we can preserve Mohammedanism in Europe.

▼ QUESTIONS ON SOURCES

1. What message is the cartoonist trying to put over in Source A? **[3 marks]**

2. Examine Source B. To what extent do Lord John Russell and Cobden agree? To what extent do they disagree? **[7 marks]**

3. Using your own knowledge and the evidence in these sources, explain why Britain went to war with Russia in 1854. **[15 marks]**

Further Reading

Books in the Access to History *series*

Try *The Concert of Europe: International Relations 1814–70* by J. Lowe.

General

The best book on the causes of the war is *The Origins of the Crimean War* by D. Goldfrank (Longman, 1994). *The Crimean War* by P. Kerr (Channel Four, 1996) accompanied a television series and examines the war itself in some detail. *The Crimean War: British Grand Strategy against Russia, 1853–56* by A. Lambert (Manchester University Press, 1990) is fascinating.

5

ITALIAN UNIFICATION

KEY ISSUES:
What were the
obstacles to Italian
unification? Why did it
come about?

POINTS TO CONSIDER

In 1870 Rome became the capital of Italy. Its acquisition from the
Pope was the final phase of a prolonged Italian struggle to become an
independent and united nation. Italians call the unification movement
the *Risorgimento* (literally 'resurgence' or 'rebirth'). The progress of
the *Risorgimento* was never smooth and it did not come about
according to anyone's preconceived plan. This chapter will examine
the tortuous process of Italian unification and in particular the roles
played by Mazzini, Cavour and Garibaldi.

ISSUE:
What was the state of
Italy in 1815?

1 Italy in 1815

a) The impact of the Napoleonic occupation

A united Italy had not existed since the 6th century. By the late 18th
century there were 11 states in the Italian peninsula which had
become one of the most underdeveloped regions in western Europe.
By 1799 the French had conquered most of Italy and remained in
control until 1814. The French occupation had important effects.

▼ State boundaries were rearranged a number of times ending up with
Italy divided into three parts: one part, including Piedmont, was annexed
to France; one part became the Kingdom of Italy, ruled by Napoleon on
behalf of his son; and the rest became the Kingdom of Naples, ruled first
by Napoleon's brother Joseph and then by General Murat.

▼ The power and influence of the Pope and the Catholic Church were
reduced.

▼ A growing number of middle-class Italians held responsible posts in the
army and in the civil service.

▼ Peasants were freed from their old feudal ties and obligations.

▼ A start was made on improving communications.

▼ Italian laws were standardised and more enlightened French legal codes
introduced.

▼ Elected assemblies were set up, giving the middle class a chance for
political participation.

France gave Italy a modicum of unity. This unity might have been
artificial and imposed from outside but at least it existed,
demonstrating that the dream of a united Italy could become a

reality. Ironically, opposition to French rule also helped promote nationalist development. French tax collection, repressive police and anti-clerical measures, and conscription provoked hostility. This took the form of secret societies, and also occasionally mass risings by peasantry led by priests and nobles.

What did Italian nationalism owe to Napoleonic rule?

b) The Vienna settlement: 1814–15

The Vienna peacemakers had two main aims in Italy. One was to prevent France regaining control of Italy at a future date. The other was to suppress revolutionary or nationalist movements which might be a danger to established governments. Both these aims were achieved by making sure that Austria effectively controlled the peninsula. Lombardy and Venetia, the rich and strategically important parts of northern Italy, were placed under Austrian rule. Austrian dominance in Italy was reinforced by installing members of the Habsburg family as the ruling sovereigns of most other Italian states. In many respects, the 1815 peace settlement redrew the map of Italy so that it resembled the Italy of pre-Napoleonic times, reinstating most of the ruling families dispossessed during the French occupation. These restored monarchs quickly re-established themselves as absolute rulers, abandoning most of the Napoleonic developments.

There was no suggestion at Vienna of establishing an Italian Confederation under Austrian control as was done with Germany. Italy, in Metternich's view, was no more than a 'geographical expression'. Even within the various states there were regional antagonisms. Differences in interests and outlook divided the cities of Rome and Venice, for example, from their rural territories. The Republic of Genoa was to prove a difficult mouthful for Piedmont to swallow. Equally hostile were the islanders of Sicily to mainland government from Naples. Given the strength of local loyalties, the notion of a united Italy seemed little more than political fantasy in 1815. In Metternich's view, this was how it should remain.

> ### ECONOMIC BACKWARDNESS
> About 90 per cent of Italians worked on the land. There was little industry anywhere. The south was poorer and far more backward than the north. Poor communications and the multiplicity of customs barriers and systems of currency did not help economic advance.

2 The growth of opposition: 1815–48

> **ISSUE:**
> **How strong were the forces of nationalism and liberalism in the period 1815–48?**

a) Secret societies

Secret societies became the focal point for individuals with grievances against the restored monarchies. The most important society was the Carbonari but there were several other groups. Most society members were middle class – army officers, students, lawyers and teachers. They were divided into many small groups on a local basis and had their

THE CARBONARI (LITERALLY: CHARCOAL-BURNERS)
In theory this was an international society with its headquarters in Paris. In reality, it was most active in Italy, particularly in the south. Carbonari members did not agree about the means to achieve their ends or even about the ends themselves. It was left to individual groups to decide their own particular policies and methods.

Q

What were the main nationalist ideas pre-1848?

own passwords and rituals. They also had diverse aims. Some radicals wanted to overthrow the existing political and social situation. Others dreamt of Italy becoming a single nation with a democratically elected parliament. Most simply wished for local constitutional reform. The only thing they had in common was a desire to overthrow the absolute monarchs and liberate Italy from Austria's grip.

b) The revolutions of 1820–1 and 1831

While the revolutionary programmes of 1820–1 and 1831 often included ideas for a united Italy, the aims of the rebels were not primarily nationalist: rather they were liberal demands for constitutional rule. A few unpopular rulers were unseated or forced to accept liberal reform. However, the revolutionary success was only temporary. Austrian troops quickly restored order and reactionary governments strengthened their hold. The secret societies, with their poor organisation and lack of common purpose, were not up to the task of directing a great national revival. The most serious weakness was the failure to generate mass support. The middle-class liberals who led the risings, fearing social upheaval and suspicious of democracy, refused to court popular involvement. Thus, the peasant masses often welcomed back their 'legitimate' rulers.

c) Giuseppe Mazzini

Mazzini was born in Genoa in 1805. After studying law, he joined the Carbonari in 1827. Imprisoned in 1830, he determined to dedicate his life to working for Italian unification. His disappointment with the objectives and methods of the Carbonari prompted him to develop a new approach to Italy's problems. After his release from prison in 1831, he settled in Marseilles where he launched his new society, Young Italy. Believing that 'the nation is the God-appointed instrument for the welfare of the human race', Mazzini addressed himself to the people not only of Italy but of Europe. He envisaged a 'united states of Europe' in which each nation would have its own special mission in the cause of humanity. However, his overriding aim was to create a republican nation state in Italy. Italy could then be the model for nationalist revolution throughout Europe. He believed that Italians must achieve national unity by their own efforts. ('Italy will make itself.') He envisaged writers, composers and teachers inspiring Italian nationalism while Young Italy prepared the way for a people's war of national liberation against Austria and the petty despots. He looked to the educated middle class and urban artisans for support. He had little faith in the peasantry and thus little interest in land reform which might have brought the rural masses on to his side. Once the revolution had

Figure 1 Italian revolutions
1820–1 and 1831

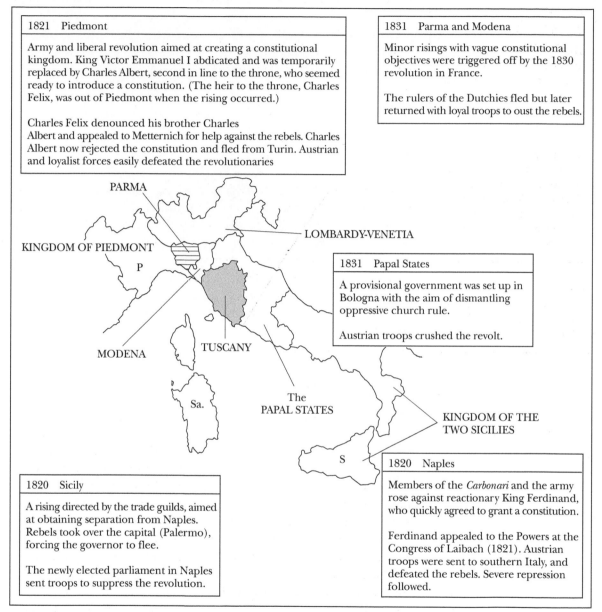

1821   Piedmont

Army and liberal revolution aimed at creating a constitutional kingdom. King Victor Emmanuel I abdicated and was temporarily replaced by Charles Albert, second in line to the throne, who seemed ready to introduce a constitution. (The heir to the throne, Charles Felix, was out of Piedmont when the rising occurred.)

Charles Felix denounced his brother Charles Albert and appealed to Metternich for help against the rebels. Charles Albert now rejected the constitution and fled from Turin. Austrian and loyalist forces easily defeated the revolutionaries

1831   Parma and Modena

Minor risings with vague constitutional objectives were triggered off by the 1830 revolution in France.

The rulers of the Dutchies fled but later returned with loyal troops to oust the rebels.

PARMA

LOMBARDY-VENETIA

KINGDOM OF PIEDMONT

P

1831   Papal States

A provisional government was set up in Bologna with the aim of dismantling oppressive church rule.

Austrian troops crushed the revolt.

MODENA

TUSCANY

Sa.

The
PAPAL STATES

KINGDOM OF THE
TWO SICILIES

S

1820   Sicily

A rising directed by the trade guilds, aimed at obtaining separation from Naples. Rebels took over the capital (Palermo), forcing the governor to flee.

The newly elected parliament in Naples sent troops to suppress the revolution.

1820   Naples

Members of the *Carbonari* and the army rose against reactionary King Ferdinand, who quickly agreed to grant a constitution.

Ferdinand appealed to the Powers at the Congress of Laibach (1821). Austrian troops were sent to southern Italy, and defeated the rebels. Severe repression followed.

occurred, it would be followed by the election of a national assembly which would carry through the revolutionary programme. Those who joined Young Italy (the maximum age for membership was 40) had to swear to dedicate themselves wholly and for ever to the endeavour to make Italy 'one free, independent republican nation'.

Mazzini spent 1831–3 organising Young Italy. Propaganda materials were distributed through Piedmont, Tuscany and the Papal States.

Figure 2 Mazzini

'Young Italy' is a brotherhood of Italians who believe in a law of progress and duty, and are convinced that Italy is destined to become one nation...They join this Association with the firm intention of consecrating both thought and action to the great aim of reconstituting Italy as one independent sovereign nation of free men and equals.

'Young Italy' is republican and unitarian – republican because theoretically every nation is destined, by the law of God and humanity, to form a free and equal community of brothers; and the republican form of government is the only form of government which ensures this future...

'Young Italy' is unitarian, because without unity there is no true nation: because without unity there is no real strength; and Italy, surrounded as she is by powerful, united and jealous nations, has need of strength above all things...

The means by which 'Young Italy' proposes to reach its aims are education and revolution, to be adopted simultaneously and made to harmonise with each other. Education must ever be directed to teach, by example, word and pen, the necessity of revolution. Revolution, whenever it can be realised, must be so conducted as to render it a means of national education.

ACTIVITY

Read the Young Italy source, written by Mazzini. Answer the following questions:

1. What seem to have been the main aims of Young Italy?

2. How did Mazzini think Young Italy would achieve its aims?

However, Mazzini's attempt at starting the national war of liberation in Piedmont in 1833 with 200 men bordered on the farcical and was easily crushed. An effort to incite insurrection in 1834 also ended in total failure. In 1836 Mazzini was forced to disband Young Italy and spent most of his later life in impoverished exile. Always dressed in black, in mourning for the failed revolution, he became the archetypal romantic revolutionary, winning admiration and even devotion from most who met him. As a revolutionary leader, he was a failure. His movement was too intellectual and too idealistic to be a practical or popular blueprint for revolution. His writings had only a limited circulation. His extreme views alienated much potential middle-class support and he had no strategy for winning over the peasantry. Mazzini estimated the membership of Young Italy at 50,000 but most historians think this an overestimate. However, as the leading propagandist of Italian unity, his influence on a section of Italian patriots, and on his greatest disciple Garibaldi, was enormous – and greatly feared by established rulers. His radical movement largely replaced the old secret societies in Piedmont and the north. His name was known throughout Italy and much of Europe. His writings helped put the idea of a united Italy firmly on the political agenda.

d) Vincenzo Gioberti

Gioberti, an exiled Piedmontese priest and ex-Mazzinian, presented a different solution to the Italian problem. In his work *Of the Moral and Civil Primacy of the Italians*, published in 1843, he dismissed total unity as 'madness', rejected revolutionary methods and saw no future for republicanism in Italy. Instead, he placed his hopes in the Pope, whom he envisaged as the president of a federation of existing Italian states.

e) Cesare Balbo

In his book of the *Aspirations of Italy* (1844), Balbo agreed with Gioberti that a united democratic Italy was undesirable. He accepted the idea of a federation of Italian states but saw no special role for the Pope. He emphasised the expulsion of Austria from Italy as the first step to political change and claimed that the only Italian state capable of achieving this feat was Piedmont. He thus advocated that its king should assume the leadership of a new Italian federation.

ITALY 1820–46

1820 risings in Sicily and Naples;
1821 Piedmont revolt;
1831 risings in central Italy: Young Italy established;
1833 failure of Young Italy rising in Piedmont;
1846 Pius IX became Pope.

ISSUE:
Why did the 1848 revolutions start and fail?

Other forces supporting unification:
▽ The idea of an independent Italy captured the minds of writers, historians and composers and the 1830s and 1840s saw the publication/ production of many works – poems, novels, plays, operas – which emphasised Italy's glorious past.
▽ Liberal economists, hopeful that economic integration would result in Italian unity, pressed for a customs union and supported the building of a national railway network.

f) Pope Pius IX

In 1846 Pius IX become Pope. While far from the wholehearted liberal he was initially taken for, at least he was not an out-and-out reactionary. Pius began with a grand gesture to the liberals, granting an amnesty to 2,000 or so political prisoners in the Papal States. Administrative, education and legal reforms followed. In 1847 Pius ended censorship of the press. He also created an advisory body, members of which were elected and included non-clergy. Reform in the Papal States was imitated in other areas. Popular enthusiasm for the papacy, and for the *Risorgimento*, rose to great heights. It suddenly seemed as though Gioberti's ideas might come to fruition and that Italy might unite under a papal federation.

3 The revolutions of 1848–9

a) The causes

By the late 1840s liberal demands for constitutions and political freedom, and nationalist demands for Italian unity and independence from Austria, were bound up with an economic crisis. Disastrous harvests in 1846 and 1847 in Italy produced food shortages in both rural and urban areas, creating a potential revolutionary situation. Italian states were thus unsettled before news of the February revolution in Paris and the March revolution in Vienna reached the peninsula. Metternich's fall seemed to give Italy a real opportunity to determine its own future without the fear of Austrian troops. The fact that there was an apparently liberal pope and a king in Piedmont ready to support Italian unification gave hope to liberals and nationalists alike. Many historians have stressed the 1848 revolutions as evidence of the growing national consciousness in Italy. Certainly an 'Italian' patriotism played a part in the risings. But historian Denis Mack Smith has stressed the deep divisions – between radicals and moderates, between urban and rural population – and argued that the degree of national consciousness should not be exaggerated. Local grievances were usually more important than Italian nationalism in sparking off risings.

b) Charles Albert and Piedmont

In March 1848 Charles Albert was persuaded to declare war on Austria. The Italian war of liberation seemed to have really begun. Mazzini arrived in Milan. The new liberal ministry of King Ferdinand of Naples sent troops north to Lombardy. Tuscany and the Papal States also seemed ready to offer support. However the 'alliance' of Italians was more apparent than real. From the start there was scarcely any cohesion among the disparate Italian movements. Charles Albert was more concerned to annex Lombardy and Venetia (and Modena and Parma) than to pursue the goal of a united Italy. Then, in April, Pope Pius IX decided to dissociate himself from the war, making it clear that papal forces would not fight against Austria. He also drew back from the idea that he should head an Italian federation. He called on Italians 'to abide in close attachment to their respective sovereigns' and attacked the ideas of Mazzini. The Catholic Church thus turned its back on liberalism and henceforward was to be a major stumbling block in the way of unification. For Charles Albert and other loyal Catholics the loss of papal support was a bitter blow. The Pope's action was followed by that of the King of Naples.

In July Charles Albert's army was defeated by the Austrians at Custozza. An armistice was signed and Piedmont withdrew from Lombardy, leaving it in Austrian hands. The Venetians quickly renounced their union with Piedmont, re-established the Venetian Republic and prepared to continue the war with Austria. Charles Albert, hoping (in vain) that France would assist him, re-entered the war against Austria in March 1849. Heavily defeated at the battle of Novara in April, he abdicated in favour of his son Victor Emmanuel II. The Austrians, concerned about possible French intervention and wishing to strengthen the new king against radical forces, treated Piedmont leniently.

c) The Roman Republic

In Rome the murder of Count Rossi, the Pope's unpopular chief minister, in November 1848 was followed by rioting. The Pope fled to Naples while the government he left behind announced a programme of reform, including the holding of a meeting of elected representatives from all parts of Italy. This met in February 1849. It quickly proclaimed the overthrow of the temporal power of the pope and the establishment of a Roman Republic. Mazzini, who reached Rome in March, was appointed head of the new government. Italians from all over the peninsular were attracted to Rome to defend the new Republic. Meanwhile the Pope appealed to France, Austria, Spain and Naples for help. The decisive campaign was undertaken by 20,000 French troops. Louis Napoleon, recently elected President of France, wanted to win

Why did the 1848–9
Italian revolutions all
fail to achieve their
objectives?

domestic Catholic support by restoring the Pope. Hopes that French troops would be welcomed by the Romans proved unfounded. Garibaldi led a gallant defence of Rome before the city finally fell in July 1849. (Garibaldi and Mazzini both escaped.) A far more reactionary government than before was now set up in the Papal States. Only when all signs of liberal reform had been obliterated did the Pope return to Rome in April 1850. He was cheered through the streets by the same crowds who had cheered for the Roman Republic a year before.

d) The effects of the failure of the 1848–9 revolutions

By 1849 the hopes of liberals and the nationalists – in most cases one and the same – had collapsed. Apart from the *Statuto*, granted to Piedmont by Charles Albert, none of the constitutions obtained from their rulers by the revolutionaries survived. None of the rulers forced out of their states had been kept out for long. Austria seemed more firmly in control of north and central Italy than ever. The Pope had now established a reactionary regime and was defended by French troops. In the south King Ferdinand II had re-established his authority on the mainland and in Sicily. Idealistic nationalists had assumed that a spontaneous popular rising would bring the reactionary powers of darkness crushing down and result in a united and free Italy. The lesson of 1848–9 appeared to be that romantic idealism could not succeed against the existing order unless supported by force. The Lombard revolutionary Pallavinco said: 'To defeat cannon and soldiers, cannon and soldiers are needed. Arms are needed and not Mazzinian pratings. Piedmont has soldiers and cannons. Therefore I am Piedmontese.' Nationalists of various hues reached a similar conclusion: if Italy was to be liberated it would be by the military strength of Piedmont, the one 'liberal' (ish) and 'Italian' monarchy in the peninsular. Gioberti renounced his idea of a papal federation in favour of Piedmont. Garibaldi, the military hero of the Roman Republic, saw Victor Emmanuel as the King of a united Italy. Victor Emmanuel, for his part, hoped to marry a policy of extending Piedmontese influence in Italy with the legitimising idea of nationalism. But after defeat in 1848–9 nationalist hopes and Piedmontese expansionist dreams seemed far from realisation.

> ### *Reasons for the failure of the 1848–9 revolutions*
>
> ▼ The military superiority of Austria was crucial in ensuring the revolutions' failure.
> ▼ The revolutionaries' hopes of French support did not materialise.
> ▼ Pope Pius IX turned his back on the Italian liberal and nationalist movements.
> ▼ Popular involvement from the peasant masses was not encouraged by the liberal revolutionaries. In most cases peasants found little or no improvement in their lives under the new governments. Social reform was not a liberal priority. Thus rulers who had been forced to flee were often welcomed back quite sincerely by the ordinary people.
> ▼ Most of the revolutions were characterised by local grievances and rivalries rather than by a concerted national effort to unite. Most 'Italians' still felt loyalty to their town or region rather than to 'Italy'. There was little cooperation between revolutionary groups and little inter-state support. The confusion of ideologies is reflected in the different provisional governments which were set up. These were moderate, extremist, liberal, republican or monarchist in varying combinations. Everywhere liberals and radicals were in conflict – and radicals were at odds amongst themselves!

See Figure 2 on Page 89

ACTIVITY

Look at the box above listing reasons for the failure of the revolutions. Place the reasons in a top five order. Justify why you have number one first and number five last.

4 Piedmont and Cavour 1848–60

a) Piedmont

ISSUE:
Why did Piedmont play such an important role in Italian unification?

Piedmontese kings after 1814 had not been renowned for their liberalism. Victor Emmanuel I (1814–21) and Charles Felix (1821–31) were reactionary, absolute monarchs. Charles Albert (1831–49), introverted and excessively devout, began his reign as a reactionary, alienating revolutionaries like Mazzini and Garibaldi. But he did introduce some social and economic reforms and by the 1840s liberalising influences crept into Piedmont, not least a comparatively free press. In March 1848 the King, apparently throwing in his lot with the liberal nationalists, granted a constitution (the *Statuto*) and went to war with Austria. His defeat and abdication brought Victor Emmanuel II to the throne.

THE STATUTO: MARCH 1848

The Piedmont constitution created a – limited – parliament. The upper house was appointed by the king. The lower house was elected. The king retained most of his existing rights. Parliament had no direct control over the government. It was far more important for ministers to have the king's support than a parliamentary majority. Less than 3 per cent of the population had the vote. Nevertheless the *Statuto* offered a few – wealthy – citizens opportunities for political participation, opportunities which were not possible elsewhere in Italy.

THE NATIONAL SOCIETY

During the 1850s many Italians rejected the ideals of Mazzini. His methods had clearly failed and it seemed appropriate to seek an alternative. The new direction which emerged was articulated and developed by Pallavicino, founder of the National Society which emerged in 1857. Pallavicino invested his hopes for Italian unification in the Piedmontese monarchy. The National Society attracted liberals, hardened revolutionaries like Garibaldi, and ex-republicans like Manin, president of the 1848–9 Venetian Republic. Although the society had only a few thousand members, its influence was

Piedmont attracted the hopes of liberals and nationalists after 1849 for several reasons:

▼ Alone among Italian states after 1849, it possessed a constitution – a great symbol to liberals – and a comparatively free press.
▼ Piedmont had twice gone to war with Austria in 1848–9.
▼ Piedmont was the most prosperous region in Italy.

During the 1850s Piedmont attracted some 200,000 political refugees – liberals, nationalists and republicans – from other parts of Italy. This gave the state a cosmopolitan nationalist flavour. It also added to the nationalist pressure on the government.

b) Victor Emmanuel and Azeglio

The new king was 29-year-old Victor Emmanuel II. Likeable and courageous, he was also shrewd and politically skilful. Some saw him as a cautious conservative: others thought him a cautious liberal. (In reality, he was probably just cautious!) His main aims were to speed up the recovery of Piedmont and to build up its army so that it had the means to fight Austria again. The King and Azeglio, appointed Prime Minister in 1849, set Piedmont on a moderate conservative path. Azeglio was not dependent on popular support. When the radical majority condemned the proposed peace with Austria, Victor Emmanuel dissolved parliament. When new elections in July 1849 returned a majority opposed to peace, the King again dissolved parliament and a peace treaty was signed with Austria in August. The autumn election, after much royal and ministerial interference, finally secured a majority ready to support Azeglio. The *Statuto* remained intact – just! During Azeglio's premiership the most important legislation was the abolition of the extensive privileges enjoyed by the Catholic Church in Piedmont. This anti-clerical policy, which continued under Cavour, enraged devout Catholics. In November 1852 Cavour replaced Azeglio following devious political manoeuvring.

c) The importance of Cavour

Cavour was a liberal nationalist. But he was no revolutionary and his hopes for Italian unification were tempered by his loyalty to the Piedmontese monarchy, his rejection of democracy and his sense of practical politics. In 1852 by bringing his own centre-right supporters into coalition with a centre-left group, he produced the *connubio* (marriage) of Piedmont's politically moderate middle ground. This enabled him to remain firmly in control of government, resisting the opposition of both the clerical right and the radical left. Victor Emmanuel, who actively disliked Cavour, had no option but to make him Prime Minister. Henceforward, he proved indispensable.

An ambitious and sometimes ruthless opportunist, Cavour's policy was based on the notion that the end justifies the means. While he believed in parliamentary institutions (he was an effective debater and skilled politician), he had no faith in democracy. He often acted without parliamentary approval and without consulting cabinet colleagues. He rigged elections and bribed newspaper editors.

> (Continued)
> substantial. Cavour, who was suspicious of the democratic aims of some of its members, could not ignore an association capable of raising 20,000 volunteers.

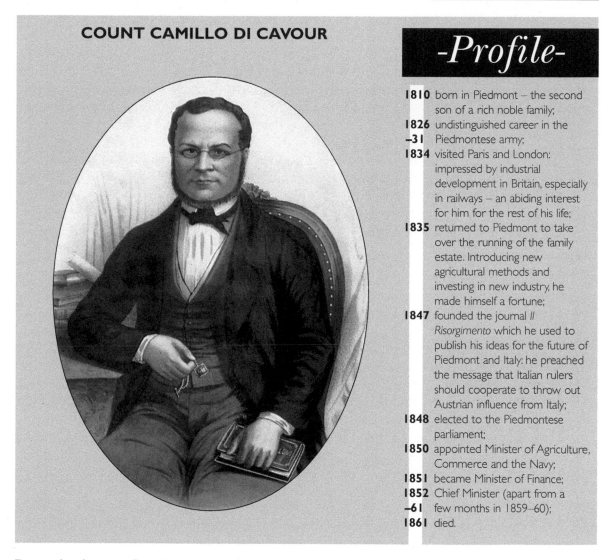

COUNT CAMILLO DI CAVOUR

-Profile-

1810 born in Piedmont – the second son of a rich noble family;

1826 –31 undistinguished career in the Piedmontese army;

1834 visited Paris and London: impressed by industrial development in Britain, especially in railways – an abiding interest for him for the rest of his life;

1835 returned to Piedmont to take over the running of the family estate. Introducing new agricultural methods and investing in new industry, he made himself a fortune;

1847 founded the journal *Il Risorgimento* which he used to publish his ideas for the future of Piedmont and Italy: he preached the message that Italian rulers should cooperate to throw out Austrian influence from Italy;

1848 elected to the Piedmontese parliament;

1850 appointed Minister of Agriculture, Commerce and the Navy;

1851 became Minister of Finance;

1852 –61 Chief Minister (apart from a few months in 1859–60);

1861 died.

Determined to confine the vote to the wealthiest citizens, he was vehemently opposed to the revolutionary republicanism of the Mazzini-type. Indeed, he was even prepared to make common cause with Austria to discredit Mazzini. Not surprisingly Mazzini regarded Cavour with gravest distrust.

ECONOMIC MODERNISATION IN PIEDMONT

Cavour placed great emphasis on Piedmont's economic development.

▼ He concluded trade treaties with France, Britain and Belgium.
▼ Piedmont's merchant fleet was enlarged.
▼ He supported the use of the latest techniques in both farming and industry.
▼ He encouraged improvements in communications. By 1860 Piedmont possessed 800km of rail track – almost as much as the rest of the entire Italian peninsula.

Compared with western Europe, Piedmont's economic development was slow but compared with the other Italian states it was considerable.

Was Cavour an Italian nationalist working always with his eyes on the prize of a unitary state? Or did he wish merely to expand the power and prestige of Piedmont?

Why was the Crimean War an important factor in the unification of Italy?

Cavour was to play a crucial role in Italian unification. However, unification did not come about according to any carefully conceived plan on his part. Indeed, pre-1860 he did not conceive of the possibility of Italy as a unitary state. He thought northern and southern Italy had little in common and identified the idea of unity with Mazzini's republican programme. In most respects, he supported traditional Piedmontese aims: to free Italy from Austrian influence and to strengthen Piedmont's influence by annexing territory in north and central Italy. He was prepared to cooperate with, but was not wholeheartedly in support of the aims of, the National Society which were more radical than he wished. 'Manin's [a National Society leader] ideas are always a trifle far-fetched,' wrote Cavour privately. 'He wants the unity of Italy and other such rubbish – nonetheless in practice all this may prove useful.' Cavour could – and did – not ignore nationalist pressure. Aware that there were pressures for constitutional reform in Piedmont and even support for separatism in Genoa and Sardinia, he realised that one way of diffusing these movements was to undertake a popular nationalist policy. While he did not take seriously the ideal of national unification, he realised he could use its appeal to achieve – more limited – Piedmontese expansionist aims.

Cavour soon realised that exploiting nationalist feeling and modernising Piedmont would not be enough to defeat Austria and win dominance over north Italy. This could only be done with foreign help. After 1852 he did his best to bring the Italian question into the forefront of European politics and to persuade Britain and France that Austrian misrule in Italy justified their intervention. In 1855 Piedmont joined Britain and France in the war against Russia, sending troops to the Crimea. (2,000 Piedmontese soldiers died.) At the Paris Peace Conference in 1856 Cavour failed to win support for his plans to extend Piedmont's power at the expense of Austria or the central Italian duchies. He returned home empty-handed and disappointed. But at least he had made important personal contacts, especially with Napoleon III. The Crimean War helped Cavour's cause in another way. It left Austria isolated in Europe. Britain and France were angry she had not helped them in the war. Russia was angry at what she saw as Austria's 'betrayal'. After 1856 Cavour committed himself to the goal of securing an alliance with France, the new arbiter of European affairs.

d) The Pact of Plombières

Napoleon III told Cavour he wanted 'to do something for Italy'. He had maintained a long interest in Italian affairs and in Italian nationalism. In 1830 he led a conspiracy which planned to proclaim his cousin King of Italy. The plot failed and Napoleon III was expelled from Rome. Keen to follow in the steps of his uncle Napoleon Bonaparte (who had declared on St Helena that he had hoped to free the Italians) and keen to act as the champion of liberal causes and the patron of the 'principle of nationality', his wish to help the Italians was undoubtedly sincere. However, Napoleon III's policy was shaped by a variety of other motives. He hoped to see the power of Austria reduced, to secure a revision of the 1815 settlement, and to restore France's international prestige. He also believed that support for Italian independence would be popular in France. Given Austria's isolation after 1856, the time for Napoleon III to 'do something for Italy' seemed opportune. Exactly what he wanted to do, however, is unclear: his plans, fluid, devious, and secret, are difficult to unravel. He certainly did not want to create a strong, unified Italian state. Such a state might represent a threat to France. However, a federation of Italian states with an enlarged Piedmont acting as a French satellite was an attractive proposition.

Oddly enough it was an assassination attempt on Napoleon III by the Italian nationalist Orsini in January 1858 which persuaded him to 'do something'. At his trial Orsini made an impassioned plea for Italian freedom which so impressed Napoleon III that he made arrangements for a secret meeting with Cavour to discuss the Italian question. The meeting took place at Plombières in July 1858. Both Napoleon and Cavour were natural conspirators and both were in their element. After lengthy negotiations a deal was struck.

A formal – secret – treaty, largely incorporating the arrangements reached at Plombières, was signed in January 1859. Napoleon and Cavour did not agree about everything. Whereas Cavour had hopes of adding Parma, Modena, Tuscany and part of the Papal States to Piedmont, Napoleon III's idea was to form a separate central Italian kingdom, to be ruled by his cousin who was to marry Victor Emmanuel's daughter. He also hoped that the Pope would be made president of an Italian federation.

e) War against Austria

Things turned out rather differently from what the two men had planned. To put the whole scheme into operation Cavour and Napoleon III needed to provoke Austria into war. Cavour began by writing an emotional anti-Austrian speech for Victor Emmanuel to deliver at the opening of parliament in January 1859. A few weeks later the Piedmontese army was mobilised. However, all seemed lost when Russia and Britain intervened in an attempt to preserve the peace. Napoleon III lost his nerve and in April joined the other powers in asking Piedmont to demobilise. In the nick of time, Austria

---

THE PLOMBIÈRES PACT

▼ Cavour would provoke Austria into war. France would then send 200,000 troops to help Piedmont evict the Austrians from Lombardy and Venetia.

▼ Lombardy and Venetia would be annexed to Piedmont.

▼ France would take Savoy and Nice from Piedmont.

▼ There would be a marriage linking the two royal families.

came to Piedmont's rescue. Emperor Francis Joseph, determined to humiliate Piedmont and to demonstrate that she had given way to Austria and not to the other European powers, issued an ultimatum demanding that Piedmont's army be returned to a peacetime footing. The ultimatum was rejected. Thus, on 29 April Austria declared war. Victor Emmanuel immediately issued a proclamation: 'People of Italy! Austria assails Piedmont...I fight for the right of the whole nation...I have no other ambition than to be the first soldier of Italian independence.' The proclamation had only a limited effect. Few Italians outside Piedmont rallied to his cause and Piedmont managed to raise only 60,000 men. However, Napoleon III kept his word and declared war on Austria. Over 100,000 French troops, ineptly led by Napoleon III, soon crossed the Alps. The Austrian army, equally poorly led, allowed France to concentrate its forces. Two brutal battles decided the first war of Italian unification: Magenta (4 June) and Solferino (24 June). Both were victories for France: Piedmontese troops took little part in the fighting. The losses were horrendous: at Solferino Austria suffered 22,000 casualties and France 17,000.

The war provoked popular disturbances across central Italy. The rulers of Tuscany, Parma and Modena were forced to quit their states and in the Romagna, part of the Papal States, the authority of the Pope was challenged. The rebels in these regions set up provisional governments and sought fusion with Piedmont. For Napoleon III, however, events were moving too fast. Anxious about the heavy casualties, the lack of support for the war in France, the threat of a Prussian army mobilising on the Rhine, apparently in support of Austria, he was also concerned at the situation in central Italy. He distrusted Cavour's activities in Tuscany and feared developments in the Papal States. (The seizure of the Romagna by members of the National Society was not popular with French Catholics.) Moreover, Austrian forces had withdrawn into the Quadrilateral fortresses and Napoleon III feared getting involved in another Crimean situation.

Ignoring the arrangements made at Plombières, Napoleon III concluded an armistice with Austria at Villafranca on 11 July 1859. Austria, fearful of a Hungarian rising and wary of Russia, was more than happy to make peace. The armistice was drawn up without any consultation between France and Piedmont. Lombardy (to save Habsburg susceptibilities) was to be ceded to France to pass on to Piedmont. Venetia would remain Austrian, and the rulers of Tuscany and Modena were to be restored (although it was not clear how this was to be achieved). Nothing was said about Parma or the Romagna. Cavour, furious at the arrangements, tried to persuade Victor Emmanuel to fight on alone. When the King sensibly refused, Cavour resigned.

Figure 3 The Unification of Italy 1859–70

Legend:
- Piedmont in 1859
- Annexed to Piedmont, August 1859
- Ceded to France by Piedmont, April 1860
- Annexed to Piedmont, April 1860
- Annexed to Piedmont, November 1860
- Ceded to France and passed by Napoleon III to Italy, July 1866
- Taken over by Kingdom of Italy as new capital, October 1870

PIEDMONT EXPANSION

1852 Cavour replaced Azeglio as Prime Minister in Piedmont;

1857 formation of the National Society;

1858 meeting at Plombières;

1859 April: war declared between Austria and Piedmont;
June: French victories at Magenta and Solferino;
July: Armistice at Villafranca: Lombardy ceded to Piedmont; Cavour resigned;

1860 January: Cavour returned as Prime Minister;
March: plebiscites in Modena, Tuscany and the Romagna favour union with Piedmont;
April: Nice and Savoy ceded to France.

f) Central Italy

That Napoleon III's 'betrayal' at Villafranca did not end the process of unification was largely due to the work of nationalists in central Italy. The provisional governments set up in Tuscany, Parma, Modena and the Romagna, all strongly influenced by the National Society, arranged for the election of assemblies. These assemblies all voted for union with Piedmont. Austria was in no position to restore the old rulers by force as she had done in the past. Victor Emmanuel, aware of Napoleon III's opposition, decided not to annex central Italy immediately. The Treaty of Zurich signed between France, Piedmont and Austria in November 1859 upheld the rights of the old rulers in principle but contained no practical provisions for their reinstatement. Given the mutual distrust between Austria and France, the idea of settling the question of the central Italian states by a

European congress quickly collapsed. Everywhere in central Italy, the popular mood was unmistakable. The former rulers were not acceptable and the call was for union with Piedmont. This was the situation when Cavour returned to power in January 1860.

Fortunately for Cavour, Napoleon III was now ready to accept Piedmontese expansion in central Italy, provided Savoy and Nice were ceded to France. It was agreed that plebiscites, based on universal manhood suffrage, should be held in all the states concerned. The plebiscites took place in March 1860. Strenuous propaganda in favour of fusion ensured that in each area the majority in favour of annexation to Piedmont was overwhelming: in Tuscany, for example, 366,571 voted for union: 14,925 voted against. In April (French-speaking) Savoy and (Italian-speaking) Nice were handed over to France after huge majorities voted in favour. In Nice the results looked suspicious: 24,484 voted in favour and only 160 against. The plebiscites, concessions to the idea of direct expression of popular will, ensured that Austria was powerless. As a result of war and diplomacy, Piedmont's area and population had doubled.

ISSUE:
How important to the cause of Italian unification was Garibaldi's contribution?

5 Garibaldi and 'the Thousand'

A Dutch artist who saw Garibaldi in Rome in April 1849 described him as follows:

> It was the first time I saw the man whose name everyone in Rome knew and in whom many had placed their hopes… Of middle height, well made, broad shouldered, his square chest, which gives a sense of power to his structure, well marked under the uniform – he stood there before us; his blue eyes, ranging to violet, surveyed in one glance the whole group. Those eyes had something remarkable, as well by their colour as by the frankness – I know of no better word for it – of their expression. They curiously contrasted with those dark, sparkling eyes of his Italian soldiers, no less than his light chestnut brown hair, which fell loosely over his neck onto his shoulders, contrasted with their shining black curls. His face was burnt red, and covered with freckles through the influence of the sun. A heavy moustache and a light brown beard ending in two points gave a martial expression to that open oval face. But most striking of all was the nose, with its exceedingly broad root, which has caused Garibaldi to be given the name of Leone, and indeed, made one think of a lion; a resemblance which, according to his soldiers, was still more conspicuous in a fight, when his eyes shot forth flames and his hair waved as a mane above his temples.

ACTIVITY

Account for the different images presented of Garibaldi in the 'Profile' and in the written source by the Dutch artist.

GIUSEPPE GARIBALDI

Figure 4
Garibaldi in 1849

-Profile-

1807 born a French citizen in Nice; his parents were Italian and he always regarded himself as Italian; he became a sailor like his father;

1831 joined the Young Italy movement;

1833 following the failure of a plot against the Piedmontese king, Garibaldi fled the country before he came to trial (at which he was sentenced to death); he settled in Brazil, where he soon became involved in revolutionary activity;

1834 moved to Uruguay; commanded the Uruguayan navy and a legion of red-shirted guerrillas which helped Uruguay win victory in a long war against Argentina;

1848 returned home and offered his services to King Charles Albert;

1849 his defence of Rome against French attack, although ultimately a failure, established him as an Italian hero; he led the 5,000 men who survived the fighting north. His wife who had accompanied him everywhere during the past ten years, died on the way; he managed to reach Piedmont; briefly imprisoned, he was freed on condition he left Italy;

1849 lived in Tangier, the USA and
−54 Peru;

1854 bought land on the small island of Caprera off the coast of Sardinia; taking up farming, he kept in touch with affairs through the National Society;

1859 played an important part in the fighting in northern Italy;

1860 his 'Thousand' seized control in Sicily and Naples;

1870 offered his services to the new French republic: commanding a guerrilla army, he had some success against the Germans;

1871 elected to the French National Assembly but soon returned to Caprera;

1882 died.

a) Garibaldi

By April 1860, northern and central Italy, apart from Venetia, had been united under Victor Emmanuel. Cavour would have happily stopped there: further unification would only make international intervention more likely. However, Garibaldi thought differently. Like other Italian nationalists, he dreamed of uniting the whole peninsula. By 1860 he had become a romantic hero, both in England, where a biscuit was called after him, and in Italy. Ill-educated, impetuous, charismatic, and first and foremost a soldier, he was very different from the wily politician Cavour. Initially a supporter of Mazzini, he abandoned his republican ideals but remained devoted to the cause of Italian unity. His main interest, apart from fighting, was women of whom he collected a large number, including three wives and innumerable mistresses. Scandal and gossip followed him everywhere but could not obscure his ability as a guerrilla leader. He inspired devotion among his men and a near-religious adoration among the masses. Unlike the idealist Mazzini, Garibaldi was essentially practical: his achievements rested upon his actions rather than his thoughts.

b) Sicily

In April 1860 a revolt broke out in Sicily. It arose in part from the excitement generated by the events in Italy in 1859–60. But a more important cause was the disappointment felt at the conservatism of the new King Francis II. Sicilian peasants soon joined the revolt. Their motives were entirely local: initially, they were more opposed to the landlords, who were raising rents and charging them for the privilege of grinding corn, than they were against the Neapolitan troops who were sent to restore order.

Garibaldi, who had been planning action against France in Nice, the loss of which was a severe blow to Italian nationalists, now set about raising a force to invade Sicily. Hoping to spark a nationalist uprising that would unite the whole of Italy, he asked Cavour for support. That support was not forthcoming. Cavour was not convinced that conquering Sicily and Naples was desirable, even if it could be done. He believed that the south was too backward and not ready for amalgamation with Piedmont. Moreover, foreign governments might be tempted to interfere if too much was done too quickly. He thus made it clear that Garibaldi did not have Piedmont's official backing. However, he did not publically veto Garibaldi's plan or prevent his departure. He was aware that the King supported Garibaldi as did Piedmontese public opinion. Elections were in progress in Piedmont and Cavour feared that open opposition to Garibaldi would lead to a loss of support for his government. Cavour reckoned there might be benefits whatever happened: if Garibaldi's scheme failed Piedmont would be well rid of him; if it succeeded Piedmont might derive some advantage.

In May 1860, with 1,089 young, mainly middle-class, red-shirted volunteers, a thousand rifles, no ammunition and virtually no help from Piedmont, Garibaldi, the self-proclaimed champion of 'Victor Emmanuel and Italy', set sail for Sicily in two old paddle steamers. He seemed to stand little chance of success. The Sicilian revolt had already failed. King Francis II of Naples had 25,000 troops in Sicily, another 16,000 in Calabria and 40,000 defending Naples. However, after landing unopposed in Sicily, Garibaldi set about winning over the peasants by promising land redistribution and tax reduction. Gathering recruits, he advanced on Palermo. At Calatafimi, he defeated a much stronger Neapolitan army. ('Here we either make Italy or die,' he declared before launching a suicidally courageous attack.) In July Neapolitan troops withdrew to Naples and Sicily was his. Appointing himself 'dictator', he immediately set about preparing for an assault on the mainland. He showed little concern for the Sicilian peasants whose contribution to his success had been so important. Indeed, he suppressed a number of new peasant revolts, thus winning the support of the landowners. Fearing – correctly – that Cavour might prevent him using the island as a base for an attack on Naples, he did not immediately hand over Sicily to Victor Emmanuel.

> Was the unification of Italy in 1859-61 the result of accident? **Q**

c) Naples

The situation was now highly complex. In Naples King Francis II conceded to a constitution, brought in liberal ministers and appealed to France for aid. Napoleon III, wary of Britain, refused support. Meanwhile, Cavour, displeased at Garibaldi's success in Sicily and fearing he might have similar success in Naples, pursued at least three – contradictory – policies. Victor Emmanuel's actions were equally devious and occasionally at odds with those of Cavour. On a personal level, Cavour did not like or trust Garibaldi and feared that he might get too much credit for uniting Italy if he continued unchecked: he wanted the credit to go to Piedmont and Victor Emmanuel.

An attempt by Cavour to arrange a revolution in Naples in favour of Victor Emmanuel before Garibaldi arrived failed. Orders were also given to the Piedmontese navy to stop Garibaldi from crossing the Straits of Messina. On the evening of 18–19 August, Garibaldi, dodging the Piedmontese ships, ferried 3,360 men to the mainland. Winning the support of poor peasants, he headed north. Bourbon military opposition in the south swiftly collapsed. King Francis II fled from his capital. On 7 September, Garibaldi entered Naples to a hero's welcome. For the next two months he ruled the Kingdom of Naples as a dictator.

d) Italy united

Garibaldi now aimed to advance on Rome. However, Neapolitan military resistance north of Naples hindered his plans. This delay gave Cavour time to regain the upper hand. He knew that Garibaldi's march on Rome might well provoke war with Napoleon who considered himself the Pope's protector. Cavour was also worried by the growing popularity of Garibaldi not only in southern but also in northern Italy. The 'Thousand' had swelled to over 50,000. Cavour feared that Garibaldi might lead a successful revolutionary coup, taking over Piedmont and Italy, and sweeping aside conservative institutions. The populist slogans that Garibaldi had employed in the south generated precisely the demands for social reform that Cavour was anxious to avoid. Determined to intercept Garibaldi before he reached Rome, the Piedmontese army, with Victor Emmanuel at its head, marched south. Defeating a papal army at Castelfidardo, Piedmontese forces skirted Rome and reached Neapolitan territory. Garibaldi now had the choice of acknowledging the presence of Victor Emmanuel or fighting him. The two men met on 26 October. Garibaldi saluted Victor Emmanuel as 'the first king of Italy' and handed over his conquests to the Piedmontese king. Garibaldi was offered the rank of Major General, the title of Prince, and a large pension. He refused them all and retired to Caprera with a year's supply of macaroni and little else. Both Victor Emmanuel and Cavour were delighted: as far as they were concerned Garibaldi's job was done.

Cavour now organised a plebiscite in Naples, Umbria and the Papal Marches. The voters had little alternative: unite with Piedmont or continue the present state of near anarchy. A huge majority in favour of union was returned although large numbers abstained from voting. There was also massive voting malpractice. What those who voted 'yes' thought they were voting for, is not altogether clear. After all a united Italy could take several forms: it could be a federal state in which the regions retained considerable autonomy or it could be – as it became – a centralised state, dominated by Piedmont. Nevertheless, the Kingdom of Italy was proclaimed in March 1861. It did not include all the peninsula: the area round Rome remained under papal control while Venetia was still Austrian. But otherwise unification was almost complete. The British politician W. E. Gladstone declared it 'one of the greatest marvels of our time'.

Q Was Cavour a master planner or merely a skilled opportunist?

ITALIAN UNIFICATION 1860–1

1860 April: revolt in Sicily; May: Garibaldi and 'the Thousand' landed in Sicily; August: Garibaldi invaded the Kingdom of Naples; October: Garibaldi presented the Kingdom of the Two Sicilies to Victor Emmanuel II;
1861 Kingdom of Italy proclaimed.

ISSUE: How successful were Italian governments (1860–70) in 'making Italians'?

6 Italy 1861–70

The new united kingdom of Italy, officially in existence from March 1861, had to face the future without the talents of Cavour who died unexpectedly in June 1861. Italy was, in fact, far from united. It had been formed hastily, imperfectly and against the wishes of many

'Italians'. Azeglio's famous epigram, 'We have made Italy, now we must make Italians', points to the new challenge for the governments of Italy. Those governments, led by a succession of undistinguished conservatives, have often been criticised. But in fairness, they faced huge problems.

▼ Strong local loyalties remained. Italians did not automatically become Italians just because they now lived in Italy.

▼ While there was support in the south in 1860 for liberation from the rule of an oppressive monarchy, there was not necessarily a wish for unity with the north.

▼ There were deep political divisions between republicans, monarchists and federalists.

▼ There were serious economic problems and great economic divisions.

▼ There was a huge financial deficit as a result of the wars and debts incurred in the 1850s. There was a need for new roads and railways. Money also needed to be spent on strengthening both the army and navy. High taxation was thus inevitable.

▼ Although most Italians shared a common religion, Catholicism could not play a part in making Italy given the Pope's hostility to the new state.

▼ Rome and Venetia were still not part of the new kingdom.

a) 'Piedmontisation'

Italian unification had been a takeover by Piedmont. After 1860 the Piedmontese systems were extended to – indeed imposed – upon the rest of the country.

▼ The King retained his Piedmontese title of Victor Emmanuel II – he did not become Victor Emmanuel I of Italy. The first Italian parliament, elected in 1861, met in Turin, capital of Piedmont. Few concessions were made to regional customs and traditions or to economic or political differences. Centralised government, based in Piedmont, was established and carried out by Piedmontese civil servants, politicians and soldiers.

▼ Italy adopted the Piedmontese constitution. It was thus far from democratic. Voting was restricted to literate and high tax-paying males over 25 years old – about 2 per cent of the population. The parliament was thus conservative and unrepresentative. Even by 1880 electors comprised just 8 per cent of the adult male population and Catholics generally heeded the Pope's command to abstain from voting. There were few ideological conflicts and no real political parties emerged. The leading politicians were those who were able to build broad coalitions by absorbing potential opponents into their faction through the promise of political favours. Most coalitions were short-lived: there were 28 administrations between 1860 and 1892.

GARIBALDI'S ROLE IN THE 1860S

Garibaldi became an embarrassment to the government after 1860. Determined to reunite Rome and Venetia, he was not easy to silence or shackle. In 1862 he returned to Sicily and collected some 3,000 volunteers for the conquest of Rome – still guarded by French troops. The King, afraid of damaging diplomatic relations with France, now issued a proclamation disowning the operation. Once on the mainland Garibaldi's force was defeated and he was wounded and imprisoned for a time. In 1867 he raised yet another army to capture Rome. Arrested and imprisoned on government orders, some of his men continued their march but lost several small battles to papal troops. Escaping from house arrest, Garibaldi retook command of his men. He was finally defeated by French troops defending Rome.

▼ The government appointed prefects to act as its local representatives in Italy's 53 provinces. Most were Piedmontese who often had little understanding of the places or people they were administering.

▼ Piedmont's legal system became the basis of the Italian legal system.

▼ The foreign and diplomatic services of the new Italy were based on those of Piedmont.

▼ Land confiscated from the Church and from the Bourbons passed into the hands of north Italian businessmen who often exploited it more ruthlessly than their predecessors.

▼ The introduction of Piedmontese external tariffs were often disastrous for the economies of other regions.

b) Problems in the South

As Cavour had recognised, the rivalry between north and south was the most difficult problem that the new kingdom had to settle. The south, politically, economically and socially backward, was not ready for union with Piedmont. The Italian governments dealt with the problem largely by ignoring it and by imposing a Piedmontese solution, whether it was appropriate or not. The immediate result of union with Piedmont was conscription, increased taxation, a higher cost of living and new, little understood, legal and administrative systems. It was hard to distinguish between unification and colonisation by Piedmont. Garibaldi's promise of land redistribution came to nothing.

Not surprisingly southern public opinion soon turned against Victor Emmanuel and in the 1860s law and order broke down. Garibaldi's nominees and supporters, ousted by the new regime, joined forces with Bourbon loyalists and discontented peasants in a guerrilla war.

Government offices were attacked and Piedmontese officials killed. The army retaliated. The government claimed it was fighting against 'brigands': in reality it was engaged in a savage civil war with fellow Italians. In 1863 90,000 Italian troops were committed to peacekeeping operations in the south. By 1865 the government emerged victorious but more lives were lost in the 'brigands war' than were lost in all the battles for unification itself. The civil war simply added to the plight of the impoverished peasants in the south and was also a drain on northern resources. Most northerners regarded Sicily and Naples as 'rotten' and blamed southerners for their own problems. Thus arguably unification served only to exacerbate regional separatism.

Venetia

In a secret treaty with Prussia in 1866, Italy agreed that if Prussia went to war with Austria within two months, she would follow her in declaring war on Austria, receiving Venetia for her pains. The war, which broke out within the stipulated timescale, was a disaster for Italian forces which, despite outnumbering the Austrians, were defeated on land and sea. The war damaged the prestige of the army, the King and the government and did nothing to weld the disparate parts of Italy into a nationally conscious whole. Nor was there even a Venetian uprising in support of unification. Austria's defeat by Prussia however led to Venetia being ceded to Napoleon III who quickly handed it to Italy.

Rome

Diplomatic efforts to persuade Pope Pius 1X to agree to unification failed. The Pope was opposed to the *Risorgimento* and disliked the pronounced anti-clerical policies adopted first in Piedmont and then in Italy. However, the outbreak of the Franco-Prussian war in July 1870 led to French forces being withdrawn from Rome. After Napoleon had been defeated by the Prussians, the Italian government felt it safe to take action. Victor Emmanuel sent a letter to the Pope in September, urging him to allow Rome to become the capital of Italy. In return for forfeiting his temporal power, the Pope would have complete spiritual independence, guaranteed by the Italian state. The Pope refused. As a result the government sent an army of 60,000 to occupy Rome. Papal troops fought back but on 20 September 1870 the Italian army entered Rome to the acclaim of large crowds. The Pope shut himself in the Vatican, declared himself a prisoner and refused to negotiate with the Italian government. A plebiscite was held in October. Rome voted overwhelmingly (133,681 to 1,507) for union with Italy and became the capital. The Pope was left in control of the Vatican – an independent state of 109 acres in the middle of Rome. Refusing to accept the state pension offered him, the Pope excommunicated Victor Emmanuel and his government but could not change the situation. While the King and most Italians still acknowledged the Pope as Head of the Church, Church and State in Italy were now separated – with important results. Many Italian Catholics found it difficult to support the government.

c) Success?

Mazzini was heartbroken about the course events had taken and still bemoaned the fact that the country had not become a democratic republic. But arguably Italy had some success in the 1860s. In so much as the governments failed to create the Italy which Mazzini envisaged, this was a deliberate failure. Cavour and his successors regarded Mazzini's dreams as nightmarish. Far from wanting to democratise the nation, they wanted to ensure that the new kingdom was a mirror image of the Piedmontese state and was controlled by the Piedmontese elite. To a large extent they achieved their aims. The governments were more in control of events than is sometimes supposed. Although ministries were short-lived, there was reasonable continuity if only because the most skilful politicians survived from one administration to the next. The leading politicians could claim credit for some economic advance and improvement in education. The unified (and modernised) army played an important role in 'making' Italians if only because it taught all its recruits to speak Italian. Southern Italy was kept under control and Venetia and Rome were added to the new kingdom. Perhaps, in the circumstances, this was a reasonable list of achievements.

▼ Working on Italian Unification

The key issue in this chapter is: what factors brought about Italian unification? The following boxes should provide useful summaries. What extra information might you wish to include in the boxes? Should there be any other boxes?

France's role

Napoleon III's genuine sympathy for Italian nationalism (while always tempered by a concern for French interests) was crucial. The role of the French army in 1859 was decisive in creating a united Italy.

Britain's role

Palmerston's government, echoing British public opinion, was well-disposed towards Italian unification. It thus backed Piedmont's annexation of central Italy in 1860 – a fact which helped secure Napoleon III's acquiescence.

Russia's role

After defeat in the Crimean War, Tsar Alexander II was prepared to accept Napoleon III's schemes to revise the 1815 settlement in order that the 1856 settlement might also be changed. Given her perceived 'betrayal' in the Crimean War, he was also unfavourably disposed to Austria. In March 1859 Alexander secretly agreed with Napoleon to remain neutral in the event of an Italian war and remained faithful to his promise.

Cavour's role

Cavour has generally had a good press. He has been seen as an Italian nationalist whose every diplomatic manoeuvre was designed to promote unification. This is incorrect. His chief concern in the 1850s was to extend Piedmontese power in northern Italy (this necessarily meant the removal of Austria) and to use the appeal of a united Italy as a means to this limited end. Even in early 1860, Cavour considered complete Italian unification neither possible nor desirable. However, pushed along by the course of events in southern Italy, he adapted his former aims. There is no doubt that he was a skilled opportunist. He also had the knack of persuading people that he had actually arranged things to happen in the way that they did. Once unification was achieved he gave the – misleading – impression he had always supported it.

Garibaldi's role

Garibaldi's contribution to the cause of Italian unity was huge. His adventures made him a focal point for patriotic emotion. He may seem unprincipled. From being a republican, he became a monarchist: from being a supporter of popular revolution he became a supporter of the established regime. Arguably his actions in 1860 exploited the masses rather than benefiting them. But he invariably acted in what he considered to be the best interests of Italy. He was a good, sometimes brilliant, military commander, inspiring great enthusiasm among his men. His conquest of the south in 1860, against all odds and expectations, was a major element in the unification process. He could have established himself as dictator of an independent southern Italy in 1860 but believed national unity to be more important. His greatest weakness was probably his impetuosity. 'He had a heart of gold and the brains of an ox,' said Mazzini, somewhat uncharitably.

Mazzini's role

Mazzini provided the intellectual basis for the nationalist movement, as well as the inspiration for revolution among some influential leaders, not least Garibaldi. But he did not have much popular influence.

How important was Italian nationalism?

Piedmontese expansionism, rather than nationalism, was arguably the real driving force behind unification. It can also be claimed that nationalism had triumphed despite rather than because of the attitudes of the majority of Italian people. Certainly the Italy that was created was not the Italy that many nationalists, like Mazzini, had envisaged. However, nationalism was clearly a vital element in the achievement of Italian unification between 1859–60. Even if expansionism was the true motive of Victor Emmanuel and Cavour, both viewed nationalism as a means of winning support both in Italy and in Britain and France. The National Society campaigned strongly throughout Italy arguing that it was essential for national unity that all Italians should rally round Piedmont.

Answering extended writing and essay questions on Italian Unification

Consider the following question: To what extent did Italy unite itself? To what extent did it need outside help?

Some historians think that Italy 'made itself'. They stress the importance of Italian nationalism, the role of Piedmont, and the work of individuals like Cavour and Garibaldi. Others stress the importance of the favourable international situation. You can point out what historians think. But essentially the question asks you to give your opinion. Write two paragraphs saying why the international situation was favourable. Then write two paragraphs stressing that the internal situation in Italy was also important in ensuring that the unification process was successful. Finally, reach your conclusion. Write a six-sentence paragraph summarising your views.

Answering source-based questions on Italian Unification

BABES IN THE WOOD.

Source A

Source B

THE GIANT AND THE DWARF.

"BRAVO, MY LITTLE FELLOW! YOU SHALL DO ALL THE FIGHTING, AND WE'LL DIVIDE THE GLORY!"

Source C

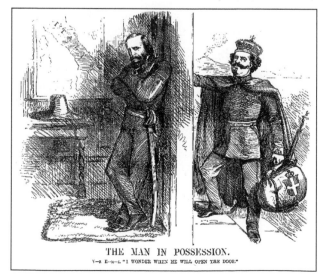

THE MAN IN POSSESSION.

V—R E—N—L "I WONDER WHEN HE WILL OPEN THE DOOR."

▼ QUESTIONS ON SOURCES

1. Examine Source A. What point is it trying to make? **[3 marks]**
2. Identify the characters in Sources B and C. What points are these sources sources trying to make? **[7 marks]**
3. Using the three cartoons and your own knowledge, explain why French involvement in 1859 helped the process of Italian unification. **[15 marks]**

Further Reading

Books in the 'Access to History' series

The Unification of Italy 1815–70 by A. Stiles is an excellent study of the topic.

General

Try *The Oxford Illustrated History of Italy*, edited by G. Holmes (OUP, 1997) and *Europe Reshaped 1848–1878* by J. A. S. Grenville (Fontana, 1976). *Italy in the Age of the Risorgimento 1790–1870* by H. Hearder (Longman 1983) and *The Italian Risorgimento* by M. Clark (Longman, 1998) are 'musts'. Biographies often make interesting reading. Try *Cavour* by H. Hearder (Longman, 1994) and *Garibaldi and his Enemies* by C. Hibbert (Penguin, 1987).

THE UNIFICATION OF GERMANY: 1815–71

CHAPTER 6

POINTS TO CONSIDER

In January 1871 King William I of Prussia became *Kaiser* (Emperor) of the new German Empire. The creation of the Empire was one of the most important developments of the 19th century. Dozens of small states which for centuries had filled the space in central Europe loosely termed 'Germany' were replaced by a single nation. The process by which Germany came to be unified has been an area of historical debate ever since. To what extent was it the result of Bismarck's diplomatic skill? How important was the Prussian army? How important was German nationalism? Was the new Empire 'created more by coal and iron than by blood and iron', as British economist J. M. Keynes claimed?

1 Germany in 1815

a) German disunity

As with 'Italy', the term 'Germany' had no real political significance in 1815. There was no single German state. In the late 18th century, some 23 million Germans were divided into 314 states, varying in size from the 115,533 square miles of the Habsburg Monarchy to the 33 square miles of Schwartzburg-Sonderhausen. All belonged to the archaic Holy Roman Empire. This, as Voltaire said, was neither Holy, Roman nor an Empire. Lacking clear natural frontiers, the Empire's boundaries included land peopled by French, Danish, Polish and Czech speakers and excluded sizeable territory with a predominantly German population. While each Holy Roman Emperor was, in theory, elected to his position, in reality only members of the Habsburg family were chosen. Habsburg control over the Holy Roman Empire, however, was little more than nominal.

b) The impact of the French Revolution and Napoleon

The French Revolution and Napoleonic conquests transformed the German political landscape. Revolutionary ideas of liberty, equality and fraternity created a new context for German politics while the Napoleonic settlement led to major territorial changes.

DIFFICULTIES IN THE WAY OF A UNITED GERMANY IN THE EARLY 19TH CENTURY

▼ 'Germany' was politically divided. Prussia and Austria were rivals for leadership.

▼ There were cultural differences between the Protestant north and the Catholic south, and between the more industrialised and liberal west and the agrarian, autocratic east.

▼ The horizons of most ordinary Germans were local and regional.

▼ 1793–1803: France took the left bank of the Rhine. Small ecclesiastical territories and ancient free cities were abolished and their lands redistributed.

▼ 1805–7: Napoleon defeated Austria (1805) and Prussia (1806). The Holy Roman Empire collapsed. Many small states were now amalgamated. In 1806–17 states were formed into the French-controlled Confederation of the Rhine.

Within the new states there was a great deal of French-inspired legal and political reform. Large sections of Germany were released from feudal restrictions for the first time. There was increased middle-class involvement in government and in administration.

c) The Prussian revival

In 1806 Prussia suffered a shattering defeat by Napoleon. As a result she lost territory, had to pay an indemnity, and was forced to reduce her army. Under the leadership of Baron Stein and Hardenburg, efforts were made to reform Prussian institutions.

▼ Prussian serfs were emancipated (1807–10).

▼ Prussia's educational system was improved at all levels.

▼ Scharnhorst and Gneisenau overhauled the army.

Prussian 'modernisation', stimulated by defeat and motivated by a desire for revenge, enabled her to become a leader in the unification movement.

d) The 1815 settlement

In 1814–5 German unification was not a practical proposition. Too many deep-seated divisions stood in the way of national unity. Perhaps the most important was the rivalry between Austria and Prussia. However, at this stage, they were content to exist side-by-side in what Austrian Foreign Minister Metternich called 'peaceful dualism'. Both powers benefited substantially from the Vienna settlement.

▼ Prussia gained part of Saxony, the Rhineland, Westphalia and Pomerania. This more than compensated for the loss of much of her Polish territory to Russia and meant that Prussia's population more than doubled to ten million. The Vienna settlement ensured that Prussia was the dominant power in northern Germany.

▼ Metternich ensured that Germany became a loose confederation of 39 states – under Austrian control. The states varied considerably in size and population.

How strong was German nationalism in the early 19th century?

▼ There was a growing sense of German identity. An educated elite, influenced by the ideas of the philosopher Herder, claimed that there was a cultural basis for German nationhood. Germans spoke a common language and had a unique cultural tradition, based on shared customs, history, and literary and artistic heritage.

▼ French occupation led to growing national resentment. Popular opinion encouraged King Frederick William III of Prussia to ally with Russia against France in 1813. Once Austria allied with Prussia, it seemed that all Germans were united in an anti-French crusade. The so-called Wars of Liberation (1813–15) have often been seen as the first collective action of the German nation.

BUT

▼ Lectures, books and pamphlets which put forward nationalistic ideas reached only a limited readership. There was no strong sense of German nationalism in 1815.

▼ The later nationalist myths of the War of Liberation bore little relation to reality. German resistance to France never became a mass national uprising. It was soon clear that the future of Germany would be decided, not by German patriots but by the particular interests of Prussia and Austria. There was no single German movement against Napoleon. South Germans tended to look to Austria for political leadership. North Germans tended to look to Prussia.

Figure 1 Germany and the Austrian Empire 1815

The German Confederation

The German Confederation was not concerned with promoting a united Germany. Indeed the rulers of the 39 separate states had no wish to see their independence limited by the establishment of a powerful central government. The Confederation's diet (or parliament) which met at Frankfurt was a permanent conference of representatives who were not elected but were sent by their governments with instructions how to act. It was presided over by the Austrian representative. The diet had very little direct control over the individual states which could refuse to accept laws as binding on them. The Confederation thus disappointed those Germans who hoped for greater national unity. It has also been much criticised by historians who think it had no place in the age of emergent nation states. It certainly failed to create genuinely 'national' institutions. Local jealousies and fiercely guarded independence meant that nothing of importance was done to unify the Confederation militarily or economically. However, the Confederation provided a framework within which German states coexisted, albeit uneasily. Metternich believed the Confederation's main purpose was to maintain the *status quo* internally and externally through a system of mutual aid in the event of rebellion or invasion. Pre-1848 this was successfully achieved.

ACTIVITY

List three reasons why German nationalists might have been optimistic in 1815 and three reasons why they might have been pessimistic.

ISSUE:
To what extent did nationalist and liberal ideas develop 1815–48?

2 The *Vormärz*: 1815–48

The years 1815–48 are often called the *Vormärz* or 'pre-March' (a prelude to the March 1848 revolution in Berlin). The period is also known as the Restoration. Metternich, associated – indeed synonymous – with the defence of the European *status quo* after 1815, had great influence. The *Vormärz* is often seen as a period of illiberality and repression. However, it also saw the development of a liberal and nationalist opposition.

a) The restoration of monarchical rule

Absolute, monarchical rule was restored in most German states in 1815. All but four were dynastic states – monarchies, duchies and principalities. However, the Federal Act of 1815 required the states sooner or later to produce constitutions. The response varied:

▼ In southern and central Germany, there was some compliance. Pre-1820 Bavaria, Baden, Württemberg and Hesse-Darmstadt introduced constitutions, creating elected assemblies. However, the monarchs continued to appoint their own ministers and retain real power. Everywhere the franchise was limited to the educated and rich.

▼ The majority of rulers, not least those of Austria and Prussia, clung to their virtually absolute power. Although the Prussian King agreed to local diets in 1823, there was no united parliament until 1847.

▼ The major German states all emerged from the years of war with better organised and more powerful bureaucracies, the result of French occupation, imitation of French methods, or simply financial necessity. The bureaucracies were active in a host of areas – social, economic, financial, legal and educational. (They ensured, for example, that educational provision in Germany was the best in Europe.) While sometimes agents of reform, they often had a repressive function, controlling public and even domestic life.

▼ Noble families continued to wield huge power, dominating the political, administrative and military institutions of most German states.

b) Nationalist and liberal developments

The defeat of Napoleon was an encouragement to German nationalism. In the decades after 1815 thousands of young, middle- and upper-class Germans longed for a united Germany to give visible form to their strongly held sense of national identity. Students joined *Burschenschaften* societies which campaigned for a united Germany while the growing 'gymnasium' movement instructed young men in drill, physical activities and the national spirit. Many nationalists were liberals and vice versa. Most liberals believed that only a united Germany could ensure that liberal aspirations would be achieved.

c) Repression

Metternich was suspicious of liberalism and nationalism: he feared they might become the basis of popular revolution which could lead to the overthrow of absolute monarchy and the end of the Austrian Empire. Fearing the danger of contagion, he believed that it was his right and duty to put down revolution anywhere in Germany. Most rulers agreed with him and thus he was able to co-ordinate repression through the Confederation. Following the murder of the reactionary writer Kotzebue by a radical student in 1819, Metternich persuaded the diet to introduce the Karlsbad Decrees. These ensured closer supervision of political activities at universities and imposed tighter censorship. Liberal newspapers were banned, a number of professors dismissed, and radical leaders imprisoned. While these measures did not eradicate national/liberal movements completely, they made it difficult for such sentiments to develop.

THE WARTBURG FESTIVAL

In 1817 nationalist students converted the Wartburg Festival from a celebration of the tercentenary of Martin Luther's stand against the Pope and the fourth anniversary of the victory at Leipzig over Napoleon into a demonstration against the princes. Given that fewer than 500 students attended the festival, its importance has often been exaggerated.

THE HAMBACH FESTIVAL

In 1832 25,000 nationalists met at the Hambach Festival in Bavaria. There was the same flag-waving and speech-making as at Wartburg in 1817 but there was a more radical edge to the demands for a united Germany. The tricolour flag, symbol of revolution, was hoisted and toasts drunk to the sovereignty of the people.

The July Revolution in Paris in 1830 sparked off riots in several German states. In Brunswick the duke was driven out and his successor forced to grant a more liberal constitution. Similar concessions were made in Saxony and Hesse-Cassel. In 1832 Metternich persuaded the diet to pass the Six Acts. These banned public meetings, tightened control of universities and the press, and obliged German princes to resist any attempt to reduce their legitimate power. A commission was established to round up student agitators who were forming themselves into a 'Young Germany' movement, dedicated to establishing a united, liberal Germany.

The pace of political debate picked up and public opinion grew bolder in the 1840s as the repression gradually relaxed. More books were published and read. Newspapers flourished. The fact that literacy in Germany was about the highest in Europe, estimated as high as 75 per cent by 1850, was an important factor. By the 1840s there were growing demands for a united Germany. The greatest support for nationalism came from the middle classes who also espoused liberalism. Most liberals envisaged a federation of states under a constitutional monarch. However, some radicals pressed for a German republic. Radicals favoured universal manhood suffrage and social reform. Enthusiastic though they were, radical groups involved only a small proportion of workers in the towns and workers on the land hardly at all.

The social question

Economic 'hard times' in the 1830s and 1840s led to general concern about the plight of the poor whose desperate situation was signalled by criminality and periodic revolt. While many blamed the forces of industrialisation for social problems, over 70 per cent of Germans still worked on the land. A rapidly growing population was one cause of increased poverty. Social crisis reinforced the disillusionment with *Vormärz* regimes.

The Rhine Crisis (1840)

Nationalism was fuelled in 1840 when it seemed that France was about to invade the German states along the Rhine. The press threw its weight behind the nationalist upsurge and there was a flurry of songs and poems such as *Deutschland über Alles*. France backed down but the Rhine Crisis put nationalism firmly on the German political agenda.

Schleswig and Holstein (1846)

In 1846 Denmark helped arouse nationalist passions. The Danish king had ruled the duchies of Schleswig and Holstein for four centuries. While Schleswig was mainly Danish-speaking, Holstein had an overwhelmingly German-speaking population and was one of the states of the German Confederation. When it seemed that the Danish King was about to incorporate both duchies into Denmark, German nationalists claimed this was a violation of the fatherland to be resisted by force if necessary. The strength of feeling was enough to persuade the Danish King to abandon his plans.

---

d) The situation in 1848

The late 1840s brought some hopeful developments for liberal nationalists.

▼ In the south-western states (especially Baden) the liberals increased their popular support and exerted considerable influence.

▼ In 1840 the conservative King Frederick William III of Prussia died. His son Frederick William IV was far less predictable. He started liberally, releasing political prisoners, abolishing censorship and extending the powers of the provincial diets. Encouraged by this, liberals began to agitate for a constitution and the calling of a single Prussian diet. Frederick William IV, aware of conservative unease, reimposed press censorship in 1843 and opposed further change. However, in 1847, hard-pressed by financial problems, he called a meeting of a united diet to vote a loan for building a railway to link East Prussia and Berlin. In return, the liberal-dominated diet demanded regular meetings. When Frederick William rejected this demand, the diet refused to vote a loan. The Prussian King then suspended the diet.

Despite growing support, nationalists, liberals and radicals had achieved very little by 1848. As long as Metternich remained in power and Prussia remained Austria's ally, there seemed little chance of changing the situation. German nationalism as a mass phenomenon tended to be reactive, erupting in response to perceived threats, especially from France, and then subsiding again. Although nationalist organisations such as the Gymnasts movement grew at an impressive rate in the mid-1840s, loyalty to individual states and dynasties remained strong. There was still a major division between the Catholic south which looked to Austria and the Protestant north which looked to Prussia.

Q Why was more not achieved on the German unity front between 1815 and 1848?

ISSUE:
To what extent did economic developments encourage German unity?

3 Germany's economic development pre-1850

a) The Prussian Customs Union

After 1815 the 39 German states managed their own economies. Innumerable customs barriers and internal tariffs restricted trade. In 1818, following pressure from Rhineland manufacturers, Prussia introduced the Prussian Customs Union. This abolished all internal tariffs and set a common external tariff for all Prussia's geographically divided territories. In 1819 Prussia moved into tariff agreements with states which were surrounded by or separated her territories, the aim being to remove as many trade barriers as possible so goods would move freely. This meant wider markets for home-produced goods at cheaper prices. Other German states, impressed by Prussia's success, either joined the Prussian Customs Union or formed opposing unions. The Middle German Commercial Union, for example, comprising Hanover, Saxony and several small states, was set up to promote its own members' trade while spoiling that of Prussia. In 1830 Hesse-Cassel, a key state in the Middle Union, ran into financial difficulties. In 1831, to the horror of her partners, she joined the Prussian Customs Union. The Middle Union soon collapsed while the Prussian Customs Union went from strength to strength.

b) The *Zollverein*

In 1834 Bavaria and Württemberg joined Prussia in the German Customs Union or *Zollverein* – an economic unit comprising 18 states with some 23 million people. By 1844 only Hanover, Oldenburg, Mecklenburg, the Hanseatic towns and Austria were not members. Within the union all internal customs barriers were dismantled and a common system of foreign protective duties applied. A start was also made in unifying both the currency and the system of weights and measures in the *Zollverein* states. The *Zollverein* strengthened German economic links and contributed to the formation of a national market. The successful economic cooperation between the states made liberal/nationalist dreams of a politically united Germany seem attainable. The *Zollverein* also helped Prussia achieve a position of economic leadership within Germany.

In what ways did the *Zollverein* contribute to German unification?

c) Railways

In 1840 Germany had only 600 miles of track. By 1850 this had increased to 4,000 miles. German economist Friedrich List viewed the development of railways as 'the firm girdle around the loins of Germany, binding her limbs together in a forceful and powerful body'.

d) Industrialisation

German, and particularly Prussian, industrialisation really took off in the 1840s. This had important consequences for German unity.

▼ The growth of industrialisation and urbanisation resulted in the growth of a commercial and industrial middle class, which tended to support German unity.

▼ Prussian economic success enhanced her status amongst the other German states.

However, Germany's industrialisation should not be exaggerated.

▼ Industry tended to be limited to certain regions – the Rhineland, Silesia and Saxony.

▼ There was still relatively little mechanisation. Fewer than five per cent of Prussia's population, for example, worked in factories.

▼ By 1850 Germany's coal and iron output was only about a tenth that of Britain.

GERMANY 1815–48	
1815	German Confederation established;
1817	Wartburg festival;
1819	Carlsbad decrees;
1832	Nationalist festival at Hambach;
1834	*Zollverein* came into operation;
1840	Frederick William IV became King of Prussia;
1847	Meeting of the Prussian United Diet in Berlin.

ACTIVITY

List three reasons why German nationalists might have been optimistic in 1848 and three reasons why they might have been pessimistic. How had things changed since 1815?

4 The 1848–9 revolutions

Note: Read pages 81–8 for the causes and main events of the 1848–9 revolutions.

ISSUE:
What impact did the 1848–9 revolutions have on Germany?

Why did the 1848–9 revolutions fail?

▼ The revolutionaries were deeply divided over the national question, social issues and on constitutional grounds. There were also deep religious, regional and class divisions.

▼ Liberal ministries had little popular support.

▼ The Frankfurt Parliament had no army or police force and no money.

▼ The revolutions failed to unseat the old rulers. Regaining their confidence, they launched counter-revolutions in the autumn of 1848, not least in Austria and Prussia.

▼ The old rulers were able to rely on the loyal support of their regular armies.

**WHAT WERE
THE RESULTS
OF THE 1848–9
REVOLUTIONS?**
▼ After 1849 liberal
constitutions were
withdrawn or revised.
Liberal ministers and
bureaucrats were
dismissed. Strict
censorship was
reintroduced.
▼ Feudal privileges were
abolished all over
Germany by 1850 and
did not return.
▼ Almost all German states
had some kind of
parliament and
constitution after 1849.
▼ The old rulers, scared by
the events of 1848–9,
made greater efforts to
introduce measures to
help both the peasantry
and the urban workers.

ISSUE:

**What were the main
developments in
Prussia in the years
1849–62?**

(Continued)
▼ Army counter-revolutionary action had a broad basis of popular
support. Large sections of the community wanted a return to law
and order.
▼ National unification foundered on the rocks of regional loyalties,
the unwillingness of sovereigns to sacrifice their power, and the
facts of power politics.

5 Developments in Prussia 1849–62

a) The Prussian Union Plan

Despite his refusal to accept the imperial crown offered by the
Frankfurt Parliament, Prussian King Frederick William was attracted
to the idea of a united Germany with himself at its head, providing he
had the consent of the princes. In 1849 General Radowitz came up
with the Prussian Union Plan. He proposed a *Kleindeutschreich*
(excluding Austria) under Prussian leadership. In addition, there
would be a 'German Union' – a confederation (similar to the old)
between the new *Reich* and the Austrian Empire. This plan was
unacceptable to Austrian Chief Minister Schwarzenberg who saw it as
a way of removing Austrian influence from Germany. But faced with
problems in the Austrian Empire in 1849, he was prepared to bide his
time. Thus Prussia, whose army was the strongest authority in
Germany in 1849, was able to pursue the plan with some success. In
March 1850 representatives from most of the German states met at
Erfurt (at Prussia's behest). 28 states agreed to the creation of the
Prussian-dominated Erfurt Union. But several crucial states,
suspicious of Prussian ambitions and fearful of Austria's reaction,
declined to join. Schwarzenberg, having suppressed the Hungarian
rising, was ready to reassert Austria's position in Germany. He now
summoned the Diet of the Confederation to meet in Frankfurt in May
1850. The response was good. Suddenly the Confederation, thought
to have been dead and buried, was alive and well. Thus by the spring
of 1850 there were two assemblies claiming to speak for Germany: the
Prussian-led Erfurt Parliament and the Austrian-led Frankfurt Diet.

A showdown soon occurred. In Hesse-Cassel, a member state of the
Erfurt Union, a rising prompted its ruler to request help from the
Frankfurt Diet. The Diet sent Bavarian troops to restore order. The
Erfurt Parliament, also claiming rights of intervention, despatched
Prussian troops. On the brink of armed conflict with Confederation
forces, Prussia backed down. At Olmütz in November 1850 Frederick
William agreed to abolish the Erfurt Union. Although this was a major

diplomatic victory for the Habsburgs, the revival of Austria was not allowed to go as far as Schwarzenberg had hoped. His proposal for an Austrian-dominated 'Middle Europe', incorporating the 70 million people of all the German states and the Habsburg Empire, was rejected. Instead, in May 1851 the old Confederation was officially restored. It seemed that the events of the past three years had been consigned to obscurity and that Austria was again supreme in German affairs.

For Prussia the 'Capitulation of Olmütz' represented a profound humiliation. However, it did not end her hopes of dominating a united Germany. Austria clearly stood in the way. In 1856 an emerging Prussian statesman, Otto von Bismarck, commented:

> Germany is clearly too small for us both; as long as an honourable arrangement concerning the influence of each cannot be concluded and carried out, we will both plough the same disputed acre...In the not too distant future we shall have to fight for our existence against Austria...it is not within our power to avoid that, since the course of events in Germany has no other solution.

ACTIVITY

Consider Bismarck's comment in 1856. Answer the following questions.

1. Does this source prove that Prussia was determined to fight Austria? Explain your answer.

2. Does this source prove that Bismarck was determined to fight Austria? Explain your answer.

b) Conservative reform

Prussia's government in the 1850s was dominated by chief minister Otto von Manteuffel. He was ready to accept limited change as long as it did not lead to any extension of parliamentary influence. He had a particular hatred of the liberal middle classes whom he saw as the real enemy of Prussian traditions. He believed the best way to strengthen the crown, stabilise society and reduce the chance of revolution was to improve the living conditions of peasants and workers. He had some success on both scores. Manteuffel had no trouble with parliament and effectively governed without it. He was reactionary in other ways: he purged liberal civil servants, imposed strict press censorship and restricted the freedom of political parties to hold meetings. Prussia in the 1850s was thus a curious mix, politically reactionary, socially reforming, and economically prosperous.

c) Prussian economic development

In the 1850s Prussian industrial production, length of railway track, and foreign trade more than doubled. These were also good years for agriculture and there was a rise in living standards. Manteuffel's ministry sought to promote economic development through the extension of the *Zollverein*. In 1849 Austria's chief minister Schwarzenberg, realising the political implications of Prussia's economic success, proposed establishing a *Zollunion* between Austria and the *Zollverein*. This move failed. So too did Schwarzenberg's

THE NATIONAL ASSOCIATION

The failure of the 1848 revolution was a serious blow to German nationalism. However, the idea of a unified state persisted in the hearts and minds of liberal-nationalists. In September 1859 the National Association was formed. Stimulated by the success of Italian nationalism in 1859, it promoted the idea that Prussia should lead the German cause (as Piedmont led the cause of Italian nationalism) and at the same time become more liberal in outlook. At its peak the National Association had only 25,000 members. It was banned in all the main German states. However, it included many influential men and had close links with a range of other organisations, not least with liberal parties which won growing support in many states, including Prussia, in the early 1860s.

GERMANY: 1848–62

1848 Outbreak of revolutions across Germany; Frankfurt Parliament set up;

1849 King Frederick William IV rejected offer of emperorship of Germany;

1850 Failure of Prussian Erfurt Union plan;

1851 German Confederation officially restored;

1861 William I became King of Prussia.

efforts in 1851 to establish an alternative customs union to include Austria and those German states still outside the *Zollverein*. Thus, while Austria clung to its political leadership of the Confederation, she was effectively isolated from the Prussian-dominated economic coalition of the German states.

d) The international situation

Prussia seemed a second-rate power in the 1850s. She avoided military conflict with Austria in 1850 and then played no role in the Crimean War but – unlike Austria – managed to keep on good terms with Russia. She might have profited from the North Italian War in 1859 if she had supported Piedmont and France against Austria. However, popular feeling in Prussia was anti-French. Prussia tried to benefit by offering Austria help in exchange for her conceding Prussia primacy in Germany. Austria's speedy defeat and willingness to make peace with Napoleon prevented Prussia's aims being realised.

e) William I

In 1858 Frederick William IV was declared insane. His brother William became regent, succeeding to the throne when Frederick William died in 1861. William I, already 63 when he became King, was to reign another 27 years. A practical man of the 'old school' with a strong sense of honour, he was a soldier by training and a conservative by instinct. At heart an absolutist, he nevertheless believed in the rule of law. On becoming regent, he dismissed Manteuffel, replacing him with a ministry containing both liberals and conservatives. The atmosphere of comparative freedom led people to talk of a 'new era'. The 1858 elections gave the moderate liberals a small majority in parliament. They hoped to play a significant role in government. William had no intention that they should.

f) Constitutional crisis: 1860–2

The strengthening of the Prussian army was one of William's main concerns: he believed it was the key to Prussia's future greatness. In 1860 Minister of War, General von Roon, introduced a bill to reform the army. This aimed to more than double the regular army's size, increase the period of service from two to three years, reduce the role played by the inefficient civilian militia (or *Landwehr*), and re-equip the troops. Roon's bill touched a number of sensitive points as far as the liberal majority in Prussia's parliament was concerned. The bill greatly increased the miltary budget. There were also fears of the army becoming a force of repression. Moreover, the civilian *Landwehr* was popular with liberals. While there was some room for compromise on detail, both sides believed that important principles were at stake. William was determined that army matters should be kept above parliamentary approval. The liberals believed that parliament should have financial control over army expenditure. Without such a right it had very little power.

The army reform bill thus led to a constitutional crisis. In 1860 parliament would only agree to approve the increased military budget for one year and would not agree to extend the term of military service. A newly elected parliament (December 1861) would not pass the money bill for the army and William would not accept two-year military service. William again dissolved parliament and replaced his liberal ministers with conservatives. The May 1862 elections were a disaster for the king and a triumph for the liberals who now had an even larger majority. In September parliament again refused to pass the army bill. William, fearing civil war, contemplated abdication. However, on 22 September on the advice of von Roon, he appointed Otto von Bismarck as chief minister. Bismarck was confident he could master the crisis.

> **JUNKER**
> A member of the Prussian aristocracy whose power rested on the ownership of large landed estates and on their traditional role as army officers and civil servants.

6 Prussia 1862–6

> **ISSUE:**
> How important was Bismarck?

a) Bismarck

Bismarck was to be the chief architect of the German Empire. In his memoirs, written in the 1890s, he depicted himself as a statesman who foresaw events and brilliantly achieved his goals. He left readers in no doubt that he was a veritable superman, working from the start of his political career for German unification. Some historians credit him with having a long-term strategy to make war on Austria and France in order to create a united Germany under Prussian control. As evidence, they cite the following words of Bismarck, allegedly spoken to Disraeli, a future British Prime Minister, in 1862:

> As soon as the army shall have been brought into such a condition to command respect, then I will take the first opportunity to declare war with Austria, burst asunder the German Confederation, bring the middle and smaller states into subjection and give Germany a national union under the leadership of Prussia.

Other historians, like A. J. P. Taylor, are not convinced. They argue that Bismarck was merely an opportunist, cleverly exploiting his enemies' mistakes and taking calculated risks which happened to be successful. Bismarck himself said: 'One must always have two irons in the fire.' He often had many more than two. In consequence, it is difficult to disentangle with any certainty his motives or the extent to

> **REALPOLITIK (POLITICAL REALISM)**
> This term is used to describe the ruthless and often cynical policies of politicians like Bismarck whose only aim was to increase the power of a state.

OTTO VON BISMARCK

Bismarck liked to present himself as a typical Junker squire. On his mother's side, however, many of his relatives were civil servants, merchants, professors and lawyers – well-educated and politically liberal. Aggressive and emotional, Bismarck's relations with William I were often stormy, their meetings sometimes degenerating into slanging matches. Bismarck once admitted: 'I am all nerves; so much so that self-control has always been the greatest task of my life and still is.' Given to melancholy, he suffered from periods of laziness, over-eating and over-drinking. He was also an inveterate womaniser and gambler. Ruthless, vindictive and unscrupulous, he could also be a charming and witty companion.

-*Profile*-

1815 born, the son of a Junker: educated in Berlin and at Göttingen University; he developed a reputation as an accomplished duellist (in one year he fought 25 duels);

1836 left university with qualifications in law and entered the civil service;

1839 disliking civil service work, he returned to manage the family estates;

1847 married and became an ultra-conservative deputy in the Prussian United Diet;

1850 served as Prussia's delegate at
–9 the diet of the Confederation;

1859 appointed Prussian Ambassador to Russia;

1862 became Prussian special envoy in France: recalled to become Minister President;

1864 war against Denmark;

1866 war against Austria;

1870 Franco-Prussian War;
–1

1871 Bismarck served as Chancellor
–90 of the new German Empire;

1898 died.

which he planned ahead. While there is no reason to doubt that he had the broad outline of what he wished to achieve in his mind from 1862, he probably did not plan in the sense of mapping out a specific set of moves. He sought instead to reach his – usually limited and clearly defined – goals by taking advantage of situations that he either helped to create or that simply presented themselves to him.

Realpolitik characterised Bismarck's political career from first to last. In his view, the end justified the means. His unscrupulous methods often brought him into conflict with William I and the Prussian military and political elites. But while many distrusted his tactics, most respected his cool judgement. Indispensable to the Prussian monarchy for nearly 30 years, he made the complex and difficult unification process appear, with hindsight, easy.

Q

Did Bismarck possess a blueprint for unification?

b) What were Bismarck's aims in 1862?

Bismarck's main aim initially was Prussian domination of north Germany rather than full national unity. He was essentially a Prussian patriot rather than a German nationalist: his loyalty was to the Prussian king – not the German people. Liberal nationalists in Prussia and in the National Society viewed him with disfavour in the early 1860s, seeing him not as a potential unifier but as an anti-liberal reactionary. However, Bismarck was not opposed to German nationalism. Aware of its popular appeal, he hoped he might be able to use it for Prussian ends. Indeed, he tended to see Prussian and German interests as one and the same. He said in 1858 there was 'nothing more German than the development of Prussia's particular interests'. Convinced that great issues are decided by might not right, he was determined to make Prussia as mighty as possible. Prussian leadership in Germany would ensure Prussian might. While he was determined to end Austrian primacy in the Confederation, he was not committed to war to make this possible. A diplomatic solution, in his view, was a preferable option.

c) What factors helped Bismarck?

In 1869 Bismarck wrote: 'I am not so arrogant as to assume that the likes of us are able to make history. My task is to keep an eye on the currents of the latter and steer my ship in them as best I can.' He steered brilliantly. However, a variety of factors enabled him to bring about German unification.

i) How important was the Prussian army?

German unification was the immediate result of three short wars – against Denmark (1864), Austria (1866) and France (1870–1). The Prussian army thus made Germany a reality. The fighting capacity of the Prussian army improved in the early 1860s thanks to the efforts and ability of War Minister von Roon and General Helmuth von Moltke, chief of the General Staff. Roon ensured that Prussian forces were increased, better trained and well armed. Under Moltke, the General Staff became the brains of the Prussian army, laying plans for mobilisation and military operations. In particular, Prussian military chiefs were quick to see the potential of railways for the rapid movement of troops.

ii) How important was the Prussian economy?

Prussian economic growth was rapid in the 1850s and 1860s. By the mid-1860s Prussia produced more coal and steel than France or Austria and had a more extensive railway network. The economic strength of Prussia gave her the military resources she needed to challenge first Austria and then France. A key industrialist was Krupp whose iron foundries in the Ruhr produced high-quality armaments.

BLOOD AND IRON

On 30 September 1862 Bismarck declared to the Prussian parliament:

> Germany does not look to Prussia's liberalism, but to its power. Bavaria, Württemberg, Baden can indulge in liberalism, but no one will expect them to undertake Prussia's role…not through speeches and majority decisions are the great questions of the day decided – that was the great mistake of 1848–9 – but by iron and blood.

This phrase, reversed to 'blood and iron', became almost synonymous with Bismarck.

Did Bismarck change Germany's destiny? **Q**

Tables 1 and 2 Statistical comparisons

	Population (million)			Per cent of labour force in manufacturing industry		Relative share of world manufacturing output		Key outputs in 1870	
	1820	1840	1870	1850	1870	1830	1860	Coal	Steel
FRANCE	30.5	34.2	36.1	20.6	22.0 [1866]	5.2	7.9	13.3	0.08
PRUSSIA/ GERMANY	10.3 26.1	14.9 32.6	19.4 40.8	c.20.0	28.0 [1882]	3.5	4.9	23.3	0.13
AUSTRIA- HUNGARY	25.5	–	34.8	14.8 [1857]	13.1 [1869]	3.2	4.2	6.3	0.02

	Austria	France	Prussia
Military			
1850	434,000	439,000	131,000
1860	306,000	608,000	201,000
1866	275,000	458,000	214,000[a]
1870	252,000	452,000	319,000[b]
Railways (kilometres in operation)			
1850	1,579	2,915	5,856[c]
1860	4,543	9,167	11,089
1870	9,589	15,544	18,876

[a] In 1866 Italy, Prussia's ally, had an army of 233,000.
[b] By 1871 the German states under Prussia's leadership could mobilise 850,000 men.
[c] The figures are for the territory of the 1871 *Reich*.

ACTIVITY

1. According to the statistics what were Prussia's a) strengths and b) weaknesses in comparison with Austria in the mid-1860s?

2. According to the statistics, what were Prussia's a) strengths and b) weaknesses in comparison with France in 1870?

Why did Prussia's economy boom?

▼ Scholars may have ascribed too much influence to the *Zollverein*. It did not provide protection for Prussian industries. Nor did it create a unified German economy.

▼ Prussia had a good education system at various levels.

▼ She possessed plentiful supplies of coal, iron and chemicals.

▼ She had a good system of communications.

▼ Historians disagree about the role played by the Prussian state. Some think it helped economic development. Others are convinced it hindered.

▼ Individuals like Alfred Krupp played an important role.

i) How important was the Zollverein?

Prussia dominated the *Zollverein* which by 1864 included virtually every German state except Austria. However, while the *Zollverein* ensured that Prussia had considerable economic influence in Germany, this was not translated into political domination. Many German states supported Austria politically to counterbalance economic subordination to Prussia. In 1866 most *Zollverein* states actually allied with Austria against Prussia.

ii) How important was German nationalism?

There is plenty of evidence to suggest that the mass of Germans had little interest in national unity. The framework of most politicians in the early 1860s was local – not 'German'. There was certainly no massive sentiment in favour of Prussian-dominated Germany. It is thus possible to claim that nationalism played little role in the unification process. However, there is no doubt that nationalist sentiment was strong among middle-class Germans who tended to lead public opinion. Books and newspapers supported the idea of national unity. There was an increased awareness of German culture – art, music, literature and history. A variety of national groups had large memberships. Moreover, fears of French expansion were still prevalent. In the early 1860s there was a liberal revival both in Prussia and across Germany. Most liberals held nationalist views. Popular nationalism, strongest in the Protestant north, was a force that could not be ignored by Bismarck or any other ruler.

> **Q** To what extent did German nationalism make unification inevitable?

iii) How important was the international situation?

▼ The fact that Prussia was a second-rate power in 1862 helped Bismarck. He was able to achieve supremacy in Germany without arousing the hostility of Prussia's neighbours.

▼ In the 1860s Britain adopted a non-interventionist posture towards continental affairs. The prevailing view was that Britain had nothing to fear from Protestant Prussia and that a strong Germany would be a useful bulwark against French or Russian expansion.

▼ Russia, concerned with reform at home, showed little interest in central Europe. Her sympathies lay with Prussia. She had still not forgiven Austria for her policy during the Crimean War and there was a growing clash of interests between the two in the Balkans.

▼ Austria's diplomatic isolation helped Bismarck. So did the fact that Austrian finances were in a perilous position. This meant she was unable to modernise her army.

BISMARCK'S PROBLEMS

▼ Prussia was in a vulnerable position. Its territories straddled across central Europe.
▼ Austria was opposed to Prussian domination of north Germany. Her population was almost twice that of Prussia and she had a larger army.
▼ The majority of German states were strongly opposed to Prussian expansion.
▼ Prussian and German liberals had little sympathy for Bismarck.

d) The constitutional crisis solved

Bismarck's appointment as chief minister was seen as a deliberate affront to the liberals. A right-wing maverick, he had no ministerial experience and was not expected to last long in power. Few realised his ability. He solved the problem of the military budget by withdrawing it, declaring that the support of parliament for the army bill was unnecessary as the army reforms could be financed from taxation. The taxes were collected and the army reorganised as if parliament did not exist. For four years and through two wars, he directed Prussian affairs without a constitutionally approved budget and in the face of fierce parliamentary opposition. New elections in 1863 gave the liberals 70 per cent of the parliamentary seats. 'Men spat on the place where I trod in the streets,' Bismarck wrote later. But he rightly judged that his opponents would avoid an appeal to force and calculated that everything would be forgiven if he achieved foreign policy success.

e) The Polish revolt (1863)

In 1863 Russian Poles rose in revolt. Unlike most European statesmen, Bismarck had little sympathy with the Catholic Poles whom he regarded as potential troublemakers in Prussia. He thus offered Russia military support. Tsar Alexander II, who had sufficient force to crush the revolt, refused the offer but an agreement known as the Alvensleben Convention permitted Russian pursuit of rebel Poles crossing into Prussia. This accord angered France and Britain and alienated liberal opinion in Germany. However, Bismarck maintained Russia's friendship. This proved useful in 1866 and in 1870–1.

f) The Danish War (1864)

In 1863 Danish King Frederick VII died without an heir. By prior international arrangement, the throne passed to Christian IX. However, the Schleswig-Holsteiners put forward their own claimant, the German Duke of Augustenburg, a move passionately supported by German nationalists. King Christian put himself in the wrong by incorporating Schleswig into Denmark in November 1863, thereby violating the 1852 Treaty of London. The German Confederation now sent an army into Holstein on behalf of the Duke of Augustenburg.

The crisis offered splendid opportunities to Bismarck. He hoped to annex the two duchies, strengthening Prussian power in north Germany and winning credit for himself into the bargain. He thus had no wish to see Augustenburg in control. Nor did he care one iota about the rights of the Germans within the duchies. 'It is not a concern of ours,' he said privately, 'whether the Germans of Holstein are happy.' He first won Austrian help. Early in 1864 Prussian and Austrian troops, acting independently of the Confederation, moved into the duchies on the grounds that the Danish King had broken the 1852 agreement. The two powers had very different aims. Austria, who supported the Augustenburg claim, was happy to pursue a policy of 'dualism' with Prussia. Bismarck, implying that he too supported Augustenburg, kept secret his own expansionist agenda. Failing to win the support of any great power, Denmark agreed that the Schleswig-Holstein matter should be resolved by the decision of a European conference. However, the London Conference (April–June 1864) failed to reach agreement. Counting on Britain's support, the Danes refused to make concessions and fighting recommenced. Despite Palmerston's boast that 'if Denmark had to fight, she would not fight alone', there was little Britain could actually do. Denmark quickly saw sense and surrendered.

g) The results of the Danish War

By the Treaty of Vienna (October 1864) the King of Denmark gave up his rights over Schleswig and Holstein which were to be jointly administered by Austria and Prussia. The question of the long-term fate of the duchies soon became a source of acute tension between the two German powers, as Bismarck may have intended. Public opinion in Germany and the duchies expected that Augustenburg would now become Duke. However, Bismarck proposed that he be installed on conditions which would have left him under Prussia's power. This was totally unacceptable to Austria. Bismarck made Austria's position in the duchies increasingly difficult and there were frequent disputes over the joint administration. By the summer of 1865 tension had reached a critical point. But neither Austria, financially bankrupt, nor Bismarck, who knew that William I was reluctant to fight a fellow German state, wanted war at this stage. In August 1865 the Convention of Gastein apparently resolved the situation. The two powers agreed that Austria would govern Holstein while Prussia administered Schleswig. Bismarck knew he could now pick a quarrel with Austria over Holstein at any time he wanted.

Historians continue to debate Bismarck's motives. Did he, as he later claimed, use the Schleswig-Holstein crisis as a means of manoeuvring Austria into open confrontation with Prussia in order to settle the problem of leadership in Germany? Or did he, whatever he said later, have no clear policy at the time except to 'allow events to ripen'? A. J. P. Taylor thought that he 'may well have hoped to manoeuvre Austria out of the duchies, perhaps even out of the headship of Germany, by diplomatic strokes…His diplomacy in this period seems rather calculated to frighten Austria than to prepare for war.'

However, by 1865 Bismarck realised that war with Austria was a distinct possibility and he did all he could to strengthen Prussia's international position. Confident that Russia and Britain would not oppose him, his main fear was France. In October 1865 he met Napoleon III at Biarritz. Historians continue to conjecture what occurred. Almost certainly nothing specific was agreed if only because neither man wanted a specific agreement. Bismarck was not prepared to offer German territory in the Rhineland in return for France's neutrality. Napoleon, calculating that a war between the two German powers would be exhausting and inconclusive, intended to remain neutral and then to turn this to good advantage by mediating between the combatants, gaining a much greater reward in the process than anything Bismarck could presently offer. Given Napoleon's anti-Austrian stance, it took little genius on Bismarck's part to secure the Emperor's good wishes.

ISSUE:

How did Bismarck win Prussian control over north Germany?

7 The Seven Weeks War and the North German Confederation

a) The approach to war

Over the winter of 1865–6 Prussian-Austrian relations deteriorated. In February 1866, the Prussian government accepted that war with Austria was inevitable. It would be fought not just to settle the fate of Schleswig and Holstein but over the issue of who should control Germany. In April 1866 Bismarck arranged an alliance with Italy to remain in force for three months. Italy was to support Prussia if war broke out during that time. In return Italy would annex Venetia. Bismarck now deliberately stoked up tension with Austria over Holstein and over proposals to reform the Confederation. Aware that it would take longer to mobilise her forces and afraid of a surprise attack, in May Austria began mobilising her troops. Prussia, claiming that she was responding to Austrian aggression, also began mobilising. While Prussia had the support of several small north German states, most large states – Saxony, Hanover, Bavaria, Württemberg and Baden – blamed Prussia for the crisis and favoured Austria.

On 1 June Austria broke off talks with Prussia over Schleswig and Holstein and appealed to the Confederation to settle the future of the duchies. This broke the terms of the Gastein Convention and Bismarck responded by occupying Holstein. Austrian troops were permitted to withdraw peacefully. To Bismarck's surprise and disappointment this did not immediately lead to war. On 10 June he proposed that the Confederation be reorganised to exclude Austria, that a national parliament be elected by universal suffrage and that all troops in north Germany should be under Prussian command. The next day Austria asked the diet to reject Prussia's proposals and to mobilise for war.

Censored by the diet, Prussia withdrew from the Confederation, declared it dissolved and invited all the German states to ally themselves with her against Austria. Instead, most began mobilising against Prussia. Bismarck now issued an ultimatum to three northern states, Hanover, Hesse-Cassel and Saxony, to side with Prussia or else be regarded as enemies. When the ultimatums were rejected, Prussian forces occupied the three states.

b) The war

The future of Bismarck, Prussia and Germany now lay with the Prussian army. General Moltke was ready. Prussian military expenditure had doubled since 1860 while that of Austria had halved. Prussian planning, particularly in the use of railways, meant that mobilisation was much more efficient than that of the Austrian army. Even so, Austria's position was far from hopeless. She had more men, 400,000 to the Prussians' 300,000, support from most of the other German states, and the advantage of a central position. However, an Italian declaration of war meant that Austria had to divide her forces. Taking the initiative, Prussian troops advanced into Bohemia. One single-track railway ran from Vienna to Bohemia. By contrast Prussia used five lines to bring her troops southwards. Moltke adopted the risky strategy of dividing his forces for faster movement, only concentrating them on the eve of battle. Fortunately for Prussia, the Austrian high command missed several opportunities to annihilate the separate Prussian armies. The major battle, involving some 500,000 men, was at Königgrätz (or Sadowa) in July. Prussian troops, armed with breech-loading needle guns, had a rate of fire five times greater than the Austrians and won a great victory. Fearing the break-up of her Empire, Austria sued for peace. Prussia was thus in a position to dictate terms. William proposed to advance on Vienna and annex Austrian land. But Bismarck, fearful that France and Russia might intervene, counselled caution. He wrote to William as follows:

> We have to avoid wounding Austria too severely; we have to avoid leaving behind in her unnecessary bitterness of feeling or desire for revenge, we ought to keep the possibility of becoming friends again. If Austria were severely injured, she would become the ally of France and of every other opponent of ours...German Austria we could neither wholly nor partly make use of. The acquisition of provinces like Austrian Silesia and part of Bohemia could not strengthen the Prussian state; it would not lead to a union of German Austria with Prussia, and Vienna could not be governed by Berlin as a mere dependency.

ACTIVITY

Examine Bismarck's letter to William. Answer the following questions:

1. Why did Bismarck favour a lenient peace with Austria?

2. What arguments might have been made against Bismarck's leniency?

At an angry meeting of the war cabinet on 23 July Bismarck got his way. (He threatened suicide if his advice was not taken!) The war was brought to a speedy end and a moderate peace concluded with Austria. Ironically, the only territory (Holstein apart) lost by Austria was in Italy where she had won substantial victories on both land and sea.

The Treaty of Prague (August 1866)

▼ Austria agreed to Prussia's annexation of Schleswig and Holstein.
▼ Prussia also annexed Hesse-Cassel, Hanover, Nassau and Frankfurt.
▼ The German Confederation was replaced by a North German Confederation comprising all the German states north of the River Main in a union dominated by Prussia.
▼ Austria surrendered Venetia to Italy (by the Treaty of Vienna – October 1866).

Figure 2 Germany and Austria-Hungary in 1867

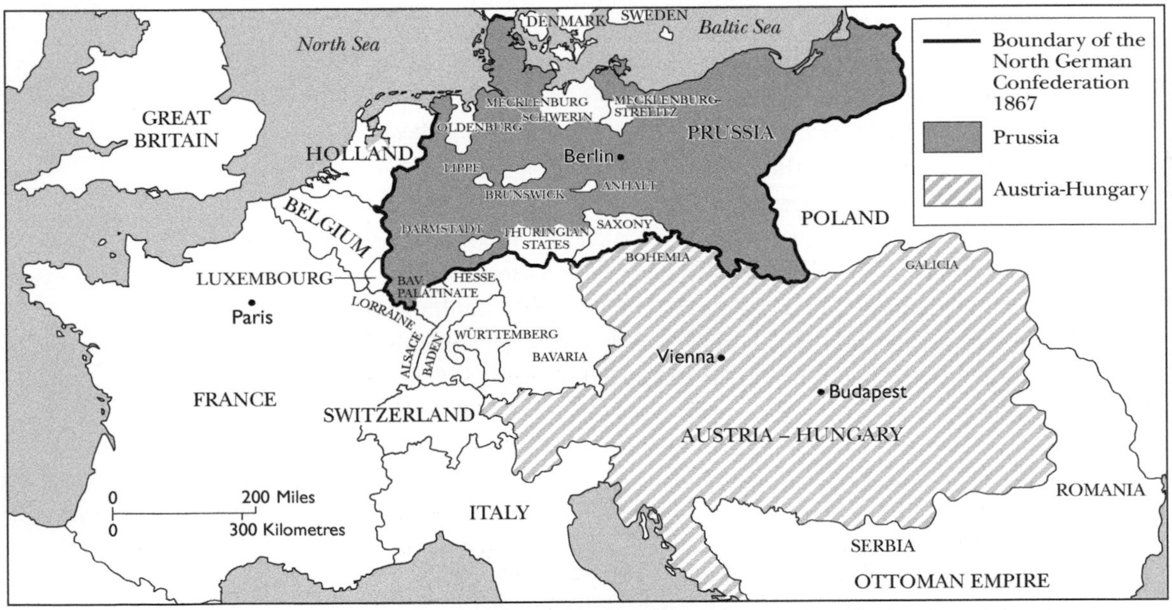

c) Southern Germany

Bismarck might have pressed for the unification of all Germany in 1866. However, as well as the threat of foreign intervention, he also feared that if Prussia absorbed too much too soon, especially the anti-Prussian Catholic south, this might be more trouble than it was worth. Four south German states – Bavaria, Württemberg, Baden and Hesse-Darmstadt – thus retained their independence. But all agreed to sign a military alliance with Prussia whereby, in the event of war, they would put their armies under the command of the Prussian king. Why the states agreed to sacrifice their military sovereignty so readily is not certain. Perhaps they were sufficiently afraid of Bismarck to feel safer in some sort of alliance with him. They also feared a possible French attack.

d) Popular support for Bismarck

The July 1866 elections to the Prussian parliament, with war fever at high pitch, resulted in a big increase in the number of conservatives (from 34 to142) while the liberal parties were reduced (from 253 to 142). The success of Bismarck's policies also won over many liberals who formed the National Liberal Party. Pledged to support Bismarck in his nationalist policy, the National Liberals were prepared to forget past conflicts. This ensured an era of harmony between Bismarck and the Prussian parliament.

The Constitution of the North German Confederation

Drafted by Bismarck, this was accepted in April 1867 and came into effect in July. It was designed to fit the requirements of Prussian power and Bismarck's own political position.

▼ The Prussian king was President of the Confederation and also the commander-in-chief. He had the power of declaring war and making peace. He appointed and could dismiss the Federal Chancellor.

▼ The Confederation had a federal structure. The various states retained control over their legal, administrative, educational and police systems, and over local taxation.

▼ The *Bundesrat* was the upper house of the Confederation's parliament. It had jurisdiction over the raising of taxes, foreign policy and the federal army. Each state was represented, according to its population size. Out of 43 votes, Prussia had 17, Saxony 4 and most of the others one each. In practice Prussia was never outvoted in the *Bundesrat*.

▼ The *Reichstag* was the lower house of the Confederation's parliament. It was elected by universal male suffrage – a giant step towards democracy. However, its powers were limited. Neither the king, his ministers, nor the *Bundesrat* were accountable to it.

▼ The Federal Chancellor was the main driving force in the Confederation. He represented the Prussian king in the *Bundesrat*. He was not responsible to the *Reichstag*.

The North German Confederation's first *Reichstag* was elected in 1867. The National Liberals were the largest single party and held the balance of power between Bismarck's conservative supporters and his various opponents. They were able to win a number of concessions from Bismarck including the right to pass an annual budget. However, this financial control was limited because it did not include control over the military budget – some 90 per cent of the Confederation's spending. Generally prepared to support Bismarck's policies, the *Reichstag* passed an impressive number of laws, including a range of unifying measures.

e) Bismarck and Germany

The Treaty of Prague brought huge gains to Prussia. Two thirds of all Germans (excluding German Austrians) were now part of the Prussian-dominated North German Confederation. Most non-Prussian north Germans quickly accepted the situation. For many liberal-nationalists there were no irreconcilable differences between Bismarck's Prussian policy and *kleindeutsch* German nationalism. Indeed, after 1866 Bismarck found himself under nationalist pressure – north and south – to complete the process of unification. Recognising that union with the southern states would strengthen Prussia in relation to both France and Austria, he was not averse to the idea and was prepared to use the rhetoric and emotion of German nationalism to help bring it about. In 1867 the four southern states were incorporated into the new *Zollparlament* – a parliament elected to discuss the policy of the *Zollverein*. This was intended to encourage closer cooperation between north and south. However, in 1868 the southern states elected a majority of delegates opposed to union with the north. Bismarck was not too concerned. He believed that in good time the southern states would fall like ripe fruit into Prussia's basket.

ISSUE:
Why did France declare war on Prussia in 1870 and what were the results?

8 The Franco-Prussian War

a) Franco-Prussian relations: 1867–70

Napoleon III was taken completely by surprise by the speed and scale of Prussia's victory. France gained nothing from the peace settlement (despite efforts to gain compensation along the River Rhine or in Belgium) and now had a very powerful eastern neighbour. Having missed the chance to check Prussia's growth of power in 1866, Napoleon needed a diplomatic and territorial success to prove that France remained Europe's greatest power. Luxembourg, ruled by the king of the Netherlands but garrisoned in part by Prussian troops, seemed Napoleon III's best bet for a showy success. In the spring of 1867 the Dutch King agreed to sell Luxembourg to France, subject to approval by the Prussian King. This, he must have known, was unlikely to be given. It suited Bismarck, given the crucial debates over the constitution of the North German Confederation, to whip up nationalist fervour. Referring to Luxemburg as 'German territory', he threatened the Dutch King with German retribution if he injured the 'national sense of honour'. However, he had no wish to start a war with France at this stage. He thus appealed to the great powers to settle the Luxembourg question. A conference in London helped defuse the crisis. Luxembourg was declared neutral under a 'collective' guarantee of the great powers. While this seemed like a compromise, the fact that there was no territorial gain for France was a heavy blow for Napoleon III.

The Luxembourg crisis seriously damaged Franco-German relations. Nevertheless, the years 1867–70 were peaceful. Bismarck was still keen to avert war. Fearful of French military strength, he was also concerned that Napoleon might find allies. Austrian Emperor Francis Joseph, hankering after regaining influence in Germany, twice met Napoleon in 1867 to see if it was possible to reach agreement. Fortunately for Bismarck, these efforts came to nothing. There was no real basis for agreement. Francis Joseph was aware that most German Austrians totally opposed a pro-French and anti-Prussian policy.

b) The Hohenzollern candidature

The episode which provoked war between Prussia and France began in 1868. Following a revolution and seeking a new king, the Spanish government made a request to Prince Leopold, a member of the Catholic branch of the same Hohenzollern family as King William I. Bismarck was a keen supporter of Leopold's candidature. William was far less enthusiastic. He knew that to proceed would provoke hostility with Napoleon III who was certain to see it as a threat to 'encircle' France. Despite his doubts, Bismarck persuaded him to support the Hohenzollern candidature. However, Leopold decided he did not wish to accept the Spanish throne and the affair seemed to be at an end. Then, as a result of pressure from Bismarck, Leopold agreed to accept after all. In June William gave his formal consent. When news of the fact leaked out, earlier than Bismarck had planned, there was uproar in Paris. The French regarded Leopold's candidature as totally unacceptable. Napoleon III, urged on by his new aggressive foreign minister, Gramont, ordered his ambassador in Berlin, Count Benedetti, to warn William that Leopold's candidacy would leave France with little option but to declare war. William, who did not want war, least of all over the Spanish candidature, assured Benedetti of Prussia's friendship and on 12 July Leopold's candidature was withdrawn.

The affair seemed to have been settled, with the diplomatic honours going to France. Bismarck spoke of humiliation and threatened resignation. He was saved by Napoleon III who now overplayed his hand. The French Emperor, goaded by the Empress

Eugenie and Gramont, demanded that William should renounce support for the Hohenzollern candidature for all time. Benedetti met William at the spa town of Bad Ems on 13 July. William refused to give the assurances demanded since he had already given his word. Even so, his reply was conciliatory. As a matter of course he instructed one of his aides to notify Bismarck, in Berlin, of the day's events in a telegram and also gave him permission to communicate details to the press. Bismarck, dining with Generals Moltke and von Roon, reduced the telegram by striking out a few words (see page 172) so that the King's message gave the impression of an unfriendly meeting and a snub to France.

As Bismarck had anticipated, the publication of the amended Ems telegram caused eruptions in France. French newspapers and crowds, convinced that French honour was at stake, demanded war. Napoleon III, urged on by his wife, his ministers, the Chamber of Deputies and public opinion, declared war on Prussia on 19 July. The German response was predictable. According to W. Carr, 'a great wave of white-hot patriotic fervour swept through the whole country including the south'. Bismarck, claiming that France was the aggressor who had 'committed a grievous sin against humanity', called upon the south German states for support in accordance with the terms of their military alliances with Prussia. Convinced that the fatherland was in danger, they agreed to support Prussia.

Q

Did Bismarck engineer the Hohenzollern candidature to ensure war with France?

FRANCO-PRUSSIAN OR FRANCO-GERMAN WAR?

Historians disagree about what to call the war. Should it be Franco-Prussian or Franco-German? Certainly Prussia dominated the German war effort. Moltke organised the strategy and Prussian troops outnumbered all other troops in the army. However, it was a genuinely German war. Most Germans were united by a hatred of France – feelings that were encouraged by government propaganda. As the war proceeded and Germans shared the pride of success, the war became something of a national crusade.

c) To what extent was Bismarck responsible for war?

Historians continue to debate how far ahead Bismarck had planned this confrontation. Given that only a great national war was likely to bring about speedy German unity, it is likely that a war against France was in his mind since 1866. Arguably he deliberately engineered the Hohenzollern candidature to provoke war. However, there is little evidence that he was set on war from 1866 or even in 1870. He certainly did not control the whole Hohenzollern affair from 1868–70. What he did do was to manipulate and take advantage of the situation. Characteristically, he conceived a range of possibilities from winning a diplomatic victory to war – provided it seemed to be brought about by French aggression. Opportunism on Bismarck's part and French blunders ensured that the Hohenzollern issue led to war. In the event France declared war on Prussia, not vice versa. If Bismarck set a trap for France, it was largely one of France's own making.

French isolation

▼ On the outbreak of war Bismarck released evidence of French designs on Belgium (an area of crucial British concern). Britain remained strictly neutral in the war. Long mistrustful of Napoleon's ambitions, if anything British sympathies were with Prussia.

▼ The presence of French troops in Rome was a barrier to French-Italian friendship.

▼ Russia had long been on good terms with Prussia. In 1868 the two countries agreed that if either was threatened by two powers, the other would come to her assistance.

▼ Austria, which might have used a Franco-Prussian war to try to regain her position in Germany, was not prepared to risk another clash with Prussia.

d) The war

German troops were quickly mobilised. French mobilisation, by contrast, was much slower. Moltke had the advantage that there were six railway lines to the French frontier: the French had two. In under three weeks some 500,000 Germans, facing fewer than 300,000 French troops, were ready to invade France. Moltke's grand strategy was initially bungled by the mistakes of his field commanders. However, Napoleon III and Marshal Bazaine snatched defeat from the jaws of victory by withdrawing 180,000 men into the fortress city of Metz. German forces encircled Metz and held the initiative.

Figure 3 Map of the Franco-Prussian War

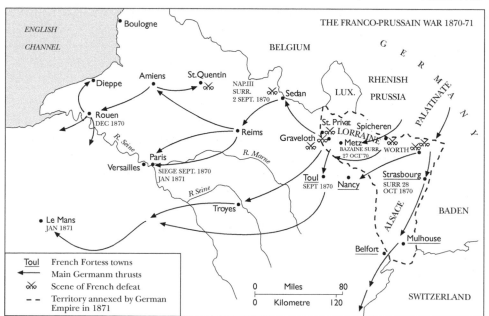

THE TREATY OF FRANKFURT (MAY 1871)

▼ The French provinces of Alsace and Lorraine were annexed by Prussia.

▼ France had to pay an indemnity of 5,000 million francs (£200 million).

▼ A German army of occupation was to remain in France until the indemnity was paid.

▼ France kept the fortress of Belfort in return for a German victory parade through Paris.

Prussian/German military advantages

▼ Moltke led an able general staff – the brain of the army. France had no general staff.

▼ The Prussians were armed with Krupp breech-loading field guns.

▼ The Prussians/Germans had more trained soldiers and recent experience of war.

▼ Germany had more people, industry and railways than France.

French military advantages

▼ French military prestige was high. French armies had acquitted themselves with credit both in the Crimean War and in north Italy in 1859.

▼ The French *chassepot* rifle was superior to the Prussian needle gun.

▼ The French possessed the *mitrailleuse*, an early form of machine gun.

Napoleon III, with an army commanded by General MacMahon, tried to rescue Bazaine's army. Intercepted by German troops, MacMahon's forces were driven back to Sedan. Here they were surrounded. 600 German guns shattered French attempts to break out of the trap. On 3 September Napoleon surrendered. The Emperor, 84,000 men, 2,700 officers and 39 generals were taken prisoner. The war should by rights have finished at this point. However, when news of the surrender reached Paris Napoleon was deposed and the new Government of National Defence determined to fight on. Thus, German forces besieged the French capital. The enthusiastic but untrained French Army of the Loire, raised to relieve Paris, was quickly defeated. Meanwhile, in October Bazaine's army in Metz finally surrendered. Eventually Paris became so short of food that the French government was forced to sign an armistice on 28 January 1871.

e) Why did Bismarck impose harsh peace terms on France?

France's loss of Alsace-Lorraine was the most controversial direct result of the war and led to long-lasting enmity between France and Germany. Why did Bismarck impose such a humiliating treaty on France, so different from the one with Austria in 1866?

▼ He believed that French defeat, irrespective of the peace terms, turned France into an irreconcilable enemy. He thus wished to ensure that France was so weakened that she could pose no threat to Germany in the future. The fortresses of Metz and Strasbourg were crucial. Metz, in

Moltke's view, was worth the equivalent of an army of 120,000 men.
▼ During the war, the German press had portrayed France as the guilty party. Justly defeated, most Germans now believed she needed to be punished.
▼ Alsace and Lorraine, rich in iron ore, were useful economically.

f) The German Empire

War against France created a tidal wave of German patriotism. Popular pressure in the four south German states for turning the wartime alliance into a permanent union grew. This strengthened Bismarck's negotiating hand with the south German rulers. Seeking to preserve Prussian influence at the same time as creating a united Germany, he was determined that the new *Reich* would have a constitution similar to that of the North German Confederation. The south German rulers, by contrast, wanted a looser confederation in which they retained more rights. Bismarck had to use all his diplomatic skill to get his way. His trump card was the threat to call on the German people to remove those rulers who stood in the way of unity. He also made some symbolic concessions – most of which meant little in practice. King Ludwig II of Bavaria, who was particularly reluctant to cooperate, was finally won over by a secret bribe: Bismarck agreed to pay him a large pension to pay off his debts. In November 1870 separate treaties were signed with each of the four south German states by which they agreed to join the German Empire. The new *Reich* was a federal state: constituent states retained their monarchies and had extensive power over internal matters. But real political power was in the hands of the Emperor, his army officers, and his hand-picked ministers of whom Bismarck, the new imperial chancellor, would be chief. (See chapter 7.)

Figure 4 William I proclaimed Emperor of Germany, 1871 (Bismarck is in the centre)

Some results of the Franco-Prussian War

▼ 'The war represents the German revolution,' said Disraeli, 'a greater political event than the French Revolution of last century…There is not a diplomatic tradition which has not been swept away…The balance of power has been entirely destroyed.'

▼ The new *Reich* would now have to cope with French desire for revenge. 'What we have gained by arms in half a year, we must protect by arms for half a century,' said Moltke.

▼ In September 1870 Italy occupied Rome.

▼ In October 1870 Russia took the opportunity provided by the war to abrogate the Black Sea clauses of the Treaty of Paris.

GERMAN UNIFICATION 1862–71

1862 Bismarck appointed Minister President (chief minister) of Prussia;

1863 Denmark incorporated Schleswig: German diet voted for action against Denmark;

1864 Austria and Prussia fought Denmark: Denmark ceded Schleswig and Holstein;

1866 Seven Weeks War: Prussia defeated Austria: North German Confederation set up;

1870 Franco-Prussian War;
–1

1871 German Empire proclaimed at Versailles.

How important was German nationalism in the creation of the Second *Reich*?

Arguably the sudden creation of the German *Reich* had little to do with nationalism and everything to do with Prussian ambition and force of arms. A realistic appreciation of Prussian interests, not an idealistic German nationalism, had inspired Bismarck towards unification. He ignored rather than exploited national feelings pre-1866. However, nationalism gave Bismarck's ambitions for Prussia a sense of moral legitimacy. After 1866 German unity, growing from the success of Prussian dynastic expansion, did become his main objective. It was a German (not a Prussian) Empire that emerged in 1871.

▼ Working on The Unification of Germany: 1815–71

By now you should have a view as to why and how German unification came about. The following factors clearly played a part:

▼ German nationalism;

▼ German (but particularly Prussian) economic growth;

▼ the international situation in the 1860s;

▼ the Prussian army;

▼ Bismarck's diplomacy.

Which of the factors do you see as most important? Which do you see as least important?

Answering extended writing and essay questions on The Unification of Germany: 1815–71

Consider the following question: 'Account for Bismarck's success in creating a German Empire in 1871.'

It is possible to argue that Bismarck did not make Germany: rather Germany made Bismarck. A variety of factors were such that Bismarck was able gain the credit for bringing about a unification which may well have developed naturally, whoever was in power. However, whatever view is taken about the 'inevitability' of German unification, it is clear that it happened as it did and when it did largely as a result of Bismarck's actions. His precise aims baffled contemporaries and continue to baffle historians. It is difficult to disentangle his motives and to decide how far he planned ahead. While it is wrong to believe he came to power in 1862 with a master plan for German unification, it is equally wrong to imagine that he had no long-term objectives and fumbled his way through events simply by good luck. He manipulated situations even if he did not always create them. He had clear aims but the exact means of achieving them were left to short-term decisions based on the situation at the time. Perhaps his main skill as a diplomat lay in his ability to isolate his enemy. He was not essentially a warmonger. For Bismarck, wars were a – risky – means to an end. However, confident in the strength of the Prussian army, he was prepared to engineer war to achieve his end.

Answering source-based questions on The Unification of Germany: 1815–71

Bad Ems, July 13, 1870

His Majesty writes to me: 'Count Benedetti spoke to me on the promenade, in order to demand from me, finally in a very importunate manner, that I should authorise him to telegraph at once that I bound myself for all future time never again to give my consent if the Hohenzollerns should renew their candidature. I refused at last somewhat sternly, as it is neither right nor possible to undertake engagements of this kind a tout jamais [for all time]. I told him that I had as yet received no news and as he was earlier informed from Paris and Madrid than myself, he could see clearly that my government had no more interest in the matter.' His Majesty has since received a letter from Prince Charles Anthony. His Majesty, having told Count Benedetti that he was awaiting news from the Prince, has decided, with reference to the above demand, on the suggestion of Count Eulenberg and myself, not to receive Count Benedetti again, but only to let him be informed through an aide-de-camp: 'That his Majesty has now received from the Prince confirmation of the news which Benedetti had already received from Paris, and had nothing further to say to the ambassador.' His Majesty leaves it to your Excellency to decide whether Benedetti's fresh demand and its rejection should be at once communicated to both our ambassadors, to foreign nations, and to the press.

Source A The message, sent by a secretary of the King from Bad Ems to Bismarck

In view of the attitude of France, our national sense of honour compelled us, in my opinion, to go to war; and if we did not act according to the demands of this feeling, we should lose the entire impetus towards our national development won in 1866...

Under this conviction I made use of the royal authorisation to publish the contents of the telegram: and in the presence of my two guests reduced the telegram by striking out words, but without adding or altering, to the following form: 'After the news of the renunciation of the hereditary Prince of Hohenzollern had been officially communicated to the imperial government of France by the royal government of Spain, the French ambassador at Ems further demanded of his Majesty the King that he would authorise him to telegraph to Paris that his Majesty the King bound himself for all future time never again to give his consent if the Hohenzollerns should renew their candidature. His Majesty the King thereupon decided not to receive the French ambassador again, and sent to tell him through the aide-de-camp on duty that his Majesty had nothing further to communicate to the ambassador.' The difference in the effect of the abbreviated text of the Ems telegram, as compared with that produced by the original was not the result of stronger words but of the form, which made the announcement appear decisive.

Source B Bismarck's Memoirs written in the 1890s.

▼ QUESTIONS ON SOURCES

1. Examine Source A. Explain why King William sent the Ems telegram to Bismarck. **[5 marks]**
2. How reliable and useful is Source B as evidence for Bismarck's actions in July 1870? **[5 marks]**
3. Using both sources and your own knowledge, assess the significance of Bismarck's 'striking out words'? **[15 marks]**

Suggested lines of response

Question 1. There are some clues in Source A.

Question 2. Bismarck was writing with the benefit of hindsight and was prone to exaggerate, dramatise and even lie in his memoirs. Nevertheless, the changes he made to the Ems telegram are accurate and he was obviously a – perhaps 'the' – crucial player in the diplomatic 'game' in July 1870.

Question 3. Why were the changes to the Ems telegram so important? To what extent did Bismarck deliberately engineer war with France?

Further Reading

Books in the 'Access to History' series

The Unification of Germany 1815–90 by A. Styles is excellent.

General

The Formation of the First German Nation-State, 1800–1871 by J. Breuilly (Macmillan, 1996) is worth reading. Try also *German History since 1800*, edited by M. Fulbrook (Arnold, 1997), *The Origins of the Wars of German Unification* by W. Carr (Longman, 1991), *Bismarck and Germany* by D. G. Williamson (Longman, 1997), and *A History of Germany 1815–1990* by W. Carr (Arnold, 1991).

KEY ISSUE:
Was Bismarck a 'good' or 'bad' thing for Germany after 1871?

POINTS TO CONSIDER

The formation of the German Empire, or *Reich*, in 1871 overthrew Europe's old balance of power system. Germany was now the continent's greatest power and seemingly in a position to dominate Europe. Otto von Bismarck dominated Germany for the two decades after 1870. His prestige as the creator of the new *Reich* was enormous and Emperor William I trusted him on most issues. What were Bismarck's aims after 1871 in both domestic and foreign policies? What problems did he face? How successful was he in dealing with the problems and achieving his aims?

ISSUE:
Who controlled the Reich?

1 The German Empire

a) The German constitution

Figure 1 Map of the German Empire 1871

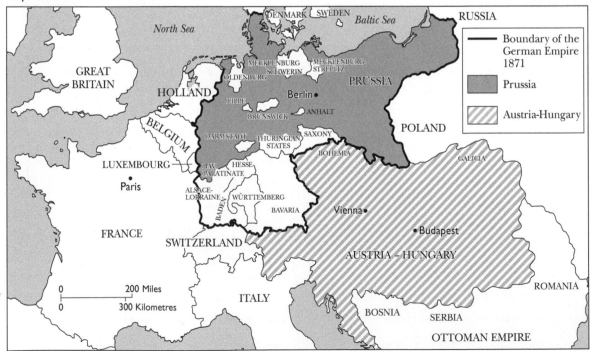

The German Empire was proclaimed on 18 January 1871 in the Palace of Versailles in France. King William I of Prussia became the new German emperor, or *kaiser*, with Bismarck as his imperial chancellor. The constitution of the *Reich* essentially incorporated the main provisions of the constitution of the North German Confederation, drawn up by Bismarck in 1867. Germany was to be a federal state. Powers and functions were divided between the central, or federal, government and 25 state governments. While no longer sovereign or free to secede, the states preserved their own constitutions, rulers, parliaments and administrative systems. (See Figure 2.) While the southern states retained some special internal rights, these were mainly decorative.

Figure 2 How was Germany ruled?

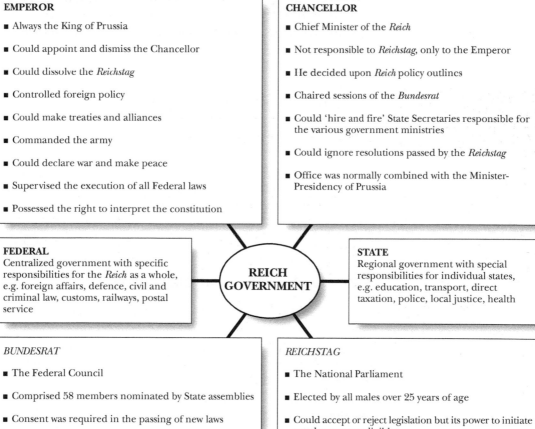

EMPEROR

- Always the King of Prussia

- Could appoint and dismiss the Chancellor

- Could dissolve the *Reichstag*

- Controlled foreign policy

- Could make treaties and alliances

- Commanded the army

- Could declare war and make peace

- Supervised the execution of all Federal laws

- Possessed the right to interpret the constitution

CHANCELLOR

- Chief Minister of the *Reich*

- Not responsible to *Reichstag*, only to the Emperor

- He decided upon *Reich* policy outlines

- Chaired sessions of the *Bundesrat*

- Could 'hire and fire' State Secretaries responsible for the various government ministries

- Could ignore resolutions passed by the *Reichstag*

- Office was normally combined with the Minister-Presidency of Prussia

FEDERAL
Centralized government with specific responsibilities for the *Reich* as a whole, e.g. foreign affairs, defence, civil and criminal law, customs, railways, postal service

REICH GOVERNMENT

STATE
Regional government with special responsibilities for individual states, e.g. education, transport, direct taxation, police, local justice, health

BUNDESRAT

- The Federal Council

- Comprised 58 members nominated by State assemblies

- Consent was required in the passing of new laws

- Theoretically able to change the constitution

- A vote of 14 against a proposal constituted a veto

- Prussia had 17 of the 58 seats

- Bavaria 6 and the smaller states one each

- In theory, it had extensive powers. In practice it usually rubber stamped the Chancellor's policies

REICHSTAG

- The National Parliament

- Elected by all males over 25 years of age

- Could accept or reject legislation but its power to initiate new laws was negligible

- State Secretaries were excluded from membership of *Reichstag* and not responsible to it

- Members were not paid

- Could approve or reject the budget

- Elected every 5 years (unless dissolved)

The German political system defies classification. Historians have variously described the *Reich* as a military monarchy, a sham-constitutional state, a Prusso-German semi-autocracy, or a constitutional monarchy. Arguably, it was all of these – and more! The complex, hybrid system can be seen (positively) as creating a delicate equilibrium with the key institutions keeping each other in check: it can also be seen (negatively) as creating major tensions, not least between monarchical and parliamentary claims to power, and between federal and state power.

b) Prussia's dominance

▼ As German emperor, the Prussian king was head of the imperial executive and civil service and supreme war lord of all the armed forces of the Empire.

▼ Prussia could block any unwelcome constitutional amendments in the *Bundesrat*.

▼ Prussia possessed 60 per cent of Germany's population and two thirds of its territory.

▼ Prussia returned 235 deputies out of a total of 397 in the *Reichstag*.

▼ The Prussian aristocracy enjoyed a dominant position in the political, military and administrative structure of the *Reich*.

However, for all the complaints about a 'Prussianisation' of Germany, the identity of 'old Prussia' was significantly diluted by its integration into the *Reich*. Prussia could no longer be governed without consideration of the wider interests of Germany. Non-Prussians held important posts in government both in the *Reich* as a whole and also in Prussia.

> **Q** To what extent was Bismarck a dictator?

Figure 3 Bismarck in 1877

c) Bismarck as Imperial Chancellor

After 1871 Bismarck was Prussian Prime Minister and Foreign Minister and *Reich* Chancellor. As such, he exercised most of the powers ascribed to the crown in the constitution, including presiding over the *Bundesrat*. Bismarck's influence over William gave him an immensely strong position which he exploited. Loathing the existence of any rival authority, he ensured that other ministers were little more than senior clerks, carrying out his orders. There was no form of collective government and nothing which resembled an imperial cabinet. His reluctance to initiate subordinates into his thought processes and his mistrust of potential rivals, encouraged him to rely more and more on his son Herbert who was Secretary of State of the Foreign Office from 1886.

After 1871 Bismarck exerted a tight grip over all aspects of policy – foreign and domestic – in the *Reich* and in Prussia. So great was his influence that he is sometimes depicted as a dictator. However, there were practical and theoretical limitations to his power, especially in domestic affairs. The fact that Germany was a federal state reduced his influence. The *Reichstag* was another constraint. His long absences from Berlin (he liked to spend time on his country estates) and his poor health (often stomach troubles arising from over-eating and over-drinking) reduced his control of day-to-day decision-making. Many contemporaries viewed him with awe – a legend in his own lifetime. Recent historians have often been less impressed. They have represented him as more a lucky opportunist than a master-planner. They have also drawn attention to his less desirable attributes – his vindictiveness, his intolerance of criticism, and his frequent use of threats and bullying to get his way. It should be said that these methods did not always succeed. After 1871 he was persistently thwarted in his efforts to shape the domestic developments of the *Reich*.

d) How democratic was Germany?

Bismarck was anxious for political power in Germany to remain in traditional hands – in those of the emperor, his army officers, his ministers – and particularly with Bismarck himself. Arguably the constitution gave little opportunity for the exercise of democracy. Bismarck regarded the *Reichstag* with some disdain – as a collection of squabbling politicians who did not reflect popular opinion. However, the *Reichstag* could withhold consent to legislation and money bills. It was thus able to exert influence – if only of a negative kind. The urgent need for legislation to establish an economic and legal framework for the Empire ensured it played a significant role. Universal male suffrage promoted the development of mass political parties with popular appeal. (See Table 2.) While these parties were in no position to form governments, Bismarck could not afford to ignore them. Although under no constitutional obligation to adopt policies approved by the *Reichstag*, he did need to secure support for his own legislative proposals. Bismarck grudgingly accepted that the cooperation of a popularly elected body was almost essential for the smooth running of a modern state. Characteristically, however, he was only ready to work with the *Reichstag* on condition that it accepted his proposals or some compromise acceptable to him. If agreement could not be reached, he usually dissolved the *Reichstag* and called for fresh elections. He was prepared to use all the means at his disposal, not least the exploitation of international crises, to swing public opinion in elections to secure the passage of contentious legislation.

Reichstag politicians have often been criticised by historians for failing to do more to exploit their potential power. However, they faced a difficult task. The balance of power was tilted sharply in favour of the monarchy and most Germans remained deeply respectful of authority, believing that it was right and proper that the emperor, or his chancellor, should rule. There was no widespread conviction that power should be in the hands of the *Reichstag*. Political parties did not expect to be the government. The most that they hoped for was that the *Reichstag* would have some influence on government decisions. Perhaps these hopes were realised. What is striking is how troublesome the *Reichstag* was for Bismarck, criticising and often thwarting his plans. Indeed, historians may have overemphasised the way that the *Reichstag* bowed to Bismarck and not emphasised enough the way that he bowed to *Reichstag* pressure. On several occasions in the 1880s he explored the possibility of changing the constitution – proof of the *Reichstag*'s influence. The *Reichstag* was thus neither a sovereign parliament nor simply a pliant instrument under Bismarck's control. It was something in between. It certainly acquired a genuine popular legitimacy and became a focal point for those whom Bismarck saw as 'enemies of the state' – Poles, Catholics and Socialists.

e) The role of the army

The army played an important role in the *Reich*, as it had done in Prussia, and generals had a huge influence on government policy. Officers owed personal loyalty to the emperor, not the state. The system of conscription ensured that all German men served for two to three years in the army. This gave the officers ample opportunity to build on the values already inculcated at school – discipline, pride in military institutions, and love of the fatherland. Given that the military budget was not subject to annual approval, the army was virtually independent of *Reichstag* control.

ACTIVITY

Brainstorm the points you might make to argue that Germany after 1871 was a) an authoritarian monarchy and b) a constitutional democracy.

German disunity

▽ The new *Reich* was a federal state. Each state had its own traditions. Each also had very real powers over education, justice, agriculture, religious matters and local government.
▽ Over 60 per cent of the population were Protestant but Catholicism was strong in Alsace-Lorraine, in south-west Germany, in the Rhineland and among the Poles.
▽ Ten per cent of the *Reich*'s population were non-German minorities.
▽ There were divisions between rich and poor.
▽ While the north and west was rapidly industrialising, the south and east remained predominantly rural.

	1870		1890
Population	41m.	Germany	49 m.
	32m.	Britain	38m.
	36m.	France	38m.
Coal (m. tons)	38	Germany	89
	118	Britain	184
	13	France	26
Steel (m. tons)	0.3	Germany	2.2
	0.6	Britain	3.6
	0.08	France	0.6
Iron Ore (m. tons)	2.9	Germany	8
	14	Britain	14
	2.6	France	3.5

Table 1 German production: 1870–90

f) German economic and social development

The results of the war against France provided a direct stimulus to the German economy. Alsace-Lorraine, for example, contained Europe's largest deposits of iron ore and production increased rapidly after 1871. The injection of the French indemnity payments into the German economy helped cause a spectacular if short-lived boom, especially in the building and railway industries. The boom assisted German banks which, in turn, provided capital for new industries such as electricity and chemicals. After 1873 the boom ended and some industries suffered hardship. Even so, industrial growth rate averaged about three per cent a year between 1873 and 1890. Coal production soared, steel production increased by some 70 per cent and the railway network doubled.

Germany's population grew from 41 million in 1871 to 49 million by 1890. Towns and cities experienced the greatest growth. Many doubled – or trebled – in size, thanks largely to migration from rural areas. Some areas, like Bavaria, remained in a sort of agrarian time-warp while others, like the Ruhr, experienced rapid industrialisation.

German society, despite all the economic changes, seems to have remained divided along traditional class lines. What mobility there was tended to be within a class rather than movements between different classes. The higher levels of the civil service and the army remained predominantly the preserve of the nobility. The most direct threat to the nobility's supremacy came from wealthy industrialists

GERMAN EDUCATION

Germany's educational system is often seen as the basis for her economic success. In terms of elementary education she led the world. Her rate of illiteracy in the 1870s was just over 1 per cent, compared with 33 per cent in Britain. Schools were used to inculcate not just literacy, but also nationalist sentiments and respect for authority.

who generally tried to emulate, rather than supersede, the nobles. While the middle classes were expanding, the mass of the population were agricultural or industrial workers. For many farm labourers life was hard and industrial employment seemed an attractive option. Thus there was a drift to the cities, even though the living and working conditions of the proletariat remained poor.

ISSUE:
How successful was Bismarck in domestic terms?

2 Bismarck's domestic policy

a) The Liberal era (1871–8)?

It is customary to divide Bismarck's domestic policies into two quite distinct phases: a 'Liberal era' pre-1879; and a conservative era thereafter. This is too simplistic. Recent research has shown that the 'turning point' in 1878–9 was not as sudden, drastic or as important as was once imagined. After 1871 Bismarck, who claimed to stand above party or sectional interest, needed a parliamentary majority. Although he was by no means a true liberal, Bismarck had little alternative but to work with the National Liberals – easily the strongest party in the *Reichstag* for most of the 1870s. (See Table 2.) In some respects the solid middle-class National Liberals were ideal allies. Most of them applauded Bismarck's success in creating a united Germany (their main aim) and were eager to help him consolidate national unity. In the 1870s a great deal of useful legislation was passed. A national system of currency was introduced, a *Reichsbank* was created, all internal tariffs were abolished and there was much legal standardisation. The National Liberals and Bismarck also united against the Catholic Church (see pages 181–84).

However, relations between Bismarck and the National Liberals were always uneasy. Politically Bismarck did not agree with their hopes for the extension of parliamentary government. He disliked having to rely on them to ensure the passage of legislation and became increasingly irritated as they opposed a number of his proposals. The army budget was a particular bone of contention. In 1867 Bismarck and the National Liberals agreed that the military budget should remain at a fixed level outside *Reichstag* control until 1872. During the Franco-Prussian War the fixed budget was extended until 1874. In 1874 Bismarck presented a law which laid down that an army of over 400,000 men would be automatically financed by federal expenditure. Given that 80 per cent of all federal expenditure was spent on the army, this threatened to seriously reduce the *Reichstag's* monetary powers. The measure was thus opposed by the National Liberals. Bismarck accused them of trying to undermine German military strength and threatened to call new elections. The National Liberals shrank from a constitutional conflict

Table 2 Germany's political parties

Party	Number of seats in *Reichstag* (1871–90)							
	1871	1874	1877	1878	1881	1884	1887	1890
The National Liberals	125	155	128	99	47	51	99	42
	The main support for this party came from the Protestant middle class. The party had two principal aims: (a) the creation of a strong nation-state and (b) the encouragement of a liberal constitutional state; the former in practice being the priority. Until 1878 the National Liberals were Bismarck's most reliable *Reichstag* allies.							
The Centre Party	63	91	93	94	100	99	98	106
	This party defended the interests of the Catholic Church.							
The Social Democratic Party	2	9	12	9	12	24	11	35
	Having close links with the trade unions, this was predominantly a working-class party. Its socialist programme aimed to fight for social reforms.							
The German Conservative Party	57	22	40	59	50	78	80	73
	This party was mainly composed of Prussian landowners. Sceptical about the unification of Germany, it came to support Bismarck after 1878.							
The Free Conservatives	37	33	38	57	28	28	41	20
	Drawn from a wider geographical and social base than the German Conservatives, the party contained not just landowners but also industrialists and professional and commercial interests. It offered Bismarck steady support.							
The Progressives	47	50	52	39	115	74	32	76
	A liberal party but one which, unlike the National Liberals, remained opposed to Bismarck's pursuit of a powerful nation-state at the expense of liberal constitutional principles.							

similar to that which had brought Bismarck to power in 1862. A compromise was reached. The military budget was fixed for seven years at a time, rather than voted for annually or fixed permanently. This was a major diminution of the *Reichstag's* power.

b) The *Kulturkampf*

Much of the 1870s was dominated by Bismarck's clash with the Catholic Church – the *Kulturkampf* – the 'struggle for culture' or the 'struggle for civilisation'. There were a number of reasons for this clash.

▼ Two thirds of Germans, mainly those in Prussia and the north were Protestant. One third – Poles, Rhinelanders and southern Germans – were Catholic.

THE NATIONAL MINORITIES

Bismarck regarded the national minorities – the Danes, French and Poles – as potential 'enemies of the State'. He thus sought to reduce their political and social influence.

▼ The Polish language was outlawed in education and law courts.

▼ Alsace-Lorraine was not granted full autonomy after 1871. Instead it became a special region under direct imperial rule with a governor and Prussian civil servants. The German language was imposed in schools and local administration. However, Bismarck did not rely solely on repression. Those French people who were unhappy with German rule were allowed to leave. 400,000 had done so by 1914. The German governors of Alsace-Lorraine made great efforts to conciliate the French-speaking provinces.

The national minorities problem was not solved. However, it does seem that the national minorities' alienation from the *Reich* probably lessened over the years. School, conscription and everyday experience 'Germanised' many minorities.

Why did Bismarck launch the *Kulturkampf*?

▼ In the late 19th century Church and State came into conflict in several countries. In 1864 Pope Pius IX's *Syllabus of Errors* had condemned as erroneous every major principle for which liberals stood. In 1870 the Vatican Council enunciated the doctrine of papal infallibility. This ruled that papal pronouncements on matters of faith and morals could not be questioned. These measures aroused great alarm in liberal circles. It seemed that Pius had declared moral war. Many of the most enlightened men of the time believed that the future of mankind was at stake. It seemed certain that militant Catholicism would interfere in the domestic affairs of states and support reactionary causes.

▼ German Catholics, aware that they were a minority in an essentially Protestant state, formed their own party – the Centre Party – in 1870. In 1871 this party won 57 seats and became the second largest party in the *Reichstag*. It was unique among German parties in drawing its support from all social strata. The party favoured greater self-rule for the component states of the *Reich*. It also objected to State interference in the Catholic Church's traditional sphere of influence – the education system.

▼ Bismarck, a sincere Protestant, had little affection for Catholicism and soon he came to view the Catholic minority with suspicion. His greatest concern in domestic policy was to unify and consolidate the new *Reich*. By 1871 he had become convinced that the Centre was a sectarian party bent on encouraging civil disobedience among Catholics whenever the policies of the State conflicted with those of the Church. His suspicions deepened when he observed how rapidly the party became a rallying point for opponents of the Empire. Bismarck tried repeatedly to persuade the Vatican and the German bishops to withdraw support from the Centre Party. Only in 1872, when it was clear that these attempts had failed, did he sever diplomatic relations with the Vatican and intensify the campaign against the Catholic Church, with the intention of subordinating Church to State. Whether he really believed that the anti-Prussian political alignment in the *Reichstag* was a Vatican-inspired conspiracy of malcontents bent on destroying the *Reich* is debateable. But the *Kulturkampf* was widely understood at the time to be a war against internal opponents of unification.

▼ It may be that the *Kulturkampf* was little more than a calculated political ploy on Bismarck's part: to put himself at the head of a popular, Protestant crusade which would be widely supported by the National Liberals and by the conservative elites in Prussia. It certainly enabled him to work closely with the National Liberals in the 1870s. They believed the *Kulturkampf* was a battle for progress against the forces of reaction.

While the *Kulturkampf* was centred on Prussia, its effects were felt thoughout the *Reich* and legislation against the Church was passed by both the Prussian *Landtag* and the *Reichstag*. In 1872 Catholic schools were brought directly under the supervision of the State. In 1872 the

Reichstag forbade the Jesuit order, whose members had always been great teachers and supporters of papal authority, to set up establishments in Germany and empowered state governments to expel individual Jesuits. In May 1873 Dr Falk, the Prussian Minister of Religion and Education, introduced a package of measures known as the May Laws. These aimed to bring the Catholic Church under State control. All candidates for the priesthood now had to attend a secular university before commencing training, and all religious appointments became subject to state approval. In 1874 obligatory civil marriage was introduced in Prussia. Clergy could be fined, imprisoned and expelled if they failed to comply with the May Laws. In 1875 the *Kulturkampf* reached a climax with laws empowering Prussia to suspend subsidies to the Church in dioceses or parishes where the clergy resisted the new legislation and all religious orders, except nursing orders, were dissolved. The legislation was enforced vigorously in Prussia by Falk. By 1876 all but two of the 12 Prussian Catholic bishops were in exile or under house arrest and more than 1,000 priests were suspended from their posts.

The results of the *Kulturkampf* were not at all what Bismarck had hoped. Attempts to repress Catholicism met with considerable opposition in Catholic areas. Only 30 out of 10,000 Prussian Catholic priests submitted to the May Laws. Catholic communities sheltered defiant priests, fought to resist discriminatory measures and fiercely maintained their religious culture and identity. Indeed, it was soon clear that the Church throve on persecution. Bismarck's hope of destroying the Centre Party backfired: the *Kulturkampf* strengthened rather than weakened his political opponents. In 1871 the Centre won 58 seats: in 1874 it won 91 seats. Bismarck's plan to head a popular Protestant crusade also failed to materialise. Protestants opposed some of the *Kulturkampf* legislation because it limited the influence of the Protestant – as well as the Catholic – Church in education.

By 1878 Bismarck accepted that the *Kulturkampf* had failed. By opening up a rift between the *Reich* and its Catholic subjects, it had increased disunity, not removed it. Anxious to have the Centre Party on his side against a potentially worse enemy – Socialism – he was ready to cut his losses and end the *Kulturkampf*. His opportunity came with the death of Pope Pius IX in 1878. Pius's successor Leo XIII was conciliatory and direct negotiations led to improved relations between Bismarck and the Catholic Church. Falk was symbolically dismissed in 1879 and some of the anti-Catholic measures were repealed: exiled clergy, for example, were allowed to return. However, the Catholic Church did not win a complete victory. Many of the May Laws remained in force: for example, civil marriage remained compulsory, Jesuits were forbidden to enter Germany, and the State continued to oversee all permanent Church appointments. Having suffered a

THE OLD CATHOLICS
Some 5,000 Catholics – they were known as 'Old Catholics' – refused to accept the decree on papal infallibility and broke with the Church. When Old Catholic teachers and professors were dismissed by Catholic bishops, Bismarck had an excellent excuse to attack the Catholic Church. Maintaining that the Prussian government was committed to the principle of religious toleration, he condemned the actions of the Catholic Church in a series of newspaper articles in 1872. This marked the start of the *Kulturkampf*.

How successful was the *Kulturkampf*?

defeat, Bismarck withdrew from a dangerous battlefield. Typically, he sought to turn failure to advantage, by henceforward harnessing Catholic political power in the *Reichstag* to the support of conservative, protectionist and anti-Socialist measures.

c) Economic protectionism

In the early 1870s Bismarck left economic matters in the hands of Delbrück, a capable administrator who continued the free trade policies of the *Zollverein*. Support for free trade was an essential principle of most National Liberals. In 1879, however, Bismarck ditched both free trade and the National Liberals. Aligning himself with the Conservative and Centre parties, he supported the introduction of tariffs, or customs duties, to protect German industry and farming. Historians continue to debate his motives. Some think he acted simply out of political opportunism. Others, more convincingly, argue that he believed protectionism to be in the best economic interests of the *Reich*. As early as 1877 Bismarck had tried to persuade National Liberals to abandon their opposition to tariff protection.

What were the economic and financial advantages of protectionism?

▼ In the late 1870s German agriculture suffered from the effects of a series of bad harvests and from the importation of cheap wheat from the USA and Russia. As the price of wheat fell, German farmers suffered. As a landowner himself, Bismarck understood the dangers of a prolonged agrarian depression.

▼ Bismarck feared that if Germany was reliant on foreign grain, she would be seriously weakened in time of war. Protectionism would aid German self-sufficiency.

▼ After 1873 industry experienced a difficult period. The slow-down in growth helped to produce a crisis of confidence in economic liberalism. Industrialists and workers looked to the government to protect their interests and alleviate their distress.

▼ The adoption of protective tariffs by France, Russia and Austria-Hungary in the late 1870s seemed to make it all the more desirable to follow suit.

▼ The federal government's revenue, raised from customs duties and indirect taxation, was proving woefully inadequate to cover the growing costs of armaments and administration. In order to make up the deficit, supplementary payments were made by individual states, a situation Bismarck found distasteful. He hoped that new tariffs would give the federal government a valuable extra source of income ensuring it was financially independent of both the states and the *Reichstag*.

What were the political advantages of supporting protectionism?

▼ By the late 1870s German landowners and industrialists were clamouring for protective tariffs. By espousing protectionist policies, Bismarck could win influential support.

▼ Bismarck and the National Liberals had never been very friendly. The National Liberals irritated Bismarck with their insistence on parliamentary rights and refusal to pass anti-Socialist laws.

▼ In the 1878 elections, the National Liberals lost some 30 seats. The combined strength of the two Conservative parties was now sufficient to outvote them in the *Reichstag*. In pursuing the protectionist case – popular with the Conservatives – Bismarck saw his chance to break with the National Liberals and broaden his political support.

▼ The tactical withdrawal that ended the *Kulturkampf* provided Bismarck with the opportunity to make some sweeping changes in his system of political alliances and to introduce a note of greater conservatism into his domestic policies.

By 1879 an all-party association for tariff reform, made up mostly of Conservatives and Centre Party members, had a majority in the *Reichstag*. Bismarck now introduced a general tariff bill. He addressed the *Reichstag* in May 1879 as follows:

> The only country [which persists in a policy of free trade] is England, and that will not last long. France and America have departed completely from this line; Austria instead of lowering her tariffs has made them higher; Russia has done the same...Therefore to be alone the dupe of an honourable conviction cannot be expected from Germany for ever. By opening wide the doors of our state to the imports of foreign countries, we have become the dumping ground for the production of those countries...Since we have become swamped by the surplus production of foreign nations, our prices have been depressed; and the development of our industries and our entire economic position has suffered in consequence. Let us finally close our doors and erect some barriers...in order to reserve for German industries at least the home market, which because of German good nature, has been exploited by foreigners...I see that those countries which have adopted protection are prospering, and that those countries which have free trade are deteriorating.

ACTIVITY

Summarise the case in favour of abandoning free trade argued by Bismarck.

In July 1879 a tariff bill passed through the *Reichstag* and duties were imposed on imports. The political results were far-reaching. Bismarck had now firmly committed himself to the Conservative camp. The National Liberal party splintered. Those who still believed in free trade and parliamentary government broke away, eventually uniting with the Progressives to form a new radical party in 1884. Other National Liberals remained loyal to Bismarck but he was no longer dependent on their backing. In that sense the 'Liberal era' was effectively at an end.

d) Bismarck and socialism

Bismarck was hostile to socialists regarding them as anarchic, revolutionary and little better than criminals. As with Catholicism, he feared the international appeal of socialist ideology. How could one be loyal both to an international organisation and to one's own country? Rather than underestimating the enemy, as with the *Kulturkampf*, it may be that he overestimated the socialist threat. Socialists were not as strong nor as revolutionary as he feared and they liked to appear. However, his fears were rational. Socialism was a threat to the kind of society Bismarck intended to maintain. Socialists did preach class warfare. Moreover, socialist support was growing. The Social Democrat party won 2 seats in the *Reichstag* in 1871: in 1877 it had 12 seats and won nearly 500,000 votes.

In 1876 Bismarck tried to pass a bill preventing the publication of socialist propaganda. It was defeated. Other measures to prosecute the SDP also failed to get through the *Reichstag*. In May 1878 an anarchist tried to assassinate Emperor William I. The would-be assassin had no proven association with the SDP but Bismarck, like many of his contemporaries, drew no clear distinction between anarchism and socialism and saw the murder attempt as part of a 'red' conspiracy. But his efforts to push through a bill against socialism were defeated by National Liberal and Centre Party members, concerned about civil liberties. A week later there was a second attempt on William's life which resulted in the Emperor being seriously wounded. Again the would-be assassin had no direct SDP link. Bismarck criticised the National Liberals for failing to pass the anti-socialist bill which might have protected the Emperor and, scenting political advantage, dissolved the *Reichstag*. His manoeuvre succeeded. The electorate, deeply shocked by the murder attempts, blamed the SDP and the National Liberals. The SDP vote fell from 493,000 in 1877 to 312,000 while the National Liberals lost 130,000 votes and 29 seats. Only by supporting anti-socialist legislation during the election campaign did they save themselves from a heavier defeat. The two Conservative parties gained 38 seats.

Bismarck now got his way in the new *Reichstag*. An anti-socialist bill, supported by Conservatives and most National Liberals, was passed in October 1878. Socialist organisations, including trade unions, were banned, their meetings were broken up and their publications outlawed. Between 1878–90 some 1,500 socialists were imprisoned. However, the anti-socialist law, far from eliminating socialism, served to rally the faithful and fortify them in their beliefs. The SDP simply went underground. Moreover, the law did not prevent SDP members from standing for election and speaking freely in both the *Reichstag* and state legislatures. After the dip in 1878, the SDP won increasing support. By 1890 it had over a million voters and 35 seats. Well-disciplined and highly-organised, it became a model for other European socialist parties. In short, Bismarck's attack on socialism was no more successful than his attack on the Catholic Church. His repressive measures may have helped increase support for the SDP and ensured that moderate and revolutionary socialist factions remained united.

e) State socialism

Bismarck did not only use repression in his efforts to destroy socialism. He hoped to wean the working classes from socialism by introducing various welfare (state socialism) measures, designed to assist German workers at times of need. These measures may not have been as cynical as some of Bismarck's critics have implied. A devout Christian, Bismarck was conscious of a moral obligation to aid those in need. There was a strong paternalist tradition in Prussia and other parts of Germany, and a general belief that one of the State's most important moral objectives was the promotion of the material well-being of its citizens. Bismarck, however, also hoped to win the support of the workers, thus cutting the ground from beneath the feet of the socialists. In a speech to the *Reichstag* in 1881 he said:

> A beginning must be made with the task of reconciling the labouring classes with the State. A remedy cannot be sought only through the repression of socialist excesses. It is necessary to have a definite advancement in the welfare of the working classes. The matter of the first importance is the care of those workers who are incapable of earning a living. Previous provision for guarding workers against the risk of falling into helplessness through incapacity caused by accident or age have not proved adequate, and the inadequacy of such provisions has been a main contributing cause driving the working classes to seek help by joining the Social Democratic movement. Whoever has a pension assured to him for his old age is more contented and easier to manage than a man who has none.

STATE SOCIALISM
1883: sickness insurance for up to 13 weeks' sick pay was introduced for three million workers and their families. The cost was to be borne jointly by employers and workers.
1884: accident insurance was introduced for injured workers. This was financed wholly by the employers.
1889: old age pensions were made available to people reaching the age of 70. This was paid for by workers, employers and the State.

These schemes added up to the most far-reaching system of social welfare introduced by any state in the late 19th century. Indeed, Bismarck's welfare provision became a model of social provision for other countries. Many historians regard 'state socialism' as his most important legacy. However, his hopes that the working class could be won over by state socialism were not fully realised. Many workers continued to labour under harsh conditions and while such conditions persisted, the Social Democrats were assured of a future. Bismarck, believing that employers must control their factories, opposed demands for state intervention to regulate working hours, limit child and female employment, and improve working conditions. Nevertheless, 'state socialism' probably did make German workers 'more contented and easier to manage'.

Figure 4 Punch cartoon 1873

3 Bismarck's foreign policy

" AU REVOIR!"

a) Bismarck's aims

In Bismarck's view, Germany was a 'satiated power' after 1871 without further territorial ambitions. Any attempt to disrupt the existing order of things by extending Germany's frontiers in any direction would unite the other great powers against her. Convinced that further wars could only threaten the security of the *Reich*, his main aim was to maintain peace. France seemed the main threat to peace. She would have resented her defeat in 1870–1 under any circumstances. The loss of Alsace-Lorraine merely sharpened the edge of that resentment. Many Frenchmen wanted revenge. France without allies did not pose a serious danger to Germany since Bismarck was confident that the German army could defeat her again if necessary. His main fear was that France might ally with either Russia or Austria. Germany might then have to fight a war on two fronts. He was determined to avoid this possibility by isolating France and remaining on good terms with both Russia and Austria. The main problem was that there was always the possibility of friction between Austria and Russia over the Balkans, where their interests were at variance.

The problem of the Balkans

The Balkans, the most troublesome area of Europe, presented major problems for Bismarck. The Turkish government's authority in many Balkan areas was only nominal. Peoples of various races and religions coexisted in a state of mutual animosity. The Slav peoples were becoming fiercely nationalistic. Russia sought to assist the Slavs to obtain independence from Turkey. As leader of the Orthodox Church, the Tsar felt a moral obligation to aid Christian Slavs if their Muslim rulers treated them too oppressively. Russia also sought to profit from Turkey's weakness. In particular, it hoped to win control of the Straits. Austria was opposed to the expansion of Russian power so close to her territories. In addition, Russia's encouragement of Slav nationalism could serve as a dangerous example to national groups within the Habsburg Empire. Austria thus sought to maintain the Ottoman Empire. She feared that if the multinational Ottoman Empire collapsed, her own similarly multinational empire might follow. Bismarck had no territorial ambitions in the Balkans: he once remarked that the area was not worth 'the healthy bones of a single Pomeranian musketeer'. However, if Austria and Russia fell out over the Balkans, Germany might have to choose between them. The fear was that the rejected suitor would find a willing ally in France.

Why were the Balkans a problem for Bismarck?

Although Bismarck faced problems, he also had a strong hand. He enjoyed far more control in the handling of foreign affairs than in domestic matters. Germany was the greatest military power in Europe and her friendship was eagerly sought by Austria and Russia, in part because of their growing antagonism in the Balkans.

THE 1875 WAR SCARE

In the early 1870s France made determined efforts to throw off the effects of defeat. Her rapid military reorganisation and the prompt repayment of the war indemnity, ensuring the riddance of the German army of occupation by 1873, surprised and alarmed Bismarck. In 1875 he reacted to French recovery and rearmament by provoking a diplomatic crisis. He prohibited the export of horses to France and in April the *Berlin Post* carried an article 'Is war in sight'? Bismarck expected that the other powers would similarly put pressure on France, discouraging her from further military expansion. He miscalculated. Britain and Russia warned Germany of her provocative actions, forcing him to offer assurances that Germany was not contemplating a war against France. The crisis thus ended in a diplomatic victory for France. Britain and Russia made it clear they would not allow Germany to destroy France.

b) The Three Emperors' League

Austria-Hungary, fearing a German-Russian agreement, took the initiative in pressing for a three emperors' alliance. Following a meeting in 1872, the Emperors of Germany, Russia and Austria reached an agreement known as the Three Emperors' League or *Dreikaiserbund*. Given that the three powers found it hard to reach agreement on any concrete objectives, the terms were somewhat vague. The Emperors identified republicanism and socialism as common enemies and promised to consult each other on matters of common interest or if a third power disturbed Europe's peace. While this was far from a cunning plan on Bismarck's part, it very much suited his purpose.

c) The Balkan crisis 1875–8

In 1875 Christian peasants in Bosnia and Herzegovina revolted against Turkish rule. In April 1876 the revolt spread to Bulgaria and in July Montenegro and Serbia declared war on Turkey. The Balkan crisis could easily damage Austro-Russian relations. Thousands of Russian volunteers joined the Serbian army amidst a wave of popular pro-Slavonic fervour. There was thus pressure for Russian intervention in the Balkans. It was likely that Austria would oppose anything which smacked of Russian expansionism. Bismarck was thus concerned: he might have to choose between his *Dreikaiserbund* partners. Determined to avoid taking sides, he had somehow to convince both Austria and Russia of Germany's good will, prevent them from quarrelling, and encourage them to find a solution to the problem.

Bismarck was helped by the fact that Tsar Alexander II and his Foreign Minister Gorchakov had no wish to find themselves in a Crimean situation again – at war with Turkey and isolated. Gorchakov, recognising that Turkey's fate concerned all the great powers (not least Britain), preferred international discussion to unilateral action. Austro-Hungarian Foreign Minister Andrassy, aware that German support was unlikely in the event of a clash with Russia, tried to collaborate with Gorchakov in an attempt to end – or at least limit the effects of – the crisis. In July the two agreed that if Turkey won she should be prevented from altering the status of Serbia and Montenegro. If she lost, they agreed to divide the spoils. Austria would get Bosnia-Herzegovina: Greece, Serbia and Montenegro would gain territory; Bulgaria, Rumelia and Albania would be made autonomous; and Russia would regain South Bessarabia.

However, Turkish atrocities in 1876 in Bulgaria (some 10,000 Bulgarians were allegedly killed) changed the situation. The atrocities stirred public opinion in both Britain and Russia with important effects. In Britain Disraeli's government was temporarily prevented from pursuing the traditional British policy of supporting Turkey against Russia. In Russia the sufferings of the Bulgarians and the defeat of Serbian and Montenegrin forces enflamed Pan-Slavist sentiment to such an extent that the Tsarist government found itself under mounting pressure to intervene on the side of the Balkan rebels. In November 1876 Tsar Alexander II declared that if his 'just demands' for the protection of Balkan Christians were not agreed to by Turkey, and the other great powers would not support him, then he was prepared to act independently. Russian and Austrian policy was suddenly out of step and both turned to Germany for support. In December 1876 the Tsar asked for an assurance of German neutrality in the event of an Austro-Russian war. Bismarck was evasive. He similarly refused Andrassy's offer of an Austro-German alliance against Russia.

In January 1877 Russia managed to buy Austrian neutrality in the event of a Russo-Turkish war by agreeing that Austria would receive Bosnia-Herzegovina, and promising that no large state would be set up in the Balkans. In April Russia declared war on Turkey. Alexander stated that his sole aim was 'the amelioration and security of the status of the oppressed Christian population of Turkey'. Courageous Turkish defence of the fortress of Plevna deprived Russia of a quick victory. It also caused British opinion to swing back in favour of the heroic Turks. Plevna finally fell in December 1877 and the Russians were able to resume their advance. By January 1878 they threatened Constantinople. In March they imposed the severe San Stefano Treaty on the Turks. This treaty significantly improved Russia's position in the Balkans.

The San Stefano treaty confirmed Andrassy's worst fears that he had been duped. The proposal to create a Big Bulgaria was seen as a cynical Russian attempt to establish a Balkan client state with a strategically-important Aegean coastline. Austria mobilised her army (but suggested a peace conference). Britain summoned troops from India and despatched the fleet to Turkish waters. Faced with Austro-British hostility and the threat of a major war, which she was in no economic or military state to fight, Russia agreed to an international conference to revise the peace terms. Bismarck, somewhat reluctantly, offered his services as the 'honest broker'. He realised he was likely to be blamed by one or the other, or even by both, of his allies for their disappointments.

> ### THE TREATY OF SAN STEFANO
> ▼ European Turkey was to be reduced to small unconnected territories by the creation of a Big Bulgaria under Russian occupation for two years.
> ▼ Turkey ceded Kars and Batum on the eastern shore of the Black Sea to Russia.
> ▼ Serbia, Montenegro and Romania were to be fully independent of Turkey.
> ▼ There was no mention of Austria-Hungary taking Bosnia-Herzegovina.

d) The Congress of Berlin: June–July 1878

The fact that the Congress – the most important meeting of the powers since 1856 – took place in Berlin was a sign of Germany's new power and Bismarck's prestige. Much preparatory work had been done before the Congress met.
▼ Russia had agreed to reduce the size of Bulgaria.
▼ Britain had agreed to guarantee Turkey's security in exchange for the island of Cyprus.

Figure 5 The Balkans 1878

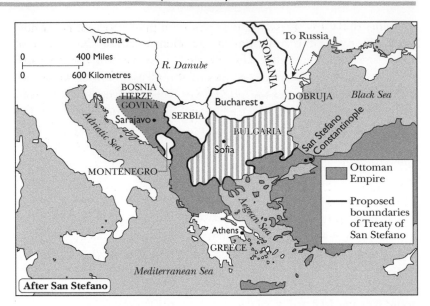

After San Stefano

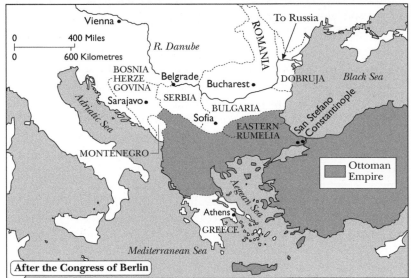

After the Congress of Berlin

THE TREATY OF BERLIN

▼ Big Bulgaria was divided into three. The northern part, Bulgaria proper, was granted complete independence under Russian supervision. To the south the province of Eastern Rumelia was to have a form of self-government under Turkish suzerainty. The third part – Macedonia – was returned to Turkish rule.

▼ Russia recovered southern Bessarabia from Romania, and gained Batum, a valuable port on the eastern edge of the Black Sea, from Turkey.

▼ Austria was to occupy Bosnia-Herzegovina.

▼ Britain gained Cyprus.

▼ The Sultan had promised to introduce reforms.

▼ Britain had agreed to support Austria's claims to occupy Bosnia-Herzegovina.

Despite these preliminary accords, the Congress was not all plain sailing. At critical moments, only Bismarck's energetic intervention saved the day.

Perhaps Britain had best reason to be pleased with the Treaty of Berlin. Disraeli's firm stand had checked Russia and Cyprus was a useful acquisition. He returned home proclaiming he had achieved 'peace with honour'. Russia, by contrast, felt she had suffered a humiliating diplomatic defeat. She had done all the fighting and then seen Britain and Austria-Hungary get away with some major spoils.

Critics of the Congress of Berlin point out that it postponed rather than solved most of the Balkan problems. The Sultan evaded implementing serious reforms. The Eastern Rumelia situation was soon to cause another crisis. The hopes of the Serbs, Romanians, Bulgars and Greeks were disappointed. Moreover, the territorial arrangements, particularly Austria's occupation of Bosnia, bitterly resented by both Turks and Serbs, contained the seeds of future Balkan wars. However, the Congress at least reasserted the concept that the fate of Turkey was a matter of concern to all the powers and could not be decided by one alone as Russia had tried to do. The Treaty of Berlin, albeit a temporary solution to the Eastern Question, did check Russian dominance of the Balkans without a war among the great powers.

For Bismarck the Congress was a mixed blessing. His main desire – that of keeping peace – had been achieved. However, Russia blamed him for her diplomatic defeat. The Pan-Slavist press was bitterly critical and Alexander II described the Congress as 'a coalition of the European powers against Russia under the leadership of Prince Bismarck'. Russo-German relations quickly deteriorated. The introduction of German protective tariffs in 1879 did not help matters, given Russia's dependence on wheat exports to Germany. By 1878–9 the *Dreikaiserbund* was well and truly dead. Bismarck was now in a potentially dangerous position. There was suddenly the real possibility of a Franco-Russian alliance.

e) The Dual Alliance

In 1878–9 it seemed to Bismarck that Germany was faced with the stark choice of continuing Russian hostility or allying with her. An alliance would sacrifice his relationship with Austria and risk enmity with Britain. His response to the pressure from Russia was to put out feelers for an alliance with Austria. In October 1879 Bismarck and Andrassy agreed to the Dual Alliance. If Germany or Austria was at war with a third power, the other partner would remain neutral unless Russia intervened. The secret alliance was to last five years. However, the option to renew the arrangement was taken up so that it became the cornerstone of German foreign policy, lasting until 1918. The Dual Alliance was something of a 'landmark'. Previous treaties had usually been concluded on the eve of wars. This was a peacetime engagement. It encouraged other powers to negotiate similar treaties until all Europe was divided into pact and counter-pact.

> ## Why did Bismarck agree to the Dual Alliance?
>
> In his *Reminiscences* Bismarck described the Dual Alliance as the fruition of a grand design cherished since 1866. There is, in fact, no evidence that he had it in mind before 1879. In reality he acted on the spur of the moment to deal with an emergency situation.
> - ▼ The Dual Alliance provided Germany with an ally with whom she could weather the storm of Russian hostility.
> - ▼ Bismarck felt he could control Austria-Hungary more than he could control Russia.
> - ▼ An alliance with a fellow German power was likely to be more popular in Germany than an alliance with Russia. It helped to win Bismarck Centre Party support.
> - ▼ The Dual Alliance was only a temporary expedient to preserve the precarious balance of power in the Balkans and to compel a more friendly Russian attitude towards both Austria-Hungary and Germany. It was not a final choice between them. Bismarck never wavered in his belief that the '*entente à trois*' was Germany's best hope.

f) The Three Emperors' Alliance

Russia, alarmed at her isolation and not anxious to ally with republican France, soon turned back to Germany. However, more than 18 months elapsed before a new *Dreikaiserbund* was signed. This was partly due to problems arising from the death of Alexander II and the accession of Tsar Alexander III. Austria-Hungary was also opposed to the entire project. However, Andrassy finally yielded to Bismarck's pressure and in June 1881 the Three Emperors' Alliance was signed. It aimed at resolving Austro-Russian disputes in the Balkans and at reassuring Russia that she did not need to seek accommodation with France.

- ▼ If Russia, Germany or Austria were at war with another power, the others would remain neutral.
- ▼ The three powers agreed to keep the entrance to the Black Sea closed to foreign warships. Thus Britain would not be free to use the Straits whenever she wished.
- ▼ The three would not permit territorial changes in the Balkans without prior, mutual agreement.
- ▼ The Balkans were to be divided into 'spheres of influence'. Russian interests were recognised in the eastern portion, Austrian interests in the western. Austria acknowledged Russian ambitions to recreate a Big Bulgaria: Russia accepted Austria's right to annex Bosnia-Herzegovina.

Although Russia continued to resent the Dual Alliance, she was pleased with the new *Dreikaiserbund*. Her partners had written off half the Balkans and had committed themselves to Russia if she came to blows with Britain. Bismarck was also pleased. His confident assertion to Emperor William that Russia would return to the fold had come to pass and the conservative alliance was restored.

g) The Triple Alliance

Bismarck, hoping to divert French attention away from Alsace-Lorraine, encouraged France to embark on colonial expansion in Africa and Asia. This had the added advantage of alienating France from Britain. In 1881, with Bismarck's support, France seized Tunis. This angered Italy who had designs on the same territory. In 1881 Italy made overtures to Austria aimed at securing an alliance. Austria had little interest in the Italian bid for closer ties but Bismarck, although having a poor opinion of Italy's strength, saw its potential. Bringing Italy closer to the Dual Alliance would secure Austria's vulnerable southern flank and deprive France of a potential ally. Accordingly, in 1882 the Triple Alliance was signed.

▼ If any of the signatories were attacked by two or more powers, the others promised to lend assistance.

▼ In the event of a war between Austria and Russia, Italy would remain neutral.

▼ If France attacked Germany, Italy would provide support to her partner.

▼ If Italy were attacked by France, both Germany and Austria agreed to back her.

h) Bismarck and colonisation

In 1881 Bismarck declared: 'So long as I am Chancellor we shall pursue no colonial policy.' However, in 1884–5 Germany was suddenly to acquire a large overseas empire. Why did Bismarck change his mind?

▼ In the early 1880s colonialism became fashionable. Many European nations were interested in carving up Africa. Enthusiastic pressure groups sprang up agitating for colonies on economic grounds and as a sign of national greatness. The German Colonial Union, founded in 1882 with support from major industrialists, did much to interest German public opinion in overseas expansion. Within Germany there was concern about the consequences of protectionist policies. Trading companies were complaining of being squeezed out of parts of Africa by foreign rivals.

▼ Bismarck had good political reasons to support German colonialism. The 1884 elections were in the offing. He needed an issue that would weaken the liberal parties. Colonialism was a convenient stick with which to beat the Radicals and Socialists and to rally support. His ploy worked: the Radicals lost 38 seats in 1884.

▼ The absence of serious difficulties with either Russia or France enabled Bismarck to embark on an energetic colonial policy.

▼ Bismarck hoped that colonies might benefit the German economy by providing new markets and raw materials.

> ## THE SITUATION IN 1884
> An Austrian agreement with Serbia in 1881 turned the country virtually into an Austrian satellite. An agreement with Romania followed in 1883. Austria-Hungary and Germany undertook to defend Romania while Romania agreed to fight if Russia attacked Austria. The Three Emperors' Alliance was renewed in 1884. In 1884 Bismarck even managed to be on tolerably good terms with France. This was the zenith of Bismarck's 'system'.

FRANCO-GERMAN RELATIONS 1884–7

In the mid-1880s Bismarck seriously considered the possibility of a lasting reconciliation with France as the best way of avoiding war on two fronts. Active cooperation with France in the colonial field was the first step. By picking quarrels with Britain over German colonial claims, he aligned Germany on France's side. The Franco-German entente reached its high water mark at the Berlin Conference of 1884–5, called to regulate the affairs of Central Africa. However, *rapprochement* with France was short-lived. In 1886 General Boulanger became French war minister and talked of a war to recover Alsace-Lorraine. Franco-German relations quickly deteriorated. To meet the French threat, Bismarck called for a 10 per cent increase in the German army.

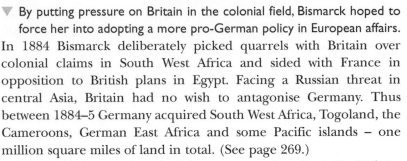

By putting pressure on Britain in the colonial field, Bismarck hoped to force her into adopting a more pro-German policy in European affairs. In 1884 Bismarck deliberately picked quarrels with Britain over colonial claims in South West Africa and sided with France in opposition to British plans in Egypt. Facing a Russian threat in central Asia, Britain had no wish to antagonise Germany. Thus between 1884–5 Germany acquired South West Africa, Togoland, the Cameroons, German East Africa and some Pacific islands – one million square miles of land in total. (See page 269.)

Bismarck's interest in colonial matters was short-lived. By 1887 he was resisting demands for further colonial expansion on the grounds of Germany's continental security. As relations with France and Russia deteriorated, he had no wish to alienate Britain. Thus he made substantial concessions to Britain when East Africa was partitioned in 1889. A German official observed that a 'good understanding with England means much more to Bismarck than the whole of east Africa'.

i) The Bulgarian crisis

A crisis in Bulgaria in 1885–6 shattered the Three Emperors' Alliance. Austria and Russia again squared up against each other in the Balkans. Bismarck refused to take sides in the dispute. He warned Austria that Germany would not help her. He also warned Russia that he would not abandon Austria.

As Austro-Russian relations worsened, Bismarck's fears of France revived. Nationalistic feelings in France were whipped up by General Boulanger. To make matters worse, Pan-Slav advisers, sympathetic to France and hostile to Germany, seemed to be exerting great influence in Russia. For domestic reasons, Bismarck may well have exaggerated the danger of war. However, he was clearly alarmed by the fear of a Franco-Russian alliance and felt that diplomatic precautions were needed to safeguard Germany.

In February 1887 the Triple Alliance was renewed on terms more favourable to Italy than those she obtained in 1882. In March 1887, with Bismarck's full backing, Britain, Austria and Italy signed the First Mediterranean Agreement, committing themselves to the maintenance of the *status quo* in the eastern Mediterranean – an action that was clearly anti-Russian.

j) The Reinsurance Treaty

How important was the Reinsurance Treaty?

Events now turned in Bismarck's favour. France, suddenly cautious, avoided Russian feelers and conservative diplomats again won the upper hand in St Petersburg. Tsar Alexander III accepted their argument that an agreement with Germany was better than nothing and in June 1887 the Reinsurance Treaty was signed. By this, if either

Russia or Germany were at war with a third power, the other would remain benevolently neutral. The provision would not apply to a war against Austria or France resulting from an attack on one of these two powers by either Russia or Germany. The Treaty, which did not contravene the Dual Alliance, can be seen as a masterpiece of diplomatic juggling on Bismarck's part. However, its importance should probably not be exaggerated. If not exactly a desperate stop-gap measure, it was hardly the cornerstone of Bismarck's system: indeed he seems to have attached little importance to it. It was simply another temporary expedient to remove his fears of a Franco-Russian alliance.

Russo-German relations did not improve much after 1887. Bismarck was partly to blame for this. In November 1887 he denied Russia access to the Berlin money market for loans to finance her industrialisation in order 'to remove the possibility that the Russians wage war against us at our cost'. In consequence, Russia simply turned to Paris where French financiers were eager to accommodate them. Nor did the Reinsurance Treaty necessarily reduce the danger of a clash over the Balkans. Indeed the Bulgarian situation continued to cause tension. Bismarck used all his influence to encourage Britain, Italy and Austria to sign the Second Mediterranean Agreement (December 1887), again guaranteeing the *status quo* in the Mediterranean and Near East. In February 1888 Bismarck published the Dual Alliance, partly to warn Russia that Germany would stand by Austria if it came to war and partly to restrain Austria by making it clear that Germany's obligations were limited to a defensive war. The publication coupled with rumours of the Mediterranean Agreement persuaded Russia to hold her hand and the Bulgarian crisis finally fizzled out.

BISMARCK'S FOREIGN POLICY

1871	Treaty of Frankfurt: Germany acquired Alsace-Lorraine;
1873	Three Emperors' League;
1875 –8	Balkan Crisis;
1878	Congress of Berlin;
1879	Dual Alliance;
1881	Three Emperors' Alliance;
1882	Triple Alliance;
1887	Reinsurance Treaty.

4 Bismarck's fall

a) Threats to Bismarck's position

ISSUE:
Why did Bismarck fall from power?

The late 1880s was a difficult period for Bismarck. Emperor William I was in his eighties and his advancing years cast a shadow over Bismarck's plans. If William died, Crown Prince Frederick, a man of liberal views who was married to the eldest daughter of Queen Victoria, would ascend the throne. It seemed likely that he would dismiss Bismarck and appoint a liberal chancellor. This would be welcome to the *Reichstag* where a majority was no longer in Bismarck's pocket.

b) William II and Bismarck

While William I lived Bismarck's hold on power was never in question. Their meetings were often stormy, but they understood each other. Usually William let Bismarck have his own way. William

THE ARMY GRANT

The friction between Bismarck and the *Reichstag* came to a head in 1887 over the renewal of the army grant or Septennates. The current Septennates were not due to expire until 1888 but the international situation alarmed the generals who pressed for an early renewal. Thus in late 1886 Bismarck asked the *Reichstag* to agree to substantial military increases. The *Reichstag* agreed but only on condition that in future it would be allowed to review military expenditure every three years. Bismarck was furious. 'The German army is an institution which cannot be dependent on short-lived *Reichstag* majorities,' he declared. Dissolving the *Reichstag*, he conjured up a picture of a revenge-seeking France, ready for war at any moment. Germany would remain in danger until the Septennates were passed and only the Conservatives and National Liberals could be relied upon to pass them. Bismarck's electoral strategem worked. The Conservatives and National Liberals won an absolute majority in 1887 and the Septennates were passed.

died in March 1888. He was succeeded by Frederick. Frederick, however, died from cancer only three months later. Frederick's 29-year-old son William II then became Emperor. Bismarck's position seemed secure again. He had cultivated the prince's friendship for several years and in public William expressed his admiration for Bismarck. But a great gulf separated the two, not least age. Treating William in a condescending manner, Bismarck assumed he would not involve himself much in matters of government. He underestimated William. Impatient, unstable, and ambitious, William was determined to rule as well as to reign, and resolved to dispense with Bismarck as soon as decently possible.

William and Bismarck were soon at odds over foreign policy. William questioned some of the basic assumptions on which Bismarck's diplomacy was based, especially the need to maintain links with Russia. They also disagreed over social policy. Unlike Bismarck, William was confident that he could win over the working class by a modest extension of the welfare system, including an end to child labour and Sunday working. Bismarck, by contrast, favoured further repression. Thus in 1889 he proposed to make the anti-socialist law permanent. William was not against renewing the law (he too feared socialism) but he wanted the measure watered down. Bismarck refused. He was then let down by the *Reichstag* which rejected his entire bill in January 1890. This was a sign that his political power was crumbling. In February 1890, with new *Reichstag* elections underway, William issued a proclamation promising new social legislation. The absence of Bismarck's countersignature from this proclamation, which he had bluntly refused to sign, caused a sensation. The election was a disaster for Bismarck. His Conservative and National Liberal allies lost 85 seats while the Radicals gained 46 seats and the Socialists won 24 seats. The 'opposition' was again in control of the *Reichstag*.

Bismarck was trapped between an emperor bent on having his own way and a hostile *Reichstag*. William refused to support his plans to reduce the *Reichstag*'s powers and in March the two quarrelled bitterly about the right of ministers to advise the monarch. At a stormy interview Bismarck nearly threw an inkpot at the Kaiser and then enraged him by letting him see a letter from Tsar Alexander III very disparaging of William's talents. William now sent Bismarck an ultimatum – resign or be dismissed. Three days later Bismarck sent a letter of resignation in which he justified his actions, claiming (wrongly) that the real difference between William and himself lay in the Kaiser's pursuit of an anti-Russian policy. This letter was not made public until after Bismarck's death. The official announcement implied that he had resigned for health reasons and that William had made every effort to persuade him to change his mind. In reality Bismarck retired with ill grace to write his memoirs and innumerable newspaper articles, invariably critical of William. Failing to exert any influence on policy, he was even heard to speak in favour of republicanism: kings, he said, were dangerous if they had real power.

c) How successful was Bismarck?

Few 19th-century figures have attracted so much attention and controversy as Bismarck. He had critics in his own time and has had many since. A few historians have claimed that his strategies and tactics were responsible for Wilhelmine and Nazi Germany. However, most contemporaries viewed, and many historians still view, him as a great statesman who achieved most of his aims, both pre- and post-1871. Defending himself against critics in 1880 he said: 'I have always acted according to the question, 'what is useful, advantageous and right for my fatherland'.' His admirers point out that no other German exerted so profound an influence on German history in the 19th century. Germany did not exist when he became Prussian chief minister in 1862. When he left office in 1890 it was Europe's strongest state. This did not happen by chance. It had much to do with his diplomatic prowess. It was unfortunate for both Europe and Germany that after 1890 his creation was in the hands of less skilful men.

▼ Working on Bismarck's Germany: 1871–90

How successful was Bismarck's domestic policy? His admirers claim:
▼ His policies helped to promote the consolidation and modernisation of Germany.
▼ The national minorities, Catholics and socialists were a threat to the *Reich*. While his campaigns against 'enemies of the State' were not successful, they were not total failures. Nor, in the context of the time, were his measures particularly repressive.
▼ For most of the 1870s he worked closely with the National Liberals, putting their – liberal – programme into place.
▼ He pioneered state socialism.
▼ His policies assisted Germany's economic development.
▼ The fact that he remained in power from 1871–90 is testimony to his political skills.
▼ While he did not approve of democracy, he did not – and could not – ignore the *Reichstag* which became a focus of German political life.
▼ He was not a dictator. His powers were far from absolute.
What points might his critics make?

Answering extended writing and essay questions on Bismarck's Germany: 1871–90

Consider the following question: How successful was Bismarck's foreign policy after 1871?

Bismarck's critics claim:

▼ He was responsible for France remaining embittered.

▼ He exaggerated the threat of a Franco-Russian alliance.

▼ His elaborate alliance system was fragile – little more than a form of crisis management.

▼ The Dual Alliance, far from being a means by which Germany could control Austria-Hungary, eventually dragged her into war in 1914.

▼ His acquisition of colonies had negative results. German colonial ambitions alienated Britain in the 1880s and more importantly thereafter when they became the basis for Germany's claim to be a world power. The colonies proved to be an expensive financial burden, costing the German taxpayer huge sums of money.

▼ His style – his frequent use of bluster and blackmail – created a legacy of distrust.

▼ His influence is often exaggerated. Economic and military strength was the basis of German power – not Bismarck's diplomatic skill. The desire of all the powers to avoid a major war was more important in ensuring peace than Bismarck's diplomacy.

Write three paragraphs answering these charges and making the case for Bismarck.

Answering source-based questions on Bismarck's Germany: 1871–90

Source A

Source A In an interview soon after his retirement, Bismarck was quoted as saying:

I had seen it [my dismissal] coming. The Emperor wished to be his own Chancellor, with no one intervening between his ministers and himself…He had ideas which I could not approve. And our characters did not harmonise. The old Emperor asked my opinion about everything and told me his own. The young one consulted other people and wished to decide for himself. I too wanted to go, though not just at the moment when he sent two messengers to hurry me. Matters of importance for the *Reich* were in progress, and I did not wish to see my achievements of a quarter of a century scattered like chaff. Yet I'm not angry with him, nor perhaps he with me.

DROPPING THE PILOT.

Source B Punch cartoon 1890

▼ QUESTIONS ON SOURCES

1. How useful and reliable is the evidence presented in Source A? **[7 marks]**

2. What does Source B suggest was the main reason for Bismarck's dismissal? **[3 marks]**

3. Using your knowledge and the two sources, explain the causes and consequences of Bismarck's dismissal. **[15 marks]**

Further Reading

Books in the Access to History series

The key texts are *The Unification of Germany, 1815–90* by A. Styles and *Rivalry and Accord: International Relations 1870–1914* by J. Lowe.

General

A History of Germany 1815–1990 by W. Carr (Edward Arnold, 1991) has two excellent chapters on Bismarck's Germany. Other good texts include *The Fontana History of Germany 1780–1918* by D. Blackbourn (Fontana, 1997), *Imperial Germany 1871–1918* by S. Lee (Routledge, 1998), *Bismarck and the German Empire 1871–1918* by L. Abrams (Routledge, 1995) and *Bismarck and Germany 1862–1890* by D. G. Williamson (Longman, 1997).

8 RUSSIA, AUSTRIA AND FRANCE C.1850–80

POINTS TO CONSIDER

In this chapter you will be considering the main political, social and economic developments in Russia, Austria and France in the third quarter of the 19th century. Did these three countries have much in common or were their developments very different? Were these years of reform or reaction? If you are examining each country in isolation it may well be worth looking back to chapters 1 and 3 to remind yourself what happened pre-1850, and also looking forward to chapter 9 to see what happened after 1880.

ISSUE:
How great a reformer was Tsar Alexander II?

1 Russia: Alexander II

Figure 1 Alexander II (1855–81) – The 'Tsar Liberator'?

a) The situation in 1855

'I am handing you command of the country in a very poor state,' Tsar Nicholas I told his son and heir Alexander II. In 1855 Russia was losing the Crimean War against Britain, France and Turkey. The war revealed the ineptness of both the Russian army and the central administration. The countryside was seething with disaffected peasants. At least Alexander, 37 years old in 1855, had been given extensive practical experience in government. He was thus well aware of Russia's problems. He realised that major changes were needed if Russia was to remain a great power and if he was to save the autocratic system – to which he was totally committed.

b) The emancipation of the Serfs

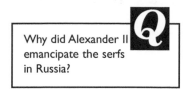
Why did Alexander II emancipate the serfs in Russia?

The peasants, over 80 per cent of Russia's 60 million people, were divided into two categories: state peasants (inhabitants of the tsar's estates) and landlords' peasants (or serfs). Both groups were technically bound to the land: they could not leave without permission. In reality, however, the state peasants had more freedom. Some owned their own land and had a large measure of control over their lives. Serfs' lives were dominated by the *mir*, the family and the noble who controlled them. The noble could seize serfs' property, sell them, and determine when and to whom they would marry. He could take serfs into domestic service at will or indeed ask almost anything else of them (but stories of sexual licence and sadistic cruelty were the exception rather than the rule). Some serfs paid rent for the land they farmed. Others paid labour by working on the lord's land – three days a week was the norm but in the worst cases it could be six days. Nobles also administered rural justice and could send troublesome serfs to Siberia or into the army.

> **THE MIR**
> The *mir* (or council), composed of the heads of families, made almost all local decisions over land use and distribution. Land was often redistributed as a family's circumstances changed. This was a disincentive for peasants to improve the land they farmed.

Problems of serfdom

▼ It was unable to deliver an increased rate of productivity which matched the rapid population growth. (This doubled between 1800–58.) The serfs thus found their traditional poverty getting worse.

▼ It no longer provided nobles with an adequate income. Many faced growing debt.

▼ It could be blamed for the relative stagnation of the Russian economy.

▼ It no longer even provided stability. There was growing peasant unrest.

Alexander II believed that little else could be reformed in Russia until serfdom was abolished. In March 1856, he told Moscow nobles:

> I have learned gentlemen, that rumours have spread among you of my intention to abolish serfdom. To refute any groundless gossip on so important a subject I consider it necessary to inform you that I have no intention of doing so immediately. But, of course, and you yourselves realise it, the existing system of serf owning cannot remain unchanged. It is better to begin abolishing serfdom from above than to wait for it to begin to abolish itself from below. I ask you, gentlemen, to think of ways of doing this. Pass on my words to the nobles for consideration.

ACTIVITY

Study Alexander's 1856 speech. What does it reveal about his motives?

As well as stressing the threat of revolution, Alexander used Russia's defeat in the Crimean War to underline the need for change. In the face of strong noble opposition, he decided to force the issue. In 1857 local committees were set up to consider reform proposals. In March 1861, the Emancipation Edict, the greatest reform in 19th-century Russia, was announced.

The main terms

▼ Serfs became free citizens. They could marry of their own free will, own property, engage in trade or business, could no longer be bought or sold, and had some legal rights.

▼ They had to continue to provide their traditional services until 1863.

▼ On average they received 25 per cent less land than they had cultivated as serfs. Landlords retained around two thirds of all land in Russia.

▼ The government paid landowners 80 per cent of the agreed price for their land. Peasants were expected to pay the remaining 20 per cent. Given that few peasants could afford to pay, the State usually met the payments. In return, the peasants repaid the government in annual instalments over 49 years. These were known as redemption payments.

▼ The *mir* was collectively responsible for paying redemption costs.

▼ Former domestic serfs received nothing except freedom.

---

c) The impact of emancipation

Why did the *mir* hold back Russian development?

Most peasants had assumed that emancipation would be a dual package of freedom and land-ownership. Thus when the terms of the edict were spelt out, joy quickly turned to anger. Peasants could not understand why they had to pay for land which they believed was theirs by right. Many genuinely believed that this was not the Tsar's intention and that the local landowners were lying to them. In 1861 there were some 500 incidents of serious rioting. Alexander was forced to intervene, stating that there was to be no emancipation except the one he had issued. Incidents of disorder declined but the peasants remained disappointed.

The situation did not improve as the details of land division were worked out. Landlords usually succeeded in retaining the best land, forcing the peasants to pay a grossly inflated price for their land. The land was given to the *mir*, not the individual peasant. There was debate within the government on the merits of the *mir* but those who wanted to set up individual peasant farming on the western model lost the argument. The *mir* system was favoured on the grounds that it was familiar and acceptable to most peasants, and because it could be collectively responsible for redemption payments. Moreover, it could now do what the lord had previously done: collect taxes, find recruits for the army, and administer justice. It also had the right to issue or withhold passports for peasants wishing to travel distances over 20 miles. The *mir* thus bound the peasants almost as firmly to their former lifestyle as serfdom had done. Moreover, it continued to distribute land – usually in scattered strips in order to ensure that no one received land of only one type and quality. Far from encouraging economic initiative, the *mir* perpetuated many of the worst elements of pre-emancipation Russia. Most peasants continued to live in poverty, a problem which was exacerbated by the remorseless rise in population.

Some historians have gone so far as to lay the blame for the revolutions of 1917 on the shortcomings of emancipation. Historian Richard Pipes, for example, sees emancipation as being too cautious, too little and too late. This is easy to say with hindsight. But given the opposition from the nobles, Alexander acted speedily and radically. Between the nobles' wish to keep all their land and the peasants' hope of freely acquiring all the land, a compromise had to be reached. Even if it failed to achieve all its aims, the Emancipation Edict remains a momentous event in Russian history.

> ### THE EFFECT OF EMANCIPATION ON THE LANDOWNERS
> Emancipation dealt a serious blow to the landowning nobility. Without serfs to rely on, many could not make their estates pay. To make ends meet they were forced to sell more land. Between 1861 and 1905 the acreage of land in noble possession fell by 41 per cent.

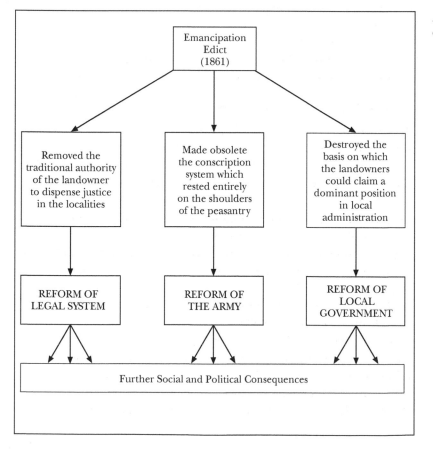

Figure 2 The impact of emancipation

To what extent did
Alexander's reforms
modify Russian autocracy?

d) Other reforms

i) Reform of the legal system, 1864

Alexander's reforms:

▼ introduced the concept of a judiciary independent of the government. Judges were required to have professional qualifications and were paid a substantial salary to avoid bribery; once appointed, it was very difficult to remove them;

▼ introduced trial by jury for criminal cases;

▼ made courts open to the public;

▼ created Justices of the Peace, appointed by the *zemstvo*, to deal with minor disputes.

The results:

▼ The police retained the power to detain anyone considered to be a threat to the state.

▼ The new system did not extend to the peasants: they were tried by separate courts.

▼ The judiciary was by and large independent and fair. The courts became trusted.

▼ The government found itself embarrassed by the jury system which frequently returned verdicts at odds with the 'official' position.

ii) Reform of the army

The Crimean War had revealed the shortcomings of the Russian army. Reform was the work of war minister Milyutin. An able administrator, he tried to humanise the military and improve its efficiency. The reforms generated much antagonism in both the army and the government. Only the support of Alexander enabled Milyutin to force them through.

▼ Military colonies (see page 27) came to an end.

▼ Most barbaric forms of punishment were abolished.

▼ Attempts were made to improve standards of literacy among the troops.

▼ All males over 20, irrespective of class, were made subject to conscription. About one quarter were chosen by ballot to serve. The length of service was reduced from 25 to 15 years (and much less for those who volunteered or who were well educated).

▼ Efforts were made to select and promote army officers on ability and merit.

The results:

▼ The reforms were vital to the recovery of Russian military prestige.

▼ The reforms represented an attack on class privileges and helped to initiate a trend towards greater social equality.

iii) Reform of local government

▼ Local councils – *zemstvos* – were set up in 1864 at two levels: province and district.

▼ *Zemstvo* members were elected for three years. All Russian males were eligible to vote and had the right to stand for election.

▼ The *zemstvos* maintained roads, arranged military conscription, supervised prisons, attended to public health, education and poor relief, and assisted with the development of industry and agriculture. They could levy local taxes to finance their activities.

▼ Municipal councils were set up in 1870. Elected by male property holders over the age of 25, they had similar responsibilties to the *zemstvos*.

The results:

▼ The *zemstvos* and municipal councils did not encroach significantly on the autocracy.

▼ The segregation of voters according to class ensured that nobles dominated the *zemstvos*. From the peasants' perspective the *zemstvos* were landowners' bodies which imposed taxes they could ill afford to pay. They showed little interest in them.

▼ Local administration improved, helping the lot of ordinary Russians. This success offered tangible proof that the Russian people had the skills to make democracy work.

iv) Educational reform

▼ Between 1861–81 the number of primary and secondary schools increased fourfold.

▼ In 1862 new schools were placed under the jurisdiction of the Ministry of Education rather than under the control of the church.

▼ After 1863 universities were given much greater freedom, including the right to import scholarly texts of any kind from abroad. Scholarships were set up to support the best students and fact-finding missions abroad were encouraged.

The results:

▼ Although there was an uneasy balance between liberal initiatives and a conservative desire to maintain control, significant progress was made in terms of both the quality of education and pupil numbers. Positive steps were made in women's education.

Relaxation of censorship

After 1855 Russia's harsh censorship laws were relaxed. Relatively liberal press laws were introduced in 1865. The number of new books published per year doubled between 1855–64 and trebled between 1864–81. In the last years of Alexander's reign, attempts were made to tighten censorship but even then it was not as severe as under Nicholas I.

> ## Economic progress
>
> ▼ Russian industrial production underwent modest expansion. Between 1865-79 the number of industrial workers more than doubled. Industrialisation was assisted by foreign investment and stimulated by the rapid development of the state railway network. In 1855 Russia had less than 700 miles of track. By 1881 there were over 14,000 miles of track.
>
> ▼ Efforts were made to encourage grain exports, Russia's chief source of foreign revenue. In 1864 exports stood at 26 million tons. By 1880 they had risen to 86 million tons.
>
> ▼ However, the Russian economy lagged behind that of more advanced countries.

Figure 3 Russian industrial progress

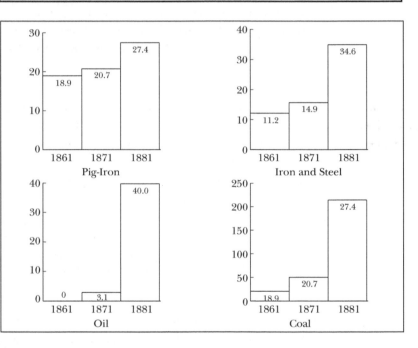

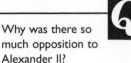

ACTIVITY

In no more than 200 words explain why the emancipation of serfdom led to other reforms.

Why was there so much opposition to Alexander II?

e) Opposition to Alexander II

i) The Intelligentsia

The greater freedom in Russia after 1855 allowed radical ideas to develop among Russia's educated classes. The intelligentsia was far from being a homogenous group. Some believed that Russia would only make progress if she adopted the main features of western civilisation, especially political liberty. Others (Slavophiles) believed that Russia had already moved too close to the west and forsaken the qualities of her own distinctive Slav culture. Slavophiles often rejected the concept of individual liberty in favour of the collective – socialist – tradition of the *mir*. Intelligentsia and radical group numbers were small, involving hundreds rather than thousands. Nevertheless, radical ideas spread, boosted by a generation of brilliant novelists and dramatists who contributed to the attack on Russian society and stressed the need for reform. Some students became totally and obsessively committed to revolutionary ends.

Influential radical 'intelligentsia' at the start of the 1860s included:

▼ Alexander Herzen: in exile in London, he edited an influential periodical *The Bell*. He advocated a type of socialism based on the *mir*. Opposed to violent change, he believed that educating the masses was the best way of achieving social revolution.

▼ Nicholas Chernyshevsky: he placed his faith in the *narod* (the people). Arrested in 1862, he wrote *What is to be done*, which embodied his ideas for a socialist state, in prison. It became the bible of radical youth. While he inspired, he did not really provide an answer to his implied question – how was revolution to occur?

▼ Mikhail Bakunin: exiled from Russia, he preached violence and destruction as the only means of achieving change.

ii) Reaction

By the mid-1860s there were growing calls for some form of parliament, particularly from the middle class. But Alexander was not prepared to give up more of his authority. When in 1865 the St Petersburg *zemstvo* demanded that a national representative body be set up, he dissolved it. In 1866 he explained his reasons.

> And now I suppose that you consider that I refuse to give up any of my powers from motives of petty ambition. I give you my imperial word that, at this very minute, at this very table, I would sign any constitution you like, if I felt that this would be for the good of Russia. But I know that, were I to do so today, tomorrow Russia would fall to pieces.

An attempt to assassinate the Tsar in 1866, attributed to the growth of radical ideas among the young, helped to spark a reactionary backlash.

▼ Count Dmitri Tolstoy became minister of education. He cracked down on schools and universities which were seen as the seedbeds of subversion. Entry to the universities was restricted and there was increased police supervision of students. The education ministry dictated curricula in schools and controlled teaching appointments.

▼ Suspected revolutionaries were exiled to Siberia.

▼ Radical journals were closed down.

▼ The powers of the *zemstvos* were reduced.

The increase in repression only increased the number of disaffected. Liberals, who essentially wanted a parliament, were pushed to the sidelines as a fierce battle developed between the government and the revolutionary movements.

THE POLISH REVOLT

Alexander began his reign with the best intentions towards his Polish subjects. However, his efforts at conciliation failed and in 1863 a serious revolt broke out in Poland. The insurgents were mainly landowners who, fortunately for Alexander, lacked the support of the peasantry. The Russian authorities dealt severely with the rebels, many of whom lost their land and freedom. Polish peasants benefited. Polish serfs were given complete emancipation with much lower redemption payments. Poland lost some of its special rights and became a mere Russian province. Efforts to force the Russian language, laws and religion on Poland united all Poles against their perceived Russian oppressors.

ALEXANDER II

1855 Alexander II became Tsar;
1861 emancipation of the serfs;
1864 the *zemstvo* established
and legal reforms
introduced;
1866 attempt to kill Alexander:
increasing reaction;
1873 *To the People*
–4
1881 Loris-Melikov proposals:
assassination of Alexander II.

iii) The populists (or narodniks)

In the early 1870s populist student groups developed. Drawing inspiration from theorists like Herzen, they invested all their hopes for change in the peasantry. They believed that the liberation of the people should be the work not of a vanguard of professional revolutionaries but of the people themselves. Their slogan, borrowed from Herzen, was 'To the People'. In 1873–4 over 2,000 students went into the countryside to preach their views. They had little success. Bemused peasants regarded the agitators with suspicion and were more likely to denounce them to the authorities than to be converted. The Populists again went to the people in 1877–8 with a similar lack of success. The government, concerned at the attempts to incite revolution, arrested hundreds of students. However in the mass trials which followed, the accused won much public support. Many were acquitted or received only light sentences.

iv) Terror

The failure of Populism to win mass support led to the emergence of small-scale groups dedicated to provoking revolution by the use of violence. One such group was Land and Liberty. In1879 an attempt on the Tsar's life – without the consent of Land and Liberty – prompted the break-up of the organisation. It split into two factions: Black Partition, which favoured peaceful methods, and People's Will, which favoured terrorism. In 1879–80 there were several more efforts to kill the Tsar. In 1880 a bomb rocked the Winter Palace in St Petersburg, killing 40 troops. The police hit back, infiltrating the People's Will and arresting many of its members. By 1881 the terrorist organisation was reduced to a few desperate men and women. Nevertheless the fanaticism of the terrorists was the tip of an iceberg of disenchantment which had spread through educated society, especially among the young.

Alexander tried to win back support. In 1880 press censorship was relaxed, political prisoners were released and Tolstoy was replaced as Minister of Education by the liberal Saburov. A Commission, headed by general Loris-Melikov, was set up with the task of countering the revolutionary movement. Loris-Melikov was convinced that conciliation was the only answer. Early in 1881 he outlined his proposals for change, including the creation of an elected body akin to a parliament. On 1 March 1881 Alexander signed the documents authorising the implementation of the Loris-Melikov proposals. On his way home to the Winter Palace he was fatally wounded by a terrorist bomb. The terrorists hoped that Alexander's death would bring down the whole tsarist system. Ironically, his murder, which caused widespread revulsion, probably strengthened tsarism. The new Tsar Alexander III held no truck with terrorists or with reform. Alexander II's assassination seemed to vindicate those who claimed that his reforms had simply incited trouble and what was needed was a dose of tough reaction.

f) Conclusion

Alexander II has often been criticised.

▼ His reforms can be seen as mere 'window dressing'. Given that he implemented more far-reaching reform than any previous tsar, this is a harsh verdict. Emancipation of the serfs transformed semi-feudal Russia into something approaching a modern state.

▼ His reforms can be seen as falling between two stools, alienating conservatives who thought he had gone too far down the reforming road, and radicals who thought he had not gone far enough. His reluctance to go further produced resentment among those who wanted change. Eventually he was to fall victim to forces which he had unwittingly released and was unable to restrain. In fairness, it is unlikely that he could ever have appeased the revolutionaries. They believed that nothing other than the complete overthrow of society would bring happiness and justice to Russia.

▼ Alexander can be criticised for not creating a parliament. But his basic motivation was to make Russia strong and, as he saw it, serve his people. While it is easy to criticise him for this stance, it is a moot point whether Russia was ready for full democratic rule. More radical reform might simply have resulted in anarchy and chaos.

2 Austria 1848–80

a) Francis Joseph and the return to absolutism

In 1848 it was far from certain what kind of political settlement would emerge in Austria out of the chaos of revolution. In late 1848 18-year-old Francis Joseph had just become emperor. Fighting was still going on in Italy and Hungary, and an Imperial parliament at Kremsier, dominated by liberals, sought to draft a new constitution which would curtail the power of the crown. Prime Minister Prince Schwarzenberg encouraged the liberals, telling the Kremsier parliament that he wanted 'constitutional monarchy sincerely and unreservedly'. In December, Schwarzenberg read out a royal address which seemed to suggest (wrongly) that the new monarch was also in favour of constitutional monarchy.

> **ISSUE:**
> How and why was Austria transformed into the Austro-Hungarian Empire?

ACTIVITY

a) Explain which phrases in the royal address would have pleased the Kremsier liberals.

b) How reliable is the royal address as a guide to Francis Joseph's future intentions?

… convinced of the need and value of free institutions expressive of the spirit of the age, we enter with due confidence, on the path leading to a salutary transformation and rejuvenation of the Monarchy as a whole. On the basis of genuine liberty, on the basis of equality of all the nations of the realm and of the equality before the law of all its citizens, and of participation of those citizens in legislation, our Fatherland may enjoy a resurrection to its old greatness and a new force. Determined to maintain the splendour of the crown undimmed…but ready to share our rights with the representatives of our peoples, we count on succeeding, with the blessing of God and in understanding with our peoples, in uniting all the regions and races of the Monarchy in one great state.

The motives of the able, unscrupulous Schwarzenberg are open to debate. Some see his support for the imperial parliament as a cynical deception but others believe that he genuinely supported moderate constitutional reform. A working parliament might be a way of bypassing the aristocracy, which he believed had proved itself incompetent as a governing elite, while simultaneously creating a more unified Empire. But while Schwarzenberg was prepared to support some limitations on the role of the emperor, he remained convinced that sovereignty must ultimately reside in the person of the monarch, not the people. Francis Joseph, despite his initial proclamation in favour of constitutionalism, agreed. He believed that a powerful monarchy, answerable only to God, was the only way to bind the disparate parts of his Empire together. On 1 March 1849 the Kremsier deputies put forward their liberal blueprint. They proposed creating a strong parliament and reducing the powers of the crown. In addition, there was a long list of the 'rights of citizens'. Schwarzenberg now informed the Kremsier delegates that the Emperor had ignored their efforts. A few days later, a new constitution, drafted by Minister of the Interior Count Stadion was declared and the Kremsier parliament dissolved. The Stadion constitution was remarkably liberal in some ways. The monarch was to share power with an elected parliament, and many of the 'rights of citizens' were retained. However, even this more modest proposal was never put into operation because Francis Joseph, growing in confidence, was determined to rule as an autocratic sovereign.

For two years, Austria effectively had no constitution. There was no parliament and the provincial diets were ignored. Francis Joseph, Schwarzenberg and the army ruled – with some success. By the end of 1850 the traditional ascendancy of the Habsburgs in Germany, Italy and Hungary seemed to have been re-established. Liberals, radicals and nationalists were silenced. Finally, on 31 December 1851 a new constitution was announced. It was known as the 'Sylvester Patent'

(*Sylvesterabend* means New Year's Eve). The patent removed all existing checks on Francis Joseph's power. An advisory council or *Reichsrat* was set up but it had no authority either to initiate or to block legislation. The patent abolished almost all tiers of elected provincial government. The Empire was to be ruled from the centre. This was more than simply a return to the pre-1848 situation: it created a more centralised and unitary system. The patent, and the death of Schwarzenberg in 1852, left the Emperor alone and absolute.

b) The 'Bach era'

The period between 1852–9 is often known as the 'Bach era', largely because during this time the new chief minister Bach, with Francis Joseph's full support, set about reforming the Empire's administration. Bach believed that the Empire should have one system of taxation, one system of law, one official language (German) and one system of overall administration. These 'reforms' were extremely unpopular with non-Germans, especially with Hungarians who experienced systematic Germanisation for the first time in their history. Even the loyal Croats, who had helped defeat the Hungarian revolt, suffered. (One Croat cynically remarked to a Hungarian: 'What you are getting as punishment, we are getting as reward.') Bach tried to impose religious as well as administrative uniformity. The Concordat of 1855 gave the Catholic Church extensive rights over education. In return, the Church preached loyalty and obedience to the emperor.

c) The October Diploma (1860) and the February Patent (1861)

Austria's defeat in Italy gave ammunition to the liberal and nationalist critics of the absolutist constitution. It also increased Austria's financial problems. European financiers refused to lend more money unless she introduced the kind of constitutional reforms which might appease the critics. In order to buy off liberal discontent and appease Europe's bankers, Francis Joseph announced a set of constitutional reforms known as the October Diploma. The old provincial diets, instruments of aristocratic influence, were reinstated. They were to work with an enlarged *Reichsrat*. The emperor was required to 'cooperate' with the diets and the *Reichsrat*. On paper, this was a major concession to state rights and to the conservative aristocracy which was deeply hostile to German centralism. Francis Joseph, however, seems to have regarded the exercise as little more than a cynical piece of constitutional sleight of hand. 'We shall indeed have a little parliamentary government,' he wrote, 'but the power remains in my hands.' The October Diploma, in fact, lasted only four months. Dissatisfied with

> **THE 1850S**
> Achievements:
> ▼ Railways expanded, industry developed and trade quadrupled.
> ▼ The administration, despite a tendency to excessive bureaucracy, was more efficient.
> Failures:
> ▼ Taxes were insufficient to meet the Empire's costs.
> ▼ Intellectual life was stifled by censorship.
> ▼ Not enough money was spent on the army.
> ▼ Austrian forces were defeated by French and Piemontese forces in Italy in 1859. Lombardy was lost. Habsburg rule in northern Italy was dealt a fatal blow.

the concessions, the Hungarians refused to recognise the diploma and demanded instead the recognition of the April Laws of 1848 which had granted them almost complete self-government.

Having dug himself into one hole, Francis Joseph appointed a new chief minister – Anton von Schmerling – who promptly dug him into another. Schmerling's immediate task was to reverse the decentralising tendencies of the October Diploma whilst declaring that no such change was occurring. Schmerling's new constitution, introduced in 1861 and known as the February Patent, was officially presented as an amendment to the October Diploma. In reality, it turned the diploma on its head, increasing the authority of the *Reichsrat* and reducing the power of the provincial diets. The latter were turned into electoral colleges for the purpose of selecting representatives for the *Reichsrat* which began to look like a parliament. It could now initiate bills and was given a right of veto over all domestic legislation. However, its ability to obstruct crown legislation was restricted by an 'emergency' clause which allowed the emperor to make law when the *Reichsrat* was not sitting. The crown also had the right to dissolve it and to appoint ministers. Foreign and military affairs remained firmly under the emperor's control.

The February Patent was opposed by those who wanted more autonomy, and the Hungarians, Croats and Czechs refused to send deputies to the *Reichsrat*. But despite their bitterness, Hungary's new leaders were not eager to repeat the experience of 1849. They rejected violence and preferred to negotiate with Francis Joseph. In 1865 the Emperor dismissed Schmerling. His successor Belcredi supported federation. The February Patent was now suspended and efforts were made to reach agreement on a new constitution. Hungarian leader Deak sought to create a 'Dual Monarchy' in which Hungarians would be given home rule while continuing to recognise a Habsburg as their legitimate sovereign.

d) The 1867 Compromise

In 1866 Austria was manoeuvred into a disastrous war by Bismarck (see chapter 6) and suffered a crushing defeat at Sadowa. The Treaty of Prague, which abolished the German Confederation, effectively ended 400 years of Habsburg authority in Germany. Events in 1866 helped Hungary's negotiating position. Francis Joseph recognised that he needed Hungarian support. Deak made it clear that the price of that support was the adoption of his Dualist constitution. Beust, who had served the King of Saxony for two decades, now became Austria's chief minister. An able diplomat, he worked out terms with Deak and Andrassy. Francis Joseph became convinced that a compromise with the Hungarians, albeit a bitter pill, might be a way of renewing the strength of the Empire. In 1867 the Compromise or *Ausgleich* became law.

HOW WAS AUSTRIA-HUNGARY GOVERNED?

▼ The Emperor of Austria (also now King of Hungary) still had great powers: he could summon or dissolve parliament, appoint ministers, and rule by decree in an emergency.

▼ There was a single imperial army and three Joint Ministers who controlled foreign policy, defence and finance. The Joint Ministers were responsible to delegations – 60 delegates each from the Austrian and Hungarian parliaments.

▼ Austria and Hungary each had their own ministers and parliaments with control over all domestic matters. Parliaments in both countries comprised an upper house, composed of nobles, churchmen and imperial appointees, and an elected lower house.

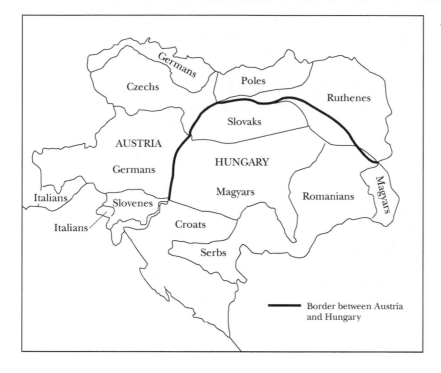

Figure 4 The Dual Monarchy

AUSTRIA

Germans

Czechs

Germans

Poles

Ruthenes

Slovaks

HUNGARY

Magyars

Magyars

Italians

Slovenes

Croats

Serbs

Romanians

Italians

Border between Austria and Hungary

Hungary, including Transylvania, Slovakia and Croatia, was now under the authority of the parliament at Budapest. Austria, including Bohemia, Galicia and Moravia, was under the jurisdiction of the *Reichsrat* in Vienna. The official language of Austria was German, of Hungary, Magyar. Effectively the Compromise ensured in Austria the supremacy of (wealthy) Germans and in Hungary the supremacy of (wealthy) Magyars. The aspirations of Czechs, Slovenes, Slovaks, Romanians and Serbs were ignored. The Compromise can thus be seen as an alliance against Slavs. Andrassy was supposed to have told an Austrian colleague: 'You look after your Slavs and we'll look after ours'. The so-called Compromise was exactly that. Although allowing the Hungarians control over their domestic affairs, it forced them to recognise that they were still part of a greater imperial entity. The settlement specified that as far as foreign and military affairs were concerned the Dual Monarchy was one entity. The emperor retained control over the appointments to the three common ministries – foreign affairs, defence and finance. In the last resort he also had the right to dissolve parliaments in both Austria and Hungary and to issue decrees that had the force of law when parliaments were not in session. These powers made it possible for him to impose his will, although he preferred cooperation with ministers who could command parliamentary majorities.

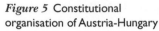

Figure 5 Constitutional organisation of Austria-Hungary

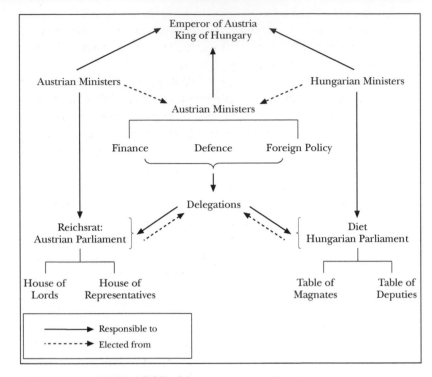

e) Political life 1867–80

The problem of containing and/or assimilating the various ethnic groups was a problem for both Austria and Hungary. The Germans and Magyars, the two dominant racial groups, made up only 40 per cent of the Dual Monarchy's population. However, the other nationalities should not all be lumped together and seen as oppressed second-class citizens. In each half of the Empire one Slav group established for itself considerable rights of self-government.

▼ In Austria, the Polish nobility were allowed to govern Galicia almost entirely as they wished. Polish was recognised as the only official language within the province.

▼ In Hungary, the Croats were given significant rights of self-government in 1868. A Croatian assembly sat in Zagreb and debated in Croatian – the language of education, administration and the railways. The Croats thus became junior partners of the Magyars.

Austria

▼ The 1867 Austrian constitution was not very democratic. Only 60 per cent of the adult male population could vote. The voting system favoured the wealthy and the Germans.

▼ A strong German liberal party emerged. Although Francis Joseph regarded the liberals with some suspicion, he had little option but to rely on them for parliamentary support. They won a number of concessions – a freer press, freer trade, and reduction of the influence of the Catholic Church.

▼ The Czech question was the key issue in Austrian politics after 1867. The Czechs resented the Compromise, resented being ruled by Germans, and resented the fact that German was the language of officials, even in the predominantly Czech areas of Bohemia and Moravia. Czech nationalists pressed for more autonomy. Refusing to recognise the legitimacy of the new constitution, they boycotted the *Reichsrat*. In 1871 the Emperor, in an effort to appease the Czechs, agreed that Bohemia and Moravia should be governed by a parliament based in Prague. In effect the Dual Monarchy would become a Triple Monarchy. This proposal aroused a storm of opposition. Germans in Bohemia and Moravia protested. Army and civil service leaders claimed that the measure would weaken the Empire. Crucially, Hungarian leaders attacked the proposals as a violation of the compromise. Forced to choose between the Magyars and the Czechs, Francis Joseph sided with the former. The reform proposals were – permanently – shelved. The Czechs were thus embittered. Their leaders boycotted parliamentary life for most of the 1870s.

▼ In 1879 Francis Joseph broke with the liberals who had lost electoral support and whom he suspected of trying to reduce his powers. He appointed his friend Count Taaffe as prime minister. Taaffe managed to win the support of conservative Germans, Poles and Czechs – the so-called 'iron ring'. Czech support had to be 'bought'. In 1880 Taaffe introduced a law which established that government officials in Bohemia and Moravia must use the Czech language when dealing with Czechs. Taaffe's iron ring survived until 1893.

Hungary

▼ Hungary was dominated by the Magyar nobility. Hungary's electoral law allowed only 6 per cent of the adult male population to vote. The Magyars, with less than half the population, obtained over 90 per cent of the seats in the Hungarian parliament.

▼ Tisza, chief minister from 1875–90, consolidated the power of the Hungarian ruling class. There was increased centralisation. A new penal code in 1878 punished severely those spreading socialist and nationalist propaganda.

▼ The Magyars began a deliberate policy of 'Magyarisation' aimed at assimilating the various ethnic groups, including the Germans, into the dominant Magyar culture. The main institution for such ethnic engineering was the educational system. By the 1880s the Hungarian

AUSTRIA-HUNGARY 1848–67

1848 Francis Joseph became Emperor;
1849 Defeat of Hungarian Revolt;
1851 Sylvester Patent;
1859 Austria defeated in North Italy: lost Lombardy;
1860 October Diploma;
1866 Austria defeated by Prussia in Seven Weeks War;
1867 Compromise introduced.

To test your understanding, consider the following question: 'Why was there so much constitutional change in the Habsburg Empire between 1848 and 1867?'

Suggested lines of response:

▼ Why was the Austrian Empire so difficult to govern?

▼ How important were the views of Francis Joseph?

▼ How important were Austria's defeats in 1859 and 1866?

language was compulsory in all secondary schools and universities. Becoming Hungarian was the passport to economic, social and political advancement. By 1880 over 90 per cent of all state officials and judges were Magyars.

Social and Economic Conditions

▼ There were great regional differences between the poor regions (for example, Galicia and Slovakia) and the rich regions (for example, Bohemia and Silesia).

▼ There was considerable railway development.

▼ The more enterprising landowners modernised farm techniques and increased productivity. Hungary exported cereal produce across Europe.

▼ By 1880 Austria-Hungary was Europe's fourth greatest industrial power.

f) Conclusion

Many see the 1867 Compromise as containing the seeds of the end of the Habsburg Empire. Perhaps the main problem was not so much the Compromise itself but the fact that Francis Joseph, yielding to German-Magyar pressure, was unwilling to grant other compromises. A federal state under Habsburg rule might have been stronger than the Dual Monarchy. Nevertheless, for all its faults, the Compromise helped the survival of the Habsburg Empire as a major power. Francis Joseph continued to inspire loyalty among his subjects. It was he who embodied the political unity that existed within the Empire.

ISSUE:
Why was Louis Napoleon able to become Emperor? How successful was he?

3   France 1848–80

a) President Louis Napoleon

Louis Napoleon returned to France in 1848. Following success in the September 1848 elections, he was allowed to take his place in the Constituent Assembly. In the Assembly, he made a poor impression. A poor public speaker, he cut a somewhat comic figure with his large head and short legs. This worked in his favour. Many leading politicians underestimated him. Thiers, for example, said: 'He is a noodle whom anyone can twist round his finger.' Once it was decided to elect a president by a national vote, Louis Napoleon won the support of many politicians who thought they had found a useful figurehead whom they could control. In the campaign none of the leading candidates was in a position to fight a well-organised campaign. Only Louis Napoleon tried, spending a large part of his personal fortune persuading newspapers to print supportive articles and launching a large-scale poster campaign. He had the advantage of his name and the emotional associations it had in the minds of many French people. To Catholics, he promised an end to godless anti-clericalism; to nationalists he promised glory and respect abroad; to the poor he promised better times ahead; to the 'haves' he promised order and strong government. In November 1848 he won 5,400,000 votes – 75 per cent of the vote.

As President, Louis Napoleon projected himself as a strong and enlightened leader, above faction. Parliamentary conflicts were

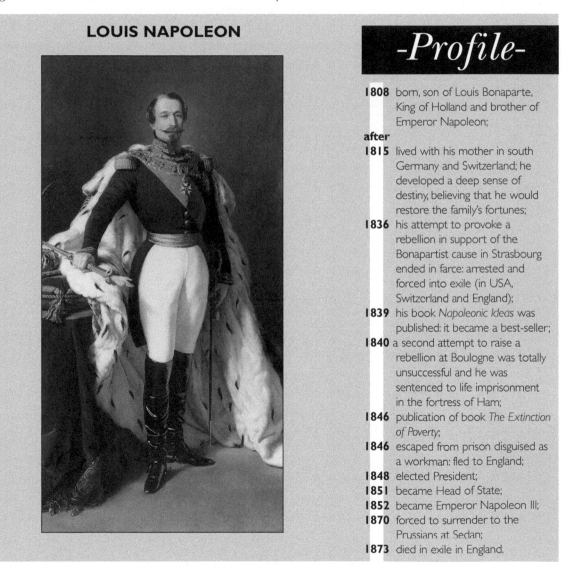

LOUIS NAPOLEON

-Profile-

1808 born, son of Louis Bonaparte, King of Holland and brother of Emperor Napoleon;

after

1815 lived with his mother in south Germany and Switzerland; he developed a deep sense of destiny, believing that he would restore the family's fortunes;

1836 his attempt to provoke a rebellion in support of the Bonapartist cause in Strasbourg ended in farce: arrested and forced into exile (in USA, Switzerland and England);

1839 his book *Napoleonic Ideas* was published: it became a best-seller;

1840 a second attempt to raise a rebellion at Boulogne was totally unsuccessful and he was sentenced to life imprisonment in the fortress of Ham;

1846 publication of book *The Extinction of Poverty*;

1846 escaped from prison disguised as a workman: fled to England;

1848 elected President;

1851 became Head of State;

1852 became Emperor Napoleon III;

1870 forced to surrender to the Prussians at Sedan;

1873 died in exile in England.

depicted as squabbles of lesser men who placed their own interests before those of France. His response to events and his policy initiatives were designed to win him popular acclaim.

▼ In 1849 he embarked on an extensive tour of France. A cholera epidemic gave him his chance to display his courage and his genuine concern for the poor. He won the affection of the masses, who appreciated his attentions and personal charm.

▼ In 1849 he sent troops to Italy to help re-establish the Pope in Rome. The move was popular with the predominantly Catholic peasantry.

▼ In June 1849 a radical republican rising in Paris was quickly crushed, reinforcing Louis Napoleon's association with firm government.

▼ The *Loi Falloux* (1850) made religion a compulsory subject in all schools and permitted the development of church schools. Again Louis Napoleon acted in accordance with the wishes of the Catholic majority.

▼ He engineered the promotion of his supporters into positions of influence.

The major limiting factor to the growth of Louis Napoleon's power was the constitution. This debarred the immediate re-election of a president. Thus the 1852 presidential election would mark the end of his career in high office. When attempts to persuade the Assembly to extend his presidency failed, he determined to change the constitution himself. Meticulous plans were made for a coup to take place on 2 December 1851, the anniversary of Napoleon I's coronation and also of his great victory at Austerlitz. The coup was a brilliant success. Politicians who might have organised opposition were arrested; key public buildings in Paris were occupied by troops; opposition newspaper offices were closed down; and large numbers of troops were brought into Paris in case of trouble. Some half-hearted attempts to raise barricades were violently repressed – at the official cost of 215 lives. Later in December Frenchmen were asked to approve the constitutional changes, including a new parliamentary system and a 10-year period of office for the president, in a referendum. 7,500,000 voted 'yes'. 600,000 voted 'no'. 'France has realised that I broke the law only to do what was right,' said Louis Napoleon. 'The votes of over seven million have just granted me absolution.' Most Frenchmen showed little concern for the end of the Republic. By 1851 Louis Napoleon seemed to stand for prosperity, progress, unity, order, patriotism and the maintenance of Christianity.

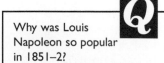

Why was Louis Napoleon so popular in 1851–2?

In March 1852 voters went to the polls to elect a new legislative chamber. Local prefects, acting as political agents on behalf of official 'Bonapartist' candidates, ensured an overwhelming public endorsement for Louis Napoleon. Of the 261 representatives only eight declared themselves in opposition to the new regime. In December 1852 another plebiscite was held to determine whether the people agreed to the Republic being turned into an Empire, with Louis Napoleon as Emperor for life. 7,800,000 voted in favour and 250,000 voted against. Even allowing for some two million abstentions,

Louis Napoleon's political system and personal leadership had the clear approval of the French people. Thus, on 1 December 1852 the Second Empire came into being. The fact that Louis Napoleon took the title Napoleon III emphasised his claim to legitimacy. (Napoleon I's son was regarded as Napoleon II, although he had never ruled in France.)

b) Napoleon III

i) His character

Napoleon III remains something of an enigma – 'the Sphinx of the Tuileries' said Metternich. Bismarck, less impressed, claimed he was a sham – a sphinx without a riddle! He can be seen as simply an upstart adventurer, lacking in steadfastness and clear and consistent aims. Victor Hugo dubbed him 'Napoleon the small'. Marx described him as a 'fool'. However, he can be viewed more positively. He had his own powerful, if peculiar, political philosophy and real political qualities. So in tune was he with the feelings and desires of most Frenchmen, he remained in power for 22 years. If his regime had not collapsed in 1870 it might have been seen as one of the rare examples of a political system that changed from near dictatorship to parliamentary liberalism without a major upheaval. But even his warmest admirers have to accept that his rule ended in ignominy – for which Napoleon III himself was much to blame. At best he can be seen as a blend of rare qualities and fatal flaws. In truth, he was a man of massive contradictions.

▼ He was mix of conservative and radical.
▼ While essentially a humane man, he was prepared to repress his opponents.
▼ He was authoritarian but he did not try to create a one-party state – or even a party!
▼ An adventurer and an opportunist, he was also a man with genuine ideals.
▼ Keen to be seen as heir of Napoleon I, his aims and skills were very different.

ii) His aims

Napoleon III certainly enjoyed power for its own sake. But arguably he regarded power as a means to an end – not an end in itself.

▼ He genuinely believed that his mission was to complete the task begun by his uncle Napoleon I. However, he carefully rewrote the Napoleonic legend to meet the aspirations of mid-19th-century France. While it revived memories of past glories, the Second Empire was no slavish imitation of the first.
▼ He saw France in the 1840s as being weak and lacking a sense of direction – a situation brought about by the political system which

encouraged wrangles between parties and factions. He felt that strong leadership was necessary. Strong government, in his view, could only exist if it was based on the will of the people.

▼ He believed that economic expansion and prosperity would end class conflict. While a prisoner in Ham, he became interested in finding a strategy to do away with poverty. He was prepared to experiment with new economic policies.

▼ He hoped to increase French influence abroad by supporting rising nationalism.

In short, he wished to see a politically united, stable, prosperous France restored to a place of pre-eminence in the world. But he had no precise blueprint for achieving his aims. For all its appeal to Napoleon's past, Bonapartism had no set ideology. The Emperor felt free to change his policies as the occasion required.

Figure 6 Punch cartoon

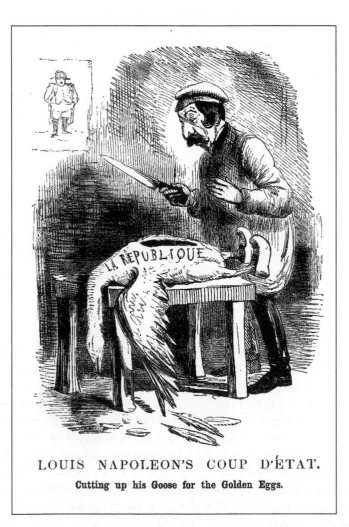

LOUIS NAPOLEON'S COUP D'ÉTAT.

Cutting up his Goose for the Golden Eggs.

ACTIVITY

Examine Figure 6.

a) What points is the cartoon trying to make?

b) What is the apparent bias of the cartoonist?

c) The authoritarian empire: 1852–9

The constitution

▼ Nearly all power was placed in the hands of the President (later Emperor). He nominated all state officials, proposed all new legislation, controlled the army and alone had power to make war and foreign treaties.

▼ The Council of State consisted of 40 members, nominated by the Emperor. Its function was to draw up the legislation proposed by the Emperor.

▼ The two houses of parliament, the Senate and the Legislative Chamber, were simply consultative. They could initiate nothing of importance.

▼ The Legislative Chamber had 261 members and was elected by universal male suffrage for up to six years. It met for just three months a year to discuss legislation drawn up by the Council of State.

▼ The Senate had a maximum of 150 members, appointed for life by the Emperor.

This new constitution was almost identical to the system devised for the first Napoleon in 1800. The similarity was no accident. As Napoleon III himself explained:

> I have taken as a model the political institutions which have, since the beginning of the century, and in similar circumstances, consolidated a society which had been upset and which raised France to a high degree of prosperity and greatness…In a word, I said to myself: since, for fifty years, France has only gone on because of the administrative, judicial, religious and financial organisation of the Consulate and the Empire, why should we not also adopt the political institutions of the period?

i) Limits to Napoleon III's power

▼ The Senate and the Chamber were not totally subservient.

▼ Universal suffrage ensured that all Frenchmen were involved in voting in elections for the Chamber and in the plebiscites that were held from time to time on major issues.

▼ Central to the Napoleonic vision of politics was a loathing of political parties, which were thought to encourage disunity. Thus, no attempt was made to build up a Bonapartist party. Instead, Napoleon III attempted to utilise the talents of the 'best men' available, irrespective of their past politics. He did not demand that they 'believed' in him, before appointing them to posts of responsibility. He merely required an acceptance of his regime and a promise to work in the best interests of France. Thus Napoleon's takeover did not result in massive changes in the people 'at the top'. While some of his personal followers were appointed to

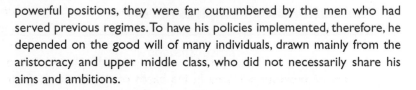

To what extent was Napoleon III's regime a dictatorship?

powerful positions, they were far outnumbered by the men who had served previous regimes. To have his policies implemented, therefore, he depended on the good will of many individuals, drawn mainly from the aristocracy and upper middle class, who did not necessarily share his aims and ambitions.

ii) The success of the authoritarian empire

Napoleon provided strong leadership. He ruled with the help of a handful of advisers – mainly relatives and old friends, some of real talent. The closest to him was his half-brother the Duc de Morny. In 1853 the group was joined by Napoleon's wife Eugenie – a strong-willed, devout Catholic, whose influence grew as the years passed. Napoleon sought to do more than simply preserve stability and order. He was very open to the possibility of change if he could be persuaded that the change was in a direction desired by the majority of his subjects. He accepted that his government had responsibility for the welfare of the poor and made efforts to woo the working class – for example, by clearing slums and meeting delegates of workers to listen to grievances. For much of the 1850s, helped by full employment and rising prosperity, he seems to have enjoyed huge support. The 1857 elections returned a massive government majority. The electoral system was in part rigged: towns were joined to rural constituencies to swamp radical working-class voters; and prefects and mayors ensured that official candidates were well supported.

d) The liberal empire: 1859–70

The changes to the political system in the early 1860s, while relatively small, indicated that Napoleon III intended to move towards a less dictatorial style of government as and when the time was right to do so. The 1869–70 changes still left him with huge powers. He could appoint and dismiss ministers. He nominated the Senate whose members could veto legislation passed by the Chamber. If the Assembly failed to support his policy, he could go over their heads and consult the people directly by holding a plebiscite. Nevertheless, the 1869–70 changes were important. Ministers, now responsible to the Assembly, needed to command majority support in the two houses. Early in 1870 a new ministry was formed with Olivier, a republican and ex-opponent of Napoleon, as premier. In May 1870 the French people were asked to agree to what was in effect a new constitution. 7,336,000 voted 'yes' and 1,560,000 voted 'no'.

Some think that the political changes of the 1860s were simply an attempt to buy off mounting opposition. In 1863 Napoleon III's opponents won two million votes and 35 seats. Of the 22 largest towns in France, 18, including Paris, fell to the republicans. As unemployment rose in the 1860s, there was growing unrest among industrial workers. In the 1869 elections 43 per cent of the votes cast went against official candidates. Many newspapers called for changes in the system. A wave of public meetings in Paris in 1869–70 showed the appeal of revolutionary ideas to a sizeable minority. By 1869 labour unrest in Paris, Lyon and Marseille was becoming endemic. All this raised fears of revolution if something was not done. However, the notion that the liberal empire was a direct result of growing opposition is mistaken. While opposition was growing, Napoleon III was not in serious danger. He had a massive majority in the Chamber. The liberal reform stemmed from genuine conviction – not political pressure. Napoleon III always claimed that the dictatorship he set up in 1852 was a temporary expedient. When he began to liberalise in 1860, the initiative came largely from him. Apart from the Duc de Morny, no other senior politician in his entourage supported constitutional reform. Morny's death in 1865 was a major blow to Napoleon III's plans. Often in great pain as a result of serious gallstone problems, he found it hard to force ministers to implement policies in which they did not believe. Only after the 1869 election did he summon sufficient energy to introduce the power-sharing policy that he had been meaning to follow for some time.

One other factor may have influenced his decision: the long-term survival of his regime. Given his failing health, he feared that he might not be able to guarantee the succession of his young son. The move towards constitutional government may have been a deliberate attempt to ensure support for the regime in the event of his retirement or death.

THE LIBERAL EMPIRE 1859–70

1859 a general amnesty was granted to all political opponents still under sentence following the December 1851 coup;

1860 –1 the Senate and Chamber were given the right to debate the government's proposals; the Chamber was also given increased influence over the budget. newspapers were allowed to report parliamentary debates, as long as they did so in full;

1864 strikes were legalised;

1867 the Senate and Chamber were given the right to question government ministers and to receive parliamentary replies to their questions;

1868 control of the press was relaxed; the laws controlling public meetings were also virtually abandoned; Workers were allowed to form trade unions;

1869 –70 the Chamber was accorded full parliamentary status with the right to initiate legislation; ministers were made responsible to parliament.

Q Was the liberalisation of the Empire part of Napoleon III's long-term plan?

Napoleon III and the Catholic Church

In 1852 the Catholic hierarchy, fearful of radical republicanism, welcomed the Second Empire and won from it valuable concessions. Church control over education was extended. Clerical salaries were increased and religious orders were tolerated. Napoleon III carefully cultivated the Catholic Church – an important ally in ensuring peasant support. However, his desire to champion the Catholic cause became harder to sustain once the Pope (in 1864) declared himself to be opposed to modern 'errors' such as liberalism and nationalism. Moreover, Catholic control of education posed an implicit threat to Bonapartism if only because it deepened existing ideological divisions. Many Frenchmen were deeply anti-clerical. In 1863 the new minister of education, Duroy, set about trying to rescue education from church control. The number of secular schools was increased and he even proposed establishing secular secondary schools for girls. The clergy, who saw educating girls as the key to the religious devotion of future generations, objected strongly. Fearful of losing Catholic support, Napoleon III jettisoned Duroy in 1869.

e) How much economic progress occurred in the Second Empire?

i) A new banking system

Napoleon III believed that prosperity was more important to the masses than the possession of abstract political rights. A disciple of the economic philosopher the Comte de Saint-Simon, he believed the key to creating additional wealth was the availability of plentiful credit. This would encourage entrepreneurs to begin new ventures. This, in turn, would provide more jobs, which would increase people's spending power, so encouraging entrepreneurs to start more ventures. In 1852 the banking system in France was in the hands of a few rich families, like the Rothschilds, who were reluctant to lend money unless there was a high degree of security. In 1852–3 therefore, Napoleon III supported the creation of three new banks. The most important was the Crédit Mobilier, run by the Pereire brothers, close associates of the Emperor. This bank looked to attract and invest the savings of ordinary French people, not just the wealthy. It helped provide the capital for many of the spectacular projects which took place in the Second Empire. However, in 1867 the Crédit Mobilier collapsed, partly as a result of opposition from the old banks. Hundreds of thousands of small investors lost money.

ii) Railway development

While over 1700 kms of track had been laid down pre-1848, there had been no government 'grand design'. Railways simply linked towns which were likely to generate enough traffic to justify the expenditure. Napoleon III, by contrast, tried to create a railway system which would link all regions of France together, making it possible to move people and goods quickly and cheaply. By 1870 some 17,700 kilometres of railway had been built.

iii) Urban renewal

Under Napoleon a huge programme of urban renewal occurred. In Paris in particular, a conscious effort was made to create a capital that was in keeping with the new Napoleonic age. The detailed work was entrusted to Baron Haussmann. The central idea in the remodelling of the capital was that there should be a series of long, straight and broad roads radiating from a central square, with a large number of interconnecting roads and squares. New buildings – shops, offices, houses – were built in an architectural pattern prescribed by the authorities. A new sewer system, a pure water supply and gas lighting were also part of the grand design. The rebuilding provided a huge amount of employment opportunities and also added greatly to the regime's prestige as Paris became the civic showpiece of Europe. However, some contemporaries attacked Haussmann's high and mighty attitude and the unorthodox means he used to raise money for his venture. Later critics have pointed out that the new Paris was often only one street deep: behind the boulevards were the remains of the old city – overcrowded, insanitary and dilapidated. Arguably Haussmann and Napoleon were more interested in appearances than the conditions in which the poor lived. The 20,000 houses demolished in the rebuilding programme had provided cheap accommodation for Paris's rapidly growing population. No attempt was made to provide affordable houses for the labouring poor.

iv) Overseas investment

A large proportion of French capital was invested in overseas ventures. The most famous of these was the Suez Canal (completed in 1869), engineered by Ferdinand de Lesseps.

v) Industrialisation

Industrial production increased by 50 per cent between 1851–70. Iron and coal output more than quadrupled. But across the industrial sector as a whole annual growth was similar to that for the reign of Louis-Philippe. Other areas, not least Germany, had greater industrial success. The France of 1870 was structurally very similar to the France of 1848. Two thirds of the people still earned their living from the land. Large factories were few and far between, and less than 10 per cent of the workforce was employed in heavy industry.

vi) The impact of free trade

Napoleon III was convinced that free trade would ensure prosperity for France. However, his free trade vision was fiercely opposed by most French industrialists who feared British competition. Nevertheless, in 1860 Napoleon III agreed to a free trade treaty with Britain. Eight more free trade treaties with other European states followed. Ironically, despite the heated debate at the time, historians have failed to identify, with certainty, any major results of free trade. While some firms went out of business (supposedly) because of foreign competition, French industry was not destroyed. Indeed, it may have benefited from the increase in economic activity that followed the lowering of tariffs. French trade more than doubled between 1855–70.

f) Napoleon III's foreign policy

Napoleon's aims in foreign policy:
▼ to restore France to her traditional place as the leading European power;
▼ to destroy the 1815 settlement as this was a continuing symbol of France's defeat;
▼ to support emerging nationalisms and make France the protector of new nations;
▼ to win popularity in France by success abroad;
▼ to maintain peace but not necessarily to abandon small-scale military enterprises.

Success in the 1850s and early 1860s:
▼ Success in the Crimean War (see chapter 4) helped French prestige;
▼ In the years 1856–63 Napoleon's prestige was at its height; a short period of Franco-Russian friendship reinforced the feeling that France was again Europe's leading power;
▼ French forces were successful in Italy against the Austrians in 1859 (see chapter 5); France gained Nice and Savoy;
▼ Napoleon III had some success in extending the French Empire overseas. By 1857 Algeria was conquered. Other colonies were established in West Africa and Indo-China.

Failure in the 1860s:
▼ French policy in Italy (see chapter 5) alienated Italian nationalists;
▼ When the Russian Poles rose in revolt in 1863 Napoleon III alienated Tsar Alexander II by his pro-Polish speeches, while offering no practical aid to the rebels;
▼ Napoleon III's efforts to establish an empire in Mexico were an embarrassing fiasco;
▼ Napoleon III misjudged the 1866 Prusso-Austrian crisis (see chapter 6); anticipating a long war, he stood on the sidelines while Austria was crushed; his belated claims for compensation in the Rhineland, Belgium and Luxembourg got nowhere;
▼ By 1870 France was diplomatically isolated and facing a strong new German neighbour.
▼ To some extent Napoleon III was unfortunate. His declining health made it difficult for him to concentrate on anything for long. Moreover, in Bismarck he found himself up against an able adversary. But he brought much of his misfortune upon himself. He believed that he was born lucky and that if he kept trying he would run into a lucky streak. This false confidence was often a substitute for careful thought.

The Franco-Prussian War
In 1870 the Hohenzollern candidature issue and the Ems telegram (see pages 165–6 and 172) resulted in the Franco-Prussian War. The Empress Eugenie, the court circle, French newspapers and politicians pushed Napoleon III into a war he did not really want to fight. The war, declared on 19 July, was always likely to be a disaster. Germany had huge trained reserves and a powerful officer corps. Attempts by Napoleon III in the 1860s to bolster French military strength by widening conscription had foundered on opposition from generals who rejected the value of conscripts, and on the Emperor's reluctance to alienate the peasants. Moreover, Napoleon III's clumsy diplomacy had ensured that France was diplomatically isolated. With key units in Rome and Algeria and a railway network clogged up by men and equipment, it took France two weeks to assemble 200,000 men. Rather than marching on Berlin, French forces found themselves defending their own country. The ageing and sick Emperor compounded his errors by taking personal command of the army, thus bearing personal blame for the military defeats which by September 3 1870 had forced his surrender at Sedan. This brought down his regime. After spending some time as a prisoner in Germany, he went into exile in England where he died in 1873.

g) Napoleon III and the Second Empire: conclusion

Many of those who have written about the Second Empire have been less than flattering. Napoleon III can be seen as promising much but achieving little. He can be criticised for replacing a democratic republic with an oppressive authoritarian regime, and for doing little to help the 'have nots'. Some see the disastrous war of 1870 as the fitting finale to a corrupt, incompetent regime. But Napoleon III has his admirers. Arguably the catastrophe of 1870 obscured many of his achievements. He can be seen as a far-sighted and pragmatic leader, keen to reconcile the desire for liberty and democracy with the principle of order. His view was that a leader must work with and not against the fundamental forces of his age. He saw nationalism and political representation as such forces. As a champion of the principle of nationality he had a significant impact on the reshaping of mid-19th-century Europe. By the 1860s the Second Empire seemed to be evolving in a liberal direction. His use of plebiscites and manhood suffrage at election times gave the masses a sense of participation. His rule seemed to guarantee political and economic stability. Under Napoleon III most French people enjoyed increased prosperity. The 1870 plebiscite indicated he still had huge support, despite a decade of serious foreign policy blunders on his part.

Q 'He promised much but achieved little.' Is this a fair epitaph for Napoleon III?

h) The Third Republic 1870–1

i) The siege of Paris

The collapse of the Second Empire in September 1870 resulted in the mob taking to the streets of Paris. A Republic – the third in French history – was proclaimed. Moderate politicians in the Legislative Chamber declared a provisional government of national defence. Its leaders were republicans who had been opposed to Napoleon III. Encouraged by popular support in Paris, the new government determined not to surrender to Prussia. Declaring its intention to wage 'war to the death', it hoped to inspire the same national effort which had liberated France from her enemies in 1792. Parisians of all classes joined the National Guard to defend the capital. However, the new government faced a huge challenge. By the end of September German troops had surrounded the city. All hope for the relief of Paris lay with the new minister of the interior, Gambetta, who made a dramatic escape from the city in a balloon in October. While he succeeded in recruiting new provincial armies, the men were inexperienced and inefficiently led. They posed little threat to the disciplined Germans besieging Paris. Within the city there was great hardship as food and fuel supplies began to run out. Cats, dogs, rats and the animals of the zoos were eaten by hungry Parisians. To compound their misery, German artillery began a regular bombardment. On 28 January 1871

France agreed armistice terms. Paris capitulated and the war, in which 150,000 Frenchmen had died, was over.

ii) The Commune

In February 1871 elections were held for a new national assembly. The assembly was overwhelmingly monarchist. Most peasants remained suspicious of radical urban ideas. The experienced politician Adolphe Thiers (1797–1877) became head of the new – no longer provisional – government which met in Bordeaux. He faced huge difficulties.

▼ He had to make peace with Germany. By the terms of the Treaty of Frankfurt (signed in May 1871) France lost Alsace-Lorraine and had to pay 5,000 million francs to Germany. German forces would remain on French soil until the indemnity was paid.

▼ Paris was seething with discontent. Most Parisians regarded the armistice as an act of treachery and had little confidence in Thiers's regime. Thiers, in turn, was suspicious of Paris where revolutions had caused changes of government in 1789, 1814, 1830, 1848 and 1870. He had little sympathy with Parisians. Three of his actions alienated Paris.

▼ The assembly moved from Bordeaux to Versailles, not Paris.

▼ In early March the pay of the Parisian National Guard, 250,000 strong, was suspended. It provided the only income for thousands made redundant by economic disruption.

▼ The assembly ordered the immediate payment of rents and commercial bills 'frozen' for the duration of the war. Many Parisians were thus threatened with bankruptcy or eviction.

By March Paris was a potential powder keg. On 18 March Thiers ordered regular troops to enter Paris and seize some 400 cannon held by the National Guard. There was violence and two generals were murdered by a mob. Thiers now withdrew his administration and loyal troops from Paris to Versailles. The Central Committee of the National Guard suddenly found it held power in Paris. On 26 March elections took place in Paris to form a municipal government – the Commune. Its name identified it with the spirit of the French Revolution and the Paris Commune of 1793. Composed of various radical groups, especially Jacobins and Socialists, and both working- and middle-class elements, it was to govern Paris for 73 days. Bitter internal feuding meant it was unable to agree on any real programme. Recent historians have debunked the Commune's socialist credentials. While it created cooperative workshops, its leaders were far from out-and-out socialist revolutionaries and there was no coherent assault upon capitalism. Commune leaders were largely preoccupied with military matters. In fact, real power continued to rest with the National Guard which was not unanimous in recognising the Commune's authority.

To what extent was Thiers to blame for the Commune?

Why did France not become a monarchy after 1871?

SOME RESULTS OF THE COMMUNE

▼ It discredited the 'left' in France for a whole generation.

▼ Some think the Commune injected a permanent and bitter rift into French politics (although arguably the Commune was proof that the rift was already there).

▼ Thiers had successfully tamed Paris. It was never again to decide the fate of France.

To Thiers the Commune was a revolutionary challenge to his government which he was determined to crush. Most Frenchmen supported him. Aided by the German release of 400,000 French prisoners-of-war, government forces besieged Paris, finally breaking into the city on 21 May. In the seven days which followed – 'bloody week' – Paris was recaptured street by street. The communards murdered hostages, including the Archbishop of Paris, and set fire to parts of the city. Government troops took few prisoners. The final death toll was around 25,000. In the aftermath some 25,000 Parisians were imprisoned or transported to overseas penal settlements. The 'right's' harsh revenge helped give the Commune a tragic grandeur, at least in the 'left's' eyes, which it did not deserve.

i) The provisional republic: 1871–77

i) Monarchist division

Given that some 400 monarchists were elected in February 1871 out of a total of some 650 delegates, it seemed likely that France would re-establish a constitutional monarchy. However, the monarchists were divided: a minority supported the Bourbon claimant, the Count of Chambord; the majority supported the Orleanist claimant, the Count of Paris. A compromise solution was eventually worked out. Orleanists accepted that the 53-year-old and childless Chambord could become king on the understanding that he would be succeeded by the Count of Paris. However, this solution was scuppered by Chambord. Although he agreed to the principles of parliamentary government, he refused to accept the tricolour as the national flag, preferring the royalist white flag. Such was the attachment of most French people, including most Orleanists, to the flag of the revolution that Chambord's stubborn stand effectively made a Bourbon restoration impossible.

ii) Thiers

Thiers, 'Chief of the Executive Power', ruled well. In addition to the great achievement of paying off the war indemnity to Germany in 1873 he pleased the middle classes by rejecting proposals for an income tax, and by favouring a return to economic protectionism. In late 1872 Thiers, previously an Orleanist, declared himself in favour of a Republic – 'the form of government which divides us least'. This incensed the monarchists and in July 1873 they forced Thiers' resignation. However, the monarchists' position was weakening. Their electoral success in 1871 was something of a freak result. Most peasants had voted for monarchist candidates because they had wanted peace and stability, not because they particularly wanted a king. After 1871 the monarchist tide quickly ebbed. Republicans won 99 of the first 114 seats contested in by-elections and a monarchical restoration grew increasingly unlikely as the Bourbons and Orleanists continued to squabble. In 1873 Marshal MacMahon, a devout Catholic and ultra-conservative, became president. MacMahon's government, often referred to as the 'Republic of Dukes' (it included seven dukes), made determined efforts to salvage the monarchists' declining cause.

iii) The 1875 constitution

By a single vote (353–352) and after vehement debate, the Chamber voted that MacMahon should be entitled 'President of the Republic'. But the additional laws that made up the 'Constitution of 1875' were designed to strengthen the electoral chances of the conservative/ monarchist parties. The president, whose period of office had been fixed at seven years in 1874, became eligible for re-election at the end of his term. Instead of being elected directly by the people, he was to be elected by a majority of the two houses of the National Assembly. An upper chamber (Senate) was instituted, with 75 of its members chosen for life and 225 elected for nine years. The president and Senate were intended to counterbalance the Chamber, elected by universal suffrage every four years. The president, Chamber and Senate could each initiate legislation. The constitution also gave the president the power to dissolve the Chamber before its term expired. It was thus not clear where real power lay.

iv) The crisis of 16 May 1877

The 1876 elections were a major disappointment to MacMahon. Some two thirds of the Chamber deputies were republican. However, conservative groups controlled the Senate. MacMahon and the Chamber soon clashed. Faced with a political deadlock, the President, acting within his constitutional powers, appointed an unrepresentative administration under the conservative Duc de Broglie in May 1877 and dissolved the Assembly. (Republicans described this as a 'coup'.) MacMahon dismissed 70 prefects, 226 sub-prefects, and 1743 mayors in an attempt to secure maximum local influence in favour of conservative candidates. Leading republicans such as Gambetta and Grévy retaliated by fighting an energetic election campaign. The republicans lost a few seats but easily retained control of the Chamber. MacMahon struggled on with a succession of ministers for a few months but the Chamber would pass no legislation. In December 1877 he was forced to capitulate and accepted another republican administration. Henceforward the Chamber would have to approve ministerial appointments. While the President retained the power to dissolve the Chamber, this power was never used again. In 1879 the republicans even won control of the Senate. They proceeded to fill the civil service and judiciary with their supporters. When they proposed to replace a number of generals, MacMahon resigned and Grévy became president. The Third Republic was now firmly in republican hands.

THE 'OPPORTUNIST' REPUBLICANS

By the mid-1870s most republican leaders adhered to the principle of Thiers that 'the Republic will be conservative or it will not be at all'. By abandoning their radicalism, they were branded as 'opportunists'. The opportunists won support from the lower middle classes and from peasants. Many of their deputies were ex-Orleanists or ex-Bonapartists. While there were various shades of republican opinion, most republicans were anti-clerical, wanting the education system to be free of all religious influences.

FRANCE 1851–77

1851 Louis Napoleon's coup d'état;

1852 Louis Napoleon proclaimed Emperor as Napoleon III;

1870 Franco-Prussian War: end of Second Empire: Republic proclaimed;

1871 end of Franco-Prussian War: the Commune;

1875 constitution of the Third Republic;

1877 failure of the 'coup' of 16 May.

▼ Working on Austria: c.1850–80

Historians have different views about the success of Austria after 1848. What points might you make to suggest that Austria was reasonably successful? What points might you make to suggest that she was failing?

Answering extended writing and essay questions on Russia: c.1850–80

Consider the following view of Alexander II's reign: 'He promised much but delivered little.' Discuss this view.

The best approach to this question is first to consider Alexander's aims and then to consider his achievements. It is worth noting that his main concern was to streamline the autocracy in order to ensure its survival. He did not intend to introduce a more liberal constitutional system. From a radical perspective, therefore, he did not promise a great deal! Ironically, his reforms perhaps went further than he intended. Emancipation of the serfs removed the mechanism which had regulated Russian society for centuries. Major reform was now required to establish a new framework. The issue was not whether there would be other reforms but how they would be planned and implemented. My answer to this question might be that he did not promise much but in the end delivered a lot! But do not simply agree with my conclusion – or for that matter with the quote in the question. Have the courage to come up with your own answer. You might argue, for example, that he did not promise or deliver much. You might even argue he promised a great deal and lived up to expectations!

Answering source-based questions on France 1848–77

ALL BUT HATCHED!

Source B

SCENE FROM "THE PRESIDENT'S PROGRESS."
(Suggested by HOGARTH.*)*

▼ QUESTIONS ON SOURCES

1. Examine Source A. What point is the cartoonist trying to make? **[3 marks]**

2. Examine Source B. Identify the characters. What point is the cartoonist trying to make? **[7 marks]**

3. Using both sources and your own knowledge, explain why Napolean III came to power in France in 1852. **[15 marks]**

Further Reading

Books in the Access to History series

All the following are highly recommended: *France: Monarchy, Republic and Empire 1814–70* and *France: The Third Republic 1870–1914*, both by K. Randell, *Russia 1815–81* by R. Sherman and *The Habsburg Empire* by N. Pelling.

General

As an introduction try *Europe Reshaped 1848–1878* by J. A. S. Grenville (Fontana, 1976). On Russia try *Russia in the Age of Reaction and Reform 1801–1881* by D. Saunders (Longman, 1992) and *Rulers and Subjects: Government and People in Russia 1801–1991* by J. Gooding (Edward Arnold, 1996). On Austria try *The Decline and Fall of the Habsburg Empire 1815–1918* by A. Sked (Longman, 1989) and *The Habsburg Monarchy* by R. Okey (Macmillan, 2000). On France try *France 1814–1914* by R. Tombs (Longman, 1996), *Second Empire and Commune: France 1848–71* by W. H. C. Smith (Longman, 1996), and *Napoleon III and the Second Empire* by R. D. Price (Routledge, 1997).

9 GERMANY, FRANCE AND RUSSIA 1880–1914

POINTS TO CONSIDER

Europe was the world's most successful continent in 1880 and arguably became stronger and richer still between 1880 and 1914. Only the USA could, and increasingly did, pose a challenge to European dominance. However, it is difficult to generalise about Europe as a whole. There were major social, economic and political differences between the various countries. Different countries, therefore, faced different challenges. This chapter, after a general introduction, will examine the challenges facing Germany, France and Russia in the period 1880–1914.

KEY ISSUE:
How serious were the social, economic and political problems in France, Germany, and Russia in the years 1880–1914?

1 General European trends 1880–1914

a) What were the main economic and social trends?

i) Population growth

Between 1850–1914 Europe's population increased from 226 million to 468 million. This was the result of both a decline in death rate and a rise in birth rate. Large families remained the norm until the early 20th century. Europe's poorest areas tended to have the largest population growth. The growth would have been even greater but for the emigration of many Europeans, especially to the USA and South America. The mass exodus – over one million Europeans a year – was the greatest transfer of population in the world's history. The motives of the emigrants, mainly men, were complex – a mixture of the 'push' of adverse conditions at home and the 'pull' of better prospects overseas.

Table 1 Population table

Year (approx in some cases)	USA	Great Britain	Germany	France	Russia
1870	39.9	26.1	41.1	36.1	84.5
1900	76.1	37.0	56.4	38.5	132.9
1910	92.4	40.8	64.9	39.2	160.7

ii) Industrialisation

Western and northern Europe were far more industrialised than eastern and southern Europe. By 1914 Germany had overtaken Britain in coal and iron production and did even better in what is sometimes termed the 'second industrial revolution' – the production of steel, chemicals and electricity. Increasingly, industrialisation in Germany and elsewhere was characterised by large-scale production. Although European industry was growing rapidly, Europe's share of world manufacturing output was decreasing, due to the massive expansion of the American economy.

Share of world industrial production (percentages)					
	USA	Great Britain	Germany	France	Russia	All Others
1870	23	32	13	10	4	18
1896–1900	30	20	17	7	5	21
1910	36	14	16	6	6	22

Table 2 Share of world industrial production

iii) Urbanisation

As industry grew, so did towns and cities. They proved to be less turbulent than many contemporaries had feared (or hoped!). Schools, social and sports clubs, trade unions, churches and political parties helped the new urban populations to integrate. As towns grew, so did service sector jobs – in health, education, transport, etc. New methods of retail distribution helped meet the increasing demands of urban consumers.

iv) Agriculture

Most Europeans still worked on the land in 1880. Farming methods in many parts of southern and eastern Europe remained the same as they had been for generations.

v) Communications

Cheap and rapid forms of transport – railways, trams, steamships – were increasingly available. Automobiles began to be produced in the 1890s and by 1914 aeroplanes were no longer a novelty. Telegraph and telephone services continued to develop and in 1901 Marconi sent the first radio signals across the Atlantic.

vi) Trade

By the late 19th century there was a truly international economy in which Europe played a crucial role. By 1914 the imports and exports of Britain, France, Germany, Belgium, Holland and Denmark accounted for half the world's trade. Most countries, with the exception of Britain, had high tariffs to protect both their industries and agriculture.

RISING LIVING STANDARDS

Across Europe there were massive gaps between the 'haves' and 'have-nots'. Even in the most advanced countries, many still lived in abject poverty. However, ordinary Europeans experienced a rise in living standards and a longer life expectancy.

▼ Industrial workers saw a reduction in the average hours of work.

▼ By 1914 several countries had introduced old age pensions and national insurance schemes for workers.

▼ Despite occasional 'slumps', 1880–1914 was a period of sustained economic expansion.

▼ Food prices were falling and Europeans could enjoy a wide range of overseas products, thanks to improvements in transport and new technology (for example, refrigeration).

▼ Medicine was increasingly scientific in both its methods of diagnosis and its developments of cures and anaesthetics. There was a marked reduction in infant deaths.

▼ Most governments insisted on minimum standards of hygiene and building in cities.

▼ Industrial workers had more leisure time. Some families were able to afford a holiday and men (in particular) involved themselves in a variety of sports and hobbies.

vii) Education

By 1914 primary education was free and compulsory almost everywhere in western Europe. Most of those who lived in industrial societies were literate. This, coupled with technical advances, led to a great increase in sales of newspapers and magazines. The political and advertising power of the cheap popular press was immense. The thirst for knowledge seemed insatiable and there was an enormous demand for books of all kinds. The spread of knowledge and new ideas speeded up the erosion of old certainties.

viii) Women's status

Women's status was slowly changing. Although very few women had the right to vote, upper- and middle-class women had more freedom. Many were limiting their child-bearing, thus liberating themselves for other activities. The expansion of women's education enabled women to enter careers which had previously been an all-male preserve. Madame Curie, for example, became a world famous scientist. For those who did not reach the heights of Curie, there were new jobs as teachers or office workers. However, peasant and working-class women were still tied to the home or continued to work for very low wages in factories, on farms or as domestic servants.

b) What were the main political trends?

i) Monarchy

Most countries still had a monarch. The only republics by 1914 were France, Switzerland, Portugal and San Marino. While some kings had limited political influence, the Russian tsars and the German and Austro-Hungarian emperors wielded huge power.

ii) The elite

In most states wealthy elites, whether traditional landowners or new industrialists, held leading positions in the government, army and civil service. However, the old aristocracy was losing some of its control, even in conservative Russia and Austria-Hungary.

iii) Parliamentary democracy

▼ Only Russia, Turkey and Montenegro did not have a parliament in 1900.

▼ Only Finland and Norway allowed women to vote.

▼ Only Spain and Sweden shared Britain's two-party system. Elsewhere there was a spate of parties. Governments, therefore, were invariably coalitions of various groups.

▼ Not everyone favoured parliamentary democracy. Some on the right believed it led to weak government. Some on the left associated it with the middle class and attacked politicians for not representing the real interests of the people.

iv) The growth of the State

Most governments now concerned themselves with issues like social welfare and education. This led to the growth of bureaucracies and an increase in cost. However, the greatest expenditure of most states still went on the armed forces.

v) The liberal decline

In the 1860s and 1870s liberal parties had seemed to carry all before them, taking power in one country after another and introducing their characteristic policies – parliamentary rule, civil liberties and free trade. However, in the late 19th century, the liberals declined. Some think the Great Depression, which began in 1873, was the beginning of the end for the liberals. While not particularly 'great', the depression reduced economic growth and perhaps led to a growing distrust of both liberal politicians and free trade. New extreme forces on both the left and right emerged, affecting almost every country in Europe.

The nationalities problem

Minority ethnic groups, who clamoured for home rule or complete independence, posed problems for many existing states. Some governments tried to appease the minorities by concessions: others attempted to impose the dominant language and culture. Ironically both policies tended to stimulate rather than reduce minority national consciousness.

---

vi) Mass nationalism

For much of the 19th century nationalism had been regarded as the ideology of the left. It had been associated with liberalism and a desire to overthrow conservative regimes and create states which reflected the wishes of the nation. However, once nation states had been formed, conservative forces sought to harness – perhaps exploit – nationalist sentiment. It could be used, for example, to combat the destabilising politics of socialism. Most governments set out to promote a sense of national identity in the mass of their people, particularly through education, military service (most states had conscription), and the creation of national symbols – festivals, heroes and anthems.

vii) Racism

A growing interest in race led numbers of European academics to try to define race and categorise racial characteristics. In the 1850s, for example, a Frenchmen, Count de Gobineau, argued that different races were physically and psychologically different. History, in Gobineau's view, was essentially a race struggle and the rise and fall of civilisations was racially determined. All the high cultures in the world were the work

THE INFLUENCE OF THE CHURCH

▼ Most Europeans remained devout Christians.

▼ Established churches, whether Catholic, Protestant or Orthodox, urged obedience to the law and vouched for the legitimacy of society and the State.

▼ The Church remained a major social, educational and charitable institution.

▼ The Church helped foster a sense of nationhood not only among majorities in nation states but also among national minorities (for example, the Poles in Russia).

However, the church was under attack:

▼ All churches, and even religion itself, were threatened by the progress of science. Charles Darwin's *Origin of Species* (1859), which put forward the idea of evolution, provided ammunition for the opponents of religion.

▼ The hold of organised religion on the urban working classes was weak.

▼ Some left-wing politicians were vehemently anti-clerical and wished to reduce or destroy altogether the power of the established Church.

of the 'Aryan', which equated with, but was not quite the same as, the 'Germanic', race. Charles Darwin's *Origin of Species* provided further ammunition for the race cause. Darwin himself said little about racial theories: his book was concerned with plants and animals. But his theory of natural selection as the means of evolution was adopted – and adapted – by many scholars. 'Social Darwinists' were soon claiming that races and nations needed to be fit to survive and rule. Not surprisingly German nationalists believed that the Aryans/Germans were the 'fittest' race. Russians assumed that the Slav race was God's chosen race on earth while Britons extolled the virtues of the Anglo-Saxon race.

viii) Anti-Semitism

Anti-Semitism was strong in many parts of eastern Europe, not least in Russia where there was a large Jewish population. Russian Jews not only suffered segregation and discrimination but were also liable to face violent assault. In the late 19th century, thousands of Russian Jews emigrated to the USA, Germany, Austria-Hungary, France and Britain. This encouraged the development of anti-Semitic tendencies in western and central Europe. Anti-Semitism in the past had been essentially religious (Jews were disliked for being 'Christ killers'). In the late 19th century it became increasingly racial. A host of late 19th century scholars helped make anti-Semitism fashionable and respectable. Pamphleteers, newspaper editors and politicians presented anti-Semitic views to the public. So did artists and musicians, like the German, Richard Wagner. Amongst the most prominent anti-Semitic writers was Wagner's son-in-law Houston Stewart Chamberlain. Chamberlain published his most influential work – *Foundations of the Nineteenth Century* – in 1899 claiming that the Jews were an evil race, conspiring to attain world domination and threatening German greatness. His book, a best-seller, even drew praise from Kaiser Wilhelm II. By the 1890s, many Germans regarded the Jews, never more than one per cent of the German population, as a threat to the purity of the nation. In France Jews also became a convenient scapegoat for virtually everything perceived to be wrong in society. In Austria the Christian Socialist Party became a mass party on the strength of its anti-Semitic propaganda.

ix) The rise of socialism

By the late 19th century, most socialists were influenced by the ideas of Karl Marx. Marx, a German Jew, spent most of his later life in Britain where he wrote *Das Kapital*, published in 1867. All history, Marx thought, was the history of class struggles. He claimed there was a growing gulf between the middle class (or *bourgeoisie*) who owned all the capital and the industrial working class (or *proletariat*). He believed that the exploited workers would inevitably rise up and overthrow the bourgeoisie and the capitalist system. The state, declared Marx, would then regulate the economy in the interests of the proletariat. Eventually there would be a classless society based on public ownership of the essential means of production.

Marx died in 1883 but his ideas, publicised by his collaborator, Frederick Engels, lived on, becoming something of a substitute religion for many working men. Those workers who espoused Marxism and who felt themselves to be terribly exploited, as indeed many were, looked forward to ultimate victory and a socialist millennium. Marxist doctrines underpinned the policies of the various socialist parties which began to play an active role in most European countries in the late 19th century. However, socialist leaders – most of whom were middle-class intellectuals, not workers – were divided on how best to achieve Marxist ends. While some extremists advocated violent revolution, moderates believed the best way to improve the lot of the proletariat was to work within the system and to cooperate with other parties to bring about social reform.

Socialist trade unions were similarly divided. Some were mainly concerned with trying to get higher wages and to reduce the working hours of their members: others were more revolutionary. *Syndicalists* – strong in France, Spain and Italy – believed that the general strike was the weapon which would destroy the capitalist system. While general strikes occurred in several countries, notably Italy, government authorities invariably stood firm: they had no intention of surrendering power to militant workers. The effectiveness of the general strike was thus a myth – albeit an inspiring one for some workers and intellectuals. Nevertheless, the strike was a powerful weapon. Railway workers and miners, in particular, could hold states to ransom.

Socialism seemed to pose a serious threat to the established order:

▼ Socialist doctrine threatened the overthrow of the ruling classes;

▼ Conservatives associated socialism with the chaos of the Paris Commune in 1871;

▼ Socialism's internationalist claims – 'workers of the world, unite' – seemed to threaten the existence of nation states.

Concerned about the potential appeal of socialism, conservative governments adopted a variety of strategies to counter it. Some, like Russia, used repression. Another strategy was to introduce legislation which improved the lot of the workers, as Bismarck attempted in Germany in the 1880s. These strategies did not stop socialist parties winning support but arguably did reduce the potential for revolution.

x) The anarchist threat

Anarchists posed another threat to the establishment. A Frenchman, Pierre Joseph Proudhon, one of the founders of anarchism, had claimed that 'property is theft'. He also opposed all traditional forms of government. His ideal society consisted of small communities running their own affairs with little or no central administration. In

---

MARXIST MISCONCEPTIONS

By 1900 it was – or should have been – apparent that Marx had got most things wrong – not least the notion that the capitalist system was on the point of collapse.

▼ His assumption that the proletariat would be loyal to their class proved to be naive. In practice, many workers were indifferent or hostile to socialism. Moreover, there were significant inequalities between different sub-groups of workers according to particular industries or local conditions. Workers found it even harder to unite internationally.

▼ Marx believed that industrialisation and middle-class revolution must precede the proletarian revolution. Thus his ideas did not seem to have much potential in countries like Russia where there was little industry. Ironically, proletarian revolution was to achieve its greatest success in Russia.

▼ Marx believed that the proletariat would become poorer and poorer. Instead standards of living were rising for most workers.

the late 19th century, Proudhon's influence spread and anarchists such as Bakunin in Russia declared war on all institutions – the State, capitalism, and religion. Bakunin supported the use of terror to sweep away existing institutions. Between 1893 and 1900 President Carnot of France, Empress Elisabeth of Austria-Hungary, and King Umberto of Italy were killed by anarchist terrorists. However, such terrorist acts did little to win anarchist support. In many respects anarchism and socialism were in competition with each other. Their aims were incompatible: socialists aimed to capture the State while anarchists aimed to destroy it. However, anarchism and socialism were not totally seperate movements. Some anarchists had socialist leanings and some socialists admired anarchist theory – and action. While the working class generally preferred socialism, the anarchists gave the socialists a run for their money in Spain and Italy.

xi) Right v. left

In most European countries there were deep political divisions. These divisions were often based on class. However, religion, race and nationality were similarly divisive. In an attempt to explain the divisions, historians brand particular groups as right or left wing. The left – anarchists, socialists, and radical liberals – wanted to change society, particularly in the interests of the 'have-nots'. The right tended to be nationalistic, conservative, and often favoured strong authoritarian government. However this right-left divide is somewhat crude. In reality, there were many different brands of 'right' and 'left', and groups termed 'right' and 'left' often had very little in common.

ACTIVITY

Brainstorm three or four reasons why European governments were often prepared to take vigorous political action against socialists and anarchists.

ISSUE:
Was Wilhelmine Germany 'modern' or 'backward'?

2 Wilhelmine Germany

a) What were the main social and economic developments in Germany?

In the late 19th century Germany became a great industrial nation. The statistics speak for themselves. Between 1870 and 1914 coal production increased by over 200 per cent (compared with Britain's 58 per cent) while steel production rose an incredible 80-fold (only 22-fold in Britain.) After 1890 the electrical industry was perhaps Germany's greatest economic achievement, producing over a third of the world's electrical goods by 1914. There were similar advances in the chemical industry.

Figure 1 Rate of economic growth 1880–1900

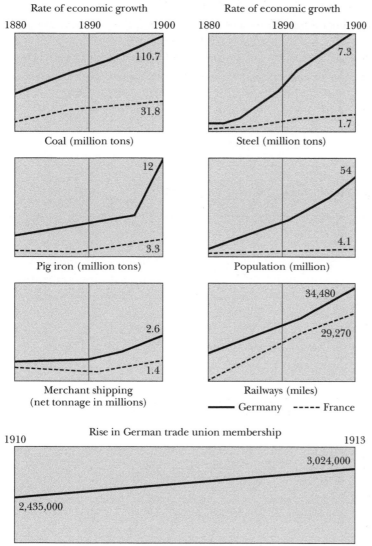

Rate of economic growth

1880   1890   1900

110.7

31.8

Coal (million tons)

Rate of economic growth

1880   1890   1900

7.3

1.7

Steel (million tons)

12

3.3

Pig iron (million tons)

54

4.1

Population (million)

2.6

1.4

Merchant shipping
(net tonnage in millions)

34,480

29,270

Railways (miles)

—— Germany   - - - - France

Rise in German trade union membership

1910   1913

3,024,000

2,435,000

Trade union membership

Industrialisation and urbanisation produced a huge proletariat. Some industrialists, concerned about their workers' welfare, provided housing and health services. In return, they expected the workforce to display loyalty, sometimes banning workers from joining trade unions. Even so, trade unions arose and demanded – and often won – higher pay and better working conditions. Despite growing industrialisation, over one third of Germans continued to work on the land. Many farmers, great and small alike, were hostile to the values of industrial society.

FACTORS ENCOURAGING GERMANY'S ECONOMIC EXPANSION

▼ An excellent education system including technical colleges and universities.

▼ Population growth – the population grew from 49 to 65 million between 1890–1910.

▼ Capital – German banks were prepared to invest heavily in German industry.

▼ Mineral resources – Germany had massive amounts of coal and iron ore.

▼ A good transport system, including navigable rivers, railways and canals.

▼ Cartels – many industries were organised into cartels – large companies that were able to fix prices and do away with the hazards of competition.

How strong was German nationalism?

German nationalism was strong. Urbanisation, education, better communications, and military service all helped to wear down provincial isolation and promote a German identity. But Germany was not totally united. It remained a nation of 25 states and territories, some of which were hostile to Prussia, the dominant state, and resisted assimilation into a national German culture. Moreover over six per cent of the population were Poles, Danes and French who had little loyalty to Germany.

b) How was Germany governed?

The Prussian state government

Prussia's archaic constitution, dating from 1850, ensured that conservative landowners (*junkers*) and industrialists remained in control, dominating the Prussian parliament and the civil service. In 1908 socialists, with 23 per cent of the vote, won seven seats in the Prussian parliament. Conservatives, with 16 per cent of the vote, won 212 seats. (Most German states were far more democratic than Prussia.)

The role of the army

The army played a key role in German politics and society. Many Germans saw the army as the symbol of German greatness, and extolled its virtues. Troops took an oath of personal loyalty to the Kaiser rather than to the State, and in many respects were independent of any control other than the Kaiser's.

Table 3 Reichstag election results

	1890	1893	1898	1903	1907	1912
Conservatives	73	72	56	54	60	43
Independent Conservatives	20	28	23	21	24	14
National Liberals	423	53	46	51	54	45
Liberal Progressives	66	37	41	31	42	42
German People's Party	10	11	7	9	7	–
Centre Party	106	96	102	100	105	91
Social Democrats	35	44	56	81	43	110
Nationalities: e.g. Poles, Danes	38	35	34	32	29	33
Others	7	21	41	22	33	19

c) What did Germany's main political parties stand for?

▼ The two conservative parties and the various right-wing splinter parties generally wished to maintain the existing order.

▼ The liberal parties wanted to create a genuine parliamentary democracy in which the government was directly responsible to the *Reichstag*, not to the Kaiser.

▼ The Centre Party had been formed to uphold the interests of the Catholic Church. Its members' socio-political views ranged from reactionary conservatism to progressive social reform. Its parliamentary strength was such that it usually enjoyed a pivotal role in German politics.

▼ The rise of the Social Democrats (the SPD) was the major political phenomenon of the era. The party was liberated by the lapse of the anti-socialist laws in 1890. While some SPD members wanted to smash the capitalist system, most were prepared to work with other parties to achieve social reform. In 1912 the SDP won almost 35 per cent of the vote and became the largest single party in the *Reichstag*. How to treat the party and its ideas were to be crucial issues for Wilhelm II and his Chancellors.

d) How important was Kaiser William II?

William II became Kaiser in 1888 and remained so until 1918. Some historians think he was responsible for all the misfortunes of his 30-year reign. He can be seen as immature, erratic, and prone to errors of judgement. 'The Kaiser is like a balloon,' said Bismarck. 'If you do not hold fast to the string, you never know where he will be off to.' Believing himself only accountable to God, he took a personal, interfering interest in almost every subject from ship design to theatrical productions. His love of military ceremonial verged on the pathological. Some historians think that if he was not clinically insane, he was deeply disturbed. He surrounded himself at court with odd characters, including a homosexually-inclined spiritualist. He frequently selected key officials for personal rather than political reasons: such men were often inadequate. William can be viewed sympathetically. The sufferings of his childhood (complications at his birth resulted in a withered left arm) and the lack of parental affection may explain his character. His military bearing may well have been a cover for a basic lack of confidence. Some scholars see him as an intelligent, energetic, and enthusiastic ruler. Others relegate him to the sidelines, arguing that his life was an endless whirl of state occasions, military manoeuvres, cruises, and hunting trips, and that his social duties meant that he did not have command of the detail of the government's work. They claim that while he may have meddled, he did

INTEREST GROUPS

Germany experienced a growth of economic and ideological interest groups. By 1914 Germany had the largest trade union movement in Europe. Farmers and industrialists also had pressure groups. Bodies like the Pan-German League and the Naval League embraced a range of ultra-nationalist and expansionist demands and were a symptom of growing political participation, especially on the part of the middle class. Historian William Carr believed that these right-wing pressure groups, through their propaganda and mass support, 'exerted more influence on the government than did the *Reichstag*'.

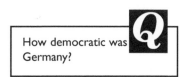

How democratic was Germany?

Figure 2 Kaiser William II

not have the ability or strength of character to determine the course of German policy. However, most historians think William played a vital role. Since he appointed and dismissed all members of the *Reich* and Prussian executives, he determined the parameters of what was and what was not possible. No major decision could be taken without his agreement.

e) What were the main political events?

After Bismarck's fall in 1890 politics in Germany became fluid and unpredictable. None of the chancellors who succeeded him had his authority. Accountable first and foremost to the Kaiser, their political survival was dependent upon his support. William's erratic interferences did not make life easy. Bismarck's immediate successor was Caprivi, a Prussian soldier who wanted to stand above parties and particular interests. More astute and independent-minded than William had bargained for, Caprivi embarked on a 'new course', taking a more conciliatory attitude to previously hostile forces, not least the Centre Party and the SDP. Winning a fair amount of backing from the *Reichstag*, he pushed through a number of social measures, including the prohibition of Sunday working and measures limiting child and female labour. He also negotiated a series of treaties which reduced German tariffs on agricultural goods in return for favourable rates for German manufactured goods. Welcomed by most Germans, the new tariff policy, which resulted in lower food prices, incurred the wrath of landholding interests which formed the Agrarian League in 1893. The League attacked Caprivi for his 'socialist' policies and demanded tariff protection for German farmers. For a few years William II continued his conciliatory policy towards socialism, in the hope that concessions would woo the moderates away from extremist policies. However, in 1894 William, fearful of the growing strength of the SDP, changed his mind and determined to stand firm against socialism. Caprivi refused to support a new anti-socialist bill and resigned.

Caprivi's successor Chlodwig, Prince of Hohenlohe-Schillingsfürst, was 75 years old. Although viewed as a stop-gap, he retained power until 1900. He was not expected to oppose the Kaiser's policies and lived up to this expectation. For several years William was the most decisive figure in the government, dictating most aspects of policy through loyal ministers like Tirpitz, navy secretary, and Bülow, foreign minister. The Kaiser's colonial and naval expansionist policies won support in the *Reichstag*. However, his efforts to take firm anti-socialist action met with little success. In 1900 Bülow became chancellor. Playing the part of an old-fashioned courtier, he retained the Kaiser's support through flattery. Caprivi's policy of making concessions to the workers was revived. For example, workers' entitlement to pension and insurance benefits was extended. However, responding to pressure from the Agrarian League, Bülow's government raised agricultural tariffs. This was unpopular with industrial workers because it meant a rise in food prices.

A crisis arose in 1908 following an article in the *Daily Telegraph* in which William expressed his wish for closer relations with Britain. *Reichstag* members questioned William's right to make such important policy statements. The Kaiser was forced to promise that in future he would respect the constitution, although arguably he had done nothing much wrong! For some months there was talk of constitutional changes to reduce the Kaiser's power. But nothing was done since the *Reichstag* could not agree on any acceptable alternative. In 1909 Bülow, having lost William's trust in the *Daily Telegraph* affair and unable to command a clear majority in the *Reichstag*, resigned. He was replaced by Bethmann-Hollweg – a hard-working, conservative bureaucrat.

The government's relations with the *Reichstag* continued to prove difficult. Right-wing parties – the Conservatives, Free Conservatives and National Liberals – which traditionally supported the government were in decline. In 1887 these parties won 55 per cent of the *Reichstag* seats. In 1912 they had only 26 per cent of the seats. This made it hard to obtain majority support. In 1913 there was a crisis over an incident at Zabern, a town in Alsace. Soldiers had dealt roughly with townspeople and those who subsequently demonstrated against the army's actions were rounded up and imprisoned by soldiers. There were public and official protests. The army defended itself by claiming to be accountable to the Kaiser alone. Only when the Alsace governor threatened to resign did William act. Rather than punish the soldiers concerned, he ordered them to be sent away on manoeuvres. In the *Reichstag*, all parties but the Conservatives joined the protests but achieved nothing. Bethmann-Hollweg stood by the Kaiser, receiving a massive vote of no confidence in the *Reichstag* for his pains. However, he retained William's confidence and thus remained as chancellor. While the Zabern incident showed that William could not ignore public opinion, it forcefully underlined the power of the Kaiser and the army.

f) Modern or backward?

By 1914 Germany was still in most respects an authoritarian monarchy, in which both William II and the old elites, particularly the army, retained their power. William claimed that 'there is only one Ruler in the Reich and I am he'. In Prussia, in particular, his position was almost unassailable. However, while the balance of power probably still rested with conservative forces in 1914, their right to govern was under threat and their right to govern as they would have liked was already being curtailed by popular forces. Neither the Kaiser nor his ministers could ignore the *Reichstag*. They needed – and often found it hard – to patch up working majorities in order to pass legislation. The *Reichstag*, with its increasing SDP presence, extended its right to debate government policy. Criticisms of William were commonplace and the German press had considerable freedom. Nor was William in a position to take firm action against his critics. While he might dream of using the army to strike against the SDP, none of his chancellors considered it: the risk would have been too great. There was thus something of a political stalemate in Germany which sometimes made for weak and confused government.

To what extent the Kaiser's powers were under threat is debatable. The middle classes were still solidly on the side of the establishment. The forces of law and order were very strong in imperial Germany and its economic wellbeing reduced discontent. While a majority of *Reichstag* members favoured constitutional changes of some sort, most had great respect for the monarchy and made no move to force the pace towards more parliamentary government. While there was much political tension and frustration in Germany in 1914 it is unlikely that a democratic revolution was in the offing.

In short, Wilhelmine Germany is difficult to sum up. The country, deeply divided by cleavages based upon geography, ethnicity, class, and religion, was also a house divided against itself politically. On the one hand it was a great modern state with the strongest economy in Europe and parliamentary democracy of a sort, with liberals and socialists in the majority, its people enjoying more freedom than most Europeans. On the other it was still governed by an old-style authoritarian regime, dismissive of public opinion. It is thus possible to argue that there was potential in Germany for future democratic development. It is also possible to argue that William's rule paved the way for Hitler.

ACTIVITY

Test your grasp of this section by answering the question, 'to what extent was Germany economically "modern" but politically "backward"?'

Suggested line of response

▼ No problems with the first part of the question. Germany was economically 'modern' (by the standards of the time). Stress her industrial strength.

▼ The 'politically backward' is more difficult. You will first need to define 'backward'. For the sake of argument, it is perhaps best to assume that 'backward' means autocratic rather than democratic. Even then, the question is not easy! It needs a 'yes' and 'no' type response. Yes…Germany was autocratic…No…Germany was a democracy of sorts.

3 France: the Third Republic

In 1870–1 France had suffered two severe shocks: defeat at the hands of Prussia; and a short-lived civil war (the Paris Commune). Despite a remarkably swift economic recovery, many French people felt a deep sense of national humiliation. The Third Republic came into existence as a result of the events in 1870–1. Perhaps because of this it was never particularly popular. Yet it survived. Why?

a) The social and economic situation

> ### On the negative side:
>
> ▼ French industrial progress was not as great as that of Germany.
> ▼ French industry was hampered by the loss of Alsace-Lorraine with its iron ore deposits.
> ▼ The French population hardly grew. In 1871 there were 37 million people. In 1911 there were only 39 million – a rise of less than 10 per cent. (Germany's population increased by over 50 per cent in the same period.)
> ▼ The proletariat was increasingly militant.

> ### On the positive side:
>
> ▼ The economy was diversified. Its traditional strengths – the production of food, wine, and luxury items – remained. Heavy industry grew rapidly and new industries – electricity, chemicals and automobiles – also developed.
> ▼ High tariffs succeeded in protecting French producers.
> ▼ From 1897 France enjoyed a period of prosperity. The period became known as *la belle époque* – the good old days. The standard of living rose. So did life expectancy: it was higher than in Germany in 1914.
> ▼ Paris was the cultural and artistic capital of Europe.
> ▼ Society was reasonably stable. More than half the population still worked on the land. The nobility was economically and politically insignificant. The mass of French farmers owned their own – small – farms. They provided a solid core to French society.

Why were there so many French prime ministers in the period?

b) How was France governed?

After 1871 there was a proliferation of political parties and a lack of party discipline. Politicians used various labels to get themselves elected: this was often no guideline to how they would behave in the Assembly. Individual deputies supported or deserted a ministry often for purely personal or local reasons. In consequence, the Chamber of Deputies was rarely able to produce a clear majority and governments changed with startling rapidity. (There were 50 ministries in 40 years.) Change did not usually mean significant differences of policy: indeed most governments came and went without managing to carry out any major measures. However, while ministries fell, individuals often stayed in – sometimes a different – office. There were important differences between right and left, which at times of crisis tended to polarise into two irreconcilable camps. These divisions were as much based on religion as class. The right, which had the support of the Catholic Church, was nationalist, often anti-Semitic and preferred order and strong government to democracy. It saw the army as the most important symbol of national unity and the means of hope of revenge against Germany. Some right-wing leaders wanted to restore the French monarchy. The left defended the Republic and tended to be anti-clerical. Despite tensions between right and left, deputies in the centre usually held the balance of power.

Republican measures: 1879–85

The Republicans were not fully in control of the Third Republic until 1879. (See page 231.) Thereafter they showed little interest in extensive social reform. Respecting the rights of property, they had no wish to take from the rich and give to the poor. Their early legislation contained much that was essentially symbolic: the return of the Assembly to Paris from Versailles (1879); an amnesty to surviving communards (1879–80); the observance of 14 July – Bastille Day – as a national holiday; and the adoption of the *Marseillaise* as the national anthem (1880). There was some political reform in the early 1880s. The Senate was made more representative. Freedom of the press was firmly established and trade unions legalised. Recruitment to important posts in the civil service was carried out by competitive examination, not patronage. Jules Ferry, Minister of Education from 1879–83, set out to free education from Catholic control. In 1882 primary education became compulsory and was provided free. Teachers became employees of the State and religious education was prohibited in state schools. The attack on Catholic influence also included the banning of the Jesuit order, the setting up of state secondary schools for girls, the legalisation of divorce and the introduction of civil marriage.

---

c) How serious was the right-wing threat?

Figure 3 General Georges Boulanger (his name translates as Baker)

i) General Boulanger

In 1886 the 48-year-old General Boulanger was appointed minister of war. He proved a good self-publicist and cut a romantic, dashing image. When he was denounced by Bismarck for planning a war of revenge against Germany, he became a national hero. Many on the right saw him as a new Napoleon – a pure patriot who rose above the sordid interests of corrupt politicians. When Boulanger lost his post in 1887, his popular support seemed to threaten the Republic. In 1888 he stood as candidate in seven by-elections, winning six of them and resigning each time so that he could stand as a candidate in the next one. He demanded the creation of a new form of government – essentially dictatorship – that would work for the 'unity, the greatness and the prosperity of the fatherland'. His victories came to a climax in 1889 when he triumphed in a by-election in Paris. Had he put himself at the head of an enthusiastic mob, he might well have overthrown the government. However, his nerve failed him and when the government started proceedings against him for treason, he fled to Belgium where he committed suicide in 1891. Although Boulanger's support quickly collapsed after 1889, the extent of that support showed how powerful were the – mixed – forces which rejected the Republic.

ii) The Panama scandal

In 1881 Ferdinand de Lesseps, the man responsible for the Suez Canal, launched a scheme to build a Panama Canal. Unfortunately, his project ran into financial difficulties and the Panama Canal Company was forced into liquidation in 1889. Many small investors lost their life savings. In 1892 it was revealed that the Canal Company's interests had been promoted by dishonest finance and bribing politicians. The scandal aroused great cynicism about those in public life and damaged the prestige of the Republic. It also helped to increase anti-Semitism largely because two Jews had carried out much of the bribery. The French Jewish community was small, only 80,000-strong in the 1890s. But right-wing groups, anxious to find a scapegoat for France's problems, targeted the Jews, claiming they were deliberately undermining French values.

iii) The Dreyfus affair

In 1894 Dreyfus, the first Jew attached to the French General Staff, was arrested and tried for passing secrets to Germany. Army leaders, aware that there was a high-level spy and keen to convict someone, found him guilty and he was sentenced to life imprisonment on Devil's Island. His conviction did not cause much of a stir at the time apart from those who thought he should have been shot. However, by 1897 it was clear that Dreyfus had been convicted on flimsy evidence and that the trial had been improperly conducted. Major Picquart, the new head of intelligence, discovered evidence that the man who had really been selling military secrets was Major Esterhazy. As more evidence came to light in 1898, Esterhazy demanded a trial to clear his name. Thanks to the fabricated evidence of Colonel Henry of the intelligence branch, he was rapidly acquitted.

The radical paper *L'Aurore* now printed an article by novelist Emile Zola which accused individual army officers of perverting the course of justice. This caused a sensation. Dreyfus became a symbol, bitterly dividing the 'political' nation – newspapers, politicans and intellectuals. The left generally supported Dreyfus. The right, believing that the army's prestige was more important than the guilt or innocence of one man (especially a Jew!), were against him. Events now turned in Dreyfus's favour. Colonel Henry admitted incriminating Dreyfus and committed suicide. Esterhazy, realising the game was up, confessed his guilt. Although it was now clear that the army leadership had colluded in finding Dreyfus guilty, anti-Dreyfusards still resisted the truth. They asserted that the whole Dreyfus affair was an international Jewish conspiracy to discredit the French army. Such was the passion generated by the affair that some feared an army coup. Instead, a strong radical government, led by Waldeck-Rousseau, came to power. This government, the first anywhere in the world to contain a socialist, was determined to defend republican institutions and to see justice was done. Unrest in the army was quelled and some officers were purged. In 1899 Dreyfus was brought home and retried by the army. Again found guilty, he was released because of 'extenuating circumstances'. The government now stepped in and gave Dreyfus a full pardon.

The Dreyfus affair embittered French political life for many years. The right became more anti-Republican and more anti-Semitic: the left, believing the Catholic Church had been behind the affair, became more anti-clerical. The radicals, who dominated politics down to 1914, passed a number of measures against the Church. In 1901 all religious orders were dissolved and their property confiscated. In 1905 a separation law ended state support of the Catholic Church which now had to pay its own clerical salaries.

After 1900 the right-wing threat died down but did not entirely disappear. The members of Charles Maurras' *Action Française* were nationalist, anti-Semitic, and anti-parliamentarian, believing that the restoration of the monarchy was the way to France's salvation.

d) How serious was the left-wing threat?

The French proletariat was relatively small and most French farmers had little time for the doctrines of Marx. The Paris Commune had dealt a severe blow to the French left. Nevertheless socialist ideas spread after 1880. Some socialists favoured working by legal means within the existing parliamentary system. Extremists, by contrast, favoured revolution. By 1900 there were several small squabbling socialist parties. In 1904–5 the main socialist groups agreed to form a united party. Although the new party reaffirmed its commitment to 'socialising the means of production', it was prepared to work within the parliamentary system. It had some success, winning 54 seats in 1906 and 103 seats in 1914. Some socialist leaders were given ministerial office.

The main trade union organisation, the *CGT*, advocated revolutionary syndicalism, believing that a general strike was the best way to destroy the capitalist system. After 1906 there was a spate of violent strikes, which resulted in destruction of property and loss of life. Clemenceau's government (1906–9) used troops to break the strikes and arrested the leaders of the *CGT*.

e) Conclusion

Few French people seemed to have had much affection for the Third Republic or its politicians whom they regarded as rogues or crooks. Many on the right wanted stronger leadership, while revolutionary socialists wanted to smash the bourgeois system. The Republic seemed to totter from one crisis to another. Yet somehow it survived. Arguably, it did so because it was the form of government which divided people

ACTIVITY

To test your understanding, consider the following question: 'Why did the politics of the Third Republic appear so unstable?'

Suggested line of response:

▼ France was divided politically. The Third Republic reflected the left-right divisions.
▼ There were a large number of parties. Governments found it hard to obtain an overall majority and thus came and went with monotonous regularity.
▼ Examine the right- and left-wing threats.
▼ Appearances may be wrong. Was the Republic more stable than it sometimes seems?

the least. When faced with a choice, the majority preferred the Republic to the prospect of a more right-wing or a more left-wing regime. By 1914 the right-wing threat had subsided and on the left syndicalists represented only a tiny minority of the population.

Did the Third Republic's successes outweigh its failures? Arguably they did. The fact that it survived was itself a major achievement. On the economic front, France had made sound progress and there had been a measure of social reform in areas of public health, working conditions and national insurance. France was successful in other ways. Many French people were proud of their artistic, cultural and intellectual achievements, and of their Empire – second only to that of Britain.

4 Tsarist Russia

ISSUES:

What problems faced Russia? How successful was the government in dealing with these? Was Russia on the verge of revolution in 1914?

In the late 19th century Russia lagged behind most other powerful countries in Europe. This backwardness was even apparent in Russia's calendar which was thirteen days behind that of the rest of Europe. It is often assumed that backwardness somehow caused the revolutions of 1917. This assumption is at best a gross simplification. Backwardness does not inevitably lead to revolution. Indeed, it usually does not. Precisely how backward Russia was is also debatable. Nevertheless, Russia faced major problems.

Figure 4 The Russian Empire in 1905

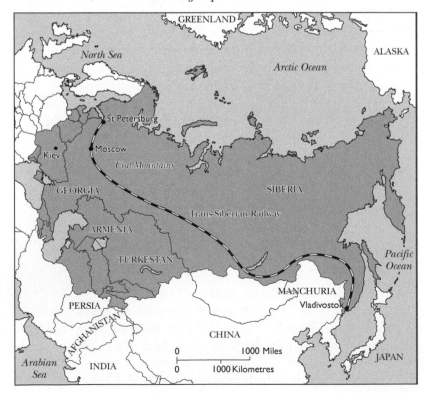

a) The problem of size

Russia was the world's largest country in area in 1890, comprising one sixth of the world's land surface. Russia's size might appear to be a strength. It was also a weakness. One problem was the sheer difficulty of communication. Orders from the government in St Petersburg, often never found their way to remote corners of the empire. The fact that Russia was an empire was another problem. Less than half of the population actually considered themselves Russian and some of the hundred or more nationalities – for example the Poles and Finns – wanted independence. In the late 19th century Russian governments tried to force non-Russian people to adopt the Russian language and culture and the Orthodox religion. This unpopular policy was known as Russification.

Great Russian	55.6	Lithuanian	1.2
Ukrainian	22.45	Armenian	1.2
Polish	7.9	Romanian/Moldavian	1.1
White Russian	5.8	Estonian	1.0
Jewish (defined by faith)	5.0	Mordvinian	1.0
Kirgiz/Kaisats	4.0	Georgian	0.8
Tartar	3.4	Tadzhik	0.3
Finnish	3.1	Turkmenian	0.3
German	1.8	Greek	0.2
Latvian	1.4	Bulgarian	0.2
Bashkir	1.3		

Table 4 Diagram showing major nationalities in Russia

b) What economic and social problems did Russia have?

i) The economic situation

Russia was still essentially an agricultural country – and a country which in many areas had still not had an agricultural revolution. The vast majority of peasants belonged to a *mir*, a type of commune, in which land was collectively, not individually, held. Land was regularly redistributed, according to a family's influence or size. Thus farmers had no incentive to be efficient. If they farmed their land well, their strips might be taken over by another family. An additional problem was that there were too many peasants and not enough land to go round. Between 1877 and 1917 Russia's population grew by 50 per cent: the amount of additional land increased by only 10 per cent. The solution to the agricultural problems was for Russia to industrialise. The surplus population could then move into the towns and industry

RUSSIA'S INDUSTRIAL PROGRESS

▼ In the late 19th century, a series of ministers of finance – especially Sergei de Witte (1892–1903) – promoted industrialisation.

▼ Russian governments supported the building of railways. By 1905 some 40,000 miles had been constructed, including the 4,000-mile-long Trans-Siberian railway (built between 1891 and 1904) which ran from St Petersburg to Vladivostok.

▼ Railway building helped open up Russia's huge mineral wealth and also encouraged industries like coal, oil, iron and steel.

▼ In the 1890s industrial output expanded at an annual rate of eight per cent.

▼ Russia was successful in attracting huge investment from abroad.

would produce the fertilisers and machines that farmers needed. Unfortunately Russia, despite being rich in natural resources, was industrially backward. However, she was making some progress.

ii) The social situation

Marxist historians once described Russian society as *feudal*. Feudal is a difficult term to define. By one definition a feudal society has a weak ruler, a strong nobility, a weak middle class, large numbers of serfs, and no proletariat. By this definition late 19th-century Russia was *not* feudal.

▼ Tsars were far from weak and Russian nobles far from strong. While some nobles were incredibly rich, the nobility was under the thumb of the tsar, not the reverse. Nor was the nobility united. By no means all were Russian (many were Polish) and not all were great landowners. By 1905 over half the hereditary nobility owned no land. Nor were all the nobility hereditary. Many were service nobility, holding a title simply because of the job they held. Lenin's father, for example, was a noble because he was a school inspector.

▼ There was a growing – and increasingly influential – middle class.

▼ Over 80 per cent of Russians were peasants – not serfs. In 1861 Alexander II had emancipated the serfs. They had to pay over a 49-year period for the land they had been 'given'. The *mir* was responsible for collecting the repayment. All peasants were thus effectively tied to the *mir* and were not allowed to leave without the permission of the village elders. Most peasants were illiterate and lived in extreme poverty. Nevertheless, some, by luck or hard work, were bettering themselves, usually by obtaining more land. By 1905 some 75 per cent of Russia's cultivated land was under peasant control.

▼ As Russian industry developed, so the proletariat developed. Russian workers suffered similar conditions to workers in every other industrialising country, working long hours for low wages. Living conditions in the growing towns were dreadful.

c) Russia's political problems

The tsar held total – absolute – power. In 1880 Russia had the dubious distinction of being one of only three European countries without a parliament. The tsar ruled with the assistance of his personally chosen ministers, a large army, a small secret police (the *Okhrana*), and the support of the Orthodox Church which used its spiritual authority to teach the Russian people that the tsar was God's representative on earth.

Russia was an autocracy. However, it was not as restrictive as is sometimes implied.

▼ Russia's bureaucracy was inefficient. There was simply not enough government at grass roots level. This limited the government's effectiveness.

▼ Although Russia was seen as a police state, it had relatively few police. While revolutionaries were sent to Siberia, conditions there were much better than under Stalin.

▼ Democracy of sorts did exist in Russia. In 1864 local government councils or *zemstvos* were set up to control, among other things, education and health. In 1870 municipal councils were set up.

d) Russian revolutionaries

In 1881 revolutionaries assassinated Tsar Alexander II. His murder solved nothing. His son Alexander III, an uncompromising autocrat, hit back at the revolutionaries. All thoughts of creating a parliament ended. Harsh repressive policies forced revolutionary groups underground. But they did not disappear. By the early 20th century there were several such groups.

Social Revolutionaries (SRs)

The SRs, the largest revolutionary group, pinned their hopes on a peasant-based revolution. Weakened by disagreements amongst themselves, the only thing that all SRs had in common was opposition to the tsarist system and a belief in land redistribution. Some SRs supported terrorist means to achieve their ends.

Social Democrats (SDs)

Other revolutionaries based their hopes on the proletariat. The first Russian Marxist was Plekhanov. In 1898 he founded the Social Democratic Party. 'Party' was a grand name. Only nine delegates, none of them workers, were present at the party's launch. Opposed to the use of terror, Plekhanov accepted Marx's view that proletariat success was inevitable: it was simply a question of waiting for it to happen. Some of his followers were less patient, not least Vladimir Ilych Ulyanov, better known by his alias Lenin. Son of a prosperous middle-class family, Lenin became a revolutionary while still a student. After being arrested and spending a few years in Siberia, he went into exile in Britain and Switzerland where he became editor of the Marxist newspaper – *Iskra* (the spark). In 1902 he published a pamphlet, *What is to be Done?*. He concluded that Russian Marxists should try to 'push' history in the right (i.e. left!) direction. He envisaged that an elite group of well-led revolutionaries, with himself as leader, could do the pushing.

SOME MISCONCEPTIONS ABOUT THE RUSSIAN POLITICAL SITUATION

▼ Many of the men who rose to the fore pre-1914 were not from the hereditary nobility. Merit, not social rank, was increasingly important. By 1897 only 51 per cent of army officers and 30 per cent of the civil service were nobles by birth.

▼ Russian tsars were not simply reactionaries. Some tsars, such as Alexander II, helped promote Russia's modernisation.

BOLSHEVIKS AND MENSHEVIKS

In 1903 the SDs split. At a meeting in London a majority of the delegates supported Lenin. Lenin's 'party' thus became known as *Bolsheviks* (the majority). Lenin's opponents – including Plekhanov who accused him of dictatorial ambitions – were called *Mensheviks* (the minority).

Q Why did middle-class Russians often join revolutionary groups?

Figure 5 Photograph of Nicholas and Alexandra

In 1894 Nicholas II succeeded his father Alexander III. He is often seen as a weak, indecisive man, very much under the control of Alexandra, his forceful German-born wife. In fairness to Nicholas, he inherited a difficult situation. He tried to do his job conscientiously and did appoint some capable ministers. In some respects he was just unlucky. His bad luck was shown at his coronation when, through no fault of his own, hundreds of people were crushed to death. He was unlucky that his only son Alexis suffered from haemophilia. However, Nicholas brought some of the bad luck on himself. 'I shall defend the principle of autocracy as unswervingly as my deceased father,' he said in January 1895. He continued the repressive policies of Alexander III, including Russification measures.

The following description of Nicholas II was written in 1912 by Count Witte, Minister of Finance from 1892–1903 and Prime Minister in 1905:

> A ruler who cannot be trusted, who approves today what he will reject tomorrow, is incapable of steering the ship of state into a quiet harbour. His outstanding failing is his sad lack of willpower. Though he means well and is not unintelligent, this shortcoming disqualifies him totally as the unlimited autocratic ruler of the Russian people.

Note: Nicholas disliked and distrusted Witte, sacking him in 1903 and again in 1905.

ACTIVITY

Why might Witte's evidence be considered a) reliable b) unreliable?

e) Why was there a revolution in 1905? (Was it a 'revolution'?)

A series of bad harvests and an industrial slump led to rising discontent in the early 1900s. There were major peasant uprisings and several leading government ministers were murdered by SR terrorists. In 1904 Russia went to war with Japan. The conflict was essentially about which country would control Manchuria and Korea. Russia had major difficulties in fighting in the Far East and her forces were defeated on both land and sea. The Russo-Japanese war exacerbated Russia's economic problems and destroyed confidence in the government. In the autumn of 1904 middle-class liberals launched a campaign demanding a parliament. On 22 January 1905 Father Gapon led a peaceful demonstration of some 200,000 people to the Winter Palace, hoping to present a petition to the Tsar asking for a redress of workers' grievances. Troops opened fire on the marchers and hundreds of people were killed or wounded on Bloody Sunday. Until now, most Russians had blamed Nicholas's ministers for the troubles. Now many blamed Nicholas himself, damaging his image as the father of his people. Ironically Nicholas had not been in the palace or ordered the 'massacre'.

Over the following months, discontent in Russia grew. There were more assassinations; liberals kept up their demands for a parliament; strikes became commonplace; peasants seized land; and in non-Russian areas there were calls for independence. As law and order broke down, Nicholas could not count on the loyalty of the armed forces. His best troops were fighting against Japan. Crews in the Black Sea fleet actually mutinied. In July the SRs set up an 'All Russian Peasant Union'. In October workers' leaders formed councils or *soviets*, the most important of which was in St Petersburg, to try to co-ordinate strike action. Many leading revolutionaries, such as Lenin, were in exile when the disturbances began. The revolution, if that is what it was, occurred in spite – rather than because – of them.

Russia seemed to be falling apart. However, Nicholas now handled matters with some skill. Dismissing a number of unpopular ministers, he brought back Witte. Witte first made peace with Japan. The Treaty of Portsmouth was far from glorious. Japan won most of the disputed land but at least loyal troops could now return to deal with the troubles at home. Witte then insisted that Nicholas must agree to set up a parliament. In the 1905 October Manifesto Nicholas reluctantly agreed to do so. He also granted a host of civil liberties including the rights of free speech and free assembly. These concessions, while pleasing many of the liberals, did not end the 'revolution'. In November 1905 there was a general strike in St Petersburg and in December an armed uprising in Moscow. What finally brought the troubles to an end was force. In December 1905 the St Petersburg soviet was dispersed and most of its leaders arrested. The Moscow rising was crushed: 500–1,000 people were killed in the fighting. Over the winter of 1905–6 loyal troops brutally restored order in the countryside. By 1906 it was clear that Nicholas's government had survived. The revolution had failed. However, it did bring about one major change. Henceforward Russia would have a parliament, the *Duma*.

f) Was Russia on the way to becoming a constitutional monarchy?

Between 1906 and 1914 there were four *dumas*. Arguably, however, there was little that amounted to real democracy in Russia.

▽ The Fundamental Laws of May 1906 declared that the tsar still controlled the armed forces and raising taxes. He had the power to dissolve the *duma* and could rule by decree when it was not in session. Moreover he still chose his own ministers.

▽ The *duma* was merely the lower house of a two-chamber legislative body. The upper house was mainly appointed by the tsar.

ANTI-SEMITISM IN RUSSIA

There was considerable anti-Semitism at all levels of Russian society from the tsar downwards. The 5 million Jews faced massive discrimination, for example in employment and education. They also faced *pogroms*. Mobs would attack Jewish houses and shops – looting, beating and frequently killing the inhabitants. Police sometimes encouraged, and rarely intervened to stop, the attacks. Between 1880–1914 some two million Jews emigrated from Russia. Those that remained often became revolutionaries. A socialist Russia offered Jews the hope of obtaining the same rights as other citizens.

▼ The electoral system ensured that the rich had much more voting power than the poor.

▼ The first two *dumas* were too radical for Nicholas's taste and were quickly dissolved. The Tsar's government now tampered with the electoral laws, essentially depriving peasants and industrial workers of the vote. The conservative-dominated third *duma*, which met in late 1907, was prepared to work with Peter Stolypin, Nicholas's new chief minister. The fourth *duma*, elected in 1912, was even more conservative.

However, while Russia was still an autocracy, she had embarked on the democratic road. After 1907 the *duma* had some influence on ministerial decision-making. It exerted its right to question ministers and to discuss state finances. The third *duma* played a constructive role in promoting education expansion and land reform. Arguably the *duma* had made a promising start which might, given time, have blossomed into a more representative and powerful parliamentary system.

g) Was Russia a repressive police state?

Repression continued. Between 1905–9 over 2,500 people were executed. Trade unions were harassed and striking workers sometimes shot, for example at the Lena goldfields in 1912. Censorship continued and the *Okhrana* was still active. Revolutionaries like Lenin and Trotsky chose to remain in exile rather than risk imprisonment in Siberia. However, the extent of the repression can be exaggerated. There was relatively little censorship. Moreover, left-wing parties could and did contest *duma* elections, even though the odds were stacked against them. Tough action against revolutionaries was in response to equally tough action by the revolutionaries. In 1908 alone, some 1,800 police were killed by terrorists. In 1911 Prime Minister Stolypin was assassinated.

h) How successful were the land reforms?

Stolypin was determined to create a class of prosperous peasant farmers (*kulaks*) who, he hoped, would support the tsar and be a barrier to future revolution. After 1906 the government encouraged peasants to buy their own land from the *mirs* or from rich landowners. A land bank was set up to loan money to peasants. Peasants were also encouraged, with government aid, to move from overcrowded regions to the empty spaces of Siberia and central Asia. By 1914 about 40 per cent of peasants in European Russia had separated from the *mir* and owned their own land. By 1914 revolutionary activity among the peasants seemed to be at a low level. Lenin was not alone among revolutionaries in fearing that the land reforms might achieve their political ends. However, perhaps the impact of the land reforms should not be rated too highly. The relative prosperity of the peasants after 1910 was due to a series of good harvests and rise in grain prices, not to Stolypin's reform. Most peasants still belonged to the *mir*, preferring the relative security of communal to individual farming. Moreover, while some peasants prospered, they did so at the expense of others. Poorer peasants, some of whom became landless labourers, resented the wealth of the *kulaks*. By European standards, most Russian peasants remained dreadfully poor.

i) How important was Russia's industrial development?

Russian industrial development, aided by huge foreign loans, continued after 1905. The country had a trade and budget surplus and the living and working conditions of most workers were improving. The fact that Russia was starting to harness its vast industrial potential alarmed Germany. However, in 1914 Russia was still essentially an agrarian society, with nearly 80 per cent of its population dependent on the land. While living conditions were improving, most workers were still poor. From 1912 there was growing industrial discontent. The fact that the proletariat was increasing meant that there was more potential for Marxist revolution.

j) Was Russia on the verge of revolution in 1914?

Although the Russian regime remained essentially reactionary, inefficient and oppressive, it is hard to believe that revolution was imminent in 1914 as Marxist historians once claimed. Lenin was despondent – and with good reason. Revolutionary support was minimal. The Bolsheviks, for example, had fewer than 10,000 members and the movement was riddled with police informers. SR and Menshevik leaders were similarly despondent. Nicholas II retained the support of the armed forces, the Orthodox Church, and the police. Moreover, he seemed to have recovered his popularity among ordinary Russians. In 1913 he celebrated the tercentenary of the Romanov family and wherever he went was greeted with apparent affection. However, while revolution was not the inevitable fate of tsarist Russia, there were still serious social, economic and political problems. 'Of the major governments of Europe none had so little credit with the people it would shortly have to lead in war as that of Nicholas II,' says historian Hans Rogger.

RUSSIA 1894–1911

1894	Nicholas II became tsar;
1905	Bloody Sunday Massacre;
1905 –6	'revolution';
1906	the first Russian *duma*;
1907 –11	Stolypin was prime minister.

ACTIVITY

Examine Tables 5 a)–f). Answer the following questions:

a) In what way do the statistics suggest that Russia's economy by 1914 was **i)** strong, and **ii)** weak?

b) Why might these statistics not tell the whole truth about Russia's economic per-formance?

Tables 5 Diagrams showing
Russia's economic performance

a) The Russian balance of trade (in millions of roubles)

	Imports	Exports	Balance
1871–80	488	454	–34
1881–90	472	622	+150
1891–1900	535	660	+125
1901–10	887	1,073	+186

(In pre-1914 Russia the rouble was worth approximately 10p.)

b) The Russian economy: annual production (in millions of tons)

	Coal	Pig iron	Oil	Grain*
1880	3.2	0.42	0.5	34
1890	5.9	0.89	3.9	36
1900	16.1	2.66	10.2	56
1910	26.8	2.99	9.4	74
1913	35.4	4.12	9.1	90

(*European Russia only)

c) Foreign investment in Russia (roubles)

1893	2,500,000
1897	80,000,000
1898	130,000,000
1913	2,200,000,000

d) Industrial growth rate 1880–1914 (average % per year)

Russia	3.5
Germany	3.75
USA	2.75
UK	1

e) Industrial production 1914 (millions of tons)

	Russia	France	Germany	USA	Great Britain	Russian ranking
Coal	36	40	190	517	292	5th
Pig iron	4.6	5.2	16.8	31	10.4	5th
Steel	4.8	4.6	18.3	31.8	7.8	4th

Russia also ranked second in world oil production, fourth in goldmining.

f) Growth of Russian railways (in kilometres)

1881	1891	1900	1913
21.228	31.219	53.234	70.156

▼ Working on Germany, France and Russia 1880–1914

Your reading of the chapter should enable you to come up with answers to the following questions. Note that there are no right or wrong answers. Have the confidence to reach your own conclusion, which should, of course, be based on good evidence.

1. Which of Germany, France and Russia faced the most serious problems in the period 1890–1914?
2. Which country was most successful at dealing with its problems?
3. Which regime was most in danger of collapse in 1914?

Answering source-based questions on Germany, France and Russia 1880–1914

Sire – We, working men and inhabitants of St Petersburg, our wives and our children and our helpless old parents, come to You, Sire, to seek for truth, justice and protection. We have been made beggars; we are oppressed; we are near to death…The moment has come for us when death would be better than the prolongation of our intolerable sufferings. We have stopped work and have told our masters that we shall not start again until they comply with our demands. We ask but little: to reduce the working day to eight hours, to provide a minimum wage of a rouble a day, and to abolish overtime…Officials have brought the country to complete ruin and involved it in shameful war. We working men have no voice in the way the enormous amounts raised from us in taxes are spent…Destroy the wall between Yourself and Your people. Give orders that elections to a Constituent Assembly be carried out under conditions of universal, equal and secret suffrage.

Source A Extract from Gapon's petition in 1905

A painful day! There have been serious disorders in Petersburg because workmen wanted to come up to the Winter Palace. Troops had to open fire in several places in the city; there were many killed and wounded. God, how painful and sad! Mama arrived from town, straight to Mass. I lunched with the others. Went for a walk with Misha. Mama stayed overnight.

Source B Nicholas II's diary entry for 22 January 1905

Source C Alexandra Kollontai, a female Bolshevik, who marched with the demonstrators and reached the square in front of the Winter Palace

> I noticed that mounted troops stood drawn up in front of the Winter Palace itself, but everyone thought that it did not mean anything in particular. All the workers were peaceful and expectant. They wanted the Tsar or one of his highest, gold-braided ministers to come before the people and take the humble petition…At first I saw the children who were hit [by rifle fire] and dragged down from the trees…We heard the clatter of hooves. The Cossacks rode right into the crowd and slashed with their sabres like madmen. A terrible confusion arose.

▼ QUESTIONS ON SOURCES

1. According to Source A why were the people marching? **[3 marks]**
2. To what extent are Sources B and C reliable? **[7 marks]**
3. Using all the sources and your own knowledge explain what happened on 'Bloody Sunday' and assess the importance of the events. **[15 marks]**

Further Reading

Books in the Access to History series.

The key texts are *France: The Third Republic 1870–1914* by K. Randell, *From Bismarck to Hitler: Germany 1890–1933* by G. Layton and *Reaction and Revolutions: Russia 1881–1924* by M. Lynch.

General

The relevant chapters in the following books are particularly good: *Europe 1880–1945* by J. M. Roberts (Longman, 1989) and *Years of Change: Europe 1890–1945* by R. Wolfson and J. Laver (Hodder & Stoughton, 1996). On developments in France try *France 1870–1919* by R. Gildea (Longman, 1996) and *France 1814–1914* by R. Tombs (Longman, 1996). On Germany try *A History of Germany 1815–1990* by W. Carr (Edward Arnold, 1991), and *Imperial Germany: 1871–1918* by S. Lee (Routledge, 1998). On Russia, try *Russia in the Age of Modernisation and Revolution 1881–1917* by H. Rogger (Longman, 1983) and *The Russian Revolution* by R. Service (Macmillan, 1999).

THE ORIGINS OF THE FIRST WORLD WAR

CHAPTER 10

POINTS TO CONSIDER

This chapter examines the causes of the First World War. The first three sections deal with the problems in foreign affairs between 1890 and 1914. Section 4 deals with the events in July/August 1914 which sparked off war. Sections 5 and 6 attempt to apportion responsibility. Proceed slowly, section-by-section, and by the end you should have your own answer to the key question: who or what was to blame for the First World War?

On 28 June 1914, Archduke Francis Ferdinand, heir to the throne of Austria-Hungary, was assassinated in the Bosnian town of Sarajevo. Several other royals were murdered in the 1890–1914 period, including the Empress of Austria (1898), the King of Italy (1900), the King and Queen of Serbia (1903), and the King of Greece (1913). These murders did not trigger war. Francis Ferdinand's assassination was different: within six weeks most of Europe was at war. Since 1914 historians have held many different views about the origins of the war. Some think that such a great event must have had great causes. But others have seen the war as simply an accident, triggered by a series of unfortunate events in July 1914. The question of responsibility for the war is another contentious area. In 1919 the victorious Allies blamed the war on German aggression. However, British wartime Prime Minister Lloyd George was soon arguing that no country wanted war and no country was wholly to blame for it. This chapter will try to explain why Francis Ferdinand's murder sparked off war. It will also try to decide who or what was to blame.

KEY ISSUE:
Was the First World War an accident or an accident waiting to happen?

Table 1 The strengths of the powers in 1900

The strengths of the European powers in 1900						
	Austria-Hungary	France	Germany	Great Britain	Italy	Russia
Population	45,015,000	38,641,333	56,367,176	41,605,323	32,450,000	132,960,000
Men in regular army	397,316	589,541	585,266	280,733	261,728	860,000
Annual value of foreign trade (£)	151,599,000	460,408,000	545,205,000	877,448,917	132,970,000	141,799,000
Merchant fleet (net tonnage)	313,698	1,037,720	1,941,645	9,304,108	945,000	633,820
1st-class battleships	–	13	14	38	9	13
2nd-class battleships	6	10	–	11	5	10

1 Colonial rivalry

For much of the 19th century European powers had relatively little interest in colonies. In the period 1815–70 only France and Britain were involved in overseas expansion. While Britain annexed large territories, she did so somewhat reluctantly. Some British statesmen regarded colonies as 'millstones round our necks'. However, in the last three decades of the century things changed. European states began to extend their control over huge parts of Africa and Asia. Almost any territory, however worthless, was considered worthy of annexation. 'Expansion is everything,' said British imperialist Cecil Rhodes. 'I would annex the planets if I could.' Between 1870–1900 Britain added four and a quarter million square miles and 66 million people to her empire; France added three and a half million square miles and 26 million people; Russia added half a million square miles and 6.5 million people. Germany acquired a new empire of one million square miles and 13 million people. Belgium and Italy also gained considerable territory in Africa.

ACTIVITY

Examine Table 1. Given the statistics, which power was Europe's a) strongest and b) weakest power in 1900. Justify your answer.

a) What caused the 'New Imperialism'?

i) Economic motivation

As early as 1902 J. A. Hobson, an English radical, argued that the 'disastrous folly' of imperialism was the result of certain interests – armament firms, big business, bankers – promoting the growth of empire for their own selfish enrichment. Lenin, the Russian revolutionary, went further, claiming that imperialism arose out of modern capitalism which had become dominated by monopolistic combines. These combines, anxious to invest capital abroad and to control raw materials, supported the acquisition of colonies. Hobson's and Lenin's arguments are no longer convincing. In reality, the export of capital had little connection with imperial expansion. France, for example, invested less than seven per cent of her foreign capital in her colonies. Lenin's view that European industry was dominated by huge combines also does not square with reality. Britain, which had the largest empire, had few large combines. The European combines that did exist did not have much influence over, or even always support, their countries' imperial policies.

This is not to say there were no economic motives underpinning imperial expansion. In the late 19th century the search for markets became increasingly competitive. Most countries, except Britain, had high tariffs, protecting their own goods. Britain feared she might be shut out of potential markets if other countries acquired too much of the colonial cake. Interestingly, European countries obtained only a fraction of their raw materials from their colonies and colonial trade was a small part of their total foreign commerce, largely because of the low purchasing power of colonial peoples. Most colonies turned out to be economic liabilities. Nevertheless, at the time most did see future economic advantages in colonies.

ii) Security

In part new imperialism grew out of the diplomatic situation in Europe after 1871. France sought prestige abroad as consolation for the loss of Alsace-Lorraine. Britain, apprehensive of France's colonial ambitions, took measures to safeguard her own interests. Her concern for the security of the route to India, for example, led her to occupying Egypt. Control over an area had its own consequences, not least a desire to control neighbouring districts in the interests of security or the wish to forestall moves by other European powers. Thus, Britain's occupation of Egypt led to a desire to control the Sudan in order to protect Egypt's southern border and the source of the River Nile.

iii) Nationalism

Imperialism became closely linked to national prestige. Colonies came to be regarded as status symbols. It was not just governments and the elite who were enthusiastic about colonies. The nationalistic masses applauded and generally backed imperial expansion. Societies sprang up which supported imperialism and pushed governments into yet more colonial acquisitions. The popular press, best-selling authors and song writers all reflected and/or created enthusiasm for empire.

The most profound of the ideas underlying imperialism was Social Darwinism. Social Darwinists took Darwin's ideas on evolution and applied them to international relations. Countries were in a perpetual struggle for existence: only the strongest and 'fittest' survived. States must increase their empires or be overtaken by others. The following is part of a speech by the British Prime Minister Lord Salisbury in 1898:

ACTIVITY

Study Lord Salisbury's speech. What are the strengths and weaknesses of this source as evidence of Britain's view of the world towards the end of the 19th century?

You may roughly divide the nations of the world as the living and the dying. On one side you have great countries of enormous power growing in power every year, growing in wealth, growing in dominion, growing in the perfection of their organisation. Railways have given to them the power to concentrate upon any one point the whole military force of their population and to assemble armies of a magnitude and power never dreamed of in the generations that have gone by. Science has placed in the hands of those armies weapons ever growing in their efficacy of destruction…By the side of these splendid organisations, of which nothing seems to diminish the force and which present rival claims which the future may only be able by a bloody arbitrament to adjust – by the side of these are a number of communities which I can only describe as dying.

iv) Humanitarian concerns

Many Europeans believed it was the duty of the 'advanced' peoples to bring civilisation to those less fortunate. Imperial administrations were often sincerely desirous of bringing benefits to their colonies, for example, by getting rid of slavery. In terms of pressure groups, missionary societies played as important a role as financial interests. About 40,000 Roman Catholic and 20,000 Protestant missionaries went to Asia and Africa with the notion of Christianising and civilising.

v) Accident

In the colonial stampede, actions were often simply reactions to events – not clearly rationalised policies. The impetus for expansion frequently came from men on the spot – missionaries, soldiers, explorers and businessmen – rather than from political leaders in Europe. The creation of a vast French empire in West Africa, for example, was largely the work of the French colonial army, often acting contrary to instructions from Paris.

b) The scramble for Africa

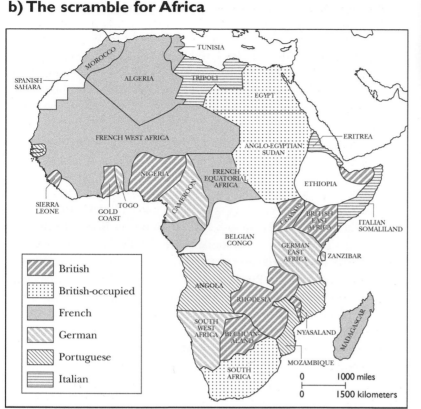

Figure 1 Africa in 1914

British

British-occupied

French

German

Portuguese

Italian

The European partition of Africa was accomplished in about twenty years between 1880 and 1900. In 1880 only about one tenth of Africa had been annexed by European states. By 1900 only one tenth had not fallen under European rule.

The main African troublespots in the 1890s

▼ **Italian ambitions in Ethiopia:** these ambitions were dashed in 1896 when an Italian army of 25,000 men was defeated at the battle of Adowa. A humiliated Italy was forced to recognise the independence of Ethiopia.

▼ **Anglo-French rivalry over the Sudan:** in 1898 there was a confrontation between a French expedition and a much larger British army at Fashoda. The French eventually had to back down and give up all claims to land along the Nile.

▼ **The Boer War:** in 1899 Britain went to war against the Boers in Transvaal. The war, which finally ended in victory for Britain, dragged on until 1902.

ISSUE:

What were the main results of the 'struggle' for China?

c) The 'struggle' for China

Between 1895–1905 China became the main focus of international rivalry. With a population of over 400 million, China seemed to offer tremendous economic potential. European, American and Japanese businesses became engaged in a battle for contracts and concessions for mining rights or railway construction. Success in securing economic concessions was seen as a reflection of political influence. The 'struggle for China' thus became a battle for prestige as much as for material gain.

In the case of Japan and Russia, political considerations went beyond mere prestige. Russia, for a variety of economic and strategic reasons, was determined to win control over the Chinese provinces of Manchuria and Korea. Japan also had ambitions in Korea. In the late 19th century Japan had quickly modernised and by the 1890s possessed a strong army and navy. Japan's victory in a war against China in 1894–5 had major repercussions. Russia protested that Japan's gains threatened her own interests and Japan was forced to abandon her claims to the Liaotung peninsula. Russia now looked to become China's protector. In return, the Chinese government agreed to allow Russia to build a railway across Manchuria. In 1898 China also granted Russia a 25-year lease on the Liaotung peninsula, including Port Arthur.

Other European powers also sought to carve out 'spheres of interest'. In 1897 Germany seized Kiaochow. France was most active in the south in areas adjacent to her empire in Indo-China. Britain sought to preserve her long-established position in central China. In 1900 anti-foreigner riots swept through China. The most dramatic event of the Boxer rebellion was the seven-week siege of the foreign legations, or embassies, in Peking. European rivalry was – temporarily – forgotten and an international force marched on Peking, relieving the legations and taking harsh reprisals against the rebels. It seemed that China might now be partitioned amongst the powers. However, Britain and the USA were opposed to carving up China, supporting instead an open-door policy by which all the powers would give up demands for exclusive rights in their spheres of interest.

Russia, still hoping to create a 'special relationship' with China, obtained even more economic concessions in Manchuria in 1900–1. Japan, concerned at Russian policy, offered Russia a free hand in Manchuria in exchange for a free Japanese hand in Korea. Russia rejected this. When further negotiations proved inconclusive, Japan launched a surprise attack on the Russian fleet at Port Arthur in February 1904. This was the start of the Russo-Japanese War. Japanese quickly occupied Korea and besieged Port Arthur. The town was finally captured in January 1905 and the Japanese went on to defeat the main Russian army at Mukden. In May 1905, the Russian Baltic

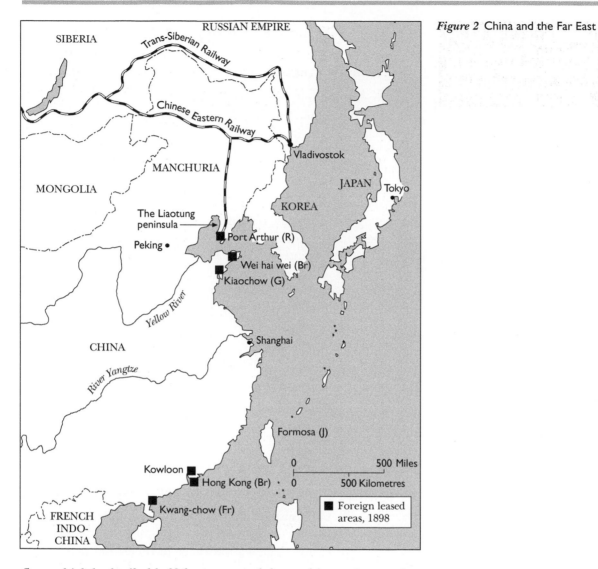

Figure 2 China and the Far East

fleet, which had sailed half the way round the world, was destroyed at the battle of Tsushima. Russia was now forced to make peace, accepting that Korea was a Japanese sphere of influence. The Russo-Japanese war brought to an end the possibility of Russian domination of northern China. After 1905 China's territorial integrity ceased to be of major concern to the great powers.

d) How serious were the colonial rivalries?

Between 1880–1905 colonial rivalries, on occasions, seriously damaged relations between the European powers. However, arguably imperial rivalries provided a safety valve through which the great powers could let off steam – at a safe distance – without harming each other too much.

ISSUE:
What impact did
Germany have on
international relations
post-1890?

2 European relations 1890–1907

a) Bismarck's legacy

The creation of the German Empire in 1871 ushered in a new era in European diplomacy. Having created the German Empire, Bismarck's main objective was its security. He thought the best guarantee was peace. A French war of revenge to recover Alsace-Lorraine posed a threat to peace. However, France by herself was not a serious danger. Danger would only arise if France managed to ally with either Austria-Hungary or Russia. If Austria and Russia went to war over their competing interests in the Balkans, France might have the opportunity of allying with either of the two powers. Bismarck, therefore, worked to maintain good relations with Russia and Austria and to reduce friction in the Balkans. The international situation in 1879 led him to sign the *Dual Alliance* with Austria. (See pages 193–4). Both countries promised to give the other full support if either were attacked by Russia. In 1882 Italy joined Germany and Austria to form the Triple Alliance. Fearing that Russia might ally with France, Bismarck signed the Reinsurance Treaty with Russia in 1887. However, William II, who came to power in 1888, questioned the need for the Russian alliance.

Opinions are still divided about Bismarck's legacy. Although he had kept France isolated, she remained embittered. By 1890 his elaborate alliance system appeared to be fragile. Bismarck's African adventures also had undesirable long-term consequences, whetting the German public's appetite for colonies and worsening relations with Britain. Bismarck can thus be seen as bequeathing serious problems to his successors. However, his admirers point out that he succeeded in co-operating with both Austria-Hungary and Russia and was generally on good terms with Britain. Given astute handling, his 'system' was workable. Russia, for example, was eager to renew the Reinsurance Treaty in 1890. Under Bismarck, Germany enjoyed security and Europe was blessed with 20 years of peace. His successors threw away his legacy. Unlike him, they failed to limit and control both their own and Austrian ambitions. It is unfair to blame Bismarck for their failure.

b) Germany's 'new course'

The 'new course' which Bismarck's successor Caprivi pursued from 1890–94 was intended to simplify German policy by eliminating the complex commitments contained within the Bismarckian system. The most crucial decision – to reject Russia's proposal to renew the Reinsurance Treaty – was taken on the grounds that it was incompatible with Germany's commitment to Austria-Hungary and that it would anger Britain, whom Germany hoped to persuade to join the Triple Alliance. In 1890 an Anglo-German agreement was reached by which Germany gained Heligoland, an island in the North Sea, in return for giving up rights in Zanzibar and East Africa. Russia and France, fearing that an Anglo-German alliance existed, felt even more isolated. This fear gradually drew them together. The process was slow and certainly not inevitable if only because Tsar Alexander III was reluctant to ally with republican France.

c) The Franco-Russian Alliance

The initiative for an alliance came from France. French financial aid helped smooth relations and in 1891 serious negotiations began. A major difficulty was that France wanted a specific alliance directed against Germany while Russia wanted a general agreement against Britain. Eventually two separate agreements were made. The 1891 political agreement was anti-British in intent, aligning France with Russia in imperial disputes. In the 1892 military convention, France and Russia promised mutual support if either were attacked by Germany. France had at last broken out of the quarantine imposed on her by Bismarck. Germany now faced the prospect of a two-front war.

d) Anglo-German relations 1890–96

At the time the German government did not regard the Franco-Russian Alliance as particularly dangerous. Indeed it hoped that the alliance might force Britain to join the Triple Alliance. The prospects of an alliance seemed good. Britain, generally anti-French and anti-Russian, felt somewhat isolated. However, fearing being drawn into a European war for the sake of German interests, Britain wanted German friendship – not a full-blown alliance. Having failed to secure a British alliance, German leaders resorted to pressure and coercion. The culmination of this type of diplomacy was the Kruger telegram in January 1896. This followed the Jameson raid in 1895 which aimed to provoke an uprising against the Boers in Transvaal. As thousands of Germans were active in Transvaal's commercial life, the German government was quite right to express concern. But its manner of proceeding was clumsy. William's telegram to Kruger, the Boer president, supporting Transvaal's independence, was seen as a gross interference in British imperial affairs. By 1896 Anglo-German relations, so good in 1890, had deteriorated badly.

ISSUE:

What were the main
aims of *weltpolitik*?

THE GERMAN NAVY

If Germany was to be a great
world power, William believed
she needed a great navy. Thus,
in 1898 and 1900 Germany
passed two Navy Laws
designed to create a powerful
battle fleet. This fleet was to
be used as 'the lever of
weltpolitik'. If Germany could
'influence' (i.e. threaten)
Britain, she could influence
the entire world.

e) *Weltpolitik*

In 1896 William II proclaimed that 'nothing must henceforth be
settled in the world without the intervention of Germany and the
German Emperor'. This is often seen as the start of a new 'world
policy' (*weltpolitik*) which was, by intent, a rejection of Bismarck's
'continental policy'. The emphasis was now on overseas expansion.
Bülow, the new German foreign minister, declared in 1897: 'we don't
want to put anyone else in the shade, but we too demand a place in
the sun'. William desperately wanted Germany to be a world power
like Britain. Many Germans agreed with him. By the late 1890s there
were three powerful organisations devoted to the promotion of
German world power – the Pan-German League, the German
Colonial League, and the Navy League.

German historian Fritz Fischer claimed that there was a sort of
master plan to *weltpolitik*. He detected three main elements in it: one
was the navy which would demonstrate Germany's status as a world
power, thereby rallying popular support behind the Kaiser; the
second was the plan for a great Central African empire comprising
the Congo and the Portuguese colonies of Angola and Mozambique;
and the third was the scheme for a German-dominated Central
European economic zone comprising Austria-Hungary, the Balkan
states, and the Ottoman Empire. Related to this scheme was the plan
to link the whole area together by a railway from Berlin to Baghdad.
However, Fischer's critics point to the fact that *weltpolitik* seems to
have consisted of three unrelated projects, suggesting a lack of
coherence in policy rather than a master plan. They think that
behind the pursuit of *weltpolitik* there lay no more than a vague
longing to be a world power. Bülow's basic aim seems to have been to
impress both public opinion and William by a few cheap successes, in
which appearances counted for more than realities. Thus German
foreign policy after 1897 was largely a 'public relations' exercise.
Contemporaries tended to attribute the vagaries of German
diplomacy to the Kaiser. In this they were partly correct. William was
a complex character whose moods were liable to change very rapidly.
(This changeability was very evident in his love-hate relationship with
Britain.) However, while the Kaiser did have considerable powers, he
did not devote himself solely to foreign policy. Foreign ministers had
much more day-to-day control of affairs. Thus, William was not the
only one to blame for the lack of clear aims in German diplomacy.

f) British policy 1898–1902

German imperial ambitions, and the creation of a big German navy,
were bound to be seen as challenges by Britain. For Germany, a fleet
was a luxury: for Britain it was essential. Determined to maintain its

naval supremacy, Britain commenced a major ship-building programme. The German naval threat inevitably increased suspicion and worsened Anglo-German relations. British and German public opinion, influenced by – or influencing – the popular press, echoed government feeling. In Germany Anglophobia probably reached its height during the Boer War (see opposite). By 1902 the British public had become increasingly anti-German. Disappointed with Germany, Britain turned to Japan to help check Russian ambitions in China. The 1902 Anglo-Japanese Alliance seemed to mark the end of policy of avoiding 'entangling alliances' in peace time. However, Britain was still isolated from her continental rivals.

g) The Anglo-French Entente

The Anglo-Japanese Alliance acted as a catalyst for improved Anglo-French relations. Given the mounting tension between Russia and Japan, both Britain and France feared they might be drawn into this conflict as allies of the main protagonists. An agreement of some kind thus seemed necessary. This came in 1904 when both countries settled most of their outstanding colonial problems. In return for France accepting British supremacy in Egypt, Britain accepted that Morocco was a French sphere of influence. The *Entente Cordiale* was not an alliance: no enemy was singled out and no joint action was planned. However, the entente did indicate a mutual desire to end past friction and a willingness to cooperate in the future. Although not anti-German in intent, the entente had serious implications for Germany.

WHY NOT?

France (to Russia). "AREN'T YOU GOING TO DANCE WITH MR. BULL?"
Russia. "I THINK I SHOULD RATHER LIKE TO, IF HE WOULDN'T TREAD ON MY TOES."
France. "OH, BUT HE WON'T. HE'S IMPROVED IMMENSELY. I FIND HIM ADORABLE!"

> ### THE BOER WAR
> From 1899–1902 Britain was at war with the Boers in South Africa. 300,000 British troops eventually crushed 60,000 Boers. Most of Europe sympathised with the Boer underdogs. There was even talk of a Continental league against Britain. Suddenly Britain's 'splendid isolation' seemed less than splendid. In these circumstances, Colonial Secretary Joseph Chamberlain proposed an Anglo-German alliance. Chamberlain's attempts at an alliance failed. Britain would still not join the Triple Alliance – Germany's objective. Germany would not join an anti-Russian alliance – Britain's objective.

Figure 3 Punch cartoon 1905

> ## ACTIVITY
>
> Examine Figure 3. Answer the following questions:
>
> **a)** Identify the countries represented in the 1905 cartoon.
>
> **b)** Comment on John Bull's relationships with the three 'women'.

h) The first Moroccan crisis 1905–6

German ministers were prepared to provoke a crisis over France's hope of making Morocco a French sphere of influence. In March 1905 William II landed at the Moroccan port of Tangiers and dramatically declared his intention of upholding Morocco's independence. In April the German government demanded an international conference to review the question of Morocco. German policy was operating on two levels. On the surface the Germans were demanding 'fair shares for all' and the right to be consulted about Morocco's fate. But their hidden aim was to weaken, if not destroy, the Anglo-French Entente. This was to be achieved by demonstrating that Britain was not a worthwhile ally. France, it was assumed, would be outvoted at the international conference since other nations would prefer the principle of 'open door' to French predominance in Morocco. France would be so humiliated that its leaders would recognise that cooperation with Germany, not Britain, was essential. To accomplish this, it was necessary to keep up tension until the French government gave in to German demands. This aggressive policy was pursued through the summer of 1905, backed by the unspoken threat of war.

Germany's actions created a panic in France and the French cabinet accepted German demands for a conference that would meet in 1906 at Algeciras. Germany had thus won a diplomatic victory. However, the Algeciras Conference itself was far from a triumph. Britain, as she had done throughout the crisis, backed France. Only Austria supported Germany and France secured a strong position in Morocco, effectively controlling both the economy and the police of the country. Algeciras was thus a severe blow to German prestige. Moreover, far from weakening the Anglo-French entente, the Morocco crisis strengthened it. Friendship with France became a basic principle of Britain's new Liberal government. Sir Edward Grey, the foreign secretary, authorised 'military conversations' in 1906 to consider how Britain might aid France if she was attacked by Germany.

i) The Triple Entente

Grey, convinced that Germany was a potential threat, determined to improve relations with Russia. Negotiations for an Anglo-Russian agreement began in 1906. They covered three disputed regions: Persia, Tibet and Afghanistan. Agreement was reached in 1907. Persia was divided into three zones: a northern Russian zone; a southern British zone; and a neutral zone separating the two. Both countries agreed not to meddle to the disadvantage of the other in the internal affairs of Tibet and Afghanistan. Although Russia cheated on the Persian agreement, Grey strove hard to maintain good relations. This was a sign that Europe, not the Empire, was now the focal point of British policy.

j) The situation in 1907

By 1907, Europe was divided into two blocs. This meant that Germany was far less secure that she had been in 1890. German policy-makers were largely to blame for this state of affairs. Between 1897–1907 Bülow and the Kaiser had conducted an ill-judged and often provocative policy. *Weltpolitik* had added little, except a few Pacific islands, to Germany's overseas empire. The construction of a large fleet had alienated Britain, ending any chance of an Anglo-German alliance. By 1907 Germany's only firm ally was Austria-Hungary. Although the Triple Alliance was regularly renewed, Germany had little faith in Italy – with good cause. In 1902 Italy and France had reached an agreement whereby each assured the other of neutrality if either were attacked.

> **THE MAIN EVENTS: 1890–1907**
>
> **1894** Franco-Russian Alliance;
> **1898** first German Navy Law;
> **1899** Boer War;
> **–1902**
> **1904** Anglo-French Entente;
> **1905** first Moroccan crisis;
> **1906** Algeciras Conference;
> **1907** Triple Entente.

3 Increasing tension: 1908–1913

> **ISSUE:**
> What were the main European crises between 1908 and 1913?

a) The 1908 Bosnian crisis

An agreement between Austria-Hungary and Russia in 1897 helped lessen tension in the Balkans for over 10 years. However, the situation in Serbia was a major concern for Austria-Hungary. Many Serbian politicians dreamed of uniting all Serbs in a Greater Serbia. Since there were twice as many Serbs in the Habsburg Empire and in Bosnia-Herzegovina (a province still in theory Turkish, but administered by Austria-Hungary since 1878) as there were in Serbia itself, Serbian ambitions could only be realised at Austria-Hungary's expense. In 1903 the pro-Austrian Serbian dynasty was overthrown and replaced by a pro-Russian regime. Austria-Hungary tried to bring economic pressure to bear on the landlocked Serbia, worsening relations between the two states.

Meanwhile, Russia, after failure in the Far East, turned her attention back to the Balkans. She was particularly keen to ensure that her warships had access from the Black Sea to the Mediterranean via the Straits. In September 1908 Izvolsky, the Russian foreign minister met Aehrenthal, the Austro-Hungarian foreign minister. Aehrenthal was receptive to the idea of a 'deal' with Russia since he was considering a project of his own – the annexation of Bosnia-Herzegovina. A new regime, the Young Turks, had just come to power in Turkey, dedicated to the revival of Ottoman power. Restoring Bosnia to full Turkish rule was one of the Young Turks' objectives. Austrian annexation of the provinces would prevent this and also end Serbia's hopes of winning them. In return for Austrian support on the Straits issue, Izvolsky agreed to Austria's annexation of Bosnia.

When Austria-Hungary jumped the gun and announced the annexation of Bosnia in October 1908 the Russian government denied any knowledge of Izvolsky's 'deal' and instructed him to support Serbia and oppose Austria-Hungary's action. Izvolsky, claiming that he had been tricked by Aehrenthal, called for an international conference to discuss the situation. Austria-Hungary rejected this call. Tension mounted when Turkey demanded compensation and Serbia threatened war. In January 1909 Germany promised Austria-Hungary full support. Tension continued until March 1909 when Russia reluctantly recognised the annexation of Bosnia. Her hopes of securing free passage through the Straits came to nothing and she was left humiliated and angry.

Serbia had no option but to back down and recognise Bosnia's annexation. Although the Serbian government promised to be a good neighbour, secret organisations, like the 'Black Hand', linked Serbian patriots in Bosnia with nationalists in Serbia. Several Habsburg officials in Bosnia were murdered by Serb terrorists.

The Bosnian crisis exacerbated Balkan problems. The fact that Germany had given full backing to Austria-Hungary ensured that relations between Germany and Russia deteriorated rapidly. By 1909 Bismarck must have been turning in his grave. Germany had not prompted the Bosnian crisis but felt she had no alternative but to support her only ally: it now seemed that the Austrian tail was wagging the German dog.

b) Anglo-German naval rivalry

In 1906 Britain launched *Dreadnought*, a new battleship superior to everything else afloat in terms of speed, firepower and strength. Germany soon had its own *Dreadnought* programme and Britain's massive naval supremacy seemingly no longer counted. Britain now had to reconstruct its lead from scratch. In 1908 the Liberal government, after proposing to reduce naval expenditure (at a time when Germany was increasing its fleet), was forced to yield to public pressure and accept the demand for eight new battleships. Attempts to reach agreement with Germany on reducing naval building failed. Thus the expensive naval race continued, seriously damaging Anglo-German relations.

c) The second Moroccan crisis 1911

In May 1911 French troops occupied the Moroccan capital Fez, following the outbreak of a revolt. A French takeover of Morocco, which would contravene the 1906 Algeciras agreement, was now widely expected. In July 1911 a German gunboat, the *Panther*, arrived at the Moroccan port of Agadir, ostensibly to protect German lives and property. Its real aim was to 'persuade' France to give Germany territorial compensation in return for German recognition of a French protectorate over Morocco. The German foreign minister Kiderlen hoped to pull off 'a great stroke', winning both a prestige victory for Germany and also French goodwill.

The French government was conciliatory. It hoped to improve relations with Germany and was prepared to pay what it considered a fair price for Germany's goodwill; but Kiderlen's demand for the whole of the French Congo made an amicable settlement impossible. His main miscalculation, however, was in ignoring Britain. Worried that German power was being used to blackmail France, Britain was not prepared to ignore the *Panther* incident. In late July, Lloyd George, a powerful Cabinet member, hitherto noted for his pro-German sentiments, declared that Britain was ready to support France to the hilt. The British fleet was put on alert and war between Britain and Germany seemed a possibility. The crisis soon ended. A Franco-German accord was signed in November by which Germany only obtained two meagre strips of territory in the French Congo. Kiderlen's heavy-handed methods had resulted in limited German gains and only at the price of increasing tension.

d) The Balkan Wars

Figure 4 The Balkans in 1912 (left – before the Balkan Wars) and 1913 (right – after the Balkan Wars)

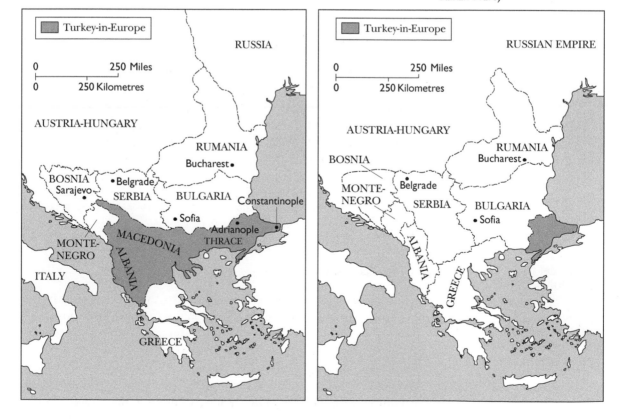

In 1911 Italy, in pursuit of her ambitions in Tripoli (modern Libya), went to war with Turkey. Italian success encouraged the expansionist ambitions of the small Balkan states. In the spring of 1912 Serbia allied with Bulgaria. Greece and Montenegro joined the alliance, called the Balkan League, in the autumn. The Balkan League states had virtually nothing in common except a desire to drive the Turks out of Macedonia and divide the spoil amongst themselves. In October 1912 the Balkan League went to war against Turkey. The Turks were quickly defeated and driven out of Europe (except Constantinople). An armistice was signed in December 1912. The peace treaty had only just been signed at London in May 1913 when Bulgaria, angry at being cheated out of some of its territorial gains, attacked Serbia. Greece, Romania and Turkey now joined the Second Balkan War on Serbia's side. Bulgaria's troops were swiftly routed and she was forced to surrender most of her gains from the First Balkan War.

What were the main results of the Balkan Wars?

▼ Although she managed to keep a toehold in Europe, Turkey had lost the bulk of her European territory. Facing the prospect of attack from Greece and Bulgaria, she looked for a strong protector and found one in Germany. After 1913 German advisers wielded considerable influence in Turkey.

▼ Bulgaria was left weakened and resentful.

▼ The Balkan Wars had been an unexpected and dangerous crisis for the great powers. They had tried to defuse the crisis by influencing the peace settlement which met in London in 1912–13. The main source of great power tension was Austria-Hungary's determination to create an independent Albania to prevent Serbia acquiring an outlet on the Adriatic. By threatening war, Austria-Hungary achieved her ambition.

▼ By 1913 Serbia had doubled its population and seemed nearer realising her aim of creating a Greater Serbia.

▼ Many Austro-Hungarian leaders thought it was essential to 'smash' Serbia if the Habsburg Empire was to survive.

MAIN EVENTS:
1908–13

1908 Bosnian Crisis;
1911 Second Moroccan Crisis;
1912 First Balkan War;
1913 Second Balkan War.

e) The arms race

In 1912 Lord Haldane, the British minister of war, went on a special mission to Germany, hoping to end the naval race. His mission failed. Instead, Germany embarked on a more ambitious naval programme. In 1912 the *Reichstag* also agreed to increase the German army by more than 30 per cent with plans for further increases. Not surprisingly this provoked the entente powers into reviewing their own military strength. In 1913 France extended military conscription from two to three years. Russia also embarked on an ambitious army expansion programme.

ACTIVITY

Consider the following question: 'Why were events in the Balkans so threatening in the period 1908–1913?'

Suggested line of response
▼ Stress that there were two power blocs in Europe, each suspicious of the other.
▼ Stress that the great powers had conflicting aims in the Balkans.
▼ Examine the 1908 crisis.
▼ Examine the Balkan wars 1912–13.

---

4 The July Crisis

a) The Sarajevo assassination

ISSUE:
Why did Francis Ferdinand's assassination lead to war?

Few people in early 1914 envisaged the outbreak of a major war. The Balkan Wars had passed without triggering great power conflict. Then, on 28 June that year Archduke Francis Ferdinand, heir to the Austro-Hungarian throne, visited Sarajevo, the major town in Bosnia. The trip was ill-conceived. Serbian terrorist groups, who had known months in advance of the visit, had plenty of time to make assassination plans. On 28 June there were at least half a dozen Bosnian terrorists in Sarajevo hoping for an opportunity to kill Francis Ferdinand. The first assassination attempt – a bomb attack on the Archduke's car – failed. However, a wrong turning by the imperial chauffeur resulted in Gavrilo Princip being in a position, through sheer chance, to shoot Francis Ferdinand and his wife.

The assassination shocked Europe. A showdown between Austria-Hungary and Serbia now seemed inevitable. Though Princip was Bosnian and therefore an Austro-Hungarian subject, it was suspected that he and the other terrorists had received both their weapons and encouragement from Serbia. The assassination thus provided Austria-Hungary with a perfect excuse for military action against Serbia. Hotzendorf, chief of the Austrian general staff, Count Berchtold, the foreign minister and Emperor Francis Joseph all agreed that Austria-Hungary's prestige, and perhaps survival, demanded that severe reprisals be taken against Serbia – even if this meant risking war with Russia.

b) The 'blank cheque'

On the 5–6 July both the Kaiser and his chancellor Bethmann-Hollweg promised full German support for Austria-Hungary in whatever measures she took against Serbia. This was the so-called 'blank

WHY DID IT TAKE AUSTRIA-HUNGARY SO LONG TO ACT?

▼ Austria-Hungary had hoped to find clear evidence that the Serbian government was involved in the assassination. It failed to find such evidence. Ironically, the complicity of Serb officials, if not the Serbian government, is undeniable. Colonel Dimitrijević, the Serbian military intelligence chief, was aware of the assassination plan but did not expect it to succeed! Serbian officials also allowed the armed assassins to cross into Bosnia. However, Serbian Prime Minister Nicola Pašić was not implicated in the assassination. Indeed, there was bitter enmity between himself and Dimitrijević.

▼ Not until 16 July did the Austrians persuade Hungarian ministers of the need for military action.

▼ A state visit to Russia by French President Poincaré and French Prime Minister Viviani was scheduled to take place between 20–23 July. Austria-Hungary did not want to give Russian and French leaders the opportunity to plan together. Not until Poincaré and Viviani were safely embarked on board ship for their return journey to France did the Habsburg government act.

cheque'. Indeed William and Bethmann-Hollweg went further: both recommended immediate action against Serbia. They assumed that Nicholas II would not support the assassination of a fellow monarch; they also assumed that Russia would not act without French support, which she was unlikely to obtain. The German government, hoping to achieve a great diplomatic victory, was thus prepared to risk – although it did not expect – a general European war. Despite being urged by Germany to 'act at once', Austria-Hungary did nothing. Indeed, for three weeks there was little indication that Europe was moving towards a major crisis. The Kaiser departed for a yachting holiday. There was no frantic planning for war in Germany. Nor was there any alarm in Britain, France or Russia. Indeed, there was no real crisis until 23 July.

c) The ultimatum

The ultimatum, presented by Austria-Hungary to Serbia on 23 July, shocked several foreign ministers by its severity. Grey later described it as 'the most formidable document I had ever seen addressed by one state to another that was independent'. The ten demands, which Austria was certain Serbia would reject, had to be accepted in their entirety within a 48-hour time limit. The Serbian government's cleverly worded reply on 25 July seemed conciliatory – even to William II. However, the Serbs rejected the key demand – to let Habsburg officials into Serbia to participate in an enquiry into Francis Ferdinand's death. Boosted by assurances of Russian support, the Serbian government was prepared to risk, and indeed expected, war. Since Serbia had not unconditionally accepted the ultimatum, Austria immediately severed diplomatic relations and ordered the mobilisation of most of its army.

d) The worsening crisis

Russia's decision to support Serbia on 24–25 July was crucial. Sazonov, the Russian foreign minister, interpreted the Austrian ultimatum as a deliberate provocation. A fellow Slav state was apparently being threatened by the 'Germanic' powers. Russian prestige in the Balkans was at stake: if Serbia was abandoned, Russia's position in the Balkans would 'collapse utterly'. Determined to stand firm, the Russian government agreed to begin extensive military measures. Sir Edward Grey, suddenly realising the seriousness of the situation, sent a series of desperate appeals to Berlin on 27 July, hoping to secure German support for an international conference to try to resolve the crisis. Germany and Austria-Hungary rejected these appeals: Austria had no faith in great power conferences and no intention of allowing Britain to mediate. On 28 July Austria-Hungary declared war on Serbia and the next day her gunboats bombarded Belgrade.

Both the Kaiser, who had just returned from his cruise, and Bethmann-Hollweg now showed some signs of having second thoughts. On 29–30 July Bethmann-Hollweg made some short-lived efforts to restrain Austria. But events were now moving too fast for statesmen to control them. Military leaders began taking over the decision-making.

On 28 July Russia ordered partial mobilisation to deter Austria. The Russian general staff, aware that partial mobilisation would hamper the effectiveness of a general mobilisation should this become necessary, pressed for full mobilisation. Russia's leadership, still hoping to avert war with Germany, hesitated. Nicholas II sent a telegram to William on 29 July appealing for his help in avoiding war. While William's reply was friendly, the German ambassador made it clear that *any* Russian mobilisation, however partial, would provoke German mobilisation. On 29–30 July Nicholas and his ministers debated whether to order a full or partial mobilisation. There was really no debate. The only object of partial mobilisation had been to appease Germany. Now that Germany had refused to be appeased, the alternatives were full mobilisation or nothing. On 30 July Nicholas II, with French support, agreed to full mobilisation. Neither Russia nor France appreciated that this decision made war inevitable. They still hoped that Germany and Austria might be prepared to negotiate a settlement. German military plans scuttled these hopes.

THE SCHLIEFFEN PLAN

Germany had only one plan to deal with a major war. This plan had been devised by von Schlieffen, Chief of the General Staff from 1891–1908. As a solution to the problem of fighting a two-front war, Schlieffen had planned a massive opening assault on France with only a holding action on the eastern front. His plan sought to capitalise on Russia's slowness in mobilising her massive resources. By the time Russia was ready to move, the Germans hoped to have defeated France so that troops could be transferred eastwards. If Russia were allowed to mobilise, the success of the Schlieffen plan would be endangered.

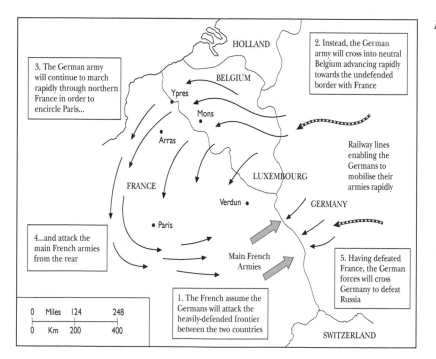

Figure 5 The Schlieffen Plan

**MAIN EVENTS
SUMMER 1914**

June 28 assassination of
Francis Ferdinand;
July 5–6 German 'blank
cheque' to Austria-
Hungary;
July 23 Austro-Hungarian
ultimatum to Serbia;
July 28 Austria-Hungary
declared war on Serbia;
August 1 Germany
declared war on Russia;
August 3 Germany
declared war on France;
August 4 Britain declared
war on Germany.

e) War!

Germany now demanded that Russia cease all military activities aimed against Germany and Austria-Hungary within 12 hours. In the absence of a reply, Germany declared war on Russia on 1 August and began to mobilise her troops. France was asked for a promise of neutrality: when no such promise was received Germany declared war on France on 3 August. Meanwhile, on 2 August the German government demanded a passage for its troops through Belgium. The Germans were prepared to guarantee Belgium's independence. The Belgian government rejected Germany's 'request'. German troops thus invaded Belgium. The violation of Belgium's neutrality, guaranteed by the great powers in 1839, had a major impact on Britain. While Grey and Prime Minister Asquith wanted Britain to go to war to support France, at least half the cabinet were opposed to intervention. However, virtually all the cabinet agreed that Britain should fight to defend Belgium. The 'left' were concerned about upholding small countries and international law. The 'right' appreciated that Belgium was strategically important: for centuries, it had been a prime objective of British policy to ensure that no strong power controlled the Low Countries. Britain now demanded the withdrawal of German troops from Belgium. When this ultimatum was disregarded, Britain declared war on Germany on 4 August.

Not until 6 August did Austria-Hungary declare war on Russia and not until 12 August did Britain and France declare war on Austria-Hungary. By then, all the great powers of Europe, save Italy, were at war. Italy, fearful of the British fleet, found good excuses for not honouring her Triple Alliance commitments. Everyone expected that the war would be short. The German Crown Prince looked forward to a 'bright and jolly war'.

5 Which country was most to blame for the war?

a) German responsibility

In 1919 Germany was forced to accept Article 231 of the Versailles Treaty (the so-called War Guilt clause):

> The Allied and Associated Governments affirm and Germany accepts the responsibility of Germany and her allies for causing all the loss and damage to which the Allied and Associated Governments and their nationals have been subjected as a consequence of the war imposed upon them by the aggression of Germany and her allies.

ISSUES:
Did Germany will the war? Were other countries more or equally to blame?

FISCHER'S MAIN CLAIMS
▼ Fearing the success of socialism in Germany, the traditional ruling classes pursued a prestige policy on a world scale. Their aim was to distract opinion from domestic

In the years after 1919 most Germans argued that this was unfair. German historians generally concluded that no single power was responsible for the – largely accidental – war. However, in the 1960s German historian Fritz Fischer stirred up a hornet's nest when he blamed Germany for starting the war.

Even if Fischer's thesis is rejected (as it should be!), it is still possible to hold Germany responsible for the war.

▽ Germany's aggressive pursuit of *weltpolitik* soured international relations after 1897 and frightened France, Russia and Britain into a defensive alignment.

▽ German policy increased tension (eg. in 1905 and 1911).

▽ Germany encouraged Austria-Hungary to take a tough line in July 1914.

▽ In 1914 the idea of a preventive war seemed desirable to some German military leaders. Germany was encircled and Russia was getting stronger.

▽ Germany rejected Britain's proposal for a conference of powers in July 1914.

▽ As a result of the Schlieffen Plan, German mobilisation meant war.

▽ By invading Belgium, Germany ensured that Britain would enter the war.

b) Austrian responsibility

▽ The Habsburg government exaggerated the Serbian threat. Serbia had only a tenth of Austria-Hungary's population. She had suffered heavy casualties in the Balkan Wars and both her army and finances were in a terrible state.

▽ In 1913–14 it was Austria-Hungary, rather than Serbia, which pursued a consistently belligerent policy. On no fewer than 25 occasions in 1913–14 the Austro-Hungarian chief of staff, Hotzendorf, urged war against Serbia.

▽ Austria sought to benefit from the Sarajevo murder. It needed little prompting from Germany.

▽ Austria contributed to the crisis by the delay between the Sarajevo murder and the ultimatum to Serbia. A rapid strike against Serbia might have averted war.

▽ Austria was the first power to resort to force by attacking Serbia.

c) Russian responsibility

▽ Russia was unable (and perhaps unwilling) to restrain Serb/Slav nationalism.

▽ Russia's promise of support influenced Serbia's decision to reject the Austrian ultimatum.

▽ Russia's decision to mobilise had terrible consequences.

(Continued)
tensions and to rally people behind the established order.

▽ Germany pre-1914 had expansionist aims not dissimilar to those of Hitler.

▽ A war council in December 1912 (attended by the Kaiser) determined that Germany should launch an expansionist war at the first favourable opportunity.

▽ Germany hoped and expected that war would result from its backing of Austria-Hungary in July 1914.

CRITICISMS OF FISCHER'S THESIS

▽ Both Bülow and Bethmann-Hollweg explicitly dismissed war as a solution to the internal socialist problem.

▽ Germany did not pursue a coherent policy in the years before 1914.

▽ The German government did not decide on war in December 1912. The war council was an irregular one, at which the chancellor was not present.

▽ Germany made no concerted preparations for war after 1912. She gave surprisingly little support to Austria-Hungary in 1912–13.

▽ By focusing only on Germany, Fischer distorts the picture of the diplomatic situation in July 1914. Policy-making in other countries was equally important.

d) French responsibility

It is hard to blame France for the outbreak of war. By 1890 agitation to win back Alsace-Lorraine had subsided and thereafter France showed no desire for a war of revenge. In 1914 French public opinion seemed very pacific. While France did promise Russia support in 1914, she did not encourage Russia to fight. The French President and Prime Minister were both literally at sea from 23–29 July and played a minor role in events. In the end Germany declared war on France, not the reverse.

e) British responsibility

Sir Edward Grey has been blamed for not doing more to work for peace. But it is difficult to see what more he could have done. The view that he might have restrained German action by making it clear that Britain would support France is a red herring. German leaders expected – and were not too concerned about – British intervention! The British Expeditionary Force was only 150,000 strong (half the size of the Belgian army) and seemed unlikely to disrupt the Schlieffen Plan.

f) Serbian responsibility

▼ Her aggressive expansionism unsettled the Balkans prior to 1914.
▼ The Serbian government could have accepted the Austrian ultimatum.

g) Conclusion

It seems unlikely that any country planned or wanted a general war in 1914. Fischer's view – that the war was deliberately begun by Germany – is unconvincing. Bethmann-Hollweg, asked by Bülow soon after the outbreak of the war, how it had come about, replied: 'If only I knew.' However, while not being entirely responsible for the war, it does seem that Germany was more to blame than any other power. Opportunism, so often a feature of German diplomacy after 1890, marked German statesmanship in July 1914. The 'blank cheque' to Austria-Hungary indicated that Germany was willing to risk a general war. German leaders embarked upon this extraordinarily dangerous strategy with an almost nonchalant attitude. Thus, by late July Germany had to choose between war or diplomatic humiliation. This dilemma was very much of Germany's own making. In Lowe's view, 'it is difficult to find a single constructive move for peace that Germany made throughout the July Crisis'.

ACTIVITY

Divide into six teams – Germany, Austria-Hungary, Russia, Britain, France and Serbia. The job of each team is twofold: a) to prepare the defence case for their country; b) to devise a number of questions they would like to put to the opposing teams/countries. Each country should then take its turn in the 'dock'. The captain of each team should first read out the defence statement. Questions from the other teams then follow. The teams take it in turn to bat. At the end, each team should decide who was most to blame, giving a mark of 6 to the country they consider most responsible for the war, 5 for the next, etc.. Take a Eurovision Song Contest-style vote to see which country gets the highest vote and thus is seen as most to blame for the war.

6 What were the main causes of the war?

a) How important was the Balkan situation?

Austria-Hungary and Russia's conflicting Balkan ambitions had heightened tensions for many years. However, by 1914 the crucial issue was the conflict between Austria and Serbia. Serbian nationalism was a potential threat to the Habsburg Empire. Serbia's sense of grievance at the Austrian annexation of Bosnia-Herzegovina was matched by Austrian alarm at Serbia's expansion as a result of the Balkan Wars. In the final analysis the First World War began as a fight for the future of the Balkans. Austria-Hungary and Germany made a bid for control. Russia resolved to stop them.

b) How important was the alliance system?

The fact that an Austro-Serbian dispute escalated into a general war had something to do with the alliance system. The alliances can be seen as both a reflection of insecurity and a contribution towards it. Arguably the alliance system reduced the flexibility of the great powers' response to crises. Germany's lack of a flexible response in 1914 ensured that her reply to a threat from Russia was to invade France! However, it is possible to exaggerate the rigidity of the alliance system both during the July Crisis and before. In August 1914, Italy, for example, refused to support her partners in the Triple Alliance. The Triple Entente was not even an alliance. Britain had no precise commitments. In 1914 no one knew for certain what Britain's response to the crisis would be. This is hardly surprising: until Germany invaded Belgium the British cabinet was deeply divided over Britain's course of action. Interestingly, while many historians after 1914 argued that the alliance system made war inevitable, many contemporaries believed that, by creating a balance of power, it helped maintain peace.

c) How important was 'international anarchy'?

After 1918 politicians as far apart as Lenin and US President Woodrow Wilson believed that the existence of nation states, pursuing their own interests rather than collaborating in the interests of Europe as a whole, was bound eventually to lead to war. 'International anarchy' was thus blamed for the outbreak of war. However, 'international anarchy' had been a fact of life in European affairs since at least 1871, during which time Europe had enjoyed over 40 years of peace. Old-style diplomacy had partitioned Africa peacefully and demarcated the interests of the powers in China. Moreover, pre-1914 European powers tended to act in 'concert' to avert the threat to peace: there was a tradition of responding to crises by convening international conferences to seek collective solutions. Conferences had met in 1906 and 1912–13. The breakdown of the 'concert' in 1914 was more a symptom of the growing tension than a cause of that tension.

d) How important was the arms race?

It has been claimed that there was a European arms race pre-1914 and that this led inevitably to war. However, if arms races led inevitably to war, the world would not have survived the Cold War. Arguably the wealth of arms in Europe in 1914 might have acted as a deterrent. Moreover, most European powers did not actually increase the size of their armies until after 1912. In many respects this was more an effect than a cause of tension. However, there is no doubt that Russia's army reforms, due to be completed in 1917, caused immense anxiety in Germany, so much so that a preventive war against Russia made sense to some German military leaders. Nor is there any doubt that Anglo-German naval rivalry helped poison relations between the two countries. Britain's willingness to go to war in 1914 owed much to the anti-German feelings generated by the naval race.

e) How important was military mobilisation?

Military mobilisation – or 'war by timetable' as A. J. P. Taylor called it – played a vital role in bringing about war in July/August 1914. Taylor argued that the outbreak of war was provoked almost entirely by rival plans for mobilisation. The Schlieffen Plan collapsed if Germany allowed Russia time to mobilise. Germany's chance of victory depended on speed. To enable quick mobilisation, elaborate railway timetables had been calculated: these could not be easily amended without throwing everything into total confusion. German mobilisation plans meant almost immediate war. Germany's plans – albeit especially crucial – were not unique: the war plans of all the great powers hinged upon railway timetables and rapid deployment of men. It was assumed – wrongly – that the side which mobilised quickly and struck the first blow would triumph. In late July, therefore, as mobilisation got underway, diplomats found they had little freedom of manoeuvre.

f) How important was capitalist competition?

Marxist historians' claims

▼ Politicians were puppets of great industrialists and financiers.

▼ Industrialists, especially armaments manufacturers, had a vested interest in provoking war to increase their profits.

▼ Frenzied competition amongst commercial rivals for markets and for raw materials inevitably brought about an 'imperialist war'.

The anti-Marxist view

▼ There is no evidence that industrialists and financiers were pressing for war. Indeed, well aware that they stood to lose rather than to gain, most were opposed to war.

▼ The view that capitalist states were bound to become involved in wars with other powers over access to colonial raw materials does not fit the facts. For much of the period the main rivalries were between Britain and France and Russia – not between Britain and Germany. The fact that Britain's imperial rivalries with France and Russia were resolved makes untenable all general assertions about such rivalries leading to war. Indeed, by 1914 most of the imperial issues had been settled.

g) How important was nationalism?

Nationalism was a powerful force in virtually every European country. It was fostered by mass education, the popular press and right-wing pressure groups. Social Darwinist theories about the survival of the fittest spilled over into nationalist thinking. Many Germans, for example, assumed that they were the fittest race. Some dreamed of uniting all Germans in a greater German state and then dominating 'inferior' races in eastern Europe. Pan-Slavism also had racist overtones. Balkan nationalism – especially the fact that political frontiers did not correspond to national groups – was also a major problem.

Ironically, most people in Europe voted for socialist and liberal – not nationalist – parties pre-1914 and across Europe there was a strong international peace movement which conducted a vigorous propaganda campaign. However, peace demonstrations in European cities ended in late July 1914 – to be replaced by cheering, patriotic crowds as national loyalty replaced class solidarity. The overwhelming impression in August 1914 is of nations united and of men going cheerfully to war. Apparent national consensus helped mobilise support which sustained and possibly trapped governments in 1914.

h) How important were domestic crises?

It has been suggested that Germany, Austria-Hungary and Russia, faced with serious problems at home, wanted war to unite their nations and avoid revolution. This view is unhelpful. It was the worsening international situation, not domestic developments, that explains why the war came when it did. The threat perceived by governments was not revolution from within but invasion from outside.

i) Was the war an accident or an accident waiting to happen?

Some historians see Europe in 1914 as a powder keg waiting to explode. Others are sceptical. A. J. P. Taylor saw few great causes of the war.

> It is the fashion nowadays to seek profound causes for great events. But perhaps the First World War had no profound causes. For thirty years past, international diplomacy, the balance of power, the alliances and the accumulation of armed might produced peace. Suddenly the situation was turned around and the very forces which had produced the long peace now produced a great war. In much the same way, a motorist who for thirty years has been doing the right thing to avoid accidents makes a mistake one day and has a crash. In July 1914 things went wrong.

Taylor claimed that the war was an accident: if anything was to blame, it was simply railway timetables. Certainly deep-rooted explanations, by themselves, fail to explain why war broke out when it did. If Francis Ferdinand had not been assassinated in 1914 there would not have been a war. However, only by understanding developments prior to 1914 is it possible to understand why a local war between Austria-Hungary and Serbia led almost instantly into a general European war. The war may have been an accident but it was also an accident waiting to happen.

j) Conclusion

In 1914 all the great powers thought that their vital interests were at stake – interests for which it was worth risking defeat, dismemberment and impoverishment. All claimed they were fighting a war of self-defence and so in a sense they were: all were motivated more by insecurity and by fear of others expanding than by a desire to expand themselves. All believed that the war would be short and that attack was the best form of defence. All got it wrong: the war was not short and defence was to prove the best form of defence. Had European leaders realised the horrors that lay ahead, they surely would not have acted as they did in 1914.

▼ Working on The Origins of the First World War

In trying to work out what caused anything in history, it is always useful to consider:

▼ What were the main long-term causes (preconditions)?

▼ What were the main medium-term causes (precipitants)?

▼ What were the main short-term causes (triggers)?

There may well be debate about what exactly is a precondition as opposed to a precipitant and what exactly is a precipitant as opposed to a trigger! Do not worry about this. The divisions are partly cosmetic. The main thing is that they may help structure your thoughts. Try to work out what you think were the main preconditions, precipitants and triggers which resulted in the First World War. Did any of the preconditions mean that war was likely or inevitable? To what extent did war seem imminent by early 1914? Could/should the war have been averted in 1914?

Answering extended writing and essay questions on The Origins of the First World War

Consider the following question: 'To what extent should Germany be held responsible for the start of the First World War?'

One way to approach this question is first to consider the historiographical debates. What have been historians' views about German responsibility? Fischer's views are particularly important. Then you might use the plan outlined in the previous section and examine Germany's policy in the long-term, medium-term, and short-term. You will also need to say something about the responsibility of other countries. If Germany was not responsible, who or what was? Finally you will have to reach a conclusion. Have the courage to say what you think. What is your main evidence for arguing as you do?

Answering source-based questions on The Origins of the First World War

Source A General Hotzendorf, chief of the Austro-Hungarian general staff, in July 1914

This is not the crime of a single fanatic; assassination represents Serbia's declaration of war on Austria-Hungary...If we miss this occasion, the monarchy will be exposed to new explosions of South Slav, Czech, Russian, Romanian, and Italian aspirations...Austria-Hungary must wage war for political reasons.

Source B A report of the conversation between William II and the Austrian ambassador Count Szogyeny in Berlin on 5 July 1914 which Szogyeny sent to Berchtold, the Austrian foreign minister

...the Kaiser authorised me to inform our gracious majesty that we might in this case, as in all others, rely upon Germany's full support...he did not doubt in the least that Herr von Bethmann-Hollweg would agree with him. Especially as far as our action against Serbia was concerned. But it was the Kaiser's opinion that this action must not be delayed. Russia's attitude will no doubt be hostile, but for this he had for years prepared, and should a war between Austria-Hungary and Russia be unavoidable, we might be convinced that Germany, our old faithful ally, would stand at our side. Russia at the present time was in no way prepared for war, and would think twice before it appealed to arms...if we had really recognised the necessity of warlike action against Serbia, he [the Kaiser] would regret if we did not make use of the present moment, which is all in our favour.

Source C The following was written by Jagow, the German secretary of state, to Prince Lichnowsky, the German ambassador in London, on 18 July 1914.

Austria no longer intends to tolerate the sapping activities of the Serbians, and just as little does she intend to tolerate longer the continuously provocative attitude of her small neighbour at Belgrade...She fully realises that she has neglected many opportunities, and that she is still able to act, though in a few years she may no longer be able to do so. Austria is now going to force a showdown with Serbia, and has told us so...Nor have we at the present time forced Austria to her decision. But we neither could nor should attempt to stay her hand. If we should do that, Austria would have the right to reproach us (and we ourselves) with having deprived her of her last chance of political rehabilitation. And then the process of her wasting away and of her internal decay would be still further accelerated. Her standing in the Balkans would be gone forever. You will undoubtedly agree with me that the absolute establishment of the Russian hegemony in the Balkans is, indirectly, not permissible, even for us. The maintenance of Austria...is a necessity for us both for internal and external reasons. That she cannot be maintained forever, I will willingly admit...

We must attempt to localise the conflict between Austria and Serbia. Whether we shall succeed in this will depend first on Russia, and

(Continued)

secondly on the moderating influence of Russia's allies. The more determined Austria shows herself, the more energetically we support her, so much the more quiet will Russia remain. To be sure, there will be some agitation in St Petersburg, but, on the whole, Russia is not ready to strike at present. Nor will France or England be anxious for war at the present time. According to all competent observation, Russia will be prepared to fight in a few years. Then she will crush us by the number of her soldiers: then she will have built her Baltic Sea fleet and her strategic railroads.

▼ QUESTIONS ON SOURCES

1. Examine Source A. Explain the comment: 'Austria-Hungary must wage war for political reasons.' **[3 marks]**
2. Examine Sources B and C. How reliable are these sources as evidence for Germany's decision-making in foreign policy in July 1914? **[7 marks]**
3. Using the sources and your own knowledge, consider the validity of the view that Germany was responsible for the outbreak of the First World War. **[15 marks]**

Points to note about the questions

Question 1 Why were some Austrians keen to pick a quarrel with Serbia?

Question 2 William's words are being reported. Might Szogyeny have changed the emphasis of what was said? How important was Jagow? Did his views echo those of the Kaiser?

Question 3 Source A tends to put Austria-Hungary in the dock. Sources B and C indicate that Germany was ready to risk war in July 1914. But do they prove Germany's 'war guilt'? What other reasons might be given as evidence for German responsibility?

Further Reading

Books in the **Access to History** *series*
Rivalry and Accord: International Relations 1870–1914 by J. Lowe is excellent.

General
Try *The Outbreak of the First World War: 1914 in Perspective* by D. Stevenson (Macmillan, 1997) and *The Origins of the First World War* by G. Martel (Longman, 1996). More detailed studies include *The Origins of the First World War* by J. Joll (Longman, 1992), *Decisions for War, 1914* by K. Wilson (ed.) (University College Press, 1995) and *The Origins of the First World War* by H. W. Koch (ed.) (Macmillan, 1984).

GLOSSARY

Nationalism   9
The Jesuits   14
The Eastern Question   50
The Carbonari   114
Federation   118
The National Society (Italy)   122
The National Association (Germany)   152
Junker   153
Realpolitik (Political Realism)   153
The Old Catholics   183
The *mir*   203

INDEX

Aberdeen, Lord 57–8, 97–103, 105
Africa 269, 280, 288
Alexander I, Tsar 26–8, 35–6, 38, 41–7, 60
Alexander II, Tsar 137, 158, 191, 194, 202–11, 227, 232, 256–7
Alexander III, Tsar 194, 196, 198, 210
Alsace-Lorraine 168–9, 178–9, 182, 195–6, 229, 249, 267, 286
Anarchism 91, 241–2
Anti-Semitism 240, 253, 259
Arms race 280, 288
Austria (-Hungary after 1867) 8–9, 20–5, 33–4, 36–40, 42–7, 50–9, 63, 73–80, 83–4, 90–1, 95, 97, 99, 101–8, 113–5, 117–129, 135, 137, 141–5, 147–53, 155–62, 164, 167, 184–5, 189–97, 200, 211–8, 227, 238, 242, 265, 272, 277–8, 280–7, 290, 292–3
Baden 144, 147, 155, 160, 162
Balkans 11, 95, 103, 107, 189–94, 197, 272, 279–80, 285–7
Bavaria 39, 82, 87, 144, 148, 150, 155, 160, 162, 169, 179
Belgium 11, 53–4, 164, 227, 237, 266, 283–4, 286–7
Berlin 67, 191–3
Bethmann-Hollweg 247, 281–3, 285–6
Bismarck, Otto 141, 151, 153–72, 174–94, 221, 241, 245–6, 272, 274
Bloody Sunday 258–9, 263–4
Boer War 269, 275
Bosnia-Herzegovina 191–4, 277–8, 281–2, 287

Boulanger 196, 251
Britain 7–8, 10, 25, 33–4, 38, 40, 42–9, 51–9, 65, 82, 88, 91, 94–110, 124, 126, 131, 136, 138, 157–60, 167, 179, 190–2, 194–7, 200, 236–7, 247, 254, 265–7, 269–70, 272–9, 284–8, 293
Bulgaria 190–2, 196–7, 280
Bulow 246–7, 274, 277, 285–6
Canning, George 45–9, 52
Carbonari 10, 13, 114–5
Castlereagh 33–4, 37–8, 41–6, 48, 60–1
Catholic Church 11–2, 14, 21, 70, 96–7, 112, 119, 122, 180–4, 199, 213, 225, 245, 250, 253
Cavour 122–8, 130–2, 136–7
Charles X, King 13–5, 53
China 270–1, 288
Colonies 195, 200, 227, 266–71
Commune 229–30, 241, 249, 253
Compromise (1867) 214–5, 217–8
Congress System 41–8, 58
Crimean War 30, 94–110, 124, 137, 152, 157, 168, 202, 204, 206, 227
Croats 73, 76, 79–80, 216
Czechs 63, 73, 77–8, 83–4, 141, 215, 217
December Revolution 27–8
Denmark 84–7, 141 147, 155, 158–9, 182, 237, 244
Dreyfus 252–3
Duel Alliance 193–5, 197, 200, 272
Duma 259–60
Eastern Question 50, 58, 96, 107–8, 193

France, 5–19, 33–8, 40–1, 43–8, 51–8, 62–3, 65, 68–72, 81, 91, 94–110, 112, 119–121, 124–128, 131, 136, 138, 141–3, 152, 155–8, 160, 164–70, 179, 182, 184, 189, 194–8, 200, 218–31, 236–8, 241, 249–54, 265–70, 272–3, 275–80, 282–4, 286, 289, 293
Francis Ferdinand, Archduke 265, 281 –2, 290
Francis Joseph, Emperor 79, 100, 103, 126, 165, 211–8, 281
Franco-Prussian War 135, 166–70, 180, 227
Frankfurt 39, 82–4, 86–8, 144, 149–50, 168, 229
Frederick William IV, King 84–8, 100, 147,150, 152
French Revolution 5–7, 10–2, 41
Garibaldi 117, 120–1, 123, 128–34, 137–8
German Confederation 9, 23, 39, 81–4, 144–5, 147, 150–3, 158–60, 162
Germany 9–11, 36, 38–40, 62–3, 81–8, 107, 141–72, 174–94, 228–30, 236–7, 242–9, 251–2, 265–6, 270, 272–4, 277–80, 282–93
Greece 46, 51–2, 95, 190, 193, 265, 280
Grey, Sir Edward 276, 282, 284, 286
Guizot 68
Hohenzollern Candidature 165–6, 227
Holland 10, 53–4, 237
Holy Alliance 42, 45, 47–9, 58, 101
Hungary 9, 23–4, 63, 76, 79–80, 90, 211–8

Industrialisation   8, 64–5, 149, 237, 242–3, 255

Italy   9–11, 337, 36–7, 40, 44–5, 55, 62–3, 73, 76–8, 88–9, 107, 109, 112–139, 160–2, 170, 195–7, 211–3, 220, 227, 241, 265–6, 269, 277, 279, 284, 287

Japan   258–9, 270–1, 275

Jesuits   13–5, 183, 250

July Revolution   15–6, 18, 53, 146

Kossuth   24, 74–5, 79

Kulturkampf   181–6

Lenin   257, 259–61, 266, 287

Liberalism   10, 40, 46, 63, 65, 73, 81, 88, 91, 121, 145, 225, 239

Lombardy   40, 77, 79–80 89 113, 119–20, 125–6

Louis XVIII, King   12–3, 34

Louis-Philippe   15–9, 53–7, 62, 68–9, 71, 74

Luxembourg   164–5, 227

Marx, Karl   64, 66, 87, 240–1, 253, 257, 261, 289

Mazzini   91, 112, 114–7, 119–123, 130, 136–8

Mehemet Ali   51, 56–7

Metternich   21–5, 33–4, 37–40, 42–7, 51, 59–60, 74–5, 84, 113, 115, 118, 142, 144–7, 221

Mir   203–5, 208–9, 256, 260

Moldavia   52, 98–105, 102–5, 108

Moltke, Helmuth   155, 16l, 166–70

Morocco   276, 278–9

Naples   6, 10, 27, 33, 40, 43–5, 62, 89, 112–3, 115, 119, 130–2, 134

Napoleon Bonaparte   5, 9, 11–2, 26, 33–41, 112, 125, 141–3, 145, 220–1, 223

Napoleon III, Emperor   17–8, 72, 96–102, 106, 108–9, 119, 124–8, 131–2, 135–7, 160, 164–8, 218–28

National Liberals   163, 180–2, 184–5, 198–9, 247

National Society (Italy)   122, 124, 127, 129, 138

Nationalism   9, 20, 40, 63, 66, 73, 81, 89–91, 118, 120, 138, 143, 145–6, 157, 239, 244, 267, 289

Nicholas I, Tsar   27–30, 52, 56–8, 79, 90, 96–101, 105, 202, 207

Nicholas II, Tsar   258–61, 283

North German Confederation   162–4, 169

Ottoman Empire – see Turkey

Palmerston, Lord   53–8, 91, 98–100, 102, 105–6, 152

Papal States   89, 91, 115, 119–20, 125–6

Paris   14–5, 18, 34, 37–8, 43, 49, 67–71, 106–7, 168, 220, 224–5, 228–30, 250–1

Piedmont   10, 43, 77–80, 94, 103, 108, 112–3, 115, 117–38, 152

Pius 1X, Pope   80, 118–21, 126, 132, 135, 182–3

Poland   9, 11, 26–7, 30, 36, 38–40, 54, 79, 83–4, 102, 141, 158, 181–2, 209,216, 227, 244, 247

Portugal   10, 27, 34, 38, 43, 48–9

Prussia   7–8, 33, 35–6, 38–40, 42–4, 47, 53–4, 57–8, 83–8, 90–1, 99, 102–3, 108, 135, 141–5, 147–71, 176, 187, 244, 247

Reichstag   175–8, 180–7, 197–9, 244–8, 280

Reinsurance Treaty   196–7, 272

Romania   195, 215, 280

Rome   72, 112–3, 119–20, 125, 132–3, 135–6, 170, 220

Russia   6–7, 25–30, 33–6, 38, 40, 43–7, 50–9, 63, 79, 88, 90–1, 94–110, 124, 126, 137, 142, 157–8, 160, 167, 170, 184–5, 189–98, 200, 202–11, 236–8, 241, 254–66, 270–3, 276–8, 280–1, 283, 285, 287–90, 292–3

Russo-Japanese War   270–1

Sarajevo   265, 281, 285

Saxony   36, 38–9, 87, 142, 146, 148–9, 160–1

Schleswig-Holstein   84–5, 87–8, 147, 158–60, 162

Schlieffen Plan   283, 286, 288

Schwarzenberg, Prince   150–1, 211–3

Serbia   73, 190–1, 193, 195, 215, 265, 277–8, 280–2, 285–7, 290, 292

Sicily   10, 62, 89, 113, 115, 120, 130–1, 133–4

Socialism   10, 66, 186–8, 199, 229, 240–2, 246, 252

Spain   6, 27, 33–4, 37, 43, 45–6, 48–9, 119, 165, 241

Stolypin   260–1

Sweden   37, 106

Talleyrand   35, 37–8, 40, 54,

Thiers,   15–7, 229–30

Third Republic   228–31, 249–54

Triple Alliance   195–6, 272–3, 277, 284, 287

Troppau, Congress of   44–6

Turkey   46, 50–2, 56–7, 94–110, 189, 191–3, 238, 274, 277–9

Tuscany   40, 89, 115, 119, 125–8

Venice/Venetia   40, 77, 80, 89, 113, 115, 119, 122, 125–6, 132–3, 135–6, 162

Victor Emmanuel II, King   119–122, 126–7, 130–3, 135, 138

Vienna   23, 67, 74, 76, 78–80, 86, 100

Vienna Peace Settlement   7, 33–41, 47, 91, 113, 142

Weltpolitik   274, 277, 285

William 1, Kaiser   141, 152–4, 159, 161–2, 166, 169, 174, 176, 186, 197

William 11, Kaiser   198–200, 245–8, 272–3, 276, 282–3, 292

Zemstvo   206–7, 209

Zollverein   148, 151–2, 156–7, 164, 184